Ways of Seeing International Organisations

For decades, the field of scholarship that studies the law and practice of international organisations – also known as international institutional law – has been marked by an intellectual quietism. Most of the scholarship tends to focus narrowly on providing 'legal' answers to 'legal' questions. For that reason, perspectives rarely engage with the insights of critical traditions of legal thought (for instance, feminist, postcolonial, or political economy-oriented perspectives) or with interdisciplinary contributions produced outside the field. *Ways of Seeing International Organisations* challenges the narrow gaze of the field by bringing together authors across multiple disciplines to reflect on the need for 'new' perspectives in international institutional law. Highlighting the limits of mainstream approaches, the authors instead interrogate international organisations as pivots in processes of world-making. To achieve this, the volume is organised around four fundamental themes: expertise; structure; performance; and capital. This title is also available as Open Access on Cambridge Core.

NEGAR MANSOURI is a postdoctoral researcher at Copenhagen Business School. She holds a PhD (with the highest distinction) and an MA in international law from the Geneva Graduate Institute, an MA in public international law from Shahid Beheshti University (Tehran, Iran), and an LLB from Imam Khomeini International University (Qazvin, Iran).

DANIEL R. QUIROGA-VILLAMARÍN is currently an Ernst Mach Fellow at the University of Vienna (Austria). He holds a PhD in international law with a minor in international history and politics with the highest distinction from the Geneva Graduate Institute (Switzerland). He also holds a MA from the same institution and a BA in law from the University of the Andes (Bogotá, Colombia).

In drawing together diverse disciplinary perspectives and traditions of thought to pluralize and complicate 'ways of seeing' international organizations, this wonderfully rich volume advances both scholarship on international organizations themselves, and more wide-ranging inquiries about the connections between legal forms, institutional arrangements, and epistemology in international law.

Megan Donaldson Associate Professor of Public International Law, University College London

Challenging the traditional lens of international institutional law, *Ways of Seeing International Organisations* brings fresh perspectives to the field. By interrogating expertise, structures, performance, and capital, this work transcends conventional boundaries, inspiring a critical, multidisciplinary understanding of international organisations' socio-technical roles and world-ordering visions.

Sundhya Pahuja Melbourne Laureate Professor, University of Melbourne

This volume brings together a remarkable set of critical voices, both established and emergent, from the field of international organization studies. The book not only documents the variety and richness of theoretical approaches available for the critical study of international institutions and law, it also provides readers with a wealth of empirical vignettes and case studies to underline their crucial contribution. A great achievement!

Jens Steffek Professor of Transnational Governance, Technical University of Darmstadt, Germany

Engaging and provocative, this volume shows international organizations as sites of socio-technical struggle. Challenging the dominance of 'problem-solving thinking' in international institutional law, *Ways of Seeing International Organizations* draws from law, history, anthropology, and political science to provide a rich description of institutional practices and their distributive effects. A sophisticated, unconventional, and insightful take on the lives of international organizations.

René Urueña Professor of Law, University of the Andes, Colombia

LSE INTERNATIONAL STUDIES

This series, published in association with the Centre for International Studies at the London School of Economics, is centred on three main themes. First, the series is oriented around work that is transdisciplinary, which challenges disciplinary conventions and develops arguments that cannot be grasped within existing disciplines. It will include work combining a wide range of fields, including international relations, international law, political theory, history, sociology and ethics. Second, it comprises books that contain an overtly international or transnational dimension, but not necessarily focused simply within the discipline of International Relations. Finally, the series will publish books that use scholarly inquiry as a means of addressing pressing political concerns. Books in the series may be predominantly theoretical, or predominantly empirical, but all will say something of significance about political issues that exceed national boundaries.

Previous books in the series:

Culture and Order in World Politics Andrew Phillips and Christian Reus-Smit (eds.)
On Cultural Diversity: International Theory in a World of Difference Christian Reus-Smit
Socioeconomic Justice: International Intervention and Transition in Post-war Bosnia and Herzegovina Daniela Lai
The World Imagined: Collective Beliefs and Political Order in the Sinocentric, Islamic and Southeast Asian International Societies Hendrik Spruyt
How the East Was Won: Barbarian Conquerors, Universal Conquest and the Making of Modern Asia Andrew Phillips
Before the West: The Rise and Fall of Eastern World Orders Ayşe Zarakol
Capitalism, Jacobinism and International Relations: Revisiting Turkish Modernity Eren Duzgun
The Counterinsurgent Imagination: A New Intellectual History Joseph MacKay
Dying Abroad: The Political Afterlives of Migration in Europe Osman Balkan

Resisting Racial Capitalism: An Antipolitical Theory of Refusal Ida Danewid
Regional Politics in Oceania: From Colonialism and Cold War to the Pacific Century Stephanie Lawson
Fueling Sovereignty Naosuke Mukoyama
Representants and International Orders: The Staging of Political Authority Alena Drieschova

Ways of Seeing International Organisations

New Perspectives for International Institutional Law

Edited by

NEGAR MANSOURI
Copenhagen Business School

DANIEL R. QUIROGA-VILLAMARÍN
University of Vienna

CAMBRIDGE
UNIVERSITY PRESS

CAMBRIDGE
UNIVERSITY PRESS

Shaftesbury Road, Cambridge CB2 8EA, United Kingdom

One Liberty Plaza, 20th Floor, New York, NY 10006, USA

477 Williamstown Road, Port Melbourne, VIC 3207, Australia

314–321, 3rd Floor, Plot 3, Splendor Forum, Jasola District Centre, New Delhi – 110025, India

103 Penang Road, #05–06/07, Visioncrest Commercial, Singapore 238467

Cambridge University Press is part of Cambridge University Press & Assessment, a department of the University of Cambridge.

We share the University's mission to contribute to society through the pursuit of education, learning and research at the highest international levels of excellence.

www.cambridge.org
Information on this title: www.cambridge.org/9781009552622

DOI: 10.1017/9781009552646

First published 2025

A catalogue record for this publication is available from the British Library

Library of Congress Cataloging-in-Publication Data
Names: Mansouri, Negar, editor. | Quiroga-Villamarín, Daniel R., editor.
Title: Ways of seeing international organisations : new perspectives for international institutional law / edited by Negar Mansouri, Copenhagen Business School; Daniel R. Quiroga-Villamarín, University of Vienna.
Other titles: Ways of seeing international organizations
Description: Cambridge, United Kingdom ; New York, NY : Cambridge University Press, 2025. | Series: LSE International Studies | Includes bibliographical references and index.
Identifiers: LCCN 2024050628 | ISBN 9781009552622 (hardback) | ISBN 9781009552615 (paperback) | ISBN 9781009552646 (ebook)
Subjects: LCSH: International agencies – Law and legislation. | International law.
Classification: LCC KZ4850 .W39 2025 | DDC 341.2–dc23/eng/20241026
LC record available at https://lccn.loc.gov/2024050628

ISBN 978-1-009-55262-2 Hardback
ISBN 978-1-009-55261-5 Paperback

Published with the support of the Swiss National Science Foundation.

Contents

Contributors

B. S. Chimni Jindal Global University

Richard Clements Tilburg Law School; Institute for Global Law & Policy

A. Claire Cutler University of Victoria

Jan Eijking University of Oxford

Guy Fiti Sinclair University of Auckland

Miia Halme-Tuomisaari Lund University

Jan Klabbers University of Helsinki

Annabelle Littoz-Monnet Graduate Institute of International and Development Studies

Negar Mansouri Copenhagen Business School

Daniel R. Quiroga-Villamarín University of Vienna

Kiri Olivia Santer University of Bern

Tommaso Soave Central European University

Juanita Uribe Graduate Institute of International and Development Studies

Dimitri Van Den Meerssche Queen Mary University of London

Acknowledgements

The editors would like to thank Nico Krisch, Joost Pauwelyn, Camila Morales Silva, and Sylvia Nissim at the Geneva Graduate Institute for their valuable contributions to their 2021 conference 'Alternative Approaches to International Organizations in International Law: Potentials, Complexities, and Pitfalls' that led to this volume. We are also grateful to Andrew Clapham from the International Law Department and Finola O'Sullivan for their advice on the publishing process. Nothing of this would have been possible without the generous support of the Swiss National Science Foundation, which awarded us the funds required to organize the conference (Scientific Exchanges Grant 2021: 203435) and additionally funded the publication of the volume in Open Access format (Open Access Books 2024 Grant: 230054).

PART I

Thinking International Organisations Differently

1 *Seeing International Organizations Differently*

NEGAR MANSOURI AND
DANIEL R. QUIROGA-VILLAMARÍN

> Art historians have pinpointed that Vermeer painted A View of Delft from the upper storey of a building on the Schieweg [...] but the final composition is not a "photographic" representation of the view from the window on the Schieweg. He reorganized reality, changed perspective, and tonal contrast [...] Legal theories are like this: their authors decide the aspects of law they want to discuss and in highlighting some, they downplay or ignore others.
>
> Scobbie, "A View of Delft: Some Thoughts About Thinking about International Law"

Seeing Like an International Institutional Lawyer: The Ethos and Pedagogy of a Subdiscipline

What do international institutional lawyers see when they peek out from a window? If, as Kennedy argues, public international lawyers see a "world of nation-states and war" while trade lawyers see "a world of buyers and sellers,"[1] it is likely that international institutional lawyers see a world of delegated competences. They dream of interstate cooperation – and they fear the nightmare that might come with the abuse of institutional power.[2] Indeed, for the mainstream international law scholarship (MILS) on international organizations (IOs),[3] these institutions represent one of the highest summits in the history

[1] D. Kennedy, 'One, Two, Three, Many Legal Orders: Legal Pluralism and the Cosmopolitan Dream' (2006) 31 *N.Y.U. Review of Law & Social Change* 641–59. 650.

[2] See, generally, J. Steffek, *International Organization as Technocratic Utopia* (Oxford University Press, 2021).

[3] We use this acronym following B. S. Chimni, 'An Outline of a Marxist Course on Public International Law' in S. Marks (ed.), *International Law on the Left* (Cambridge University Press, 2008), pp. 53–91.

of the rational organization of global life in the "long march of mankind from the cave to the computer."[4] Accordingly, the subdiscipline has been organized around a series of fixed dichotomies and research questions that frame its field of vision.

For instance, the mainstream international legal inquiry into IOs is usually restricted to a fixed list of topics (legal personality, membership, financing, external relations, legal status of normative outputs, application of international law, etc.) and methods (interpretation of IOs' constituent instruments, the study of rulings of international and domestic courts, etc.).[5] Functionalism, as the dominant theoretical lens of lawyerly inquiry into IOs in international law, "has been developed by practitioners, responding to practical challenges, often in piecemeal fashion and through mimicry or comparison."[6] In fact, much of the subfield has developed in the form of the endless commentaries on a series of landmark rulings by international courts and arbitration bodies on the competence and legal personality of certain international institutions.[7]

In other words, a pragmatic and practice-oriented lens, underpinned by a particular understanding of the legal scholar's craft, has come to dominate the international legal inquiry into institutions. As such, the IOs' law ethos, pedagogy, and intellectual framework has remained committed to a monodisciplinary outlook.[8] A clear example of that can be found in the syllabi and textbooks that deal with the law of IOs, written often by MILS lawyers (many of them associated with the legal offices of IOs themselves) with the aim of training new generations of future IO law practitioners. As a result, "doing" IOs law has overshadowed "thinking" about international institutions. Indeed, not much has changed since Chimni wrote in 1999 that

[4] M. N. Shaw, *International Law*, Fifth ed. (Cambridge University Press, 2003), p. 1.

[5] See, for instance, H. G. Schermers and N. Blokker, *International Institutional Law: Unity within Diversity*, Sixth revised ed. (Brill, 2018).

[6] J. Klabbers, 'Theorizing International Organizations' in A. Orford and F. Hoffmann (eds.), *The Oxford Handbook of the Theory of International Law* (Oxford University Press, 2016), pp. 618–34. 618.

[7] See, for a recent restatement, C. Ryngaert, I. F. Dekker, R. A. Wessel, and J. Wouters (eds.), *Judicial Decisions on the Law of International Organizations* (Oxford University Press, 2016).

[8] N. Mansouri, 'On International Institutional Law, Its Pedagogy and the Turn to Alternative Approaches' *OpinioJuris* (October 2020).

[i]n the corpus of literature which constitutes international legal studies, there is little reflection on the role of international institutions in sustaining a particular vision of world order. While international law experts have concerned themselves with international institutions, the discussion has largely been confined to the rules of law which govern their legal status, structure and functioning, with matters of power and influence left to political scientists.[9]

As John Berger noted, the "relationship between what we see and what we know is never settled. Each evening we see the sun set. We know that the earth is turning away from it. Yet the knowledge, the explanation, never quite fits the sight."[10] With this in mind, *Ways of Seeing International Organisations* seeks to disrupt this state of disciplinary complacency. It is time, we argue, for the discipline to start seeing IOs differently. For the MILS, lenses reveal as much as they obscure. While the functionalist window has placed "norms" and "authority" at the forefront of its concerns, it has seldom interrogated IOs as *sites of socio-technical struggles*, or as *vessels of visions of world ordering*. More dramatically, the MILS perspective has settled itself with a reified set of issues or questions that "naturally" belong within "the providence of jurisprudence determined."[11]

Conversely, our volume challenges the premise that "looking" at international institutions is a neutral operation. Instead, it problematizes and pluralizes our "ways of seeing" IOs. In particular, it opens vistas to four core issues that have been overlooked (to different degrees) in the MILS literature: expertise, structures, performances, and capital.[12] To do so, we bring together voices from international law's neighboring disciplines in conversation with the heterodox traditions that have developed within the legal discipline itself. With the former, we refer to International Relations (IR),[13] history,[14] and

[9] B. S. Chimni, 'Marxism and International Law: A Contemporary Analysis' (1999) 34 *Economic and Political Weekly* 337–49. 339.

[10] J. Berger (ed.), *Ways of Seeing* (Penguin Books, 1972), p. 7.

[11] J. Austin, *The Province of Jurisprudence Determined: And, the Uses of the Study of Jurisprudence* (Hackett Pub, 1998).

[12] Berger, *Ways of Seeing.*

[13] P. J. Katzenstein, R. O. Keohane, and S. D. Krasner, 'International Organization and the Study of World Politics' (1998) 52 *International Organization* 645–85.

[14] M. Mazower, *Governing the World: The History of an Idea, 1815 to the Present* (Penguin Books, 2013); B. Reinalda, *The Routledge History of International Organizations from 1815 to the Present Day* (Routledge, 2013).

anthropology,[15] among others. With the latter, we allude to perspectives from the so-called New Stream;[16] the Feminist;[17] the Third World Approaches to International Law;[18] and the Global Administrative Law (GAL) scholarly movements.[19] By putting these two stands of literature in conversation, our edited volume pushes for an interdisciplinary opening of international institutional law that not only blurs the external boundaries of the field but also challenges some of its key internal tenets. Our goal is not only to promote diversity in the methods and methodologies used to study IOs,[20] but to actively challenge the current "common sense" way of doing things within the subfield of international institutional law.

15 R. Niezen and M. Sapignoli (eds.), *Palaces of Hope: The Anthropology of Global Organizations* (Cambridge University Press, 2017).

16 J. Klabbers, *An Introduction to International Organizations Law*, Third ed. (Cambridge University Press, 2015); J. Klabbers, 'The Cheshire Cat That Is International Law' (2020) 31 *European Journal of International Law* 269–83. 270–76. For an overview, see A. Bianchi, *International Law Theories: An Inquiry into Different Ways of Thinking* (Oxford University Press, 2016), pp. 110–62.

17 H. Charlesworth, 'The Gender of International Institutions' (1995) 89 *Proceedings of the Annual Meeting (American Society of International Law)* 79–85; H. Charlesworth and C. Chinkin, *The Boundaries of International Law: A Feminist Analysis* (Manchester University Press, 2000). Chapter 6; G. Heathcote, *Feminist Dialogues on International Law: Successes, Tensions, Futures* (Oxford University Press, 2019), pp. 133–72. For an overview, see Bianchi, *International Law Theories*, 183–204.

18 B. Rajagopal, *International Law from Below: Development, Social Movements and Third World Resistance* (Cambridge University Press, 2003), pp. 73–94; S. Pahuja, *Decolonising International Law: Development, Economic Growth and the Politics of Universality* (Cambridge University Press, 2011), pp. 10–43; B. S. Chimni, *International Law and World Order: A Critique of Contemporary Approaches*, Second ed. (Cambridge University Press, 2017), pp. 495–99. For an overview, see Bianchi, *International Law Theories*. 205–26.

19 N. Krisch and B. Kingsbury, 'Introduction: Global Governance and Global Administrative Law in the International Legal Order' (2006) 17 *European Journal of International Law* 1–13; B. Kingsbury and L. Casini, 'Global Administrative Law Dimensions of International Organizations Law' (2009) 6 *International Organizations Law Review* 319–58. See also J. E. Alvarez, *International Organizations as Law-Makers* (Oxford University Press, 2006); J. E. Alvarez, *The Impact of International Organizations on International Law* (Brill, 2016).

20 A goal we share, for instance, with F. Badache, L. R. Kimber, and L. Maertens (eds.), *International Organizations and Research Methods: An Introduction* (University of Michigan Press, 2023).

"Must Do Away with All Explanation": International Institutional Law beyond Problem Solving

Our volume is not the first – and hopefully will not be the last – call for the reimagination of the law of IOs (and international law more broadly).[21] Indeed, it builds upon – but it also departs from – the legacy of the previous attempts to renew or re-theorize the study of international institutions, from Constitutionalist approaches to the aforementioned GAL movement. Our invitation to see IOs differently, however, differs insofar as we challenge the dominance of "problem-solving thinking" in the study of international institutions in international law. For all of their intellectual innovations, Constitutionalist perspectives and GAL were also fixated on providing solutions to an increasingly complex global order through the language of European Public Law.[22] Here, again, drives for renewal may risk becoming repetitions.[23] We argue that the job of international institutional law scholars should not be reduced to merely finding "legal" answers to "legal" questions – we can perhaps leave that to judges and practitioners.[24] Instead, we investigate the ways in which IOs serve as sites of struggle for remaking the world order. In this way, *Ways of Seeing International Organisations* goes beyond the limited theoretical debate between advocates of liberal constitutionalism and those who remain faithful to functionalism.[25]

[21] The quoted phrase in the heading is from L. Wittgenstein, *Philosophical Investigations* (Basil Blackwell, 1953), p. 47 (passage 109).

[22] M. Martti, 'Between Coordination and Constitution: International Law as a German Discipline' (2011) 15 *Redescriptions: Political Thought, Conceptual History and Feminist Theory* 45. As an overview, see Bianchi, *International Law Theories*. 44–71.

[23] D. Kennedy, 'When Renewal Repeats: Thinking against the Box' in W. Brown and J. Halley (eds.), *Left Legalism/Left Critique* (Duke University Press, 2002), pp. 373–419. E. Cusato, R. Mignot-Mahdavi, S. Stolk, and R. Vos, 'In Praise of Multiplicity: Suspending the Desire to Change the World' (2024) 37 *Leiden Journal of International Law* 1–5.

[24] P. Schlag, 'Spam Jurisprudence, Air Law, and the Rank Anxiety of Nothing Happening (A Report on the State of the Art)' (2008) 97 *The Georgetown Law Journal* 803–35. 812–13.

[25] J. Klabbers and Å. Wallendahl, 'Contending Approaches to International Organizations: Between Functionalism and Constitutionalism' in J. Klabbers and Å. Wallendahl (eds.), *Research Handbook on the Law of International Organizations* (Edward Elgar Publishing, 2011), pp. 3–30. In this vein, see also N. Krisch, *Beyond Constitutionalism: The Pluralist Structure of Postnational Law* (Oxford University Press, 2010).

The dominance of "problem-solving thinking" is not exclusive to international law. In the 1980s, Robert Cox wrote extensively about the tendency in the IR neorealism of Hans Morgenthau and Kenneth Waltz, where the role of the discipline was portrayed as identifying "variations on always recurrent themes."[26] Emerging from the assumption that "the past repeats itself" based on a quantifiable rationality, theoretical frameworks such as game theory shed historicism to give way to claims of scientific prediction. Ahistoricism, abstraction, and the production of binaries lie at the core of problem-solving theories in both IR and international law. As Cox noted, a problem-solving theory "takes the world as it finds it, with the prevailing social and power relationships and the institutions into which they are organised [...] The general aim of problem-solving is to make these relationships and institutions work smoothly by dealing effectively with particular sources of trouble."[27] At the core of such theories is the division of social reality into "spheres or aspects of action," chief among them separation between the realms of "politics" and the "economy."[28] This, in turn, entails a categorization of actors into "public" and "private"; "state" and "non-state."

Similar to IR neorealism and liberal institutionalism, MILS studies global processes within the confines of regime-complexes. In this sense, doctrinal international law in general – and international institutional law in particular – remains structurally ahistorical and regime-oriented. It does not take interest in the study of historical change, nor does it interrogate how social orders emerge in the first place. The turn to social sciences in international law has not drastically changed the "problem-solving nature" of the international legal inquiry either. Over the last thirty years, the reign of the neoliberal international legal education geared towards training corporate practitioners to match the demands of global capitalism has exacerbated disciplinary and epistemological biases. The ultimate goal of teaching and research in international law programs – and in law courses on IOs, for that matter – remains finding "solutions" to "global challenges" within the existing order(s). The ideological stance that "one should know

[26] R. W. Cox, 'Social Forces, States and World Orders: Beyond International Relations Theory' (1981) 10 *Millennium: Journal of International Studies* 126–55.

[27] Ibid. 130. [28] Pahuja, *Decolonising International Law*, 11.

what's inside the box before embarking on out-of-box thinking," or that "theory is abstraction from experience or action,"[29] has eventually resulted in sidelining questions of capitalism, colonialism, everyday practices, expertise, and ideology in the day-to-day making of the "international."

For that reason, our volume does not offer a blind celebration of interdisciplinary thinking. As we have argued earlier in relation to the dominance of "problem-solving theories," realist and liberal institutionalist IR share many assumptions and shortcomings.[30] While we remain committed to interdisciplinary dialogue, we do not presume that other disciplines can simply "correct" limitations of MILS by merely adding different "methods" or "perspectives" and stirring. At the same time, in a moment of disciplinary "turf wars,"[31] calls for "counterdisciplinarity,"[32] and celebrations of narrow understandings of lawyers' *métier* (even among critical legal scholars),[33] the contributors to our edited volume remain convinced that our field has much to learn from its peers in the social sciences and the humanities.

What is more, we also envision such interdisciplinary dialogue as a two-way street.[34] As such, we hope that the increased use of social science methods in international law might also offer relevant insights on questions of law, justice, regulation, and rights for our colleagues in other departments. In this sense, we build on the burgeoning literature

29 M. Wallace, 'The Ends of Theory' in J. Herron, D. Huson, R. Strozier, and R. Pudaloff (eds.), *The Ends of Theory* (Wayne State University Press, 1996).

30 Which is unsurprising given their common intellectual roots in interwar Kelsenian positivism. See O. Jütersonke, *Morgenthau, Law and Realism* (Cambridge University Press, 2010). See further Bianchi, *International Law Theories*, 110–34.

31 T. Aalberts and I. Venzke, 'Moving beyond Interdisciplinary Turf Wars: Towards an Understanding of International Law as Practice' in J. dAspremont, T. Gazzini, A. Nollkaemper, and W. Werner (eds.), *International Law as a Profession* (Cambridge University Press, 2017), pp. 287–310.

32 M. Koskenniemi, 'Law, Teleology and International Relations: An Essay in Counterdisciplinarity' (2012) 26 *International Relations* 3–34.

33 A. Orford, 'On International Legal Method' (2013) 1 *London Review of International Law* 166–97; A. Orford, *International Law and the Politics of History* (Cambridge University Press, 2021), p. 185.

34 On the lack of cross-reading between disciplines, see J. Klabbers, 'The Formation of International Organizations Theory and Its Problems – Reflections Occasioned by Liesbet Hooghe, Tobias Lenz and Gary Marks, *A Theory of International Organization*' (2020) 19 *International Organizations Law Review* 1–26.

on the intersections of international law and history,[35] anthropology and international law,[36] and IR and international law,[37] while adding a layer of specific engagement with IOs and institutional legal questions, across these conversations. Ultimately, our volume not only promotes cross-fertilization between disciplinary departments but argues for an increasing destabilization of the intellectual boundaries that delimit the intellectual spaces we inhabit.[38]

In sum, our aim is to question and reimagine our ways of seeing IOs in international legal scholarship in general – and of international institutional law in particular. To do so, we propose a departure from finding "solutions" to global challenges, in a way doing "away with all explanation,"[39] and instead seeing what we have already grasped with new eyes. The volume invites the international law academy to reflect on world institutions in a multidimensional perspective and foregrounds questions of expertise and knowledge production; material and social structures; practices and performances; capital and classes. While our volume has no aspirations of comprehensiveness (as it cannot realistically cover all IOs, nor does it provide space for every discipline or perspective), it provides both experts and newcomers with a compelling overview of what interdisciplinary and critical methods can bring to the study of the "international" – a tentative map of the everyday struggles that are waged within IOs to make and contest world orders.

In this sense, we also depart from a robust tradition of critical social theory, which has interrogated the relationship between international institutions, knowledge production, and the making of the material world. In this sense, Marxist–Gramscian theories have been

[35] I. de la Rasilla, *International Law and History: Modern Interfaces* (Cambridge University Press, 2021). See especially pp. 283–307 on institutional approaches to the history of international law.

[36] A. Riles, 'Introduction to the Symposium on The Anthropology of International Law' (2021) 115 *AJIL Unbound* 268–71.

[37] J. L. Dunoff and M. A. Pollack (eds.), *Interdisciplinary Perspectives on International Law and International Relations: The State of the Art* (Cambridge University Press, 2013).

[38] N. M. Rajkovic, 'The Space between Us: Law, Teleology and the New Orientalism of Counterdisciplinarity' in W. Werner, M. De Hoon, and A. Galan (eds.), *The Law of International Lawyers* (Cambridge University Press, 2017), pp. 167–96.

[39] Wittgenstein, *Philosophical Investigations*. 47 (passage 109).

reappropriated and reinterpreted by international lawyers to explain the processes of capitalist expansion, the labor division among different international institutions, and the mechanisms used to contain anti-systemic movements.[40] Post-structuralism and post-poststructuralism have also offered methods for the uncovering of the trajectories of international civil servants as "people with agenda,"[41] or the intellectual history of international institutions, forging the path to more historical and multifaceted views of the "international," its making, and its contestation. Derridean, Bourdieusian, Foucauldian, or Latourian modes of deconstruction of the "social" have borne interesting insights for the language, authority, and material performance of technocratic governance.[42] As some of the chapters in this volume attest, approaches that focus solely on either the "macro" or "micro" scales of critique have limitations in their understanding of global processes and institutions. The same is true for the dichotomy between "internal" and "external" modes of critique, as Chimni argues in Chapter 3. In this vein, this volume invites readers to engage dialectically with both the "micro" and "macro" critique and the "internal" and "external" critique to interrogate the "international" forces of stability and change in the world order. By putting various modes of critique in conversation, our volume seeks to highlight the significance of methodological curiosity and of a diversity of positionalities in the scholarly inquiry into international institutions.

[40] Some examples of capitalist critique of international institutions are: C. C. Cutler and S. Gill (eds.), *New Constitutionalism and World Order* (Cambridge University Press, 2014). T. Krevor, 'The Legal Turn in Late Development Theory: The Rule of Law and the World Bank's Development Model' (2011) 52 *Harvard International Law Journal* 288–319. B. S. Chimni, 'Karl Marx, Douglass North, and Postcolonial States: The Relation between Law and Development' in P. O'Connell and U. Özsu (eds.), *Research Handbook on Law and Marxism* (Edgar, 2021). C. Schwöbel-Patel, *Marketing Global Justice: The Political Economy of International Criminal Law* (Cambridge University Press, 2021).

[41] S. Marks and A. Lang, 'People with Projects: Writing the Lives of International Lawyers' (2013) 27 *Temple International and Comparative Law Journal* 437–53.

[42] G. F. Sinclair, *To Reform the World: International Organizations and the Making of Modern States* (Oxford University Press, 2017); D. Van Den Meerssche, *The World Bank's Lawyers: The Life of International Law as Institutional Practice* (Oxford University Press, 2022); T. Soave, *The Everyday Makers of International Law: From Great Halls to Back Rooms* (Cambridge University Press, 2022).

Volume Overview: New Questions and Methods for the Study of IOs

Ways of Seeing International Organisations puts forth proposals for a decidedly non-doctrinal approach to the study of the "institutional" dimension in international law.[43] It brings together a diverse and balanced cast of scholars from international law, the social sciences, and the humanities to reflect on promises and perils of transdisciplinary methods for the study of IOs. It would not be coherent with the destabilizing ethos of our volume, however, to focus merely on intergovernmental organizations created by states through a formal constitutive instrument – as the traditional literature often does. Instead, our volume seeks to interrogate transnational institutions that actively shape the "global." For that reason, our volume also includes chapters on the role of international courts and tribunals (and, specifically, their secretariats), and certain nongovernmental organizations with transnational regulatory aspirations. Indeed, we hope our volume not only challenges the atheoretical and procedural focus of the mainstream literature on international institutional law but also disrupts – even if momentarily – the monopoly of knowledge production in this field, which has long been dominated by male European scholars, many of whom have been affiliated with IOs.[44] Indeed, that has been the motivation behind our initial sets of conversations both in person and in print, in which we sought to bring together scholars from a variety of vantage points as a way to push the line of vision of our field further ahead.

In line with its objectives, the volume is structured in two parts. The next two contributions in this part (Part I) shed light on the past and present of international institutional law and the implications of different theoretical frameworks for the "institutional" dimension of international law. For all their differences, these two authors share a concern about the limitations of the traditional ways of seeing IOs and put forward alternative ways of thinking about the role of these

[43] See D. Kennedy, 'The Move to Institutions' (1987) 8 *Cardozo Law Review* 841–988. 985. See also O. Aloni, *The League of Nations and the Protection of the Environment* (Cambridge University Press, 2021), pp. 93–94.

[44] J. Klabbers, 'Reflections on the International Telecommunication Union: International Organization as Epistemic Structures' in A. Bianchi and M. Hirsch (eds.), *International Law's Invisible Frames: Social Cognition and Knowledge Production in International Legal Processes* (Oxford University Press, 2021), pp. 200–18.

institutions in global governances. B. S. Chimni ponders on what critical theory can bring to the study of IOs – and vice versa. His call for a dialectic between internal and external critiques, in many ways, sets the stage for the subsequent theoretical or empirical interventions of our volume. Jan Klabbers, in turn, questions mainstream approaches to international institutions in the discipline of international law and in IR. Instead, he proposes a supra-functionalist approach that highlights distributive implications of global processes.

Part II, in turn, interrogates four different constellations of research themes that have been and continue to be out of the ambit of inquiry in the mainstream literature on international institutional law. For each cluster of research themes, the volume puts three chapters in conversation to ask our authors to explore different aspects of international institutions in an oscillation between *what to study* (objects of inquiry) and *how to study* (method/approach/perspective). By bringing together three different, but not necessarily divergent, perspectives, the four sections seek to open space for interdisciplinary dialogue. In all of the sections, we have included authors who were trained as lawyers, placing them in conversation with those who hail from other disciplines – and others who may feel uncomfortable with such disciplinary boundaries in the first place. The common thread that brings these sections together is that all of the contributions invite the reader to *see* the "international" in a different light.

The section "Expertise, Authority, and Knowledge Production" begins with a chapter by Annabelle Littoz-Monnet where she discusses the processes of production and circulation of knowledge through expert groups, academia, high-level commissions, or advisory committees within IOs. Richard Clements interrogates the case of the Independent Expert Review of the International Criminal Court, conceptualizing internal reform as a method of world ordering. Juanita Uribe studies the case of hidden hunger and how various UN agencies came to transform it into a governable object for policymaking. She explores how these agencies problematize the world, by aggregating knowledge through bureaucratic procedures.

The chapters in the section "Structures, Spaces, and Jurisdictions" revolve around material and normative structures within which IOs function. Some of these structures are shaped by organizational culture, some by the materiality of space, and others by constructed legal and jurisdictional boundaries. Tommaso Soave enquires into the institutional practice of international lawyers in international adjudicative settings, focusing on the ways in which legal operators function in the space between the structure and agency set by not only elastic norms but also socio-professional modalities. Kiri Olivia Santer offers an ethnographical account of how IOs and states raise claims over contested jurisdictions in cases of transnational legal conflicts, focusing on the involvement of the European Union and International Maritime Organization in the patrol of the Central Mediterranean. Daniel R. Quiroga-Villamarín concludes this section, focusing on the eminently material structures that constrain the "everyday geographies" of international ordering. To do so, he uses archival research to show what a material approach to international legal history can reveal about the interim headquarters of the League of Nations and the United Nations.

While the section "Expertise, Authority, and Knowledge Production" probes into questions of expertise and knowledge production, and the section "Structures, Spaces, and Jurisdictions" engages with material and discursive practices involved in the making of international order, the section "People, Practices, and Performance" zooms in on the quotidian experiences of international lawyers, civil servants, and independent experts within international bureaucracies as questions of gender, ideology, and professionalization in international institutions. Jan Eijking opens this section with an intervention that draws from a growing tradition of biographical and sociological approaches which sits at the crossroads of IR and international history. In particular, he focuses on the 1865 founding conference of the International Telegraph Union to understand the union from the perspective of its making. Miia Halme-Tuomisaari, in turn, follows with a reflection on what anthropology can offer to the study of international institutional law, focusing on the everyday performances of the UN Human Rights Committee. Dimitri Van den Meerssche introduces us to the Latourian critique of the lawyerly practice in international institutions. Focusing on the World Bank's legal office, he invites us to look for sites of political agency and intervention within "the situated, material, and embodied life of international law."

The section "Capital, Class, and Political Economy" explores the intertwined life and functioning of global institutions and the capitalist mode of production. It explores the ways in which international bureaucracies and their experts reconfigure production relations, integrate spheres of production and exchange, and depoliticize racial capitalism. Negar Mansouri argues that the history of the world order since the rise of capitalism to an overarching force of socio-political ordering in late seventeenth-century England has been a history of struggles between the organization of production relations by the market (laissez-faire capitalism) and organization of such relations by the bureaucratic vanguards (state capitalism). She subsequently engages with the dynamics of such struggles in three historical developments in the post-World War II global economy. Subsequently, Claire Cutler explores the notion of "resilience" as an adaptation strategy in the disciplinary operations of global neoliberal imaginaries. In particular, she studies how "resilience" is operationalized by a plethora of international institutions ranging from the World Bank and the Organization for Economic Cooperation and Development to the International Committee of the Red Cross and the UN. By drawing attention to the question "who gets what" from the resilience talk, Cutler introduces a critical political economy approach to the language of resilience in global governance. Last but not least, Daniel R. Quiroga-Villamarín offers a historical account of Ethiopian sovereignty within two key international institutions of the first half of the twentieth century: the League of Nations and the United Nations. He situates the case within the broader racial hierarchy embedded in European international legal imaginary and the United States' reaction towards it in the post-World War II era.

The volume concludes with a contribution by Guy Fiti Sinclair, in which he takes stock of the opportunities and the limitations of interdisciplinary and critical approaches to the study of international law and its institutions. He draws together some of the common threads of the volume to ponder on what the future of international institutional law might look like. Ultimately, we hope that the volume might open new ways of seeing the role of IOs in global governance – and, as such, that it offers more questions than answers for a field in need of a profound reimagination.

2 Critical Theory and International Organizations

The Need for an Integrated Approach

B. S. CHIMNI*

Emergence of Critical Approaches

This chapter underscores aspects of the study of international organizations (IOs) or international institutions that are relatively neglected by critical approaches to international law (CAIL) and calls for an integrated approach that combines what may be termed external and internal critiques and, in its backdrop, considers proposals for their reform.

A few prefatory remarks are, however, in order at first on the evolution of CAIL scholarship. For nearly a century international institutional law scholarship has been rooted in the positivist tradition of international law, whose different variants may together be termed mainstream international institutional law scholarship (MIILS).[1] MIILS has a synergistic relationship with functional and liberal approaches, which tend to present IOs as essential and neutral institutions that promote international cooperation and the global common good.[2] Their shared views are widely disseminated through standard textbooks of international law and IOs. What are neglected are the individual and collective roles of IOs in the expansion and stabilization of a hegemonic global order centered around the global capitalist system through inter alia prescribing, justifying, and legitimizing policies and practices that advance the interests of advanced capitalist states.

* I would like to thank the anonymous reviewers and the editors of this volume for their comments. The errors and infelicities are mine alone.

1 See H. G. Schermers and N. M. Blokker, *International Institutional Law* Sixth edition (Leiden: Brill Nijhoff, 2018); P. Sands, P. Klein, and D. W. Bowett, *Bowett's Law of International Institutions* (London: Sweet & Maxwell, 2009).

2 J. Klabbers, 'The Emergence of Functionalism in International Institutional Law: Colonial Inspirations', *European Journal of International Law* (2014) 25, 645–675 at 646.

An emergent MIILS was challenged in the inter-war period of the last century by Soviet scholarship using a Marxist lens and later by the classical realist approach.[3] Subsequently, after decolonization post-colonial nations questioned the role of IOs for pursuing the interests of developed nations, in particular the role of international economic organizations such as GATT, IMF, and the World Bank. There was also an effort to establish new IOs such as UNCTAD, created in 1964 and seen as anti-GATT, that argued the case of developing nations, in this case in the field of international trade.[4] UNCTAD formally adopted the principle of preferential treatment for developing nations, leading in 1966 to the addition of Part IV in GATT.[5] Since developing nations were heavily reliant on the export of primary products for their export earnings UNCTAD actively promoted price and income stabilizing international commodity agreements and international commodity organizations.[6] UNIDO was founded in 1966 to "promote and accelerate the industrialization of developing countries."[7] The G-77 was established in the same year as UNCTAD to identify, articulate, and promote the collective interests of developing nations in international economic organizations.[8] The different critical and constructive efforts culminated in the call for a new international economic order in 1974.

[3] On the Soviet approach see generally G. I. Tunkin, *Theory of International Law* (Cambridge, MA: Harvard University Press, 1974) Edited and translated by W. E. Butler. Unfortunately, the Soviet approach was too closely tied to Soviet foreign policy. On classical realist approach see H. Morgenthau, *Politics among Nations* Fifth edition, Revised (New York: Alfred A. Knopf, 1978); B. S. Chimni, *International Law and World Order: A Critique of Contemporary Approaches* Second edition (Cambridge: Cambridge University Press, 2017), chapter 2.

[4] See generally *UNCTAD at 50: A Short History* (United Nations, 2014) available at https://unctad.org/system/files/official-document/osg2014d1_en.pdf

[5] See General Principle Eight, Proceedings of the United Nations Conference on TRADE AND DEVELOPMENT, Geneva, March 23 – June 16, 1964, Volume I, FINAL ACT AND REPORT (New York: UN, 1964) pp. 10–11.

[6] B. S. Chimni, *International Commodity Agreements: A Legal Study* (London: Croom Helm, 1984).

[7] UNIDO, 'Brief History' available at www.unido.org/who-we-are/brief-history

[8] "The Group of 77 is the largest intergovernmental organization of developing countries in the United Nations, which provides the means for the countries of the South to articulate and promote their collective economic interests and enhance their joint negotiating capacity on all major international economic issues within the United Nations system, and promote South-South cooperation for development." The Group of 77 at the United Nations www.g77.org/

These initiatives and developments received support from the academia in the developing world, in particular from the first-generation proponents of Third World Approaches to International Law.[9] Meanwhile, other critical voices began to emerge. The neo-Gramscian scholar Robert Cox argued that we need "to place the process of international organisation in the framework of global change, to take the structural, diachronic approach."[10] He identified those features of IOs that sustained the rule of advanced capitalist nations: (1) they embody the rules which facilitate the expansion of hegemonic world orders; (2) they are themselves the product of the hegemonic world order; (3) they ideologically legitimate the norms of the world order; (4) they co-opt the elites from peripheral countries; and (5) they absorb counter-hegemonic ideas.[11] But even by the end of the last century there was a paucity of critical literature on IOs.[12]

However, in the last two decades the influence of both MIILS and the functionalist-liberal approaches to IOs has begun to be actively challenged by a host of critical approaches, which include a second generation of Third World Approaches to International Law, Feminist Approaches to International Law, and Neo-Marxist Approaches to International Law. There is, besides, the global administrative law initiative, which seeks to promote the democratic functioning of IOs.[13]

[9] These scholars included G. Abi-Saab, R. P. Anand, M. Bedjaoui, and T. E. Elias. See for instance M. Bedjoaui, *Toward a New International Economic Order* (New York: Holmes and Meir Publishers, 1979); A. Anghie and B. S. Chimni, 'Third World Approaches to International Law and Individual Responsibility in Internal Conflict' in Steven R. Ratner and Anne-Marie Slaughter, *The Methods of International Law* (Washington, DC: The American Society of International Law, 2004) pp. 185–211.

[10] R. W. Cox, *Approaches to World Order* (Cambridge: Cambridge University Press, 1996) p. 526; R. Falk (2016) 'On the Legacy of Robert W. Cox', *Globalizations* 13:5, 501–505, DOI: 10.1080/14747731.2016.1203050.

[11] R. W. Cox, 'Gramsci, Hegemony and International Relations: An Essay in Method' in Stephen Gill ed., *Gramsci, Historical Materialism and International Relations* (Cambridge: Cambridge University Press, 2011) pp. 49–66, at 62.

[12] A perusal of the literature shows that critical literature was very thin by the beginning of the new millennium. C. Archer, *International Organizations* Third edition (London: Routledge, 2001) pp. 112–173; B. S. Chimni, 'Marxism and International Law', *Economic and Political Weekly* (1999) 34, 337–349 at 343.

[13] See B. Kingsbury, N. Krisch, and R. B. Stewart, 'The Emergence of Global Administrative Law', *Law and Contemporary Problems* (2005) 68, 15.

Each of the critical approaches bring out particular troubling dimensions of IOs. The feminist approaches contend that IOs neglect the world of women, promoting policies and practices which reinforce institutions of patriarchy, and in this context point to among other things the absence of women in key decision-making positions.[14] The third world and Marxist approaches to international law argue that IOs are instruments of imperialism, the roots of which can be traced back to the Mandate System of the League of Nations.[15] Arguably, a transnational capitalist class has emerged in recent years that influences the work of IOs, diminishing the resistance of postcolonial nations to imperialism.[16] There are also intersectional approaches, which combine class, gender, and race standpoints to critique IOs.[17] Finally, emerging global administrative law points to the need for greater transparency and accountability in the functioning of IOs.

It deserves mention that the various critical approaches do not subscribe to the reductionist view that IOs are mere instruments of class, gender, racial, or geographical domination. There is recognition that to different degrees individual IOs also promote larger community interests. Thus, for example, whatever the critique of WHO, it would be acknowledged that it has been an important instrument of coordination in the course of the Covid 19 pandemic, providing beneficial assistance and guidance to member states.[18] The United Nations even serves as a site for the formation of counter-hegemonic coalitions (such as in the UN General Assembly [UNGA]) and strategies (discursive and legislative) to influence international agenda and outcomes. Even in the instance of international economic organizations whose mandates and design more openly support the objectives of

[14] H. Charlesworth and C. Chinkin, *The Boundaries of International Law* (Manchester: Manchester University Press, 2000).

[15] A. Anghie, *Sovereignty, Imperialism and International Law* (Cambridge: Cambridge University Press, 2003).

[16] B. S. Chimni, 'International Institutions Today: A Global Imperial State in the Making', *European Journal of International Law* (2004) 15, 1–39.

[17] For one such approach see Chimni, *International Law and World Order*.

[18] As the UN Secretary-General has pointed out, "even in the face of necessary but hard questions, it is important not to lose sight of what has gone right, thanks in part to a robust ecosystem of partnerships, as well as recent steps to strengthen WHO, the International Health Regulations (2005) and regional capacities, such as the Africa Centres for Disease Control and Prevention." *Our Common Agenda – Report of the Secretary General* (New York: UN, 2021) p. 51.

imperialism, critical approaches are not dismissive of them. For instance, there is acceptance that developing nations need IMF as a lender of last resort. The problem is not the goal of providing loans for overcoming short-term balance of payments crises but the content of the accompanying conditionality regime. Yet all things considered it can be said that IOs tend to promote the interests of dominant social classes and states in the international system. In other words, critical approaches rightly underline the class, gender, race, and geographical bias of existing IOs.

While critical approaches have made an important beginning in pointing to the deficiencies in IOs there are important aspects of their history and functioning that have received insufficient attention. First, the existing literature primarily offers an *external critique* of individual IOs with a focus on issues of biased design, the lack of adequate participation of weak states and groups, and unjust distributional outcomes. This critique needs to be strengthened in at least four ways: through factoring in the emergence of institutional complexes that necessitate a critique that goes beyond the design and operation of individual organizations; by offering a separate and detailed account of the history and participation of individual postcolonial nations in IOs; by advancing an appropriate theoretical framework that enables the effective combination of the class, gender, race critique of IOs and evolving IO complexes; and by suggesting ways to fill gaps in the existing accountability and responsibility regime found in the International Law Commission's Draft Articles on the Responsibility of International Organisations. Second, an external critique needs to be accompanied by an *internal critique* of IOs. An internal critique should inter alia review the following aspects of the functioning of an IO: the working of rules of membership, withdrawal, suspension, expulsion, voting, finance, and dispute settlement; in relation to endogenous and exogenous factors, the changing interpretations of mandates and accompanying policies and practices and their impact over time; and the role of leadership, staff recruitment policies, knowledge production, and organizational culture and how these subserve the interests of powerful states. Third, an active debate is called for on the need and usefulness of advancing proposals for the *reform* of IOs. A key question is whether organizational nihilism or organizational reform is the way forward for weak states and groups? In sum, what is needed is an integrated critical approach to IOs.

External Critique

The external critique of IOs neglects at least four important dimensions of the functioning of IOs. The first is the ongoing transmutation of IOs through the emergence of what Abbot and Faude call "hybrid institutional complexes" (HICs).[19] The historical movement is from individual IOs to "regime complexes" (consisting of an international treaty and a formal international organization) to HICs characterized by "a high degree of institutional diversity."[20] HICs are constituted by "informal inter-governmental organisations; trans-governmental networks; transnational public–private partnerships; transnational associations of sub-national governments; private transnational regulatory organisations; and other types of institutions."[21] According to Abbott and Faude, "HICs exhibit relatively greater functional differentiation, and...greater informal hierarchy. As a result, they produce different dynamics, interactions, systemic effects and outcomes."[22] Eilstrup-Sangiovanni and Westerwinter speak more broadly of the emergence of a global governance complex defined as "a system of governance composed of at least three international or transnational institutions or actors whose mandates,

[19] K. W. Abbott and B. Faude, 'Hybrid Institutional Complexes in Global Governance', *The Review of International Organizations* (2022) 17, 263–269.

[20] Ibid., p. 268.

[21] Ibid., p. 264. Abott and Faude illustrate their model with among others the climate change HIC: "The *climate change* HIC includes a range of institutions associated with the UN Framework Convention on Climate Change (UNFCCC), as well as other formal interstate institutions, including other treaties, international development banks and plurilateral 'clubs,' many led by the United States. It also encompasses IIGOs including the G7/8 and G20, multinational and regional environmental TGNs, and several transnational networks of subnational governments. In addition, PTROs set standards for private behavior, and other private organizations engage in information sharing, operational activities and finance. Finally, under the 'voluntary commitment system' initiated by the UN Secretary-General and UNFCCC, numerous states, subnational governments, public–private partnerships, firms and civil society organizations have voluntarily pledged action. Thus, the climate change HIC is far more encompassing than either the 'regime complex for climate change,' which includes only international institutions, or the 'transnational regime complex for climate change,' which includes only transnational institutions." The acronyms following each category have been deleted. Ibid., p. 267.

[22] Ibid., pp. 267 and 271.

functions and memberships overlap, and that jointly address a specific policy problem."[23] The UN Secretary-General has also spoken of the phenomenon of networked multilateralism that "draws together existing institutional capacities, overcoming fragmentation to ensure all are working together towards a common goal..."[24] He has pointed out how "networks can be flexible, allowing for variable participation by a wide range of actors and the possibility for open coalitions or small 'mini-lateral' or even 'micro-lateral' groups, growing over time to include more actors."[25]

The result of the emergence of these new developments is that engaging with single institutions or even regime complexes does not today suffice to understand the working of IOs. The inner dynamics of HICs or the like may either promote progressive orientation and practices[26] or result in impeding individual components from pursuing commonly agreed objectives.[27] For instance, in the field of climate change multiple regional and international IOs, along with corporations and subnational associations (such as cities) and civil society associations are involved. Arguably, given the vast financial resources available to corporations, and the primacy accorded to the interests of shareholders, disinformation campaigns and lobbying may be carried out negatively impacting the dynamics of the global climate change institutional complex. In other words, critical approaches must "investigate the ways that power is articulated and exercised within institutional complexes."[28]

[23] M. Eilstrup-Sangiovanni and O. Westerwinter, 'The Global Governance Complexity Cube: Varieties of Institutional Complexity in Global Governance', *The Review of International Organizations* (2022) 17, 233–262 at 238. Italics omitted. They clarify that "for a GGC to exist, institutions and actors must be involved in jointly governing an issue on a continuing basis which leads them to take account of one another's actions, even if relations between them are antagonistic. Institutions whose actions indirectly impact one another, perhaps on a one-off basis, but that do not interact continually, do not form a GGC." Ibid., p. 238.

[24] *Our Common Agenda – Report of the Secretary General*, p. 66.

[25] Ibid.

[26] It may lead to "enhanced performance, stronger complementarity of governance activities and greater policy coherence." Eilstrup-Sangiovanni and Westerwinter, 'The Global Governance Complexity Cube', p. 241.

[27] There is a view that "overlapping institutional mandates may produce gridlock as the lack of formal hierarchy yields a proliferation of veto points, and conflicting rulesets encourage noncompliance and opportunistic forum-shopping." Eilstrup-Sangiovanni and Westerwinter, 'The Global Governance Complexity Cube', p. 249.

[28] Ibid., p. 253.

Second, there is the justified lament of postcolonial theory that both mainstream and critical approaches do not study the record of participation of Global South nations, occluding the possibility of soundly assessing their place and role in IOs. The history of participation of even principal developing nations such as Brazil, China, India, Indonesia, and Nigeria are seldom reviewed and taken into consideration in theorizing or identifying problems with the functioning of contemporary IOs. Take the example of colonial India, which was an original member of the League of Nations and United Nations. Its record of participation in the period before independence in 1947 shows that formal membership alone does not promise positive outcomes.[29] That history suggests that the current relationship between postcolonial nations and IOs need to be evaluated only after locating them in deep structures of neo-colonialism.[30] There is also the need to examine whether regional organizations (e.g., African Union and ASEAN) and development organizations (e.g., the New Development Bank) established by Global South nations are able to advance their interests. Furthermore, how far do these organizations depart from the universal counterparts in terms of design, objectives, and functioning? For example, do international financial institutions established by Global South nations reject the principle of weighted voting? In short, in order to advance an effective critique of IOs or offer sound suggestions on ways of reforming them it is necessary to engage with the history of participation of Global South nations.

Third, while individual critical theories have made important contributions in pinpointing shortcomings in existing IOs from class, gender, race, and geographical standpoints there is also a need to explore intersectional approaches that can draw together the rich insights that have been advanced. The overall idea is not an arithmetic aggregation of the different critiques but the development of a more fundamental viewpoint that traces the separate critiques to deep structures that give rise to different forms of exclusion. Arguably, the deficiencies can be traced to the functioning of a patriarchal and racial global capitalist system whose inner dynamics produces negative distributive outcomes

29 R. P. Anand, 'The Formation of International Organizations and India: A Historical Study', *Leiden Journal of International Law* (2010) 23, 5–21 at 9.

30 See for example L. Dellmuth, J. A. Scholte, J. Tallberg, and S. Verhaegen, 'The Elite–Citizen Gap in International Organization Legitimacy', *American Political Science Review* (2022) 116:1, 283–300.

for subaltern groups and nations in the process of sustaining the global accumulation of capital.

Fourth, there is the need to pinpoint the weaknesses and gaps in the ILC's Draft Articles of Responsibility of International Organizations as it only deals with a narrow set of acts of omission and commission.[31] What is called for is a more inclusive rendering of the rules of legal accountability and responsibility, especially for large human rights harm caused to subaltern groups and nations through IO policies and practices.[32] One way forward is for IOs to "acknowledge customary international law obligations to provide effective remedies."[33] According to Daugirdas and Schuricht, the advantages of this move are many: "...it offers a way to apply human rights law to powerful, non-State actors – and increases the likelihood that those obligations will be implemented. And from the perspective of global administrative law, a customary obligation offers a way to cement accountability-promoting principles in a traditional source of binding law."[34] Another possibility is that member states of IOs undertake due diligence obligations.[35] These are just some suggestions. What is called for is a thorough discussion of ways in which to supplement ILC's Draft Articles.

Internal Critique

Even a comprehensive external critique of IOs will remain partial and limited if unaccompanied by a review of the internal functioning of an IO, i.e., a study of its intramural structures and everyday practices,

[31] The text of DARIO is available at https://legal.un.org/ilc/texts/instruments/english/draft_articles/9_11_2011.pdf
On "acts of omission" see J. Klabbers, 'Reflections on Role Responsibility: The Responsibility of International Organizations for Failing to Act', *European Journal of International Law* (2017) 28:4, 1133–1161.

[32] Chimni, 'International Institutions Today'.

[33] K. Daugirdas and S. Schuricht, 'Breaking the Silence: Why International Organizations Should Acknowledge Customary International Law Obligations to Provide Effective Remedies', *Law & Economics Working Papers* (2020), 166 at p. 19. https://repository.law.umich.edu/law_econ_current/166P.19.

[34] Ibid., p. 20.

[35] K. Daugirdas, 'Member States' Due Diligence Obligations to Supervise International Organizations' in Heike Krieger, Anne Peters, and Leonhard Kreuzer eds., *Due Diligence in the International Legal Order* (Oxford: Oxford University Press, 2021) p. 59.

which can play an important role in sustaining the hegemony of powerful states. The internal critique is now complicated by the emergence of HICs as a new dynamic is in play with individual IOs having to function in an institutional complex. At least seven aspects of the internal functioning of an IO deserve to be examined.

First, critical theory needs to be more alert to the fact that powerful states seek to achieve their objectives through manipulating the design features of an IO.[36] The focus of the internal critique will be more on the practice of states than the design feature per se. For example, it would examine in detail how the provisions on withdrawal from membership have been used to make an IO change direction and policies.[37] The US has deployed the withdrawal strategy on a number of occasions: It withdrew from membership of ILO (in 1977, returned in 1980), UNESCO (in 1985, returned in 2003), UNIDO (1995), UNICEF (2017), HRC (2018, returned in 2022, withdrew in 2025), and WHO (2020, returned in 2021, withdrew in 2025). It has also threatened to withdraw from WTO. A number of Global South nations have also used the provision of withdrawal to signal their dissent from policies of IOs. For example, Bolivia (2007), Ecuador (2009), Venezuela (2012), and Honduras (2024) have withdrawn from the International Centre for the Settlement of Investment Disputes (ICSID) to protest inequitable outcomes. African nations have threatened to exit the International Criminal Court (ICC) for targeting African leaders. Burundi (2017) and Philippines (2019) have already withdrawn from ICC. However, in view of the power differentials Global South nations do not have the same impact as those of the Global North.

A key design feature of any IO relates to the allocation of voting rights which can be used to gain control over the decision-making process. The constituent instruments of the IMF and World Bank are examples of IOs that adopt a weighted voting system denying

[36] For a survey of different theories of institutional design see E. Voeten, 'Making Sense of the Design of International Institutions', *Annual Review of Political Science* (2019) 22, 147–163. Available at www.annualreviews.org/doi/pdf/10.1146/annurev-polisci-041916-021108; See also B. Koremenos, C. Lipson, and D. Snidal, 'The Rational Design of International Institutions', *International Organization* (2001) 55, 761–799.

[37] I. von Borzyskowski and Felicity Vabulas, 'Hello, Goodbye: When Do States Withdraw from International Organizations?', *The Review of International Organizations* (2019) 14, 335–366.

effective participation to Global South nations. The veto powers assigned to the five permanent members in the UN Security Council is another instance. These design defects have sought to be rectified by Global South nations. Thus, for instance, Article 10 of the Charter of Economic Rights and Duties, 1974, stressed "the right to participate fully and effectively in the international decision-making process in the solution of world economic, financial and monetary problems."[38] There have also been efforts to amend the UN Charter provisions on membership and veto power in the UN Security Council;[39] the Russian vetoes after the invasion of Ukraine is likely to renew these endeavors. The challenge before critical approaches is to offer in the matrix of these formal voting structures an ethnographic account and analysis of the dynamics of the regular interactions among officials of the organization, the type of diplomatic bargaining that tends to take place, the informal processes influencing decision-making in times of crisis, and the negative effects of formal arrangements on taking impartial, equitable, and reasoned decisions.[40]

Second, in reviewing IOs, critical approaches need to distinguish different phases of the life of IOs with the inevitable ebbs and flows to capture the complex relationship between external developments in the global order and the changing interpretations of their mandates. What are required are thick histories of organizations that allow an assessment of the principal factors that influence their functioning, and the informal and formal processes through which respective mandates are adapted to address new challenges or concerns of powerful member states. For example, the World Bank has gone through at least six phases in response to external developments. Michael Goldman identifies four of these: the "'reluctant Banker' period of 1944–68; the Bank's 'rise to power' in the period of 1968–80 during which the calls for 'poverty alleviation' and meeting 'basic needs' for the 'absolute poor' reflected a new turn; the 'debt and adjustment' period of 1980–89;

[38] Article 10 of the Charter of Economic Rights and Duties of States, 1974.

[39] See generally D. Bourantónis, *The History and Politics of UN Security Council Reform* (New York: Routledge, 2005).

[40] See generally Fanny Badache, Leah R. Kimber, and Lucille Marrtens eds., *International Organizations and Research Methods: An Introduction* (Ann Arbour: University of Michigan Press, 2023); J. Eckel 'Focal Times and Spaces: How Ethnography Foregrounds the Spatiotemporality of International Organizations and Global Governance', *Global Policy* (2021) 12, 34–44.

and the 'green neoliberal' period" beginning 1989.[41] The 2007 financial crisis and Covid 19 pandemic inaugurated two subsequent phases. The different phases of the history of the IMF are inter alia reflected in its changing guidelines on conditionality. For instance, as a response to developing nations avoiding seeking loans from the organization IMF adopted new conditionality guidelines in 1979. A key feature of the new guidelines was the possibility of "pay[ing] due regard to the domestic social and political objectives, the economic priorities, and the circumstances of members including the causes of their balance of payments problems."[42] But the situation underwent change with the collapse of primary commodity prices in the early 1980s followed by the debt crisis that visited many Global South nations. Thereafter, IMF tended to neglect the 1979 guidelines.[43] The organization once again revised its conditionality guidelines in 2002 when it was without clients, now recognizing that "its programs have become unduly intrusive" and that there was a need to "reduce the number of conditions to those that are essential to the achievement of the program's objectives."[44] But post the financial and pandemic crises the IMF received a new lease of life and the earlier regime of conditionalities was essentially restored. The history of IMF also shows how the mandate can be reconfigured in practice. It was given little authority by the articles of agreement in the domain of capital controls.[45] But since it worked in

[41] M. Goldman, *Imperial Nature: The World Bank and Struggles for Social Justice in the Age of Globalization* (New Delhi: Orient Longman, 2006) p. 50. D. Van Den Meersche, *The World Bank's Lawyers: The Life of International Law as Institutional Practice* (Oxford: Oxford University Press, 2022).

[42] See Selected Decisions and Selected Documents of the IMF, Forty First Issue, July 30, 2020 available at www.imf.org/en/Publications/Selected-Decisions/selected-decisions-list

[43] T. Ferguson, *The Third World and Decision Making in the International Monetary Fund* (London: Pinter Publishers, 1988).

[44] D. D. Bradlow, *The Governance of the IMF: The Need for Comprehensive Reform* (September 2006) p. 16, available at https://digitalcommons.wcl.american.edu/fac_works_papers/20/ See also IMF, 'Guidelines on Conditionality', September 25, 2002, Selected Decisions and Selected Documents of the IMF, Forty First Issue, July 30, 2020 available at www.imf.org/en/publications/selected-decisions/description?decision=12864-(02%2F102)

[45] For justification of its role in capital controls see A. Martin, 'The IMF and Its Shifting Mandate towards Capital Movements and Capital Controls: A Legal Perspective', *Legal Issues of Economic Integration* (2017) 44, 211–235. But according to Stiglitz and Ostry the Articles of Agreement "did not give the

the interests of the advanced capitalist states the absence of mandate did not deter IMF from adopting an "institutional view" on capital controls, the latest in March 2022 (replacing an earlier view approved in 2012).[46] The reasoning that informs and legitimizes the response of the IMF – pointing to developments in the world economy – can only be tenuously justified by reference to the articles of agreement. Put differently, the mutable relationship between IMF actions, its mandate, and the global capitalist system deserve to be adequately researched.

The changing role of UNHCR is another example of how the mandate of an IO is adapted to meet either new situations or the concerns of powerful states.[47] Betts speaks of "formal and informal adaptations over time" of the UNHCR Mandate with respect to "who to protect" and "how to protect."[48] The changes in the mandate have in some cases been authorized by states, but in other instances initiated by the organization in response to changing contexts and developments, including its relationship to other organizations in the field.[49] Betts goes on to identify "five key turning points in mandate expansion": "1. prolonging its existence (1952–1956); 2. geographical expansion (1957–1967); 3. becoming a humanitarian relief agency (1990–2000); 4. assuming responsibility for IDP [internally displaced persons] protection (1998–2006); and 5. protecting victims of natural disaster (2007–2011)."[50] What critical approaches need to explore is the relationship between these different phases, the organizational stakes in modifying the mandate, and the interests of powerful states. An important variable here

IMF the authority to push for capital-market liberalisation." J. E. Stiglitz and J. D. Ostry, 'The IMF Is Still Behind the Times on Capital Controls', *Project Syndicate*, May 16, 2022 available at www.project-syndicate.org/commentary/imf-revised-capital-control-framework-still-flawed-by-joseph-e-stiglitz-and-jonathan-d-ostry-2022-05

[46] See IMF, 'Review of the Institutional View on the Liberalisation and Management of Capital Flows', Policy Paper, March 2022 available at www.imf.org/-/media/Files/Publications/PP/2022/English/PPEA2022008.ashx. For a brief comment see Stiglitz and Ostry, 'The IMF Is Still Behind the Times on Capital Controls'.

[47] The original mandate of UNHCR is to be found in the Statute of the Office of the United Nations High Commissioner for Refugees available at www.unhcr.org/4d944e589.pdf

[48] A. Betts, 'UNHCR, Autonomy and Mandate Change' in Joel Oestreich ed., *International Organizations as Self-Directed Actors: A Framework for Analysis* (New York: Routledge, 2012) pp. 118–137 at p. 118.

[49] Ibid., pp. 119, 120. [50] Ibid., p. 119.

is the voluntary nature of funding making UNHCR vulnerable to pressure from rich donor states.[51] Therefore, when Betts concludes that UNHCR "has had considerable agency to define its own destiny," the question is the factors and actors that allowed it that freedom.[52] These aspects call for close study so that the hypothesis of IOs as vehicles for pursuing the interests of powerful states can be tested.

The shifting role of the UN Security Council and UNGA in the maintenance of international peace and security in different times is an instance of the shifting responsibility of the internal organs of an IO. The emergency session of the UNGA on the Russian invasion of Ukraine called under the Uniting for Peace Resolution adopted in 1950 shows the evolution of assigned roles of internal organs of IOs over time.[53] Critical approaches must closely analyze the meaning and implications of such developments.

Third, critical approaches do not sufficiently examine the role of organizational leadership and its impact on the goals and functioning of an IO. The feminist approach to international law is an exception in this respect, but its reflections are essentially confined to the absence of women in leadership roles. While this lament is entirely appropriate the issue of leadership goes beyond the gender question. A dynamic leadership can redefine the goals of an IO. For example, Robert McNamara, who was the president of the World Bank between 1968 and 1981, played an important role in projecting a poverty agenda in a period of accelerated decolonization. The official history of the World Bank puts it in the following way: "Robert McNamara shaped the Bank as no one before him... The Bank that McNamara left in 1981 was completely transformed from the institution he had entered thirteen years earlier. It was a much larger organisation, and much more complex."[54] What did this expansion and complexity mean?

[51] B. E. Whitaker, 'Funding the International Refugee Regime: Implications for Protection', *Global Governance* (2008) 14, 241–258.

[52] Ibid., p. 137.

[53] M. Ramsden, 'Uniting for Peace: The Emergency Special Session on Ukraine', *Harvard International Law Journal* available at https://harvardilj.org/2022/04/uniting-for-peace-the-emergency-special-session-on-ukraine/

[54] World Bank: Explore History: Robert S McNamara www.worldbank.org/en/archive/history/past-presidents/robert-strange-mcnamara; See also D. Van Den Meerssche, '"The Critic Is Not the One Who Debunks, but the One Who Assembles": On Professional Performances and Material Practice,' in this volume, Chapter 12.

Did it reflect the strategy of the Bank to deal with the problems of postcolonial states? Did the poverty agenda help operationalize a neo-colonial agenda? The leadership in IOs has played an important role in other organizations such as UNHCR. According to Betts, leadership "mattered for defining the direction of the organisation's mandate."[55] The fact that the role of leadership is a significant factor can be seen from the targeting of WHO Director-General Tedros Adhanom Ghebreyesus by the Trump administration during the Covid 19 pandemic followed by a call for change in the direction and functioning of the organization. In reality, the leadership was impeded by "limitations in the mandate" and "its chronic underfunding, with 80 per cent of its $2 billion annual budget dependent on earmarked contributions, which undermines its [i.e., WHO's] independence and capacity to deliver on its mandate."[56] In sum, a critical assessment of leadership of IOs is important in sustaining the view that these serve interests of powerful states.

Fourth, critical approaches should review staff recruitment policies and everyday practices of an IO. The kind of staff that is hired, its class, gender, geographical, and disciplinary dimensions, has an important bearing on organizational culture with implications for IO policies and practices. Thus, for example, it is important to consider the profile of experts working in the World Bank and explore how far the dominance of economists has a bearing on the fact that it has not taken international human rights law seriously.[57] What role have anthropologists and sociologists played in the World Bank? What impact have they had on organizational culture? Did the generation of interdisciplinary knowledge help internalize the gender and green critiques? There are a range of other issues as well. How does the socialization and everyday work of the staff contribute to the effectiveness of an IO? How far does the fact that international civil servants are insulated from the influence of individual member states

[55] Betts, 'UNHCR, Autonomy and Mandate Change', p. 120.

[56] *Our Common Agenda – Report of the Secretary General*, pp. 50–51. See also E. Benvenisti, 'The WHO – Destined to Fail? Political Cooperation and the COVID-19 Pandemic', *American Journal of International Law* (2020) 114, 588–597.

[57] G. A. Sarfaty, 'Why Culture Matters in International Institutions: The Marginality of Human Rights at the World Bank', *American Journal of International Law* (2009) 103, 647–683.

help in maintaining the autonomy of an IO? For instance, it has been said that there is "substantial evidence that World Bank staff play an important role in facilitating implementation of investment projects."[58] In sum, what is the impact of organizational culture and staff on the working of IOs?

Fifth, there is a need to separately study the legal culture of IOs as it can determine whether certain policy initiatives and practices are seen as in accord with respective mandates. In his recent work Van den Meerssche documents how a "new normative architecture" proposed by Anne-Marie Leroy, the World Bank General Counsel from 2009 to 2016, shaped the understanding of the limits of the organization's mandate and accountability.[59] Leroy departed from the more traditional approach of predecessors like Ibrahim Shihata who insisted that the World Bank act within the constraints imposed by the mandate. Instead, she emphasized "a pragmatic 'paradigm' for legal practice."[60] It allowed Leroy to respond positively to the demands of the higher management leading to "the emergence of a new 'culture' of lawyering a flexible, dynamic, outcome-driven approach attuned to the productivities of uncertainty and the governmentality of risk."[61] This orientation was used to limit the Bank's accountability to international human rights law. She did this to restore "institutional harmony" when the World Bank Inspection Panel was seen as overstepping its role.[62]

Sixth, critical approaches should review the knowledge production function of IOs which has from the times of the League of Nations performed a crucial role in global governance; the League saw the production of information and analysis on mandate states as critical to their (colonial) administration.[63] The production of knowledge about postcolonial nations is as significant today in devising and legitimizing

[58] M. Heinzel and A. Liese, 'Managing Performance and Winning Trust. How World Bank Staff Shapes Recipient Performance', *The Review of International Organizations* (2021) 16, 625–653.

[59] D. Van Der Meerssche, 'Deformalizing International Organizations Law: The Risk Appetite of Anne-Marie Leroy', *European Journal of International Law* (2023) 34, 141–167 at 143.

[60] Ibid., at 143. [61] Ibid., at 149. [62] Ibid., at 163.

[63] A. Anghie, 'Colonialism and the Birth of International Institutions: Sovereignty, Economy, and the Mandate System of the League of Nations', *New York University Journal of International Law and Politics* (2002) 34, 513.

certain models of development.[64] For instance, the development strategies recommended by organizations such as the World Bank are based on the knowledge produced and its larger vision of development spelled out in publications such as *The World Development Report*.[65] The impact of the ideas advanced in them comes through their wide dissemination and their eventual infiltration of policy-making forums in postcolonial nations. The "law and development" project of the World Bank is another example of how knowledge is used, in this case relying additionally on the work of economic historians like Douglass North, to ensure the creation of legal institutions necessary to promote free market economies.[66] But to be sure not all production of knowledge by IOs feeds into the hegemonic enterprise. The UN, as the UN Secretary-General has observed, is "a source of reliable data and evidence, providing public and verified information to help the world understand risks and opportunities."[67] There are also initiatives underway for "better linking of knowledge centres across the United Nations system, including in its specialised agencies."[68] Such efforts need to be evaluated from the perspective of weak groups and nations.

Seventh, critical theories should devote close attention to IO–NGO–civil society relations. The UN Secretary-General has stated that "what is most needed" at present is for the UN system "directly to include civil society in their work across all the pillars of our activities."[69] He has called on "all United Nations entities…to establish a dedicated focal point for civil society, if they have not already done so."[70] Underlying this understanding are the all-affected and all-subjected principles that stress the need to give voice to all those impacted by global rules, decisions, and practices and help address democratic deficit in IOs.[71] At the same time there is a need to be alert to the

[64] A. St. Clair, 'The World Bank as a Transnational Expertized Institution', *Global Governance* (2006) 12, 77–95.

[65] See generally L. Mehta, 'The World Bank and Its Emerging Knowledge Empire', *Human Organization* (2001) 60, 189–196.

[66] B. S. Chimni, 'Karl Marx, Douglass North, and Postcolonial States: The Relation between Law and Development' in Paul O'Connell and Umut Oszu eds., *Research Handbook on Law and Marxism* (Cheltenham: Edward Elgar, 2021) pp. 319–335.

[67] *Our Common Agenda – Report of the Secretary General*, p. 74.

[68] Ibid., p. 74. [69] Ibid., p. 75. [70] Ibid.

[71] B. S. Chimni, 'The Limits of the All Affected Principle: Attending to Deep Structures', *Third World Thematics: A TWQ Journal* (2018) 3, 807;

growing presence and influence of corporates in IOs to suggest ways in which to limit their impact. Thus, for example, WHO has framed rules to limit the influence of transnational corporations in the making of its policies.[72] Finally, in instances when IOs accept the viewpoint of civil society, such as the World Bank's accommodation of its human rights and environment critiques, it is important to evaluate whether it is real and substantial.

Reform of IOs

It can be said that despite the serious and legitimate concerns expressed by critical approaches – which need to be further explored through addressing the neglected dimensions of external and internal critiques – contemporary IOs have a dual character. Even as IOs help sustain the hegemony of powerful states these also promote the common good, each IO to a different degree, through institutionalizing progressive international cooperation. If that were not the case weak nations would not have remained members of IOs or expressed concern today that the liberal international order is being dismantled. In other words, there is acknowledgment that a global order in which IOs mediate the relationship between powerful and weak states on the basis of agreed rules and established channels for communication is better than a system in which the relationship between these group of states is the direct subject of power relations. The concern of weak nations is that among other things the mandate and rules that control the functioning of IOs, especially key IOs (or their organs), favor strong states constraining among other things their policy space, limiting the possibility of promoting the welfare of their peoples.[73] The

J. von Bernstorff, 'New Responses to the Legitimacy Crisis of International Institutions: The Role of "Civil Society" and the Rise of the Principle of Participation of "The Most Affected" in International Institutional Law', *European Journal of International Law* (2021) XX, 1–33.

72 In 2016 WHO adopted a "Framework of Engagement with Non-State Actors." It recognizes the risks involved in dealing with non-state actors including "conflicts of interest" and "undue or improper influence… especially in, but not limited to, policies, norms and standard setting." Sixty-Ninth World Health Assembly, WHA 69.10, May 28, 2016, Framework of Engagement with Non-State Actors https://apps.who.int/gb/ebwha/pdf_files/wha69/a69_r10-en.pdf

73 Chimni, 'International Institutions Today'.

matter is complicated by the emergence of a transnational capitalist class which aligns the interests of elites of key Global South and Global North nations.[74] This development prevents important Global South nations from actively campaigning for reform of key IOs through a global coalitional strategy, other than to seek changes that enhance their individual influence in the global order. It is this complex situation which explains why IOs are simultaneously the subject of sanguine mainstream functionalist and liberal views and questioning critical approaches. To put it differently, while IOs have the potential to actively promote the global common good through institutionalized international cooperation, and some gains do accrue to weak nations, the promise of a just global order remains largely unfulfilled as these submit to the imperatives of sustaining a global capitalist order.[75]

But given the fact that some advantages do accrue to weak nations the idea of reform of IOs is worth pursuing so as to enhance opportunities for further gains. It could of course be argued that since IOs are primarily tools of dominance and exploitation any effort at reform will only go to legitimize them. Such a view overlooks three considerations: First, since the proposals for reform simultaneously represent a critique of the mandate, structures, and functioning of existing IOs these can help disseminate the reasons for dissatisfaction. Second, as long as the direction of proposed reforms is part of a larger vision for creating a more equitable global order such initiatives do not necessarily go to legitimize individual IOs or the global organizational order. Third, the reform project could in the face of resistance from powerful states propel the creation of new IOs that serve the interests of weak nations. In the past weak nations established organizations like UNCTAD and UNIDO for this purpose.

The more important question perhaps is whether in the present state of international relations there is less likelihood of effective collective strategies being put together by weak nations. The fact that

[74] Chimni, *International Law and World Order*, pp. 507–509.

[75] "...there is an important nuance to consider between left-wing and right-wing populist critique of IOs. While left-wing populists typically accept the need for IOs but criticize their distributive consequences, right-wing populists reject IO authority in principle." J. Tallberg, 'Legitimacy and Modes of Global Governance' in M. N. Barnett, J. C. W. Pevehouse, and K. Raustiala eds., *Global Governance in a World of Change* (Cambridge: Cambridge University Press, 2022) pp. 311–338 at p. 329.

key Global South nations are members of G-20 – and the non-aligned movement and G-77 are no longer as effective – would appear to reduce the possibility of building a coalition of weak states to bring about reform of IOs. On the other hand, we have seen the creation of a new platform and multiple organizations by BRICS nations. These contrasting developments suggest competition and collaboration between key nations of the Global North and Global South that does not eliminate the possibility of and space for reform of existing IOs. The problem with the standpoint of organizational nihilism is that it leaves the field free for dominant social forces and actors to pursue their hegemonic enterprise. It discounts the fact that sustained critique and political mobilization through a coalition of states, and global civil society, even if at times sans some key states of the Global South can help bring about changes that advantage weak nations and groups in however small ways. It must be remembered that "while weak states are often profoundly disadvantaged in the global system, they have more power than is commonly assumed, and a wide variety of strategies for exercising that power."[76] The latter range from linkage making to the act of withdrawal.

However, if IO reform is to be pursued several steps need to be taken by CAIL to create a facilitating environment.

First, there is a need to decolonize the pedagogy and study of IOs. It is crucial to expose and disseminate the role IOs play in sustaining a hegemonic global order. Such interventions must be accompanied by a critique of MIILS for ignoring the key role of ideology, power, and interests in the functioning of IOs. Likewise, attention must be drawn to the limitations of the functionalist and liberal approaches. A sustained case has to be made out for studying IOs from class, gender, race, and intersectional standpoints.

Second, when possible critical scholars should use official platforms to propose reforms in relevant IOs. For example, many leading TWAIL scholars have served or are serving as UN Special Rapporteurs on different human rights themes. These include Tendayi Achiume, Michael Fakhri, Obiora Okafor, and Balakrishnan Rajagopal. The position of Special Rapporteurs allows the authorized gathering and

[76] D. Snidal, T. Hale, E. Jones, C. Mertens, and K. Milewicz, 'The Power of the "Weak" and International Organizations', *The Review of International Organizations* (2024) https://doi.org/10.1007/s11558-024-09531-w

dissemination of important information and analysis which challenges dominant accounts and visions of the global order. It equally creates opportunities to advance proposals for reform of IOs in concerned areas even if these be modest in nature.

Third, critical approaches should assess measures taken by IOs to accommodate critiques, including in some instances the creation of new processes and mechanisms to address problems raised by academia and civil society critics.[77] Thus, for example, the World Bank created the World Bank Inspection Panel to deal with concerns of project-affected persons whose plight was raised by social movements.[78] Its design and functioning should be appraised so as to identify gaps and weaknesses in functioning.

Finally, critical approaches should advance detailed proposals for reform of IOs and call for the creation of new organizations if these can promote the interests of weak states and groups. For instance, a new IO is needed for global digital regulation as the current regime constituted by national and regional regimes and self-regulation of digital corporations cannot effectively protect the digital rights of individuals and weak states. Equally, critical approaches should propose designs and structures that can promote digital equity and justice.

Concluding Remarks: The Value of an Integrated Approach

In order to be effective, the appraisal of IOs should not simply be an extension of a critique of the global order. The specificities of the world of IOs, their mandates, structures, and functioning, need to be the basis on which any assessment must be advanced. What are called for are integrated critical studies that combine external and internal

[77] As one scholar observes, "[o]ver the past two decades old-style IOs have been refitted for new procedural standards, including transparency, participation, and accountability. These reforms have in many cases been explicitly driven by a desire to legitimize IOs in light of new governance norms and growing societal contestation. IOs have seriously expanded the institutional opportunities for civil society actors to participate in policy-making. Many IOs have also adopted public information policies that expand transparency and instituted novel accountability procedures. In addition, a growing number of IOs have sought to strengthen democratic representation through the creation of international parliamentary assemblies." Tallberg, Legitimacy and Modes, p. 329.

[78] On WB Inspection Panel see its website www.inspectionpanel.org/

evaluation of individual organizations and institutional complexes to map and illuminate over time the role inter alia of the mandate and its interpretations, design, leadership, and culture in sustaining the domination of powerful states resulting in troubling outcomes. Such detailed analysis can help assign appropriate significance to formal and informal elements and processes, underscoring that the demand for structural reform should be accompanied by suggested changes in the everyday practices and culture of an organization or organization complex. In other words, an integrated approach can capture the interaction and dynamics between the formal and non-formal elements to help identify multiple spaces for intervention and reform. It can thus help frame appropriate initiatives to realize the interests of weak states and groups.

3 *Inter-disciplinarity and the Law of International Organizations*

JAN KLABBERS*

Introduction

The law of international organizations is stuck in a rut. The legal framework governing the operation of international organizations developed in the late nineteenth and early twentieth century has not been changed since. Perhaps it was suitable once upon a time, for the world circa 1900, but whatever suitability it may once have had has long disappeared from view.[1]

The outdated nature of the legal framework, one might be tempted to think, is little more than a theoretical academic conceit. After all, international organizations continue to exist; they continue to multiply; they function more or less as they have done for over a century; and the world would decidedly be worse off without them. Indeed, states queue up to join them: no sooner has a state achieved independence than it wants to join the United Nations. No sooner has a European state achieved a certain level of economic development than it wants to join the European Union, as doing so is the smart thing to do (and withdrawing is economic suicide, as the UK is finding out). And even the stable genius that is Donald Trump, who once spent some time tweeting from the White House, saw fit, his reputation as gravedigger of international law and multilateralism notwithstanding, to have the US join international organizations. So what, then, if the theoretical framework is outdated?

And yet, there are practical ramifications – the theoretical immaturity has a 'spill-over' effect (pun intended) into the practical life of international organizations and, what is more, into our everyday lives.

* This chapter is part of the PRIVIGO project, which has received funding from the European Research Council, Grant No. 883417.

[1] See further J. Klabbers, 'The EJIL Foreword: The Transformation of International Organizations Law', (2015) 26 *European Journal of International Law* 9–82, with references.

This is most prominently visible when it comes to issues of control: international organizations operate without much political control, and without much judicial control; a point made with some regularity in the literature.[2] Hence, these highly important political actors – the institutions of global governance – can almost by definition do as they please in ways that are difficult to reconcile with basic ideas about democratic decision-making, the accountability of public power, or the cherished Rule of Law.

As a result, it should come as no surprise that many have proclaimed that the law ought to change, so as to facilitate the control over international organizations, especially perhaps when these are exercising public power. Neither is it very surprising that inspiration for the rejuvenation of international organizations is often looked for in the insights of neighbouring disciplines, in particular the discipline of International Relations (IR). And yet, much of this barks up the wrong tree. Mainstream IR, whether neo-realist or liberal-institutionalist, at its best can and does offer a deeper insight into political processes and the uses and limits of particular concepts; think only of some of the work of Robert Keohane.[3] But it often does so at the price of specific legal thought. So as a way to overcome problems of control, IR does not have all that much to offer, really, in much the same way that the brain surgeon is unlikely to find much help in the work of the surgeon specialized in knees. They may both occupy the 'same conceptual space', as Slaughter once delightfully yet misleadingly called it – but do not have all that much to teach each other.[4]

The call for inter-disciplinarity, which I was asked to address, makes sense in the abstract but is not without pitfalls. In what follows, I will explain what the problem is with international organizations law (in the section Functionalism's Limits), where and how the formation of theory should and could improve, and under what conditions which

[2] See, e.g., C. Ferstman, *International Organizations and the Fight for Accountability: The Remedies and Reparations Gap* (Oxford: Oxford University Press, 2017).

[3] Emblematic perhaps is R. Keohane, *International Institutions and State Power: Essays in International Relations Theory* (Boulder, CO: Westview, 1989). Seminal on accountability is R. Grant and R. Keohane, 'Accountability and Abuses of Power in World Politics' (2005) 99 *American Political Science Review* 29–43.

[4] A. Slaughter, 'International law in a World of Liberal States' (1995) 6 *European Journal of International Law* 503–538.

forms of inter-disciplinarity may be of assistance in arriving at a persuasive legal theory of international organizations (in the section On State-centrism and Inter-disciplinarity). In doing so, I depart from the less wide-ranging but excellent recent study by Gasbarri,[5] and will sketch my own intuitions about how to come to a proper understanding of international organizations law (in the section Towards a Supra-Functionalist Alternative). The Conclusion contains some final remarks.

Functionalism's Limits

The theory of international organizations law was effectively put in place about a century ago, after in particular Paul Reinsch and Francis Sayre had published their influential works.[6] Reinsch laid down the broad contours: under functionalism, as it came to be known, international organizations perform tasks assigned to them by their member states. These tasks are typically a-political, technical in nature (administrative, in today's language), cost member states little in terms of either loss of sovereignty or financial contributions, and yet, if all relevant sectors of social life are organized this way, world peace will be around the corner. The overwhelming functionalist sentiment is that through inter-state cooperation, swords can be turned into ploughshares.[7] To this Reinschian and still very recognizable basis, Sayre further added the idea that all forms of more than incidental inter-state cooperation, no matter their precise goal, ought to be seen as international organizations. This makes it plausible for the discipline to treat wide-ranging entities such as the World Bank and the European University Institute, or the World Health Organization, the

[5] L. Gasbarri, *The Concept of an International Organization in International Law* (Oxford: Oxford University Press, 2021).

[6] P. Reinsch, *Public International Unions, Their Work and Organization: A Study in International Administrative Law* (Boston: Ginn & Co., 1911); F. Sayre, *Experiments in International Administration* (New York: Harper, 1919). An insightful overview of the history of thinking about international organizations is J. Steffek, *International Organization as Technocratic Utopia* (Oxford: Oxford University Press, 2021).

[7] The biblical phrase is used to great effect in the title of I. Claude, *Swords into Plowshares: The Problems and Progress of International Organization*, 2nd edn (New York: Random House, 1959).

North Atlantic Treaty Organization, and the International Jute Study Group, as species of the same genus.

Functionalism's main strength is, no doubt, its normative appeal; as an explanatory theory, it has some traction – though not much, really. It can explain why Liechtenstein was refused admission to the League of Nations: not having an army of its own, Liechtenstein was considered unable to contribute to the League's function of maintaining peace and security. It can help explain why international organizations can boast certain powers (in order to facilitate their functioning) and it can explain why, as a general matter, international organizations enjoy privileges and immunities (again, in order to facilitate their functioning). But it is unable to explain why some organizations enjoy higher levels of immunities than others. And it cannot explain why some enjoy broader powers than others, or why some allow any aspirant state to join – in a telling development, Liechtenstein was warmly welcomed into the United Nations in 1990, despite still lacking an army of its own and despite the UN still having the same basic function as the League.[8]

Indeed, functionalism, for all its merits, has basic problems explaining some of the more visible or representative events happening to and within international organizations. None of these was more grim than the Rwandan genocide. During three months or so in 1994, some 800,000 Rwandans were slaughtered. The UN was timely informed; there could be no doubt that the matter fell squarely within the tasks of the UN; the death toll was exceptionally high; and yet the UN stood by idly, with no one on the Security Council wishing to even utter the word 'genocide' for fear of unleashing legal ramifications.[9] Functionalism is singularly useless here as an explanation: if ever there was something happening that would warrant UN action, this was it. And yet, nothing much happened. The most plausible explanation available in the literature is that while important states were rather lukewarm to begin with, neither did the UN itself (its secretariat, its department of peacekeeping operations) display much enthusiasm.

[8] The most plausible explanation then is that the UN has adopted a universalist rather than functionalist ambition. See Th. Grant, *Admission to the United Nations: Charter Article 4 and the Rise of Universal Organization* (Leiden: Martinus Nijhoff, 2009).

[9] M. Barnett, *Eyewitness to a Genocide: The United Nations and Rwanda* (Ithaca, NY: Cornell University Press, 2002).

This was attributed to a certain 'metal fatigue': having been shamed not long before in Somalia and having a difficult situation in the former Yugoslavia to contend with, there was just not enough interest or animus to address the Rwandan genocide.[10]

Functionalism is also unable to explain why, a few years later, the Director-General of the Organization for the Prohibition of Chemical Weapons (OPCW), Mr Bustani, was forced out of office. Bustani had been neither lazy nor corrupt, and in fact had just been re-elected for a second term as Director-General when the US started a campaign against him.[11] It is generally rumoured that the campaign was the result of Bustani proposing surprise inspections of chemical facilities not just in countries in the Middle East or Eastern Europe, but also in the US. This apparently rubbed US politicians the wrong way. A possible second explanation, sometimes whispered, is that Bustani was about to bring Iraq into the regime[12] – and if so, this would have made it so much harder to claim that Iraq was holding weapons of mass destruction, which could justify an invasion two years later. Both accounts suggest an organization (and organizational leadership) functioning very well, doing exactly what it was assigned to do. And yet, Bustani was ousted, in a manner that baffles functionalist theory: surely, one should not be ousted for effective functioning?

And functionalism would have a hard time explaining the US' *volte face* with respect to the Universal Postal Union (UPU). In 2018, the US announced its withdrawal from this classic international organization, having realized that the postal rates set by the UPU, the 'terminal dues', worked much more favourably for a country like China than for the US. In response, the UPU organized an extraordinary conference, adapted its terminal dues, and did so to the satisfaction of the US, which could happily announce not to withdraw after all. It is part of the function of the UPU to set terminal dues; yet the precise distribution thereof, and consequent allocation of costs and benefits, remains out of functionalism's reach.

[10] M. Barnett and M. Finnemore, *Rules for the World: International Organizations in Global Politics* (Princeton, NJ: Princeton University Press, 2004).

[11] J. Klabbers, 'The Bustani Case before the ILOAT: Constitutionalism in Disguise?' (2004) 53 *International and Comparative Law Quarterly* 455–464.

[12] As reported in E. Benvenisti, *The Law of Global Governance* (The Hague: Hague Academy of International Law, 2014) 153.

These three anecdotes all suggest that functionalism is insufficient. A more plausible explanation of the UN's indolence at the time of the Rwandan genocide taps into organizational sociology; the ousting of Bustani owes considerably more to naked power politics than it does to any functionalist concerns; and the UPU episode suggests that a perspective informed by institutional economics or political economy may be very welcome. These events all suggest that insights from neighbouring disciplines may help to understand them. More generally, it has been established that withdrawal, expulsion, or suspension of member states rarely is based on functionalist considerations alone. Claims concerning these matters will be dressed up in functionalist language (and sometimes not even that: surely, Zimbabwe's dismal human rights record has fairly little bearing on its capacity to contribute to the functioning of the Commonwealth), but usually owe next to nothing to concerns about the organization's functioning.[13]

Yet, the stories also suggest that, in all cases, the law played an important role (not necessarily benign) in structuring debates and discussions, and even in offering alternatives. In the Rwandan genocide, much energy went in to avoiding the term 'genocide', for fear that it would activate a legal duty to prevent and punish, under the terms of the Genocide Convention. In addition, it has been suggested that legal responsibility might rest on the UN for failing to perform in accordance with its mandate.[14] In the Bustani affair, legal procedures were required (and somewhat manipulated perhaps) to create the appearance of respectability, and Mr Bustani sought and found relief with the ILO Administrative Tribunal, which held that his dismissal had taken place unlawfully and ordered compensation. And in the UPU saga, one set of legal rules was replaced by a different set of legal rules, following established legal procedure. What is more, none of the episodes can be properly understood without taking into account the structuring role of the law: legal procedures channel the discussion, help decide which terms are considered acceptable, and help to create path dependencies. Any attempt to explain these incidents in purely

[13] A. Duxbury, *The Participation of States in International Organisations: The Role of Human Rights and Democracy* (Cambridge: Cambridge University Press, 2011).

[14] J. Klabbers, 'Reflections on Role Responsibility: The Responsibility of International Organizations for Failing to Act' (2017) 28 *European Journal of International Law* 1133–1161.

legal functionalist terms is bound to fail; but conversely, any attempt to explain these matters by ignoring the role of legal rules and procedures is likewise bound to fail.

On State-Centrism and Inter-disciplinarity

The anecdotes listed earlier, anecdotal as they may be, suggest two things of pivotal academic relevance. The first of these is the need to move beyond state-centrism. It is a remarkable and sadly ironic feature of much scholarship on international affairs, world politics, and global governance that it still tends to be highly state-centric: states are considered to be the central actors, and putative explanations are typically cast in terms of the interests of states. This is downright deceptive: states are conduits and have to be because this is how the international legal machinery is organized, but states rarely have interests of their own, beyond the ubiquitous and circular idea of the *raison d'état*. Instead, behind states there are the interests of groups and persons within the state.[15] Governments and politicians may wish to be re-elected; companies may wish to make a profit; individuals may wish to have opportunities, be protected against each other, or be free from unwarranted controls; and civil society organizations may wish to push a normative agenda. All these can be said to have interests which may or may not explain much, but states themselves, in isolation from these interest groups (*nomen est omen*...), have few interests of their own beyond perhaps sheer survival.[16]

The most obvious reason why states are given such a central role is epistemological in nature and has little to do with their actual relevance. States are few in number (some 200 or so, worldwide) and share a bunch of similar features, so they are extremely suitable for theory-building. The result is that much theorizing, by lawyers and social scientists alike, takes place in terms of state interests (and within international organizations in terms of member state preferences,

[15] R. Putnam, 'Diplomacy and Domestic Politics: The Logic of Two-Level Games' (1988) 42 *International Organization* 427–460.

[16] See further J. Klabbers, 'Rules, Institutions and Decisions: Taking Distribution Seriously', in G. Hellmann and J. Steffek (eds.), *Praxis as a Perspective on International Politics* (Bristol: Bristol University Press, 2022), pp. 127–142.

blissfully ignoring possible institutional autonomy), placing the state as the central unit – never mind that the subsequent analysis does not always elucidate what actually goes on in the world.

The state-centrism is taken to a further extreme when analysts start to count attitudes towards multilateralism or international law as meaningful in their own right, as in claims that 'state X is against multilateral institutions' or 'state X is the gravedigger of international law'.[17] Dubious as it is to think of states as having interests of their own to begin with, it is even less persuasive to think (beyond broad outlines) of states as having a position on international law in general. Surely, no state would decline the status of statehood, awarded by international law, or voluntarily forfeit the right of self-defence, a right that only makes sense (as far as states are concerned) under international law. States will not be for or against international law; they will, instead, be for or against particular sets of rules or regimes. And they will be for or against particular regimes depending on the desires, wishes, and interests of influential domestic factions.

The second lesson to be drawn from the earlier discussion is the lesson that inter-disciplinarity is needed, but much depends on how this is realized. What is clear is that individual scholars can learn from those working in different disciplines, and this, of course, makes eminent sense, and has made eminent sense from the very first days of academic specialization. Academics may think (and have to think) in little boxes, but the real world (however defined or conceptualized) cannot be expected to respect disciplinary boundaries. Clearly, being familiar with concepts, methods, and techniques, and borrowing from insights prevailing in other disciplines, can be highly beneficial. There are examples of international lawyers doing so fruitfully: think of the historically informed work of Martti Koskenniemi,[18] or the way Eyal Benvenisti sometimes weaves insights from economics into some of his legal work.[19] Likewise, some scholars active in IR make good use of jurisprudential insights and international legal

[17] S. Talmon, 'The United States under President Trump: Gravedigger of International Law' (2019) 18 *Chinese Journal of International Law* 645–668.

[18] M. Koskenniemi, *The Gentle Civilizer of Nations* (Cambridge: Cambridge University Press, 2001).

[19] See, e.g., E. Benvenisti, 'Exit and Voice in the Age of Globalization', (1999) 98 *Michigan Law Review* 167–213.

understandings, perhaps none more so than Friedrich Kratochwil[20] and Nicholas Onuf.[21] And some are formally trained in several disciplines, integrating insights from the diversity of their backgrounds into their work.[22]

This need not result in formal cooperation between representatives from different disciplines, however: such formal collaborations are usually not very insightful, and often amount to the scholar from one discipline adopting methods and insights from the other.[23] It is not necessarily the case that the results are unhelpful: for instance, lawyer Kenneth Abbott and IR scholar Duncan Snidal have done some useful work together, with Abbott adding more than just a lawyer's sense of precision.

Yet, the example of Abbott and Snidal's work also suggests that inter-disciplinary collaboration is best done (if at all) between scholars with similar sensibilities. The rationalist IR scholar and the law and economics-oriented lawyer speak much the same language; they share the same working assumptions about rationality, profit maximization, the relevance of market analogies perhaps, and thus can fruitfully communicate. Much the same applies to the critical legal scholar and the constructivist IR scholar: both will have an innate understanding of the role and relevance of language in the construction of society, the relevance of tropes and biases, and the relevance of making legal claims. But collaboration between a critical legal scholar and a rationalist IR scholar is highly unlikely – their assumptions do not match, to the point where even bare communication may be extremely difficult. Likewise, the realist IR scholar or historian can only communicate with the most self-loathing lawyer: those who feel that law is by definition epiphenomenal cannot realistically communicate, let alone collaborate, with those for whom law is something relevant, however ephemeral or ineffective it may be perhaps.

[20] F. Kratochwil, *Rules, Norms and Decisions* (Cambridge: Cambridge University Press, 1989); F. Kratochwil, *Praxis: On Acting and Knowing* (Cambridge: Cambridge University Press, 2018).

[21] N. Onuf, *World of Our Making* (London: Routledge, 2013 [1989]).

[22] One example is G. Sarfaty, *Values in Translation: Human Rights and the Culture of the World Bank* (Stanford, CA: Stanford University Press, 2012).

[23] J. Klabbers, 'The Relative Autonomy of International Law or The Forgotten Politics of Interdisciplinarity' (2004) 1 *Journal of International Law and International Relations* 35–48.

It is also worth pointing out that it is perfectly respectable (and perhaps preferable) to be eclectic in terms of theory and method and discipline.[24] As a point of departure, the established methodologies in most academic disciplines can generate useful results (leaving poor scholarship aside, but this too is not bound to any particular approach). A couple of caveats are in place, however. First, it seems that in the more 'scientific' branches of international law scholarship (and by extension international organizations law scholarship) generating hypotheses is far more popular than actually testing them. This is understandable: generating a hypothesis, whether of the critical or the rationalist variety, is relatively easy. One needs a few facts, an established method, *et voilà*, a new hypothesis is born. In an industry which places a premium on output, visibility, and whatever is understood by impact, one can see the temptation.[25] The clever hypothesis-generator can this way easily churn out a dozen or so articles every year, and given that hypotheses can generate attention (more so than verification tends to do), he[26] can also end up being among the most cited scholars, without ever doing much research, properly speaking, whether empirical, doctrinal, or historical. This is particularly endemic in the law and economics tradition but is not only visible in those circles alone.

A further caveat harks back to the earlier point about eclecticism. All methodologies, it would seem, have their blind spots. Viewing states as profit maximizers tends to block from the view the relevance of non-state actors, as well as of such concepts as altruism; viewing actors as altruists, by contrast, tends to obscure the role of power. Focusing on power as formal authority tends to hide informal power exercises; et cetera. Regardless of whether a single truth can even exist,

[24] If only to overcome Arendt's rueful observation that 'it is in the nature of academic quarrels that methodological problems are likely to overshadow more fundamental issues'. H. Arendt, *Between Past and Future* (London: Penguin, 1968) 53.

[25] The discipline of international law is surprisingly reluctant to discuss how scholarship is affected by the structure of the academic industry. For a brief attempt, see J. Klabbers, 'On Epistemic Universalism and the Melancholy of International Law' (2018) 29 *European Journal of International Law* 1057–1069. See also J. Klabbers, 'The Ethics of Inter-Disciplinarity and the Academic Industry' (2024) 93 *Nordic Journal of International Law* 132–151.

[26] These clever academic industrialists are almost exclusively male, so the male pronoun seems appropriate here.

it seems rather obvious that the same thing can look differently to different people. The theologian may view a church as a place of worship; the sociologist as a site of expression, while the architecture historian may entertain yet a different view.[27] These need not be mutually exclusive, but can well be complementary; accordingly, it is folly to ignore what those in other traditions are doing.

And perhaps the most important practical caveat is to be reminded that inter-disciplinarity is a two-way street. Since the late 1980s and early 1990s, when Abbott[28] and Slaughter[29] started to endorse collaboration between IR scholars and international lawyers, it is fair to say that international lawyers have tried hard to familiarize themselves with IR scholarship and IR scholars. International lawyers have made an effort, and have often incorporated insights gained from the study of IR. But it is also fair to say that the love has remained unrequited. With the exception of some work in the constructivist IR tradition, IR scholars have spurned the advances of international lawyers – somehow the IR practitioners seem to think that a basic understanding of the law is a luxury, a bit like getting the topography of a state right.[30] Sometimes this is rather innocent: it may not be accurate to suggest the Universal Declaration on Human Rights has been 'ratified' (instead of adopted), but nothing much usually rides on this. But sometimes it gets considerably more serious, so much so as to jeopardize their insights.

One recent example concerns an ambitious attempt to understand international organizations, positing that these creatures are often the playball between universalist and parochialist sentiments, or function versus community.[31] Plausible as this is, it would have immensely strengthened the approach if the authors had realized that for some

[27] Seminal is H. Putnam, *Ethics without Ontology* (Cambridge, MA: Harvard University Press, 2004).

[28] K. Abbott, 'Modern International Relations Theory: A Prospectus for International Lawyers' (1989) 14 *Yale Journal of International Law* 335–411.

[29] A. Slaughter, 'International Law and International Relations Theory: A Dual Agenda' (1993) 87 *American Journal of International Law* 205–239.

[30] IR scholarship uses the law (if at all) in order to present or illustrate an IR analysis – rarely the other way around, as testified by almost all contributions to J. Dunoff and M. Pollack (eds.), *Interdisciplinary Perspectives on International Law and International Relations* (Cambridge: Cambridge University Press, 2013).

[31] L. Hooghe, T. Lenz, and G. Marks, *A Theory of International Organization* (Oxford: Oxford University Press, 2019).

hundred years or so, this very tension has been managed by what lawyers refer to as the 'implied powers' doctrine. And the implied powers doctrine is by no means an esoteric doctrine, but is the widely acknowledged centrepiece of international organizations law, discussed in even the most introductory of textbooks.[32] This then raises an awkward question: why do IR scholars not consult even those most introductory of textbooks? IR scholars working on economic issues would as a matter of course open an introduction to economics to learn about Ricardo's terms of trade or the Stolper–Samuelson theorem, but when it comes to the law, doing so is apparently considered unnecessary.

This can only be based on a fundamental misunderstanding of the relevance of law, a misunderstanding that most likely can be traced to the all-too-simplistic (and rather surreal) realist IR tradition. For those who view international law as merely engaged with constraining actors from behaving in a certain manner, it must indeed seem that international law is mostly useless. But here lies the rub: any half-way sophisticated understanding of the law will realize that constraining actors is but a small part of what the law aims to do. In much the same way as in domestic societies law is more than just crime and (sometimes[33]) punishment, so too is international law far more about facilitating the interactions amongst autonomous agents (call them states, if you will), and about both enabling and possibly controlling the exercise of public power. Societies cannot function without private law (contract, property, tort, family law); societies cannot function without public law (constitutional and administrative), and much the same applies to international society, regardless of whether one thinks it is deserving of the label society or needs to be prefaced by adjectives such as anarchical.[34]

[32] See, e.g., J. Klabbers, *An Introduction to International Organizations Law*, 4th edn (Cambridge: Cambridge University Press, 2022), or N. White, *The Law of International Organisations* (Manchester: Manchester University Press, 1996), or C. F. Amerasinghe, *Principles of the Institutional Law of international Organizations*, 2nd edn (Cambridge: Cambridge University Press, 2005), or H. Schermers and N. Blokker, *International Institutional Law*, 6th edn (Leiden: Martinus Nijhoff, 2018).

[33] Edelman suggests that criminal law can never be completely enforced: it takes far too many resources to do so. See M. Edelman, *The Symbolic Uses of Politics* (Urbana, IL: University of Illinois Press, 1985 [1964]).

[34] The three branches (criminal, civil, and public) come with different ideas about accountability as well. See P. Cane, *Responsibility in Law and Morality* (Oxford: Hart, 2002).

Towards a Supra-Functionalist Alternative

International organizations lawyers have been seduced, perhaps under the influence of Sayre writing a century ago, to view international organizations as manifestations of 'the international': international organizations give effect to cooperation between states, and since cooperation is by definition considered a good thing (the alternative seemingly being the Hobbesian world of all against all where life is 'nasty, brutish, and short'), it follows that international organizations are generally considered as good things – for who could possibly argue with the promise of turning swords into ploughshares?

This view painfully ignores that international organizations are not merely manifestations of the 'international' but also 'organizations'. There must be a reason why the organizational form is preferred over alternative possibilities of establishing cooperation (think of the treaty, the congress, the informal coalition, etc.). The most obvious reason, historically defensible moreover, is that the organizational form is better suited than alternatives if two imperatives need to be met in tandem: the combination of widespread participation and permanent management. Put bluntly: the COVID crisis would have worked out rather differently if the global health regime had consisted merely of a single treaty between a few handfuls of states, with the parties meeting once a year for two days. Instead, global health requires permanent management and widespread participation: it is surely no coincidence that already in the mid-nineteenth century the organizational form was chosen to protect the West against infectious diseases originating elsewhere. Much the same applies to customs classifications, or the regulation of postal traffic – this cannot properly be done on an incidental basis or with only a few handfuls of states.

As organizations, international organizations (like all organizations) do essentially three things.[35] First, they regulate. The UPU may set terminal dues. The International Telecommunication Union (ITU) distributes radio frequencies (and much besides). The World Meteorological Organization (WMO) figures out when a storm is

[35] This builds on J. Klabbers, 'International Organizations and the Problem of Privity: Towards a Supra-Functionalist Approach', in G. Politakis et al. (eds.), *ILO 100: Law for Social Justice* (Geneva: ILO, 2019), pp. 629–646.

properly to be called a storm, and the International Civil Aviation Organization (ICAO) harmonizes safety standards.[36]

Second, as organizations (like all organizations), international organizations monitor and manage. They monitor compliance with the standards they have established but also engage in further monitoring activities: the International Organization for Migration does not just set standards and offer best practices but also studies migration patterns and collects data.[37] The WMO does not just regulate what constitutes a typhoon but also follows weather patterns, tries to predict what will happen next, and issue warnings in case of bad weather, to the point of the WMO being one of the driving forces behind the Intergovernmental Panel on Climate Change.[38]

And like all organizations, international organizations allocate costs and benefits. The terminal dues set by the UPU benefit some more than others; the distribution of radio frequencies benefits some more than others, and much the same applies to declarations of a Public Health Emergency of International Concern by the WHO or a declaration of airworthiness by the ICAO. Distributing radio frequencies or declaring a public health emergency are activities with an inevitable technical, expertise-based component: there is a reason why the ITU tends to be directed by engineers or natural scientists, and why much of the staff at WHO is medically trained. But at the same time, these tasks are inherently political: decisions will involve winners and losers.

It follows that there might be merit in not (only) viewing international organizations law through functionalist lenses but also studying how this body of rules helps to structure patterns of winners and losers; which institutional biases are inherent in institutions and carved in legal texts, and how those legal texts come about. Tracking the role of law in the distribution of costs and benefits by international organizations manifests a decidedly novel approach to the law of

[36] Intriguingly, ICAO's website declares, not without a sense of drama, that ICAO is not a global regulator, and should not be criticized for acts that remain the prerogative of sovereign states. See www.icao.int/about-icao/Pages/default.aspx (visited 26 November 2021).

[37] An excellent recent study is M. Bradley, *The International Organization for Migration: Challenges, Commitments, Complexities* (London: Routledge, 2020).

[38] L. Andonova, *Governance Entrepreneurs* (Cambridge: Cambridge University Press, 2017).

international organizations, as does the study of these processes in terms of their effects not on member states alone but on other actors as well, in particular effects on the private sector. What seems clear is that the law is not merely the final outcome of political processes, as it is so often assumed to be, but it in turn also helps channel and structure those same political processes. Political processes are embedded in legal rules – it could not be otherwise. And those legal rules therewith are not merely innocent technical devices, but help to shape political outcomes. If even war, so often seen as the antithesis of law, is recognized as a highly legally regulated affair,[39] the same applies to everyday political processes.

The insight has serious implications for the law of international organizations. It entails that the law of international organizations can no longer be plausibly viewed as a set of rules and doctrines aiming to facilitate the effective functioning of international organizations in a setting where those organizations are pitted against their member states – this, one might conclude, is sheer ideology.[40] The relevant struggle is not merely the struggle between the principals and their agent, the member states and their organization; it also pits member states against each other, organizations against each other, and, most of all, involves interests within those member states.

To provide one example among many possible examples: the outbreak of the swine flu and the WHO's response thereto owed fairly little to any conflict between the WHO and its collective member states; nor did it reflect any conflict among member states. Instead, it turned out that those whose interests were affected were mostly pharmaceutical companies. Those whose vaccines were marketable made a handsome profit; those who were less well-prepared did not.[41]

Either way, what mattered eventually (and these are the points on which the WHO received considerable flak afterwards) was the

[39] D. Kennedy, *Of War and Law* (Princeton, NJ: Princeton University Press, 2006).

[40] J. Klabbers, 'What Role for International Organizations in the Promotion of Community Interests? Reflections on the Ideology of Functionalism', in E. Benvenisti and G. Nolte (eds.), *Community Interests across International Law* (Oxford: Oxford University Press, 2018), pp. 86–100.

[41] S. Machado Ramirez, 'The WHO and the A1H1 Pandemic: Some Reflections about Third-Party Effects of International Decision-Making', in J. Klabbers (ed.), *International Organizations Engaging the World* (Cambridge: Cambridge University Press, in press).

combination of substantive decision-making and the timing thereof. Had the WHO not declared a public health emergency, its (in-)activity would not have had much impact on pharmaceutical companies. But it did, and its timing became subjected to predictable criticism: the pharmaceutical companies whose vaccines were not yet ready complained that the decision had possibly been taken prematurely. Others retorted, not unreasonably, that postponing the decision could have sacrificed human lives. Both positions are plausible enough, and decision-making of this kind often amounts to political action of the 'damned if you do, and damned if you don't' variety. The best one can hope for is a reasonable exercise of discretion and judgement by the decision-makers – what Aristotle already recognized as *phronesis*.[42]

Noteworthy in all this is that the law never is an innocent bystander. The WHO's decision-making is embedded in legal rules, granting considerable powers to its director-general. The declaration has obvious legal effects: once a public health emergency is declared, national governments can take measures they may not take otherwise; and citizens may vie for vaccines while they otherwise might be reluctant or simply indolent. Critics too have little choice but to voice their discontent in legal terms. They cannot simply claim that the WHO got it wrong because their companies or industries were badly affected; instead, their claims have to be presented in legal terms, and follow legal procedures to be heard.[43]

All this suggests, as noted earlier, that inter-disciplinary scholarship can be very useful. The study of international organizations law (and the understanding of international organizations) can be enriched by taking on board insights from neighbouring and even not so neighbouring disciplines. Examples abound. International organizations are generally seen as playing an economic role: indeed, there is an entire branch of economics studying the roles and effects of institutions, under the label 'institutional economics'.[44] This too is likely

[42] J. Klabbers, *Virtue in Global Governance: Judgment and Discretion* (Cambridge: Cambridge University Press, 2022).

[43] See further also J. Klabbers, 'Towards a Political Economy of International Organizations Law' (2023) 20 *International Organizations Law Review* 82–101.

[44] D. North, *Institutions, Institutional Change and Economic Performance* (Cambridge: Cambridge University Press, 1990); E. Ostrom, *Governing the Commons* (Cambridge: Cambridge University Press, 1990).

to enhance the lawyer's understanding. By the same token, there is scholarship studying patterns of administration, whether public administration or business administration: in essence, while there are differences between the government agency and the private company, there are also similarities, and both are institutions of some sort. Consequently, the student of international organizations may well derive insights from scholars of both public administration and business administration and related sub-disciplines such as organizational sociology. It may be relevant, e.g., that organization scholars have developed the idea that some organizations are composed of other organizations (i.e., meta-organizations[45]), something that may well apply to international organizations: meta-organizations of states. If so, the dynamics are bound to be different in some respect than with organizations composed solely of individuals: organizations have constituencies in ways that individuals do not, and for instance the idea of states as conduits may well result from this realization: states have constituencies, after all, while individuals do not – at least not in the same way. Public administration scholars and organization sociologists have also long studied patterns of distributing and sharing accountability. The problem of the 'many hands', e.g., has long informed these branches of scholarship,[46] as have ideas about the leaking away of responsibility and accountability as related to the outsourcing of authority.[47]

Historians can tell us what went into the decision-making of international organizations on specific points or what role specific organizations (or even their organs) played in particular policy domains,[48] or in politics at large.[49] Intellectual history, additionally, can tell us

[45] G. Ahrne and N. Brunsson, *Meta-organizations* (Cheltenham: Edward Elgar, 2008).

[46] M. Bovens, *The Quest for Responsibility* (Cambridge: Cambridge University Press, 1998); M. Harmon, *Responsibility as Paradox* (Thousand Oaks, CA: Sage, 1995).

[47] R. Jackall, *Moral Mazes* (Oxford: Oxford University Pres, 2010 [1988]).

[48] S. Pedersen, *The Guardians* (Oxford: Oxford University Press, 2015); P. Clavin, *Securing the World Economy* (Oxford: Oxford University Press, 2013); V. Lagendijk, *Electrifying Europe* (Amsterdam: Aksant, 2008).

[49] D. Gorman, *The Emergence of International Society in the 1920s* (Cambridge: Cambridge University Press, 2012); A. Iriye, *Global Community* (Berkeley, CA: University of California Press, 2002); E. Rosenberg, *Transnational Currents in a Shrinking World, 1870–1945* (Cambridge, MA: Harvard University Press, 2014).

about the underlying ideas, concepts, and assumptions[50] – and some good historical work contains instructive and informative elements of both.[51] Anthropologists and ethnographers can help us understand how organizational cultures, practices, and rituals affect the acts of participants and other stakeholders and of those organizations.[52]

Conclusion

If this chapter constitutes something of a manifesto, it seems fitting to offer not conclusions but rather final suggestions. Good academic work is work that has soul and is somehow connected to people of flesh and blood. That does not exclude analytical philosophy (quite the opposite), but it does, or should, limit the amounts of energy spent on trying to prove that Foucault was right, or that Latour is superior to Bourdieu or vice versa. Those are suitable topics for conversations over a glass of Armagnac on the Left Bank, but less interesting as scholarly ventures.

That is no slight on Foucault, or Latour, or Bourdieu. Instead, I hope to have suggested that a good international organizations lawyer takes careful note of the insights these scholars have to offer on, among other things, power, expertise, and social capital, as their insights can help us understand the topic of our study. But it should not derail into a race between them, or a competition, as is sometimes the case.[53]

If it is true that all theories and methods have their own blind spots, it follows (in much the same vein, really) that the best academic work is driven rarely by theory or by method but rather by curiosity. The point of academic work is not to show that the neo-realists are right, or that rational choice is methodologically superior – if only because

[50] M. Mazower, *Governing the World* (London: Allen Lane, 2012); G. Sluga and P. Clavin (eds.), *Internationalisms* (Cambridge: Cambridge University Press, 2017).

[51] The enumeration is far from exhaustive: much can be learned from diplomatic historians, social and economic historians, and cultural historians, to name a few.

[52] R. Niezen and M. Sapignoli (eds.), *Palaces of Hope: The Anthropology of Global Organizations* (Cambridge: Cambridge University Press, 2017).

[53] An excellent recent example of studying international organizations law with the help of the previously mentioned thinkers is D. van den Meerssche, *The World Bank's Lawyers: The Life of International Law as Institutional Practice* (Oxford: Oxford University Press, 2022).

much depends on the object of study and the research question. Those of us interested in the best interpretation of article 2, paragraph 7 of the UN Charter will not gain much from a law and economics approach, and neither will those of us interested in the accountability of the World Bank. But should we wish to know why some organizations have withdrawal clauses, then insights from economics may be helpful.[54] In other words, the research question should influence the choice of theory and method, rather than the other way around.

Likewise, there is little point in trying desperately to achieve a paradigm shift. True paradigms are rare, especially in the social sciences and humanities, where they might be non-existent.[55] Research funding agencies, themselves bureaucracies that should be studied as such, are keen on paradigm shifts, but that is largely a conceit drifted over from the natural sciences, and akin to the amateur football team dreaming of one day winning the Champions League. It is useful to set the bar high, but few of us will ever realize a paradigm shift – so this kind of language ought not to be taken overly seriously. A good academic study is one that tells us something we did not already know or makes us understand something we did not understand before. And as the discussion in this chapter will have made abundantly clear, there is no substitute for reading and studying widely and broadly.

[54] Classically A. Hirschman, *Exit, Voice, and Loyalty* (Cambridge, MA: Harvard University Press, 1970).

[55] This was the opinion of Thomas Kuhn, the scholar who popularized the notion of paradigm. For the record, he said little about the humanities, but held that there were no true paradigms in the social sciences, and given his own background in the natural sciences, it is not impossible that to his mind the humanities were not 'science' to begin with. Th. Kuhn, *The Structure of Scientific Revolutions*, 2nd edn (Chicago, IL: University of Chicago Press, 1970).

PART II

Ways of Seeing International Institutions

Expertise, Authority, and Knowledge Production

4 *Studying the Assembling of Expertise in Global Governance*

ANNABELLE LITTOZ-MONNET

International organisations (IOs), as well as other sites of global governance, make claims to the 'evidence-based' or 'expert-based' nature of their agendas and policy interventions, whether in health, climate, education, or development aid.[1] Global policies and programmes are largely legitimised by reference to their reliance on 'evidence', presented as reliable, scientific, and 'expert'. 'Experts' – sitting in IOs, expert groups, academia, high level commissions, or advisory committees of all sorts – indeed abound in global governance forums and produce a plethora of studies, databases, and seminal papers that form the knowledge base in given issue domains. This self-proclaimed rationalisation of the work of IOs largely goes unchallenged in academia.[2] Existing scholarship in International Relations (IR) and International Law (IL) often rehearses a narrative where IOs are seen as relying on scientific expertise to solve global problems. This view is based on two assumptions. First, the expertise of IOs is perceived to be strongly associated with science, and science itself is understood as developed independently of the circumstances of time, place, and social conditions. Second, global 'problems' are largely seen as given,

[1] S. Timmermans and A. Angell, 'Evidence-based medicine, clinical uncertainty, and learning to doctor' (2001) 42 *Journal of Health and Social Behavior* 342–59; K. P. Donovan, 'The rise of the randomistas: on the experimental turn in international aid' (2018) 47 *Economy and Society* 27–58; O. J. Sending, 'Recognition and liquid authority' (2017) 9 *International Theory* 311–28; A. Jatteau, 'Expérimenter le développement? Des économistes et leurs terrains' (2013) 93 *Genèses* 8–28.

[2] S. Jasanoff, *The Fifth Branch: Science Advisers as Policymakers* (Harvard University Press, 1998); T. F. Gieryn, 'Boundary-work and the demarcation of science from non-science: strains and interests in professional ideologies of scientists' (1983) 48 *American Sociological Review* 781–95; T. M. Porter, *Trust in Numbers: The Pursuit of Objectivity in Science and Public Life* (Princeton University Press, 1995); L. Daston and P. Galison, *Objectivity* (Princeton University Press, 2021).

existing out there for policymakers, or scholars, to address and solve them with the best knowledge and tools that they have.

Yet, the making of expertise involves decisions regarding what forms of knowledge to include and exclude. It also involves processes of assembling, which give shape to dispersed facts and knowledge and profoundly delineate what emerges as 'expertise'. Such processes are deeply political; not only are they shaped by and through epistemic controversies and contests, where financial, epistemic, and social resources are all at play, but they are also embedded in time-specific macro-epistemic conditions, which shape the contours of what forms of knowledge count.

Acknowledging that the making of expertise involves political processes of inclusion, exclusion, and assembling also has implications for how we conceive global objects of governance, those 'matters of concern', or 'problems', that IOs govern. It brings to light that such problems are themselves defined through processes of sense-making, where expertise plays a central role. Objects of governance are, indeed, interpreted and made sense of through and with knowledge and tools seen as 'expert' and relevant. Acknowledging the subtle political processes at play in the delineation of objects of governance has implications for scholars in IR and IL, who study objects such as bioethics, the law of the sea, and biodiversity, amongst others. It makes it possible to see these not just as problems in need of solving through the mobilisation of evidence, statistics, or scientific studies, but as complex and 'wicked' matters of concern that ought to be made sense of in the first place.

It is, thus, necessary to open up the black-box of knowledge-making processes in global governance and engage with the processes through which IOs produce and stabilise expertise. How do certain forms of knowledge gain the status of expertise? What kinds of evidence come to be seen as valid and relevant for governance purposes? As we know, '[e]xpertise is authoritative knowledge at a given decision point'.[3] This does not imply that 'anything goes'. Certainly, expertise also consists of substantive knowledge in a given domain.[4] But when a multitude of

[3] A. Leander and O. Wæver, 'Introduction: assembling exclusive expertise: knowledge, ignorance and conflict resolution in the Global South' in A. Leander and O. Wæver (eds.), *Assembling Exclusive Expertise: Knowledge, Ignorance and Conflict Resolution in the Global South*, (Routledge, 2018) p. 2.

[4] H. M. Collins and R. Evans, 'The third wave of science studies: studies of expertise and experience' (2002) 32 *Social Studies of Science* 235–96.

professional, scientific, or experiential knowledge forms co-exist and struggle for recognition, power dynamics and asymmetries also play out in the delineation of specific knowledge forms as expert. Thus, what is seen as expertise 'conforms to no transcendent criteria of logic or method, but frequently incorporates popular conceptions (and misconceptions) of relevance and reliability, and all too commonly reflects differences in the social and material positions of disputing parties and decisionmakers'.[5]

Thus, in this chapter, I propose some entry points to study the making and stabilisation of expertise in global governance. The approach goes beyond an exclusive focus on IOs, which are understood to be part of a broader machinery of knowledge production that involves a complex web of actors, sites, infrastructures, and power relationships. Taking the study of IOs away from international secretariats, member states, and formal negotiating structures makes it possible to examine how expert groups, think-tanks, professional organisations, large activist organisations, academic research clusters, and private actors, as well as their knowledge techniques and 'ways of seeing', participate in the production of 'expertise' in global governance.

In a first part, I outline ways in which expertise has been discussed in IR, as well as in Political Science, Sociology, and Science and Technology Studies (STS). In a second part, I shed light on specific and concrete paths through which the politics of expertise can be analysed. I argue that the power–knowledge nexus can be analysed by exploring sites and networks of knowledge production (i), infrastructures of knowledge production (ii), and relations between humans and/or things (iii). In a third part, I propose three potential methodological entry points to study the making of expertise.

IR Scholarship and Expertise

In IR, IL, and Political Science, as well as in policy circles, 'expertise' is largely seen as 'the real and substantive possession of groups of experts'.[6] Experts, thus, distinguish themselves from 'non-experts' by their possession of knowledge of facts, theories, methods, and

[5] S. Jasanoff, 'Accountability: (no?) accounting for expertise' (2003) 30 *Science and Public Policy* 157–62 at 159.

[6] H. Collins and R. Evans, *Rethinking Expertise* (University of Chicago Press, 2008) p. 2.

techniques that pertain to a discipline or professional field. Such knowledge can be gained through training and legitimised through the traditional university degree and/or through long-term professional experience in a given domain. According to this view, expertise is also isolated from the social and the political; it is a form of knowledge produced through systematic techniques, which ensure that it is 'valid', 'accurate', and 'objective'. This understanding of expertise relies on the assumption that the development of expertise is tied to that of science, and that scientific knowledge is itself developed in isolation from social and political conditions. The prevalence of this view is widely established in governmental spheres, as well as in IR and IL.[7]

Thus, if science produces true and valid knowledge, using such knowledge will also produce the right political decisions.[8] This 'rationality project' emerged in debates amongst political scientists in the 1950s, when a group of scholars developed hopes that policymakers would advance better policy agendas and programmes if they used sound evidence in the formulation of their decisions.[9] From this perspective, the development of scientific knowledge is driven by the logic of science, which is independent from the circumstances of time, place, and social conditions. If it is possible to understand reality by 'getting down to the facts', the application of science-based knowledge would seem, indeed, to be the best way to help solving policy problems. As a result, existing work on expertise is predominantly concerned with the way experts influence or shape policy, based on the assumption that the scientific and the policy spheres are neatly separated and driven by different logics.

The focus on the impacts of expert knowledge in policymaking also prevails in IR. Scholars in the field have argued that, because they deal with highly complex and technical issues, international decision-makers depend on science and technology for determining the risks and consequences associated with political action. As decision-makers seek

[7] Jasanoff, *The Fifth Branch*; Gieryn, 'Boundary-work and the demarcation of science from non-science: strains and interests in professional ideologies of scientists'; Porter, *Trust in Numbers: The Pursuit of Objectivity in Science and Public Life*; Daston and Galison, *Objectivity*.

[8] N. Caplan, 'The two-communities theory and knowledge utilization' (1979) 22 *American Behavioral Scientist* 459–70.

[9] R. E. Lane, *Political Ideology* (Free Press, 1962); D. Bell, *The End of Ideology: On the Exhaustion of Political Ideas in the Fifties* (Free Press, 1960).

information to make choices, this enables epistemic communities to provide information that favours or excludes different alternatives.[10] This approach has stimulated a research programme that seeks to identify the scope conditions of the influence of research on policy, as well as the obstacles to a better flow of scientific research to policymaking.[11] Not only does this perspective assume that knowledge and policy *are* distinct but also that they *should* be. In the hopes that policymakers advance better policy agendas and programmes, the focus was on enhancing the use of sound evidence in the formulation of their decisions.

Other accounts in Political Science and IR have focused on the mobilisation of knowledge for political purposes. Such perspectives no longer assume that knowledge is valued only as a way of rationalising decisions, but acknowledge its symbolic and legitimising role.[12] Existing insights have revealed the way policymakers use expert knowledge selectively, and sometimes misleadingly, in order to back their agendas and programmes, frame issues in a way that pushes the policy solutions they prefer, gain legitimacy, or yet expand their competences.[13] In their work on international bureaucracies, Barnett and Finnemore have revealed that expertise is central to the assertion of IOs' authority. When 'emphasising the "objective" nature of

[10] P. M. Haas, 'Introduction: epistemic communities and international policy coordination' (1992) 46 *International Organization* 1–35.

[11] A. Verdun, 'The role of the Delors Committee in the creation of EMU: an epistemic community?' (1999) 6 *Journal of European Public Policy* 308–28; P. M. Haas and C. Stevens, 'Organized science, usable knowledge, and multilateral environmental governance' in R. Lidskog and G. Sundqvist (eds.), *Governing the Air: The Dynamics of Science, Policy, and Citizen Interaction*, (The MIT Press, 2011), pp. 125–62; M. K. D. Cross, 'Rethinking epistemic communities twenty years later' (2013) 39 *Review of International Studies* 137–60.

[12] C. H. Weiss, 'The circuitry of enlightenment: diffusion of social science research to policymakers' (1986) 8 *Knowledge* 274–81; C. Boswell, *The Political Uses of Expert Knowledge: Immigration Policy and Social Research* (Cambridge University Press, 2009); D. Nelkin, 'The political impact of technical expertise' (1975) 5 *Social Studies of Science* 35–54.

[13] C. H. Weiss, 'Bureaucratic maladies and remedies' (1979) 22 *American Behavioral Scientist* 477–82; A. Littoz-Monnet (ed.), *The Politics of Expertise in International Organizations: How International Bureaucracies Produce and Mobilize Knowledge* (Routledge, 2017); A. Littoz-Monnet, 'Expanding without much ado. International bureaucratic expansion tactics in the case of bioethics' (2021) 28 *Journal of European Public Policy* 858–79.

their knowledge, staff of IOs are able to present themselves as technocrats whose advice is unaffected by partisan squabbles'.[14] While these contributions have pointed to the crucial role(s) of knowledge in politics, they assume either that expertise is externally produced and subsequently enters the political domain, or that policymakers use knowledge to pursue specific interests. Such accounts, which bracket the production of knowledge, do not point to the different forms of enmeshment between knowledge and politics in processes of knowledge-making.

'De-Blackboxing' the Making of Expertise

Sociologists of science, scholars in the field of STS, and critical scholars more broadly have problematised the view that expertise is 'objective' and 'neutral' for decades. The French sociologist Bruno Latour has pointed out that scientific knowledge enjoys no independence or claim to authority beyond the political and economic interests that helped develop the scientific claims.[15] From that perspective, science embeds and is embedded in the social and the political. As put by sociologist of science Sheila Jasanoff, '[w]hat counts as expertise ... frequently incorporates popular conceptions (and misconceptions) of relevance and reliability, and all too commonly reflects differences in the social and material positions of disputing parties and decision-makers'.[16] What counts as expert knowledge can and does change. It is embedded in time and place-specific political circumstances, power dynamics, and conceptions of what is worthwhile, valid, and relevant. The power–knowledge nexus has, of course, consequences for the way governance objects, whether human rights, biodiversity, food, or trade, are seen, governed, and regulated through the norms and practices of IL. Yet, this is often overlooked by scholars who study such issues as unproblematic problems in need of solving.

I propose later that capturing the politics of the production of knowledge and expertise requires paying attention to where and by

[14] M. Barnett and M. Finnemore, *Rules for the World: International Organizations in Global Politics* (Cornell University Press, 2004) p. 24.

[15] B. Latour, *We Have Never Been Modern* (Harvard University Press, 1993).

[16] Jasanoff, 'Accountability: (no?) accounting for expertise', 159; M. Lynch and S. Jasanoff, 'Contested identities: science, law and forensic practice' (1998) 28 *Social Studies of Science* 675–86.

whom knowledge is produced (knowledge sites and networks), infrastructures of knowledge production (material artifacts), and relations. This approach makes it possible to analyse the way expertise is produced by and through a nucleus of sites, organisations, knowledge techniques, and material artifacts, which operate in a highly enmeshed and mutually reliant space.[17]

Sites

Studying sites of knowledge-making in global governance requires paying attention to centres of knowledge production within, across, and beyond IOs. The spatiality of knowledge production is changing. Sites of knowledge production are increasingly situated outside established expert networks and are therefore increasingly dispersed. The knowledge considered as 'expert' by IOs is often produced in hybrid and informal spaces, located beyond or across traditional governmental spheres, such as boundary expert groups, high-profile academic clusters, private sites, or ephemeral 'crossing points': the events, forums, and fairs where officials, activists, experts, and regulators meet and stabilise understandings of problems. At the same time, the apparent dispersion of knowledge sites can conceal novel forms of concentration, where hierarchies persist, and which determine access, and the possession of knowledge becomes a major source of power.[18]

IOs have research departments and statistical units, which produce profuse in-house knowledge that is central to their authority and legitimacy. Still, they often set up expert groups to produce knowledge and recommendations on specific issues. Also in these groups, knowledge considered as authoritative and 'expert' is produced and stabilised. Such groups typically gather high-profile professionals, who have multiple affiliations in the policy, academic, and private spheres. Discussions within such groups typically focus on the technicality of issues, leaving aside, or at least making opaquer, their political implications. Experts tend to internalise their role as technical advisors, rather than political advocates, thus facilitating more consensual and

[17] S. Jasanoff, 'The idiom of co-production' in S. Jasanoff (ed.), *States of Knowledge: The Co-Production of Science and the Social Order* (Routledge, 2004), pp. 1–12, p. 3.

[18] C. Rikap, *Capitalism, Power and Innovation: Intellectual Monopoly Capitalism Uncovered* (Routledge, 2021).

less conflicting discussions.[19] The seemingly technical knowledge – reports, studies, guidelines – produced by expert groups then act as material manifestations of this consensus, which have their own self-perpetuating dynamics. Endowed with authority and intellectual prestige, such inscriptions stabilise the consensus reached and perpetuate its reproduction. Such reports typically become heavily cited and circulate across spheres, becoming the uncontested reference points for all governance actors in given domains.

In a number of governance domains, a limited number of influential research clusters, located in prestigious academic institutions, also maintain close ties with IOs and other sites of global governance. High-profile research clusters can also act as boundary sites; they tend to produce research in an intersected space in between academic and policy spheres. Distinct kinds of relationships work to entangle research clusters with IOs. Professionals often move between the research clusters and IOs and their expert groups, and IOs can routinely request research from the clusters. More entrenched forms of collaborations can also be observed, where IOs and academic clusters co-sponsor events, produce 'policy-scientific reports', or co-sponsor courses and trainings. The ties between policymakers and the clusters, which are typically already endowed with a high degree of resources and reputational prestige, work to further reinforce their prestige and authority. As a result, such entanglements also cement and amplify existing hierarchies, so that less prestigious academic institutions or schools hardly ever have access to IOs. IOs, for their part, boost their authority while invoking their collaborations with prestigious schools.

But IOs increasingly find partners beyond academia, in private sites. The knowledge mobilised by IOs as 'expertise' is, indeed, also increasingly produced in partnership with philanthropists' data centres, large consultancy firms, private companies' research labs, or yet large NGOs, which have their own research staff and statisticians.[20]

[19] M. Abélès and I. Bellier, 'La Commission européenne: du compromis culturel à la culture politique du compromis' (1996) 46 *Revue française de science politique* 431–56.

[20] C. Ban, L. Seabrooke, and S. Freitas, 'Grey matter in shadow banking: international organizations and expert strategies in global financial governance' (2016) 23 *Review of International Political Economy* 1001–33; A. Littoz-Monnet, 'Exclusivity and circularity in the production of global governance expertise: the making of "global mental health" knowledge'

Such sites collaborate with IOs, but also increasingly produce the data that makes up the knowledge base of global governance.[21] Private actors and their big datasets are becoming increasingly involved in processes of data collection and analysis for UN agencies.[22] Sapignoli has shown that IOs have been turning towards 'big data' through the creation of new large-scale 'data mining' strategies, thus 'making corporations hugely significant for the information-gathering objectives of global governance, often in partnership or in competition with international organizations and states'.[23] The World Bank has been incorporating data compiled by private companies into its own datasets.[24] In the field of security, 'datasets are transferred from private to public databases', eventually informing security decisions.[25] In global health, private companies, as well as data centres funded by philanthropic foundations, collect and generate big data, metrics, and a plethora of studies that interpret these numbers and make specific policy recommendations based on them.[26] As global processes

(2022) 16 *International Political Sociology* 1–20; L. Seabrooke and O. J. Sending, 'Contracting development: managerialism and consultants in intergovernmental organizations' (2020) 27 *Review of International Political Economy* 802–27.

21 J. Eckl and T. Hanrieder, 'The political economy of consulting firms in reform processes: the case of the World Health Organization' (2023) 30 *Review of International Political Economy* 1–24; A. Littoz-Monnet and X. Osorio Garate, 'Knowledge politics in global governance: philanthropists' knowledge-making practices in global health' (2023) 31 *Review of International Political Economy* 1–26; M. Tichenor and D. Sridhar, 'Metric partnerships: global burden of disease estimates within the World Bank, the World Health Organisation and the Institute for Health Metrics and Evaluation' (2020) 4 *Wellcome Open Research* 35.

22 F. Johns, 'Data mining as global governance' in R. Brownsword, E. Scotford, and K. Yeung (eds.), *The Oxford Handbook of Law, Regulation and Technology* (Oxford University Press, 2017), pp. 776–98.

23 M. Sapignoli, 'Anthropology and the AI-turn in global governance' (2021) 115 *American Journal of International Law* 4–8 at 7.

24 K. Pistor, 'Re-construction of private indicators for public purposes' in K. E. Davis, B. Kingsbury, and S. Engle Merry (eds.), *Governance by Indicators: Global Power through Quantification and Rankings* (Oxford University Press, 2012), pp. 165–79.

25 R. Bellanova and M. de Goede, 'The algorithmic regulation of security: an infrastructural perspective' (2022) 16 *Regulation & Governance* 102–18 at 102.

26 Littoz-Monnet and Osorio Garate, 'Knowledge politics in global governance'; A. Littoz-Monnet, 'Knowledge machineries and their objects of expertise: knowing bodies, moves, and moods through "mobile health" data' (2024) 4 *Global Studies Quarterly*.

of agenda-setting and prioritisation turn to digital technologies, IOs, think-tanks, and even NGOs increasingly rely on the huge datasets of the private sector, which has the resources to develop the technologies used for data collection and transformation, as well as the corporate experts who seem to have the required training to design and implement technologies for data collection, storage, and analysis. When private actors and sites produce data, metrics, and studies autonomously or in partnership with IOs, they are in a critical position to shape how objects are known. They also shape knowledge validation standards themselves, thus delineating what is considered as expertise.

Finally, the many ephemeral yet routine work meetings, fairs, conferences, consultative forums, reflection forums, and roundtables that pepper global governance in most policy domains consist of 'crossing points' where expertise is assembled and stabilised.[27] In these (often physical) spaces, policymakers, experts, private actors, activists, and consultants routinely meet and discuss. Here, the governance of problems takes place in ways that are mundane and informal, away from formal decision-making arenas. These routine meetings can act as 'field-configuring events', that provide a focal point where certain understandings are articulated. As the same data and documents, and their associated assumptions, are circulated and rehearsed, certain affirmations come to be taken for granted and appear incontestable.[28]

Despite their appearance of multi-actorness and diversity, often widely advertised by IOs when they convene such events, the meetings are often quite exclusive and structured by their own hierarchies. IOs are increasingly pressed by calls for being more participatory and inclusive, and, in response, tend to incorporate diverse and sometimes contentious voices in the consultation exercises they convene. However, IOs may orchestrate such processes until critical voices become subdued to the mainstream agenda. Civil society organisations might be represented, but large and already recognised ones can be chosen, while small, more contentious organisations can be left out. Additionally, amongst those who attend, not all have the same opportunities to speak. Some act as hosts or panellists and sit at the

[27] A. Littoz-Monnet, *Governing through Expertise: The Politics of Bioethics* (Cambridge University Press, 2020).

[28] C. Hardy and S. Maguire, 'Discourse, field-configuring events, and change in organizations and institutional fields: narratives of DDT and the Stockholm Convention' (2010) 53 *The Academy of Management Journal* 1365–92.

core of these crossing points, while others remain at their periphery. IOs may also seemingly accommodate contentious claims, while at the same time reinterpreting them in a way that tames them or subjects them to their own agendas. Examining how understandings are articulated within crossing points makes it possible to ask 'what forms of knowledge count in global ordering'.[29] As such, the workings of events reflect and might even reinforce broader social hierarchies.[30]

The dispersion of knowledge-making does not imply that such processes are flat. Certain sites, endowed with prestige and resources, sit at the core of the global knowledge machinery, while others are peripheral. Despite an apparent multiplicity, diversity, and openness, the production of knowledge in global governance tends to be highly exclusive.[31] Even when participation is seemingly broad, resources and asymmetries operate to delineate who can speak and what knowledge counts.

Material Infrastructures

IOs 'know' social reality through and with diverse 'objects of expertise',[32] whether indicators, metrics, documents, or legal tools, such as treaties, decisions, digests, and so on. Paying attention to the materiality of expertise provides another entry point to study its politics. Although the material has always been ubiquitous in our lives, for, as put by Latour, 'Society is not made up just of men, for everywhere microbes intervene and act',[33] the effects of material objects have, recently, been more widely recognised, as algorithms, models, and tools of cyber surveillance visibly 'act' autonomously.

Scholarship in the field of IR has, thus, recently been catching up with insights that are already well-established in STS, Sociology, and Political Economy, on the significance of materiality in the study of

29 L. M. Coleman, 'The making of Docile Dissent: neoliberalization and resistance in Colombia and beyond' (2013) 7 *International Political Sociology* 170–87.

30 Hardy and Maguire, 'Discourse, field-configuring events, and change in organizations and institutional fields'.

31 Littoz-Monnet, 'Exclusivity and circularity in the production of global governance expertise'.

32 A. Esguerra, 'Objects of expertise: the politics of socio-material expert knowledge in global governance' (2024) 4 *Global Studies Quarterly*.

33 B. Latour, *The Pasteurization of France* (Harvard University Press, 1988) p. 35.

knowledge and its politics. Such material artifacts, what Latour called 'inscriptions', are highly portable and endlessly reproducible. As they circulate, texts, for instance, serve to stabilise and naturalise facts.[34] Knowledge artifacts function as 'durable, more mobile traces which can be transported between locales'.[35] They do not only 'represent' cultures, ideas, and discourses. They also 'mediate ties between humans' over a long time and large distances and, as such, make transportable and perpetuate certain ways of knowing.[36] Thus, knowledge objects have been shown to have their own 'lives', as they travel and are used in ways that produce a multiplicity of meanings and political effects.[37]

Not all knowledge artifacts are materially bounded in the same way. Data, metrics, and estimates are not 'materially bounded in the ways that drones, tanks, bodies, and boats are'.[38] Rather, they acquire materiality and stability in a more processual fashion, as they circulate, are reproduced, and become performative.[39] Knowledge objects, thus, are characteristically open, question-generating, and complex. They are processes and projections rather than definitive things.[40] They become meaningful as they are captured, assembled, and acted upon.

Thus, studying the politics of the material objects considered as 'expertise' by IOs requires paying attention to the networks, relationships,

[34] T. F. Gieryn, *Cultural Boundaries of Science: Credibility on the Line* (University of Chicago Press, 1999); B. Latour and S. Woolgar, *Laboratory Life: The Social Construction of Scientific Facts* (Princeton University Press, 1979).

[35] W. Walters, 'The power of inscription: beyond social construction and deconstruction in European integration studies' (2002) 31 *Millennium* 83–108 at 91; B. Latour, *Science in Action: How to Follow Scientists and Engineers Through Society* (Harvard University Press, 1987).

[36] S. L. Star, 'The ethnography of infrastructure' (1999) 43 *American Behavioral Scientist* 377–91.

[37] C. Aradau and T. Blanke, 'Politics of prediction: security and the time/space of governmentality in the age of big data' (2017) 20 *European Journal of Social Theory* 373–91; A. Finiguerra, 'A boat's afterlife: multiple translations of migratory debris' (2023) 29 *European Journal of International Relations* 628–50; A. Leander, 'Technological agency in the co-constitution of legal expertise and the US drone program' (2013) 26 *Leiden Journal of International Law* 811–31.

[38] M. de Goede, 'The chain of security' (2018) 44 *Review of International Studies* 24–42 at 31.

[39] K. Knorr Cetina, 'Objectual practice' in K. Knorr Cetina, T. R. Schatzki, and E. von Savigny (eds.), *The Practice Turn in Contemporary Theory* (Routledge, 2001), pp. 184–97.

[40] Knorr Cetina, 'Objectual practice', p. 190.

and claims that give traction to those material systems.[41] Some scholars have therefore shifted away from a focus on knowledge artifacts towards 'knowledge infrastructures' to refer more specifically to the socio-material ensembles that underpin and shape the production of knowledge.[42] For Edwards, knowledge infrastructures are the 'robust networks of people, artifacts, and institutions that generate, share, and maintain specific knowledge about the human and natural worlds'.[43] Such works go beyond the study of immediate processes of knowledge creation and pay attention, instead, to the infrastructures that generate, organise, and shape the production of knowledge.[44] Tichenor et al.[45] for instance define infrastructures as the background structures – the materials, people, and ideas – that enable the production of certain knowledge forms. By adopting this lens, scholars have been able to go beyond the micro-processes of producing artifacts, such as numbers, documents, or forecasts, and pay attention to the broader system(s) within which certain forms of knowledge are produced.[46] Doing so reveals how such infrastructures place limits on the knowledge and imaginaries that can be produced through them. Thus, IOs use objects of expertise in specific kinds of socio-material arrangements, which have their own power dimensions and social relations that they bundle together.[47]

The increased dispersion of sites of knowledge production in global governance has been strongly entangled with transformations in the

[41] N. Anand, *Hydraulic City: Water and the Infrastructures of Citizenship in Mumbai* (Duke University Press, 2017).

[42] S. Hirsch and D. Ribes, 'Innovation and legacy in energy knowledge infrastructures' (2021) 80 *Energy Research & Social Science* 102218.

[43] P. N. Edwards, *A Vast Machine: Computer Models, Climate Data, and the Politics of Global Warming* (MIT Press, 2010) p. 17.

[44] C. Bueger, 'Making things known: epistemic practices, the United Nations, and the translation of piracy' (2015) 9 *International Political Sociology* 1–18; M. Tichenor, S. E. Merry, S. Grek, and J. Bandola-Gill, 'Global public policy in a quantified world: Sustainable Development Goals as epistemic infrastructures' (2022) 41 *Policy and Society* 431–44; Littoz-Monnet, 'Knowledge machineries and their objects of expertise'.

[45] Tichenor, Merry, Grek, and Bandola-Gill, 'Global public policy in a quantified world'.

[46] Bueger, 'Making things known'; J. Bandola-Gill, 'Our common metrics? Our common agenda report and the epistemic infrastructure of the sustainable development goals' (2023) 14 *Global Policy* 8–12; M. Langevin, 'Big data for (not so) small loans: technological infrastructures and the massification of fringe finance' (2019) 26 *Review of International Political Economy* 790–814.

[47] Langevin, 'Big data for (not so) small loans'.

materiality of knowledge-making practices. The material infrastructures and techniques through which knowledge is produced and assembled by IOs are changing. '"Big data" are increasingly used to monitor, know, and govern populations', whether in IOs, private sites, or even academia.[48] With digitalisation, new possibilities of integrating and aggregating highly disparate forms of data through new techniques have emerged.[49] Statisticians themselves are being replaced by new kinds of experts, the data analysts and software engineers often working in private companies. These novel methods of data generation, accumulation, and transformation have been associated with new kinds of 'data flows' and 'messy geographies' of knowledge-making. While such transformations have been discussed in an exciting body of scholarship, the way they affect how global problems are known and governed has been given scant attention.[50]

Relations

Studying relations between people, sites, and things also provides us with another way of studying the politics of expertise. Relations, in fact, are their own objects of study, where transactions, seen as a dynamic, unfolding process, become the primary unit of analysis rather than the constituent elements themselves.[51]

Scholars studying knowledge in global governance have focused, first, on the *circulation of people* across spheres and organisations, either simultaneously or successively.[52] Recent insights in IR and International Political Sociology (IPS) have argued that 'the concept

48 A. K. Madsen, M. Flyverbom, M. Hilbert, and E. Ruppert, 'Big data: issues for an international political sociology of data practices 1' (2016) 10 *International Political Sociology* 275–96 at 276.

49 M. Flyverbom, A. K. Madsen, and A. Rasche, 'Big data as governmentality in international development: digital traces, algorithms, and altered visibilities' (2017) 33 *The Information Society* 35–42; A. Mackenzie, 'The production of prediction: what does machine learning want?' (2015) 18 *European Journal of Cultural Studies* 429–45 at 433; J. van Dijck, 'Datafication, dataism and dataveillance: big data between scientific paradigm and ideology' (2014) 12 *Surveillance & Society* 197–208 at 198.

50 Sapignoli, 'Anthropology and the AI-turn in global governance'.

51 M. Emirbayer, 'Manifesto for a relational sociology' (1997) 103 *American Journal of Sociology* 281–317.

52 O. J. Sending, *The Politics of Expertise: Competing for Authority in Global Governance* (University of Michigan Press, 2015) p. 5.

of an epistemic community does not stand if the community and those that it is meant to advise are the same'.[53] Shifting away from a focus on scientists or experts, who would be producing expert knowledge autonomously from 'politics',[54] scholars have revealed that 'identities and behavioural patterns cut across analytical categories of epistemic communities, international organisations, or advocacy networks'.[55] From that perspective, it no longer makes sense to conceive of expertise as produced by 'experts' or scientists autonomously, as people hold multiple roles and identities, circulate between spheres and organisations, and thus can act as 'experts' while at the same time performing other roles.[56]

Individuals can, indeed, be detached from their formal affiliations and move across spheres. More often, they enjoy familiarity with different settings *simultaneously* and transfer their knowledge across these different spaces in what has been called 'identity switching'.[57] The circulation of people contributes to the circularity and exclusivity of expertise. Those who tend to occupy, simultaneously or successively, multiple positions are typically endowed with resources, be they epistemic, social, or reputational. These resources make it possible for actors to navigate spheres and organisations and put themselves in influential positions.[58] Thus, by paying attention to the professionals – often a small, circular, exclusive, and intersected nucleus of people and organisations – who produce the reports, guidelines, studies, or

53 E. Tsingou, 'Club governance and the making of global financial rules' (2015) 22 *Review of International Political Economy* 225–56 at 230.

54 Haas, 'Introduction'.

55 Sending, *The Politics of Expertise: Competing for Authority in Global Governance*, p. 5.

56 L. Seabrooke, 'Identity switching and transnational professionals' (2014) 8 *International Political Sociology* 335–37.

57 Seabrooke, 'Identity switching and transnational professionals'; L. Seabrooke and E. Tsingou, 'Power elites and everyday politics in international financial reform 2' (2009) 3 *International Political Sociology* 457–61; D. Demortain, 'Standardising through concepts: the power of scientific experts in international standard-setting' (2008) 35 *Science and Public Policy* 391–402.

58 P. Bourdieu and L. J. D. Wacquant, *An Invitation to Reflexive Sociology* (University of Chicago Press, 1992); Y. Dezalay and M. R. Madsen, 'In the "field" of transnational professionals: a post-Bourdieusian approach to transnational legal entrepreneurs' in L. Seabrooke and L. F. Henriksen (eds.), *Professional Networks in Transnational Governance* (Cambridge University Press, 2017), pp. 25–38.

numbers, which constitute the 'evidence' or 'expertise' seen as relevant in a given issue domain, one can grasp significant aspects of knowledge-making practices.

Recent scholarship reveals that expertise is articulated by diverse actors or groups in continuous relations with one another, who gather in transnational communities,[59] communities of practice,[60] professional networks,[61] or yet clubs.[62] In the legal field, such communities typically involve legal elites from the academic, policy, and private spheres. Shifting away from a focus on specific actors and their influence, such accounts have shown that whatever their specific form or configuration, such arenas or groupings act as the loci where global governance knowledge is articulated, co-produced, and stabilised, until certain understandings of problems come to be seen as natural, evident, and incontestable.[63]

Second, scholars have also focused on the *circulation and assembling of material knowledge things*. Relations can be produced, for instance, by the circulation, exchange, and citing of material objects, what Latour calls 'inscriptions'.[64] The knowledge considered as relevant for policymaking purposes in specific domains often consists of a narrow set of research findings and data. Thus, the same studies, metrics, or reports circulate in a self-referential fashion. They can be heavily cross-cited, adding to the circularity of expertise.

[59] D. Stone, 'Partners to diplomacy: transnational experts and knowledge transfer among global policy programs' in A. Littoz-Monnet (ed.), *The Politics of Expertise in International Organizations* (Routledge, 2017), pp. 93–110; M.-L. Djelic and S. Quack (eds.), *Transnational Communities: Shaping Global Economic Governance* (Cambridge University Press, 2010).

[60] Bueger, 'Making things known'.

[61] A. Cohen, 'Legal professionals or political entrepreneurs? Constitution making as a process of social construction and political mobilization' (2010) 4 *International Political Sociology* 107–23; Seabrooke and Tsingou, 'Power elites and everyday politics in international financial reform 2'; L. Seabrooke and L. F. Henriksen, 'Issue control in transnational professional and organizational networks' in L. Seabrooke and L. F. Henriksen (eds.), *Professional Networks in Transnational Governance* (Cambridge University Press, 2017), pp. 3–24.

[62] Tsingou, 'Club governance and the making of global financial rules'.

[63] A. Vauchez, 'The force of a weak field: law and lawyers in the Government of the European Union (for a renewed research agenda)' (2008) 2 *International Political Sociology* 128–44.

[64] Latour and Woolgar, *Laboratory Life: The Social Construction of Scientific Facts*.

Expert groups, private actors, IOs, and research clusters often make repeated affirmations of particular numbers or studies, resulting in the 'recursive recognition' of this knowledge over time.[65] By contrast, studies or experiential insights that do not resonate with dominant ideas or well-established norms of scientific validity, or that are simply produced by people or organisations not endowed with social or epistemic prestige, tend to be disregarded.[66] In order to be heard, one needs to speak the exclusive language and use the theoretical frameworks of the dominant.[67] As a result, a narrow body of knowledge circulates across spheres so that the same data or research becomes heavily cross-cited by everyone.[68] The circulation of knowledge goes *de pair* with the circulation of individuals described earlier. But data circulation can also act autonomously and beyond the role of specific individuals. Cross-citing and recursive recognition become inscribed in particular sites and products of expertise and tend to be self-perpetuating. What becomes interesting, here, is how and where such knowledge circulates, and the way such flows feed into the circular, but also exclusive, nature of expertise.

Methodological Entry Points

A number of methodological approaches and techniques provide entry points into studying the making of expertise in global governance. Methods and sources may be eclectic; there is no 'right' or 'wrong' when it comes to methodology. Engagement with sources can also be polymorphous. In addition, the same sources can be examined, analysed, and interpreted, with and through distinct methods.

[65] A. Broome and L. Seabrooke, 'Recursive recognition in the international political economy' (2021) 28 *Review of International Political Economy* 369–81.

[66] D. L. Sackett and W. M. Rosenberg, 'The need for evidence-based medicine' (1995) 88 *Journal of the Royal Society of Medicine* 620–24.

[67] T. Biersteker, 'Participating in transnational policy networks: targeted sanctions' in M. E. Bertucci and A. F. Lowenthal (eds.), *Scholars, Policymakers and International Affairs: Finding Common Cause* (Johns Hopkins University Press, 2014), pp. 137–54; M. Eagleton-Pierce, 'Professionalizing protest: scientific capital and advocacy in trade politics' (2018) 12 *International Political Sociology* 233–55.

[68] Littoz-Monnet, 'Exclusivity and circularity in the production of global governance expertise'.

Studying People

As expert knowledge is typically produced by a myriad of actors and networks across spheres and organisations, as discussed earlier, one possible entry point when studying the making of expertise is therefore to focus on the networks, or communities, that produce the knowledge considered as expert in a given domain. Studying such groups can prove particularly useful in order to capture enmeshments between knowledge and politics in processes of knowledge-making. It can also help identify which actors and sites are excluded from the production and assembling of expertise. Prosopographic methods, a specific biographical method which consists of examining the 'social profiles' of professionals in an issue domain – their career trajectories and relationships rather than their particular actions – is a promising avenue. A prosopographic study involves an in-depth examination of the biographies, and multiple and changing affiliations across time and locations, of those that are recognised as 'experts' in a given domain. Social profiles can be traced through an examination of CVs, online job profiles, online searches, or the authoring of documents considered as 'expert' documents. Studying the authorship and sponsorship of specific documents can prove particularly useful for identifying networks of expertise. Alternatively, mapping the phenomenon of cross-citing also reveals such networks, where specific groups of professionals cite each other in ways that can be highly circular and exclusive.[69] Expert groups, private actors, IOs, or boundary research clusters indeed make repeated affirmations of particular claims, studies, or numbers, resulting in the 'recursive recognition' of this knowledge over time.[70]

Other forms of network analysis can also be mobilised to help trace the complex entanglements between actors and sites involved in the making of expertise.[71] In order to map expertise networks, and

[69] Littoz-Monnet, 'Exclusivity and circularity in the production of global governance expertise'.

[70] Broome and Seabrooke, 'Recursive recognition in the international political economy'.

[71] J. Attride-Stirling, 'Thematic networks: an analytic tool for qualitative research' (2001) 1 *Qualitative Research* 385–405; H. Knox, M. Savage, and P. Harvey, 'Social networks and the study of relations: networks as method, metaphor and form' (2006) 35 *Economy and Society* 113–40; B. Latour, P. Jensen, T. Venturini, S. Grauwin, and D. Boullier, '"The whole is always

conceptualise the nature of the relationships between actors and sites within such networks, qualitative Visual Network Analysis (VNA) can be an interesting avenue. VNA is concerned with the *visual* rather than the structural (social) properties of networks.[72] It can be conducted with the help of different software packages, in which qualitative data gathered through interviews or observations (actors, relations, type of relations, contextual information) can be inserted, and which allows for visualisation of the continuous interplay between forces of attraction and repulsion between actors or groups of actors. This can be relevant in terms of identifying who sits at the core or at the periphery of the community of actors that produces expert knowledge. As such, it can capture existing hierarchies and power asymmetries within and beyond expert networks.

Studying Texts

The material products of expertise, whether expert reports, studies, datasets, or yet numbers, can also provide an excellent starting point to study the fabric of expertise in global governance. Discursive and genealogical forms of analysis can be particularly useful. Discursive analysis is an attempt to deconstruct the tenets or the framing of discourses. Genealogy, for its part, is a form of historical enquiry; It aims to reconstruct the past through an analysis of historical sources, texts, events, and processes.[73] This can be crucial in terms of revealing the

smaller than its parts" – a digital test of Gabriel Tardes' monads' (2012) 63 *The British Journal of Sociology* 590–615; T. Venturini, M. Jacomy, A. Meunier, and B. Latour, 'An unexpected journey: a few lessons from sciences Po médialab's experience' (2017) 4 *Big Data & Society* 2053951717720949.

72 One could also rely on quantitative forms of Social Network Analysis (SNA), which typically are used to study relational ties that link actors through flows of data or personal interactions. Yet, while formalistic methods evaluate the frequency of interactions either directly between individuals or groups or through the circulation of information and data (S. P. Borgatti, A. Mehra, D. J. Brass, and G. Labianca, 'Network analysis in the social sciences' (2009) 323 *Science* 892–95.), they focus too strongly on the density of interactions and its measurable forms (number of contacts, quantity of information exchanged), leaving aside more informal and invisible forms of relationships (Knox, Savage, and Harvey, 'Social networks and the study of relations').

73 M. Bevir, 'What is Genealogy?' (2008) 2 *Journal of the Philosophy of History* 263–75.

contingency of given knowledge forms with long lineages and open a space for alternatives.[74]

There is a diverse 'toolkit' when it comes to discursive forms of analysis, including genealogical, deconstructive, and juxtapositional forms of analysis.[75] 'Critical framing analysis', which conceives of discourse as frames, can be a promising technique. Frames are devices that actors use 'to situate events, to interpret problems, to fashion a shared understanding of the world and to galvanise possible resolutions to current plights'.[76] Examining the way experts and other actors who work with them identify and frame problems provides crucial insights into 'embedded and tacit assumptions, meanings, reasonings and patterns of action and inaction'.[77] When conducting critical framing analysis, or any other kind of discursive analysis, one may start identifying texts that constitute 'points of reference',[78] i.e., texts which are taken as a basis for all further reflections on how to govern the domain at stake. This includes the policy documents, official reports, and meeting documentation produced by IOs, or the reports and evaluations produced by expert groups, private foundations, or private actors.

Studying Sites and Infrastructures

Particularly relevant to global terrains, participant observation and ethnographic interviews provide a unique internal perspective for understanding global knowledge-making practices. Participant observation is also particularly useful for observing the varied and often contradictory conceptualisations of the 'global'.[79] Ethnographic methods have

[74] S. Borg, 'Genealogy as critique in International Relations: beyond the hermeneutics of baseless suspicion' (2018) 14 *Journal of International Political Theory* 41–59.

[75] In the genealogical method, contingency of contemporary discursive practices examined through study of past discursive practices. Juxtapositional analysis consists in juxtaposing one discursive 'truth' to events and issues that 'truth' fails to acknowledge or alternatively pairing dominant representation with alternative accounts.

[76] M. Barnett, 'Culture, strategy and foreign policy change: Israel's road to Oslo' (1999) 5 *European Journal of International Relations* 5–36 at 15.

[77] T. Wengraf, *Qualitative Research Interviewing: Biographic Narrative and Semi-structured Methods* (Sage, 2001) p. 116.

[78] N. Fairclough, *Critical Discourse Analysis* (Longman, 1995).

[79] L. Maertens, 'Ouvrir la boîte noire. Observation participante et organisations internationales' (2016) 5 *Terrains/Théories*.

proven to be promising ways to provide thick descriptions of actors, sites, and infrastructures involved in the production of knowledge and the relationships between these.[80] They can thus provide an excellent vantage point to map sites of expertise production and knowledge machineries, as well as types of relations (meetings, exchange of data, financial flows, co-organisation of events) within a knowledge machinery. Participant observation provides direct access to the machineries of knowledge production and their often-opaque dynamics. It also allows for observing the dynamics between macro and micro scales, where power and relationships of authority operate in subtle ways. This can be crucial in terms of accessing contextual information on hierarchies, resources, invisible relations, and constraints in the process of knowledge production. Observing sites, their relations, and hierarchies in these processes may result, of course, in a plethora of information. In that case, the use of systematised observation protocols – using a notebook where all actors and interactions are recorded – is important. The ethnographic process goes back and forth between the theoretical and the empirical, the abstract and the concrete.

Conclusion

Using these methodological entry points makes it possible to reveal the reasons why specific formations are in place and reintegrate power dynamics and hierarchies into the analysis of knowledge-making. Exploring global governance expertise through one of these avenues involves making a shift away from studying formal arenas, mechanisms, and actors of global governance, and instead zoom in on ways of doing politics 'by other means'.[81] The processes of knowledge production discussed here point to the political nature of expertise, and the need to understand its making as a subtle way of governing that takes place beyond the traditional spheres of decision-making. Examining the processes, boundary sites, and infrastructures of knowledge production help us understand how the co-production of science and politics operates in practice. Such enmeshment can be observed in often

[80] A. Riles, *The Network Inside Out* (University of Michigan Press, 2001).

[81] B. Latour, 'Give me a laboratory and I will raise the world' in M. Biagioli (ed.), *The Science Studies Reader* (Routledge, 1999 [1983]), pp. 141–70; M. Callon, P. Lascoumes, and Y. Barthe, *Acting in an Uncertain World: An Essay on Technical Democracy* (MIT Press, 2009) p. 68.

tangible forms when one engages with the meso- or micro-level study of processes of knowledge production. This enmeshment produces circularity and exclusivity in the making and content of global governance expertise. It thus has exclusionary effects, which cannot be dissociated from those stemming from more structural hierarchies. In addition to financial or material resources, widely accepted norms of validity also structurally delineate what forms of knowledge are seen as valuable in global governance. Certain norms act as markers of what is scientific and what is not, with the effect that knowledge that does not match these criteria tends to be dismissed as anecdotal, inconclusive, biased, or 'non-expert'. Thus, the concrete micro knowledge-making processes which embed expertise in the political can also intersect with and replicate macro-epistemic structures, both material and ideational, inscribing certain forms of expertise and the power of their protagonists in global governance. This of course has implications for the way global problems are understood and acted upon. Those knowledge forms which count as expert strongly shape how global issues are seen, governed, and regulated by IOs.

5 *Experts, Practices, Power*
The Work of International Criminal Court Reform

RICHARD CLEMENTS*

Introduction

According to Donna Harraway, '[t]here is no unmediated photograph or passive *camera obscura* in scientific accounts of bodies and machines; there are only highly specific visual possibilities, each with a wonderfully detailed, active, partial way of organizing worlds'.[1] In April 2019, four ex-Presidents of the governing body of the International Criminal Court (ICC) machine, the Assembly of States Parties (ASP), published a joint opinion piece in *Atlantic Council* to mark the twentieth anniversary of the signing of the Rome Statute. As leading figures in international criminal justice, they hoped to capture the ICC in full view, both its successes and, tentatively, its failures.[2] On one account, the ICC had achieved much in its short lifespan: 'put[ting] on notice' would-be war criminals and bringing justice to victim communities around the globe, facilitating peacebuilding efforts in Colombia, modelling 'accountability mechanisms for Syria and Myanmar', and, ultimately, placing some individuals responsible for the world's worst crimes behind bars.[3] With this 'unmediated photograph', the authors reaffirm their commitment to the ICC as an institution tasked with closing the impunity gap by prosecuting atrocity crimes and bringing justice to victims.

Yet this image also depicts problems and 'deficiencies' hampering the court's quest for justice as the prompt for the ex-Presidents'

* This chapter has gone through several iterations, and I thank the editors, Negar Mansouri and Daniel Quiroga-Villamarín, for their helpful comments and steady guidance. All errors are my own. Email: r.a.clements@uvt.nl.

1 D. Harraway, 'Situated Knowledges: The Science Question in Feminism and the Privilege of Partial Perspective' (1988) 14 *Feminist Studies* 575, 583.

2 Z. Al Hussein, B. Ugarte, C. Wenaweser, and T. Intelman, 'The International Criminal Court Needs Fixing' (*Atlantic Council*, 24 April 2019).

3 Ibid.

intervention. They highlight a gap between the court's 'unique vision' and its 'daily work': cases collapsing due to inadequate case-building and witness protection, judges declining to authorise investigations out of fear for the organisation's long-term stability, and various 'management deficiencies prevent[ing] the court from living up to its full potential'.[4] Looking beyond the court's own work, there is also the fragile political context in which it operates, especially dwindling 'diplomatic support' and the sanctions levelled against senior court figures by the first Trump administration.[5] Further afield (though omitted by the ex-Presidents) lie the protracted tensions between the ICC and African states parties over allegations of structural racism and bias, as well as serious resourcing issues resulting from successive zero-growth budgets.[6]

After this diagnosis comes the cure: a course of international organisation (IO) reform, via 'an independent assessment of the Court's functioning by a small group of independent experts'.[7] This comes after two decades of ICC reform punctuated by recurring cycles of deficiency, improvement, and renewal, ranging from small-scale reorganisations of court organs to institutionalised working groups devoted to studying and streamlining court governance.[8] Yet despite their quiet optimism about past and future reform efforts, the ex-Presidents offer little sense of how reform works beyond self-evident assumptions

[4] Ibid.

[5] Ibid. See US Executive Office of the President, Blocking Property of Certain Persons Associated with the International Criminal Court, EO 13928, 11 June 2020.

[6] R. López, 'Black Guilt, White Guilt at the International Criminal Court' in Matiangai Sirleaf (ed.), *Race and National Security* (Oxford University Press 2023) 211; S. Ford, 'Funding the ICC for Its Third Decade' in Carsten Stahn (ed.), *The International Criminal Court in its Third Decade: Reflecting on Law and Practice* (Brill Nijhoff 2023).

[7] Hussein *et al*, 'ICC Needs Fixing'. For an excellent study of the relationship between international law, institutions and reform, see G. Sinclair, *To Reform the World: International Organizations and the Making of Modern States* (Oxford University Press 2017).

[8] I have previously discussed these cycles in the context of wider narrative trends around institutional progress in R. Clements, 'From Bureaucracy to Management: The International Criminal Court's Internal Progress Narrative' (2019) 32 *Leiden Journal of International Law* 149. The reference to renewal and repetition is drawn from D. Kennedy, 'When Renewal Repeats: Thinking against the Box' (1999–2000) 32 *NYU Journal of International Law & Politics* 335, 337.

about its functional effectiveness. In this regard, they join many ICC practitioners and commentators who frequently call for court reform but rarely consider its mechanics or wider distributional effects. This chapter problematises the 'black box' of reform to think about what it entails and how it is constructed, experienced, and effected within IOs like the ICC, taking its Independent Expert Review (IER) of 2019–2020 – the follow-up to the ex-Presidents' proposal – as the expert production of a partial organisational world that entrenches existing arrangements of power among states parties.

At the heart of this discussion lies the notion of *expert reform work*. This notion seeks to reorient – theoretically and methodologically – the plane on which IOs and their legal landscapes are analysed. The phrase itself hints at its own recalibrations: *expert* because the experienced, trained professional turns out to be a more important site of institutional innovation than the IO itself or external structural forces; *reform* because experts' seemingly mundane tweaking exercises have the power to reconstitute an IO's contexts, problems, priorities, and future possibilities; and *work* because the effort of IO reform is an interpretive task performed by experts but is also the many other ideas and materials that craft an institutional reform process.

The notion of expert reform work, which is further fleshed out later, draws on Harraway's idea of partial worlds, but also actor network theory (ANT) as a lens 'that attempts to map and understand the relationship and interplay between physical or material objects and concepts' as not only a semiotic but a 'material-semiotic method' concerning 'the symbiotic relationship between people, things and ideas'.[9] The draw of actor network theory for this study of IOs derives from a 'central tenet of ANT thinking', namely that 'such systems or material-semiotic states are not static or fixed but rather are in a perpetual state of *forming and reforming*'.[10] This chapter attempts to bring this underlying premise of ANT thinking, namely that states (or institutions) are always becoming and re-becoming, to the study of IO reform itself as an expert institutional exercise involving people, documents and sites. As such, the chapter's focus on IO reform as expert

[9] P. Stokes, *Critical Concepts in Management and Organization Studies* (Palgrave Macmillan 2011) 3. See B. Latour, *Science in Action* (Oxford University Press 1987).

[10] Stokes, ibid, p. 4 (emphasis added).

work is an attempt to think through IO change as a perpetual, but no less political or pliable, process of institutional becoming.

Following the likes of Harraway and Bruno Latour, the chapter proposes that expert reform work is neither a rational science of perfectibility nor a 'god trick' that creates the organisation from nothing and nowhere.[11] It is precisely these imaginaries of reform that have led to the predictable yet lacklustre reformism of the past two decades of ICC operations. Instead, reform work often means expertly encountering and mediating myriad textual and non-textual materials, ideas, and structures in ways that allow the expert to do their job to a standard that those with a stake in the outcome deem satisfactory. Studying these encounters allows us to capture the tectonic effects of the seemingly contingent and inconsequential framings that legal reformers bring to their task, as well as the push and pull effect other materials such as institutional documents and position papers have on the process of institutional becoming.

To grasp the mechanics of this expert reform work at the ICC, I begin by summarising key aspects of the IER before centring the expert as an important node in IO reform.[12] This differs from other accounts of the expert as rational technician or handmaiden of power, situating them instead as and among a 'network of relations' between ideas and practices that rearrange the IO's context, problems, priorities, and possibilities.[13] From here, the chapter then poses a set of reflections on the IER process to attend to the expert-led and situated institution-making process that is IO reform.

Conditions for Expert Work: The Independent Expert Review

The IER will be our aid throughout. Specifically, the central axis on which this chapter turns is an obscure, yet important concept

[11] Harraway, 'Situated Knowledges'.

[12] There is a rich literature on international legal reform, see e.g. D. Kennedy, 'When Renewal Repeats: Thinking against the Box' (1999–2000) 32 *NYU Journal of International Law & Politics* 335, 337; L. Eslava and S. Pahuja, 'Between Resistance and Reform: TWAIL and the Universality of International Law' (2011) 3 *Trade Law & Development* 103. Sinclair describes international law as 'discipline, discourse and practice of reform', Sinclair, 'To Reform the World'.

[13] Stokes, 'Critical Concepts in Management'.

introduced in the opening pages of the IER experts' final report, published in September 2020. The concept in question is the 'three-layered governance model', a heuristic or interpretive device offered by the experts as a way to understand the ICC's different functions and how they relate to one another, but also a crucial component in the experts' re-imagination of the court.[14] Before discussing the model, it is necessary to go back several steps, to clarify who these experts are, and why and for whom they were conducting this analysis. In doing so, I begin to flesh out the notion of expert reform work.

In Resolution 18/7 of December 2019, the ICC ASP commissioned a 'State Party-driven review process' – the IER – to 'identify ways to strengthen the ICC and the Rome Statute system' via 'concrete, achievable and actionable recommendations aimed at enhancing the performance, efficiency and effectiveness of the Court'.[15] The ASP devised a preliminary document, the Terms of Reference to delimit the scope of the review. It also proposed that a group of nine independent experts be appointed to consider 'complex technical issues' under three clusters of 'governance', 'judiciary', and 'investigations and prosecutions'.[16] The panel was formed of international lawyers such as Richard Goldstone (the panel chair), Mónica Pinto, and Mohamed Chande Othman. Once appointed, the panel of experts commenced a nine-month period of stakeholder consultations and analysis (conducted predominantly online due to the COVID-19 pandemic). The panel's findings were published in a final report in September 2020, which became the panel's definitive statement on the conditions, constraints, and prospects for the institution. It proposed 384 recommendations across the court's organs, processes, and activities that were promptly taken up and evaluated by scholars and court officials including the ICC Prosecutor and the President of the court.[17] The ICC itself offered a detailed official response the following year.[18]

[14] ICC, 'Independent Expert Review of the International Criminal Court and the Rome Statute System: Final Report', 30 September 2020, para. 31.

[15] ASP resolution 18/7, ICC-ASP/18/Res.7, 6 December 2019, para. 6.

[16] Ibid, para. 2.

[17] E.g., OTP, Remarks of the Prosecutor on the IER Report, The Hague Working Group and the New York Working Group of the Bureau, 4th Joint Meeting, 7 October 2020; ICC, The ASP Bureau Working Group's Online Meeting on the Report of the Independent Expert Review: Preliminary Reactions of the ICC President, 7 October 2020.

[18] ICC, Overall Response of the International Criminal Court to the Independent Expert Review Final Report, 14 April 2021.

Despite its widespread promotion at the time, IER commentary has been brief. With so many recommendations, it is not surprising that the panel's findings on workplace bullying and harassment drew most attention, with many other proposals being quickly lumped together, quietly implemented, or forgotten.[19] Moreover, many scholars, including several normally critical voices, seemed indifferent to yet another effort to tinker around the edges of a system that, to them, required nothing less than structural transformation.[20] Only one scholar hinted at the three-layered governance model proposed by the expert panel as 'a new way of conceptualizing the ICC as a complex institution'.[21]

Despite general disinterest, though, studying the conditions and effects of the panel's work demonstrates why it may be important to take such reform exercises and interpretive devices seriously as recalibrations of institutional power and stakeholder interest. The experts were supposed to identify ways to 'strengthen' the ICC and the Rome Statute system, and to do so through proposals that would be 'concrete, achievable and actionable'. Already in this description, what was deemed organisationally achievable became a key limiting factor for the kind of analysis and proposals the experts could offer to the ASP. Other factors included skill and time: all appointed experts were lawyers and institution-builders and Resolution 18/7 indicates that the experts would begin their work on 1 January 2020, submitting their final report by 30 September 2020. These legal experts had to account for what was 'concrete, achievable and actionable' within nine months as criteria directing and limiting their work.

Beyond these factors, the experts also operated in, and reaffirmed, a particular historical moment. As noted at the outset, the IER appears as the latest cycle in a long history of ICC reform efforts largely initiated and justified on grounds of efficiency, effectiveness, and improved

[19] D. Guilfoyle, 'The International Criminal Court Independent Expert Review: Questions of Accountability and Culture' (EJIL Talk!, 7 October 2020), www.ejiltalk.org/the-international-criminal-court-independent-expert-review-questions-of-accountability-and-culture/; L. Sadat, 'The International Criminal Court of the Future' in Stahn (ed.), *The International Criminal Court in Its Third Decade* (Brill 2023) 444–472, at 456.

[20] See Lopez, 'Black Guilt/White Guilt'. Stahn does not directly engage with the IER but offers 'ways to re-imagine the ICC beyond [it]', C. Stahn, 'Re-imagining the ICC in a Multipolar World' in Stahn (ed.), *The International Criminal Court in Its Third Decade* (Brill 2023) 562–594, at 562.

[21] Guilfoyle, 'International Criminal Court Independent Expert Review'.

performance.[22] Already during preparatory discussions on a permanent ICC in 1995, the United Kingdom asked whether it was 'the best use of limited resources to undertake international investigations and prosecutions with all the difficulties and duplication of personnel that that involves'.[23] While these kinds of questions did not stop the court from emerging, they set the tone for the infant body: when the ICC began operations in 2002, its first Prosecutor, Luis Moreno Ocampo, stated: 'I have the chance to build the most efficient public office' for tackling anti-impunity.[24]

Such managerial concerns are themselves not context-free but were baked in over time. At the ICC, as in other modern IOs, efficiency has been justified as necessary for securing 'value for money' for stakeholders, i.e. the court's funders. Particularly in the wake of the 2008 global recession, western states as the main financial backers have become more vocal about ensuring the court's cost-effectiveness for the sake of national (read European) taxpayers.[25] This was soon translated by court leaders into the working practices and culture of the institution. In November 2012, then-ICC President, Sang-Hyun Song, reassured states parties that court officials had become 'responsible managers of the funds which the States Parties have provided'.[26] This growing connection between efficiency and the concerns of major donors is not

[22] By way of example, former ICC President Silvia Fernández de Gurmendi informed states parties upon her election in 2015 that her 'main priority' would be 'to enhance the effectiveness and efficiency of the institution', ICC, Presentation of the Court's Annual Report to the Assembly of States Parties, 18 November 2015. See also ICC, Comprehensive Report on the Reorganisation of the Registry of the International Criminal Court, August 2016, para. 38.

[23] Summary of Observations Made by the Representative of the United Kingdom of Great Britain and Northern Ireland on 3, 4, 5, 6 and 7 April 1995, Ad Hoc Committee on the Establishment of an International Criminal Court, Press Release no. 32/95, 7 April 1995, 11–12.

[24] L. Moreno Ocampo, 'The International Criminal Court' in David Crane, Leila Sadat, and Michael Sharf (eds.), *The Founders: Four Pioneering Individuals Who Launched the First Modern-Era International Criminal Tribunals* (Cambridge University Press 2018) 94–125, at 116.

[25] S. Kendall, 'Commodifying Global Justice: Economies of Accountability at the International Criminal Court' (2015) 13 *Journal of International Criminal Justice* 113.

[26] Statement of President Song to the ASP 11th Session, 14 November 2012, The Hague, p. 4, available at: https://asp.icc-cpi.int/NR/rdonlyres/0EEEED0E-5BA8-4894-8AB5-3C2C90CD301B/0/ASP11OpeningPICCSongENG.pdf.

an innate characteristic, then, but a condition that emerged out of the specific political-economic and discursive relations between court officials and states parties since the drafting of the Rome Statute. It is a particular meaning of efficiency that experts, including the IER panel, were inured to and fluent in.

These being some of the panel's background conditions and ideas, they did not explicitly constrain or determine the panel's conclusions. Within certain strands of critical scholarship, such wider forces as political or economic capacity are often deemed determinative of institutional outcomes. Yet the expert remains central as mediator: to draw on Duncan Kennedy, such external constraints around the meaning of efficiency produce within them 'the effect of necessity, the experience of legal compulsion', leaving them with a sense, though not a 'reality', that 'there is no alternative'.[27] Background conditions and ideas are thus necessarily mediated by the modalities of expertise itself: its requirements of objectivity, independence, and rational analysis. It is through these modalities that expertise bears the descriptive power to reimagine the institution. While there may be a great many pressures and forces at play during experts' efforts to reform an IO, how those pressures are assembled and articulated is part of the expert's objective function.[28] Taking the expert as a key unit of analysis, as other scholars have done,[29] thus centres the specific descriptive and imaginative power of experts in IO reform settings.

To elaborate, experts largely rely on the traits of objectivity and the techniques of rational scientific analysis to establish themselves and their findings as authoritative.[30] As Littoz-Monet acknowledges in this volume, there are multiple uses of expertise beyond its capacity to rationalise decision-making. Yet it is at least these rational claims of experts that necessitate a conceptual break or firewall between those proposing and overseeing reform and those carrying it out (never mind

[27] D. Kennedy, *A Critique of Adjudication* (Harvard University Press 1997) 161.

[28] B. Latour, *Reassembling the Social: An Introduction to Actor-Network Theory* (Oxford University Press 2005) 159.

[29] See e.g. T. Mitchell, *Rule of Experts: Egypt, Techno-Politics, Modernity* (University of California Press 2002); O. Sending, *The Politics of Expertise: Competing for Authority in Global Governance* (University of Michigan Press 2015); D. Kennedy, *A World of Struggle: How Power, Law and Expertise Shape Global Political Economy* (Princeton University Press 2016).

[30] This is no longer always the case, partiality and indeterminacy having become part of a new style of expertise of late, see Van den Meersche in this volume.

those experiencing its effects). This firewall is familiar not only from scholarship on expertise but also in the literature on the independence of IOs from their members,[31] or judicial independence from state interests.[32] Similarly, for reformers, their independence from states is deemed crucial for sound decision-making and the legitimacy of institutional processes. It was not for nothing that the ICC reform exercise was branded an *independent* expert review.

Nonetheless, claims to independence and objectivity have often been branded mere smokescreens for the hegemonic interests that remain hidden behind them.[33] These are the dynamics that David Kennedy has described as 'capture', or the idea that 'international policy-making will favour some policies and exclude others, and distribute resources from some groups to others, because the policy-making machinery has been captured by political forces committed to these results'.[34] At the ICC, capture is often closely linked to global *realpolitik*, great powers, or global distributions of capital.[35] Latent in the idea of capture is the assumption that, if kept non-ideological, 'outcomes will be in some sense neutral or benign'.[36] Yet to attend to the modalities of IO reform from within means acknowledging its own distributive potential.

This alludes to a second power of expertise, namely its constitutive power vis-à-vis the IO, emphasising the *expert* dimension of the independent review. Evidently, states parties and other stakeholders have an interest in the outcome of reform exercises given their potential effects on scrutiny of potential crimes as well as budget demands. However, these interests are not directly translatable to the organisational setup given the 'objective' expert vocabulary and

31 R. Collins and N. White, 'International Organizations and the Idea of Autonomy' in Richard Collins and Nigel White (eds), *International Organizations and the Idea of Autonomy: Institutional Independence in the International Legal Order* (Routledge 2011) 3.

32 Article 40, Rome Statute of the International Criminal Court, A/CONF.183/9, agreed 17 July 1998, entered into force 1 July 2002.

33 See T. Krever, 'Spectral Expertise' (2017) 106 *New Left Review* 148, 157.

34 D. Kennedy 'The Politics of the Invisible College: International Governance and the Politics of Expertise' (2001) 5 *European Human Rights Law Review* 463, 473.

35 See e.g. D. Bosco, *Rough Justice: The International Criminal Court in a World of Power Politics* (Oxford University Press 2014); G. Baars, *The Corporation, Law and Capitalism: A Radical Perspective on the Role of Law in the Global Political Economy* (Brill 2019) 239.

36 Kennedy, 'Politics of the Invisible College', at 466.

techniques that exist quite apart from state control.[37] Not only this, but states would find it difficult to control such reform processes in practice without being condemned by stakeholders for attempting to influence or politicise independent investigations. It is the same logic that has the court maintain such a strict division between its own objective legal functions and the political interests of its states parties, now applied to court governance as opposed to investigations.

At the ICC, states parties already play a large role in managing the court via the ASP and other internal bodies such as the Committee on Budget and Finance. Moreover, as Emma Palmer and Hannah Woolaver have shown, 'in some instances States Parties have attempted to use the ASP to influence the exercise of judicial and prosecutorial functions in cases where their interests were implicated in ongoing proceedings'.[38] Yet in reform settings, fears of such assertions of coercive power by states parties distract from the more subtle power of experts and their practices.[39] As noted earlier, the meaning acquired by efficiency through the discourse of major donor states has placed a premium on reform proposals likely to make the court more cost-effective and therefore more accountable to certain stakeholders. This discourse has since become a central component of the way experts conduct themselves when analysing and offering recommendations, namely to take account of all relevant information as well as the wider realities and challenges facing the court, or in Martti Koskenniemi's words, to 'streamline, balance, optimize [and] calculate'.[40] Taking account of such managerial factors is not to be captured by state interests, but to be a competent, pragmatic technocrat. In this way, reform work is itself capable of reconstituting and redistributing an

[37] Expertise, too, has its own processes of cultural production based on prestige, awards, and location, see A. Rasulov, 'What Is Critique? Towards a Sociology of Disciplinary Heterodoxy in Contemporary International Law' in Jean d'Aspremont, Tarcisio Gazzini, André Nollkaemper, and Wouter Werner (eds.), *International Law as a Profession* (Oxford University Press 2017) 189–221.

[38] E. Palmer and H. Woolaver, 'Challenges to the Independence of the International Criminal Court from the Assembly of States Parties' (2017) 15 *Journal of International Criminal Justice* 641, 645.

[39] M. Foucault, *Archaeology of Knowledge and the Discourse on Language* (trans. A. M. Sheridan Smith, 1972 [1969]) 135–140.

[40] M. Koskenniemi, 'Constitutionalism as Mindset: Reflections on Kantian Themes About International Law and Globalization' (2007) 8 *Theoretical Inquiries in Law* 9, 13.

organisation's resources, values, and power differentials precisely as an act of objective expertise, rather than as a repudiation of it.

This point chimes with the international law literature on expertise. According to David Kennedy, '[g]enerating a common vision of a world to be governed is both a communicative and performative work of the imagination and a technical institutional project'.[41] This is particularly visible in the context of IO reform, where expert work meets complex bureaucratic machineries. Much of what it means to be an expert concerns the visions of governance that such expert work is capable of producing. International lawyers, diplomats, policymakers, NGOs, legal advocates, and activists produce knowledge as part of their job. Such knowledge constitutes in various ways: framing an organisational context, identifying its problems, establishing narratives of success and failure, establishing 'realities' constraining the organisation, and recommending solutions.

IO reformers such as the IER panel are similar to experts and such expert work, with some distinctions. First, given how many obstacles stand in the way of proposals being accepted and implemented, reformers' recommendations and solutions may be among the least significant of their articulations as far as constituting the IO is concerned. Instead, and second, reformers are often uniquely mandated to make a diagnosis of the IO as a whole, rather than only one of its organs or as an official with a set of bounded tasks. This gives IO reformers a particularly unique opportunity to redefine the entire IO, relying on the ideas, materials, and practices assembled about them in the process without being accused of overstepping their mandate. To understand more concretely how this constitutive work *works*, I return to the panel's interpretive device, the 'three-layered governance model', to reflect further on the kind of imaginaries experts perform.

Expert Reform Work in Action: The 'Three-Layered Governance Model'

Putting aside any suggestions of bias or capture, let's imagine how nine independent experts might have inscribed efficiency – and thereby the preferences of major financial contributors – into the ICC's organisational form simply by applying their legal knowledge and

[41] Kennedy, *World of Struggle*, at 90.

objective, technical expertise. From the beginning, the expert panel confronts a dilemma. Operating on the basis of their expansive mandate across governance, judiciary, and prosecutions, the panel must reckon with how to fulfil such a mandate despite the judicial and prosecutorial independence that underwrites two of the panel's focus areas: 'judiciary' and 'investigations and prosecutions'.

As shown earlier, the firewall of independence prevents the experts from simply overriding judicial and prosecutorial independence by assertion: their findings must, after all, satisfy both the requirements of expert objectivity and the expectations of stakeholders such as court officials, state representatives, and NGOs with an interest in upholding the fundamental principles of judicial and prosecutorial independence. Independence therefore becomes a fulcrum on which the panel's framing of the IO turns. It is for this reason that the expert panel begins its final report by addressing precisely this dilemma. The report begins by recalling that 'inherent in the structure of any international court or tribunal is the dual nature of the institution: the ICC is both a judicial entity (ICC/Court) and an international organisation (ICC/IO)'.[42] This duality corresponds to the underlying rationale of judicial independence on the 'ICC/Court' level and that of state party oversight and accountability on the 'ICC/IO' level.

As IO, the ICC 'does not carry out judicial activity – it indirectly supports it', with states parties playing a 'key role'.[43] As a court, though, the panel offers a further division 'between justice and the administration of justice'.[44] This further division is also connected to the question of independence. According to the experts, justice as '[j]udicial and prosecutorial work (e.g. judgments, deliberations by judges, the prosecutor's decisions to initiate or pursue a case, investigations) require[s] absolute independence'.[45] Yet this idea of 'absolute independence' already suggests its opposite. And indeed, the administration of justice is deemed 'not [to] necessitate the same degree of independence'.[46] Why? Because 'the administration of justice is audited in national systems – the same should be the case for the ICC'.[47] To reinforce the point, and the shrinking role of independence in the division of court functions, the panel avers that 'confidentiality and independence should not be used as a way of deflecting accountability and

[42] IER Final Report, para. 26. [43] Ibid, para. 27. [44] Ibid, para. 28.
[45] Ibid. [46] Ibid, para. 29. [47] Ibid.

preventing oversight'.[48] Hence, efficiency, not independence, becomes the vehicle for assessing performance in relation to the administration of justice.

From this reframing emerges the 'three-layered governance model', in which each layer is subject to greater degrees of state oversight: a protected inner 'core' of judicial and prosecutorial activity, a 'middle layer' of partial accountability facilitated by performance indicators and a proposed Judicial Audit Committee, and an outermost layer of IO administration heavily influenced by state oversight. The model is backed up by reference to article 119 of the Rome Statute, as well as a decision of Pre-Trial Chamber II in *Prosecutor v. Ali Kushayb*, in which it states that 'the Court's statutory framework clearly distinguishes the role of the Court, as a judicial institution entrusted with the power to exercise its jurisdiction over persons for the most serious crimes of international concern; the position of the ASP, which is responsible for considering and deciding on the Court's budget; and the duties of the judiciary and Chambers'.[49] This is taken to affirm the three layers of ICC governance.

What are the experts doing by elaborating this model at the very outset of their report? While the model may be read consistently with the Rome Statute and its case law, those (two) sources say nothing of the efficiency rationale that now underpins the model. These 'primary' sources merely refer to a functional division of labour grounded in notions of judicial independence and state party control over budgetary matters. The panel's reframing is thus facilitated by a professional internalisation of efficiency, after years of efficiency measures and austerity politics, fused to a familiar legal division between Court and IO and backed by the legal framework and its jurisprudence. Collectively, it allows – or demands – that court functions be judged according to an efficiency rather than an independence rationale, altering the power differentials within the court, especially as between the Prosecutor, judges, and states parties.

Yet this work is not the experts' alone. Beyond the final report itself, this redescription of the ICC's organisational form along efficiency

[48] Ibid.

[49] Arts 38–43, Rome Statute; ICC, *Prosecutor v. Ali Kushayb*, Decision on the Defence request under article 115(b) of the Rome Statute, ICC-02/05-01/20-101, 23 July 2020, para. 8.

lines is afforded by three 'clusters' of issues first proposed by the ASP in the IER Terms of Reference mentioned earlier, namely '(a) governance; (b) judiciary; and (c) investigations and prosecutions', a triple division which appears to have been copy-and-pasted as the panel's triple conceptualisation of the court.[50] In keeping with the earlier discussion on the power of experts, a degree of interpretation and translation was required to make these issues commensurable and legible at an organisational level. Yet the Terms of Reference, as a document, directs us to the affordances of many different practices, concepts, ideas, and things in relation to one another.[51] It makes reform a much more worthy site of analysis to consider such heterogeneous elements as a Terms of Reference and the situated meaning of efficiency, as affording certain possibilities and impossibilities, rather than as the instruments of a hegemonic apparatus. This applies equally to the other crucial documents of the IER. One is the draft working paper of November 2019 that had already consolidated some issues under 'clusters' by posing certain objectives, possible actions, and useful instruments for experts to draw upon.[52] Another is the panel's own interim report of June 2020 which did not yet offer the three-layered conceptualisation of the final report, but began to situate the work of reform in a longer institutional history of optimisation, creating a placeholder for the final report that would appear three months later.[53] As Annelise Riles has argued elsewhere, 'each document – the old and the new – lean on each other to take full effect'.[54] In this way, one can sketch how experts and reformers knit together, both as expert and node, a network of interpretive and material associations.

With this expanded understanding of what such assemblages afford, other important conditions, including time and global events, re-emerge as relevant considerations for why the IER came out as

[50] ASP resolution 18/7, ICC-ASP/18/Res.7, 6 December 2019, Annex I: Terms of Reference for the Independent Expert Review of the International Criminal Court.

[51] B. Latour, 'On Actor-Network Theory: A Few Clarifications' (1996) 47 *Soziale Welt* 369.

[52] ASP, Draft working paper: Matrix over possible areas of strengthening the Court and Rome Statute system, 27 November 2019.

[53] ICC, Independent Expert Review on the International Criminal Court and the Rome Statute System: Interim Report, 30 June 2020.

[54] A. Riles, 'Models and Documents: Artefacts of International Legal Knowledge' (1999) 48 *ICLQ* 805, 813.

it did. Although approaching the question of legal interpretation from a phenomenological perspective, Duncan Kennedy considers the role of 'resources, time and skill' in lawyers' efforts to make their interpretations stick.[55] Applied to the IER, it was already noted that the panel operated within a tight timeframe of nine months: how would a process twice this length have changed or potentially undermined the chosen governance model? Moreover, their resources, though extensive and well-connected to important figures within the court, were somewhat inhibited by the COVID-19 pandemic and the constraints associated with relying on many online rather than in-person meetings. The materiality – including meeting constraints and technological possibilities – afforded by physical meetings may have caused the governance model to be discounted altogether: a circular room populated by a bank of NGO officials may be somewhat more persuasive than the appearance of individual video profiles isolated from themselves and their colleagues;[56] gaps in connectivity may cause an interruption of conversation and a return to the basic premise of judicial independence without its sub-division into judicial and administration of justice mandates. Lastly, the nine-member panel comprised experienced lawyers and institution-builders within other international criminal tribunals. They did not seek to offer a sociological, economic, or anthropological analysis, but an expertise cognisant of the legal frameworks and constraints of IO reform. This may also have affected the kinds of stakeholders the panel consulted with – court managers and transnational NGOs rather than those directly affected by the court's work. A lens that is attuned to a wider range of materials and actors, and what these collectively afford, helps to make sense of IO reform beyond theories of rational science and structural determinacy.

[55] D. Kennedy 'A Left Phenomenological Alternative to the Hart/Kelsen Theory of Legal Interpretation' in D. Kennedy, *Legal Reasoning: Collected Essays* (Davies Group Publishers 2008) 160.

[56] S. Jasanoff, 'Subjects of Reason: Goods, Markets and Competing Imaginaries of Global Governance' (2016) 4 *London Review of International Law* 361, 370; C. Schwöbel-Patel and W. Werner, 'Screen' in Jessie Hohmann and Daniel Joyce (eds.), *International Law's Objects* (OUP 2018) 419, 423. For an overview on the (new) material turn, see D. Quiroga-Villamarín, 'Domains of Objects, Rituals of Truth: Mapping Intersections between International Legal History and the New Materialisms' (2020) 8 *International Politics Reviews* 129, 130.

Work Effects: Redistributing the ICC

The discussion until now has focused largely on the sociologically enriching potential latent in approaching IO reform exercises through the notion of expert reform work: the constitutive role of experts, but also the assemblages that form them and which they re-form in turn. However, the earlier discussion on efficiency and its meaning-making potential for the ICC also hints at the wider range of distributive effects that can be surveyed when acknowledging the work of reform. This points to the wider stakes of expert reform work. The IER panel was clear about the functional intent of their governance model. Their first recommendation to the court was that 'the Three-Layered Governance Model should be used as a tool to ensure effective and efficient governance, clarify reporting lines, and improve cooperation among stakeholders'.[57] This narrow reading of the model's effects as relating only to the specific organisational purposes and components for which it was intended is consistent with the mainstream view of expertise as concerned only with functional effectiveness.[58]

The IER complicates this narrow reading of the model's effects by considering both its unintended consequences and the broader redistributions of meaning, influence, and resources it is capable of effecting across the ICC. These redistributions relate to the context, problems, priorities, and future possibilities of the organisation and are discussed in turn.[59]

Context: While experts are often said to operate within a context – 'the "drivers" that decision makers are said to ignore at their peril: technological, historical, social, economic, or political "realities"'[60] – these realities are also expert articulations that narrate a particular social milieu within which the IO is said to exist, and to which it should be directly responsive. The context of the IER was already outlined by the ex-Presidents, and the expert panel, as they

[57] IER Final Report, para. 50, Recommendation 1.

[58] R. Clements, *The Justice Factory: Management Practices at the International Criminal Court* (Cambridge University Press 2023) 23–26.

[59] G. Burrell, 'Modernism, Postmodernism and Organisational Analysis: The Contribution of Michel Foucault' in A. McKinlay and K. Starkey (eds.), *Foucault, Management and Organization Theory* (SAGE Publications 1998) 14, 25.

[60] Kennedy, *World of Struggle*, at 112.

diagnosed the judicial and administrative 'deficiencies' of the court and the need to remain efficient and effective in an unstable political landscape. The official context therefore knits together a sense of declining multilateralism with isolated court problems and the scarce resources of an austerity-prone donor community. This (and subsequent organisational imperatives) may have differed had the ex-Presidents and the panel referred to alternative contexts, such as the African Union's hostility towards the court or the tangibility of justice for victim communities.

Problems: From this context emerges a more tangible set of problems than the ex-Presidents' references to 'management deficiencies'. Kennedy reminds us that 'the idea of a "global problem" is a complex work of imagination'.[61] Within IOs, the rendering of an *organisational* problem is no different, although as we have seen, the remit for expert imagination here may also be conditioned by experts' mandate, experiences, and time. Indeed, it is part of the power of framing a problem as organisational that it directs concern towards internal structures, workflow issues, personnel, fragmentation, and underperformance. Framing the problem differently, as a problem inherent in the tensions between different visions of global justice, would demand a different analysis and alternative recommendations.[62] So too would framing the problem in terms of leadership, the court's constituencies, racial bias, or transnational capitalism.[63] As it happened, these problem frames remained unused.

Priorities: Operating in a fragile global 'context' and having identified corresponding organisational 'problems', certain activities (and solutions) are prioritised. As a result of the three-layered governance model, those measures that were most likely to deliver efficiencies for the court were prioritised. The increased oversight this model afforded to states also allowed their concerns, specifically those on whom the court financially relies, to take on greater importance. This was already acknowledged at the 1998 Rome Conference, when the conference secretary stressed that 'to secure the financial health of the Court, the

[61] Kennedy, ibid, at 95.

[62] D. Robinson, 'Inescapable Dyads: Why the International Criminal Court Cannot Win' (2015) 28 *Leiden Journal of International Law* 323.

[63] C. Schwöbel-Patel, *Marketing Global Justice: The Political Economy of International Criminal Law* (Cambridge University Press 2021).

support of major financial contributors was crucial and hence the concerns of the major contributors should be looked at more sympathetically'.[64] The issue becomes more acute when value-for-money concerns begin to funnel resources into constructing a managerial apparatus to oversee the court's administration of justice functions, including a Judicial Audit Committee and data-collection for performance indicators. These all necessitate the allocation of resources towards some concerns and away from others, including those not seen as real concerns in the first place.

Possibilities: Lastly, the cumulative effect of such contextualising, problematisation, and prioritisation is to further shape the ICC's conditions of possibility and the very institutional imaginaries that produce the court.[65] Much as Martti Koskenniemi denoted that '[t]he concepts and structures of international law… are the conditions of possibility for the existence of something like a sphere of the international', so too do expert articulations form the conditions of possibility for the organisational sphere.[66] Considering what is easier or more difficult to articulate before and after a reform exercise such as the IER may be a fruitful way of assessing the effects of this discursive work. Although the ICC itself pushed back against some of the panel's findings, including parts of its model framing, it will certainly be easier for states parties to argue in favour of greater oversight over administration of justice matters given the panel's reasoning that these are audited nationally. The ICC itself pointed out in its response to the IER final report that the model's three layers are 'inextricably linked' not hermetically closed, meaning that states and other interested actors may become more strategic in seeking to exert influence. For example, efficiency savings in the recruitment and retention of staff may disproportionately advantage those already familiar with the court's work in the Global North, shaping the types

[64] M. Arsanjani, 'Financing' in Antonio Cassese, Paola Gaeta, and John Jones (eds.), *The Rome Statute of the International Criminal Court, Volume 1* (Oxford University Press 2002) 315, 320.

[65] S. Jasanoff, 'Future Imperfect: Science, Technology and the Imaginations of Modernity' in S. Jasanoff and Sang-Hyun Kim (eds.), *Dreamscapes of Modernity: Sociotechnical Imaginaries and the Fabrication of Power* (Oxford University Press 2015) 1–33.

[66] M. Koskenniemi, *From Apology to Utopia: The Structure of International Legal Argument* (Cambridge University Press 2005 reissue) xiii.

of prosecutorial and judicial activity the court undertakes in the long term.[67] Under such circumstances, it becomes more difficult to justify reforms based on non-efficiency rationales, such as the fairness of proceedings or the court's practical effect on victims. Together, reform work points to these subterranean effects on the court's present and future activities.

Conclusion

It perhaps misses the point of re-imagining IO law to spend a chapter on one relatively obscure reform exercise. There are far more pressing issues confronting the ICC than the outworkings of its latest technical tweaking. Yet through this managerial example, I have sought to perform a double take on IO reform as an important site for studying not only how institutions change but via what modalities and materials, by what interpretive devices, and with what redistributive effects institutions like the ICC remain in a perpetual state of becoming. The IER's contribution was not only to offer a sound, rational basis for court optimisation, nor to act as handmaiden to powerful states. Rather, it was to carry out expert reform work in ways that re-formed the ICC anew by baking efficiency rationales into the division of its judicial and administrative functions.

The notion of expert reform work attends both to the forms of expert knowledge required to carry it out and the additional epistemic labour required to put abstract expectations, constraints, and mandates into organisational action. It offers an account of expert reform beyond positivist ideas of functional optimisation and more structuralist accounts of embedded and instrumentalised hegemony.[68] This also opens up the concept of work to dynamics not limited to experts and their agentic manoeuvring of materials, but also the entanglement of people, ideas, norms, and documents and what these 'nodes' afford to one another as part of organisational (re)assembly. Expanding the analytic thus does not negate but enriches the discussion on reform's distributional effects: the IER having demonstrated

[67] ICC, Overall Response of the International Criminal Court to the Independent Expert Review Final Report, 14 April 2021, para. 26.

[68] P. Bourdieu, 'The Force of Law: Toward a Sociology of the Juridical Field' (1987) 38 *Hastings Law Journal* 805.

how organisational tools, devices, documents, and ideas reshaped the context, problems, priorities, and possibilities of the ICC as an IO. Attending to the granular and the banal is perhaps where alternative IO scholarship will find new modes of engagement and new questions to ask of IOs, offering 'wonderfully detailed, active, partial ways of organizing worlds' beyond the imaginaries supplied by ICC ex-Presidents and expert reform panels.[69]

[69] Harraway, 'Situated Knowledges'.

6 *Drawing the Contours of Hidden Hunger as an Object of Governance*

JUANITA URIBE

Introduction

In the shifting context of global policy-making, International Organizations (IOs) have become powerful sources of expert authority and central sites for the exercise of power in global governance. While we have a clear understanding of how IOs deploy expertise, there has been relatively little effort among legal scholarship and International Relations (IR) to critically examine the processes by which such institutions produce and validate knowledge claims about governance objects and, in doing so, authorize certain solutions as the only ones "viable." This chapter examines the way in which the World Health Organization (WHO), Food and Agriculture Organization (FAO), and United Nations Children's Fund (UNICEF) acted as central vehicles in defining the contours of "hidden hunger" as a "matter of fact" – or as a medicalized and economized object of governance. It shows how this problematization largely authorized the prioritization of short-term responses and easily measurable programs such as food fortification[1] and vitamin supplementation in Global South countries. Rather than addressing the underlying socio-economic determinants of the problem, such responses acted as political analgesics providing temporarily relief. In highlighting how IOs' "ways of seeing" are connected to the practice of governing, the chapter sheds light on the everyday politics of rule-making.

This chapter examines how IO's knowledge practices *stabilize certain "ways of seeing" and acting upon global governance objects.*

[1] The term food fortification broadly refers to the addition of one or more nutrients to a food whether or not they are normally contained in the food. See M. Lawrence, *Food Fortification: The Evidence, Ethics, and Politics of Adding Nutrients to Food*, (Oxford University Press, 2013).

Looking at how IOs delineate the contours of objects allows us to move beyond "problem-solving" perspectives, according to which institutions' main role is to enable global cooperation and find solutions to global challenges.[2] The work of IOs is profoundly political. They make certain issues knowable and governable and, in doing so, define the world in such a way as to confer authority on some categories, actions, and actors rather than others.[3] This is especially patent at a time when, in order to make claims valid across jurisdictions, IOs rely on the acquisition and deployment of certain forms of expertise.

International legal scholarship has largely focused on analyzing the formalistic and institutional dimensions of objects of governance, be they climate change, pollution, or health.[4] From such perspectives, objects of governance are exogenous entities to be addressed and regulated through laws, conventions, and standards. However, adhering strictly to a formalistic and legal account of objects fails to capture how given visions and ways of acting upon gain traction at the expense of others. For that, we need a more textured examination of the socio-political processes that shape such objects. I propose to do so by analyzing how IOs define objects as "matters of fact," to draw on Latour's term, and how, in turn, this problematization narrows down the possible range of policy solutions.[5] In contrast to "matters of concern," which are marked by dispute and situatedness, matters of fact appear as ahistorical realities. Nonetheless, matters of fact are just as political as matters of concern; the distinction lies in how institutions approach them and how they are publicly perceived.

Empirically, I focus on the field of global food governance, more particularly on the case of "hidden" hunger, which has been defined and addressed by the international community as a form of undernutrition primarily stemming from vitamin and mineral deficiency. Such forms of hunger are qualified as "hidden" because there are no visible warning signs, so that individuals who suffer from it are not often aware of it. I explore how hidden hunger was problematized

[2] See Quiroga-Villamarín and Mansouri's introduction to this volume.

[3] O. J. Sending, *The Politics of Expertise: Competing for Authority in Global Governance*, (University of Michigan Press, 2015).

[4] C. Ryngaert, I. F. Dekker, R. A. Wessel, and J. Wouters, *Judicial Decisions on the Law of International Organizations*, (Oxford University Press, 2016).

[5] B. Latour, 'Why has critique run out of steam? From matters of fact to matters of concern', *Critical Inquiry*, 30/2 (2004), 225–48.

as a medicalized problem stemming from "a deficit" of nutrient consumption in Global South countries. Despite being a complex socio-economic and political issue directly linked to factors such as access to food, inequalities, and dominant agroindustrial models, efforts to address hidden hunger have predominantly relied on what I refer to as "political palliatives," such as food fortification and vitamin supplementation.[6] The chapter mainly focuses on the work of three particular agencies, also known as the bureaucratic machinery[7] of food and agriculture: the FAO, WHO, and UNICEF.[8] While the activities of these agencies were certainly key in mobilizing resources and bringing public attention, this chapter wants to highlight the politics inherent in their knowledge-making practices and highlight that ways of seeing problems always come at the expense of marginalizing others.

The remainder of the chapter proceeds as follows: The first section of the chapter discusses different perspectives that have scrutinized the work of IOs as machineries of social and political ordering. The second section of the chapter introduces the analytical framework of the paper, namely how IOs' problematization of objects of governance as "maters of fact" restricts the range of possible solutions and political interventions. Sections three to five delve into the empirics by unpacking how WHO, UNICEF, and the FAO delineated the contours of hidden hunger in highly exclusionary ways. On the one hand, they show how, through quantification techniques, laboratory exercises, and statistical instruments, IOs assembled a body of knowledge that defined hidden hunger in medicalized and economized terms, portraying it as an indisputable matter of fact. On the other hand, the empirical sections explore how this problematization marginalized some knowledge forms while simultaneously enabling short-term forms of political action, mainly targeting individuals in the Global South.

6 For a detailed analysis of food fortification and vitamin supplementation policies as a "magic-bullets" and "techno-fixes" see J. N. Ruxin, 'Hunger, science, and politics: FAO, WHO, and UNICEF nutrition policies 1945–1978', (University of London, 1996); A. H. Kimura, *Hidden Hunger: Gender and the Politics of Smarter Foods*, (Cornell University Press, 2013).

7 S. Ilcan and L. Phillips, 'Making food count: expert knowledge and global technologies of government', *Canadian Review of Sociology/Revue canadienne de sociologie*, 40/4 (2003), 441–61.

8 For a historical analysis of WHO, UNICEF, and the FAO's involvement in nutritional policies see Ruxin, 'Hunger, science, and politics: FAO, WHO, and UNICEF nutrition policies 1945–1978'.

The article relies on an in-depth case study. Through immersion in details of the case, I explore the ways in which IOs produced and validated knowledge claims about hidden hunger as an object worthy of global collective attention with consequences for legal outcomes. This was done through an extensive textual analysis of policy documents, reports, and websites from these IOs, as well as of academic publications in nutrition and health journals. I also conducted semi-structured interviews with policy makers and statisticians from the WHO, FAO, and UNICEF, as well as from civil society organizations.

IOs as Machines for Social and Political Ordering

The discipline of IR and some strands of legal scholarship have treated international institutions as "solvers" of different problems, such as international cooperation and information asymmetries, among others.[9] In an attempt to reintroduce the "social" into the analysis, sociological-oriented scholarship has questioned some of these premises by exploring the ways in which IOs do politics.[10] These accounts are highly attentive to the role of IOs in shaping intersubjective understandings. Barnett and Finnemore, for example, highlight that IOs are autonomous actors that "both regulate and constitute the world."[11] Other accounts have highlighted the different ways in which IOs, as purposeful actors, assemble or mobilize knowledge to achieve certain

[9] M. Zürn, 'Democratic governance beyond the nation-state: the EU and other international institutions', *European Journal of International Relations*, 6/2 (2000), 183–221; R. O. Keohane, *After Hegemony*, (Princeton University Press, 1984); S. Park, *International Organisations and Global Problems: Theories and Explanations*, (Cambridge University Press, 2018).

[10] J. Ferguson, *The Anti-Politics Machine: 'Development', Depoliticization and Bureaucratic Power in Lesotho*, (Cambridge University Press, 1990); F. Petiteville, 'Les organisations internationales dépolitisent-elles les relations internationales?', *Gouvernement et action publique*, 5/3 (2016), 113–29; B. Müller, *The Gloss of Harmony: The Politics of Policy Making in Multilateral Organisations*, (Pluto Press, 2013); O. Nay, 'International organisations and the production of hegemonic knowledge: how the World Bank and the OECD helped invent the fragile state concept', *Third World Quarterly*, 35/2 (2014), 210–31; M. Louis and L. Maertens, *Why International Organizations Hate Politics: Depoliticizing the World*, (Taylor & Francis, 2021).

[11] M. N. Barnett and M. Finnemore, *Rules for the World: International Organizations in Global Politics*, (Cornell University Press, 2004).

goals such as expanding their mandate into new areas,[12] enacting depoliticization,[13] or becoming policy relevant actors in a given field.[14] Approaching IOs as real fields of ethnographic inquiry, scholars have conceptualized them as circuits of power "where normative frameworks are produced and globally diffused, resources are distributed and knowledge circulated through transnational expert networks."[15] Similar claims have been made by international legal scholars, who have examined IOs' activities and workings in their contingent and historically situated dynamics.[16]

Following this research tradition, this chapter explores a concrete aspect of the politics of IOs object-making: the knowledge-making practices that they set up in order to problematize objects of governance, and thus govern them. Following Foucauldian-inspired scholarship in international law and IR, I seek to understand how certain practices and modes of treatment are attributed to problems.[17] Yet, rather than focusing on how certain issues enter the domain of "thought," I am interested in exploring how, more concretely, IOs actively participate in exclusionary processes of social and political ordering in the field of global food policy.[18]

Studying how IOs participate in object-making in the domain of global food governance is of relevance to international law scholarship in two main ways. On the one hand, food governance is

[12] A. Littoz-Monnet, 'Expert knowledge as a strategic resource: international bureaucrats and the shaping of bioethical standards', *International Studies Quarterly*, 61/3 (2017), 584–95.

[13] Louis and Maertens, *Why International Organizations Hate Politics*.

[14] S. Grek, 'Governing by numbers: The PISA "effect" in Europe', *Journal of Education Policy*, 24/1 (2009), 23–37.

[15] Müller, *The Gloss of Harmony: The Politics of Policy Making in Multilateral Organisations*.

[16] T. E. Aalberts, 'A Foucauldian approach to international law. Descriptive thoughts for normative issues', *European Journal of International Law*, 19/4 (2008), 870–75; T. Aalberts and B. Golder, 'On the uses of Foucault for international law', *Leiden Journal of International Law*, 25/3 (2012), 603–8; D. Kennedy, 'Challenging expert rule: the politics of global governance', *Sydney Law Review*, 17/1 (2005), 5–28.

[17] Aalberts, 'A Foucauldian approach to international law'; N. Rose and P. Miller, *Governing the Present: Administering Economic, Social and Personal Life*, (John Wiley & Sons, 2013).

[18] J. Uribe, 'Excluding through inclusion: managerial practices in the era of multistakeholder governance', *Review of International Political Economy*, 24/1 (2024), 1–24.

an area that is treated as an appendix of trade regimes and where there is a high deference to expert knowledge. Analysis of "technical standards" and trade negotiations tends to overshadow the politics of norm-making.[19] As a result, international legal scholarship has often taken food governance standards at face value, ignoring the knowledge that underpins them.[20] On the other hand, thinking about object-making and its links to knowledge also makes it possible to understand that that "universal" definitions of dietary standards or notions such as hunger often rest in uncertain and elusive grounds, thus indicating that expertise is a space of instability and constant challenge.

IOs' Power: Knowing and Acting upon Objects of Governance

In global governance, where there is an absence of democratic forms of legitimation, the recourse to knowledge constitutes one of the most advanced sources of authority.[21] Governing, indeed, increasingly takes place "outside the arena of legislative deliberation and democratic decision making"[22] and relies on claims to expertise rather than those of collective identity value and interest.[23] The consolidation of evidence-based modes of decision-making, for example, attests to the fact that governing increasingly rests on claims of efficiency and instrumental rationality rather than those of collective identity value and interest.[24] This broader turn towards rationalized forms of governance and, more broadly, the scientization of politics is particularly pronounced in policy-making transcending nation states.

[19] See, however, A. Saab, 'An international law approach to food regime theory', *Leiden Journal of International Law*, 31/2 (2018), 251–65; A. Orford, 'Food security, free trade, and the battle for the state', *International Law and International Relations*, 11 (2015), 1.

[20] N. D. Fortin, *Food Regulation: Law, Science, Policy, and Practice*, (John Wiley & Sons, 2022).

[21] Barnett and Finnemore, *Rules for the World: International Organizations in Global Politics*; J.-P. Voß and R. Freeman (eds.), *Knowing Governance*, (Palgrave Macmillan UK, 2016).

[22] S. Randeria, 'Glocalization of law: environmental justice, World Bank, NGOs and the cunning state in India', *Current Sociology*, 51/3–4 (2003), 305–28, 29.

[23] Voß and Freeman (eds.), *Knowing Governance*.

[24] Voß and Freeman (eds.), *Knowing Governance*.

In this context, IOs solidify their authority by depicting objects of governance as exogenous entities that are knowable and actionable.[25] Through the production of global indicators, metrics, rankings, and datasets, or by hiring bodies of experts, IOs strive to insulate themselves from partisan squabbles and processes of political contestation.[26] This often leads some IOs to simplify complex social activities into simple "scores," economized "facts," or ratings.[27] This process resonates with what Latour has termed "matters of fact," which are entities that are presented as uncontestable truths, fostering a perception of naturalness and inevitability.[28] Problematizing issues such as pollution, crime, or migration as matters of "fact," detached from their socio-economic and political determinants, indeed allows IOs to act as powerful global governors.[29]

Representing social problems as matters of fact requires significant effort. It is indeed intrinsically related to the availability of technologies, infrastructures, and different instruments, which translate the complexities of economic, social, and political contexts into a stabilized reality capable of orienting action. However, despite their aura of universality, "*matters of fact*" are just one exclusionary particular way of defining and thinking about global objects. Attempts to scientize often result in the exclusion and erasure of subjects and of those voices that do not conform to logics of instrumental rationality.

Similarly, presenting objects as matters of fact is not devoid of political implications. In the following section, I show how such a problematization narrows down the scope of possible solutions, limiting them to approaches that align with standardizable rationales and quantifiable results. Responses to matters of facts often come in the form of technical fixes that are perceived as straightforward and easily implementable. Such responses become favored due to their perceived feasibility and their capacity to demonstrate measurable impact and "results." These responses, however, act as what I refer to as powerful

[25] B. B. Allan, 'Producing the climate: states, scientists, and the constitution of global governance objects', *International Organization*, 71/1 (2017), 131–62.

[26] Barnett and Finnemore, *Rules for the World: International Organizations in Global Politics*.

[27] C. Shore and S. Wright, 'Governing by numbers: audit culture, rankings and the new world order', *Social Anthropology*, 23/1 (2015), 22–28.

[28] Latour, 'Why has critique run out of steam?'.

[29] Louis and Maertens, *Why International Organizations Hate Politics*.

"political palliatives," which provide surface-level and temporary relief, while overlooking responses that address the social, political, and economic root causes of problems.

Problematizing Hidden Hunger as a Matter of Fact: Science and Economics

I focus on the case of hidden hunger to show how different UN agencies characterized hidden hunger as a "matter of fact," portraying it as a medicalized problem of nutrient deficiencies mainly in the Global South, to be solved through programs such as adding nutrients to food or delivering vitamin capsules. In a first step, I examine how IOs produced a "cartography of nutritional deficiencies,"[30] by amassing a body of biochemical and statistical knowledge produced through quantification processes. In doing so, IOs perpetuated Global-North–Global-South asymmetries, wherein countries in Africa, South America, and Asia are characterized by their "deficiencies" and framed as in need of "correction" and assistance.[31] In a second step, I show how such problematization of hidden hunger subtly authorized technical responses and short-term forms of political action that largely neglected the root causes of the problem.

Until the 1980s, hidden hunger did not garner significant global attention. The focus of global discourse in the field was primarily on what was termed the "protein era," characterized by a widespread belief that a "protein gap" was the primary cause of malnutrition and hunger worldwide. However, by the 1970s, it became evident that the deficiency in protein was not the predominant nutritional issue globally.[32] Consequently, there was a shift in focus towards the role of "micronutrients," or tiny substances and particles such as vitamins and minerals, which started receiving increasing attention from the international community.[33]

In fact, at the time, the connection between these tiny nutrients and health was primarily the subject of scientific and academic inquiry.

[30] J. L. Barona, *From Hunger to Malnutrition: The Political Economy of Scientific Knowledge in Europe, 1818–1960*, (Peter Lang, 2012).
[31] Kimura, *Hidden Hunger*.
[32] D. McLaren, 'The great protein fiasco', *The Lancet*, 304/7872 (1974), 93–96.
[33] R. D. Semba, 'The rise and fall of protein malnutrition in global health', *Annals of Nutrition and Metabolism*, 69/2 (2016), 79–88.

During this era, studies conducted on a national scale began to unveil the extent of "hidden hunger," its clinical manifestations and its ramifications for health.[34] However, in 1986, a publication by Alfred Sommer of an article on Vitamin A in the *Lancet* played a pivotal role in elevating what was considered solely a "health" issue into a matter of greater social and political significance. Sommer's study not only confirmed Vitamin A's role in severe clinical conditions, as previously documented, but also highlighted its correlation with elevated childhood mortality rates.[35]

Given the relevant and potential social implications of the topic, various UN agencies convened major international conferences to advance the understanding of the impacts of nutritional deficiencies and elevate political conversations. As early as in 1974, Sommer was invited to a WHO-sponsored meeting in Indonesia to discuss his work on Vitamin A. He was also in charge of writing the 1995 WHO report on Vitamin A deficiency and its consequences, and of chairing different scientific advisory committees at the WHO and UNICEF.[36]

The 1990 Summit of Children took the issue very seriously and promised the virtual elimination of Vitamin A deficiency by the year 2000.[37] After the summit, several conferences and summits were held. One significant event was the Conference on Ending Hidden Hunger in 1991, held in Montreal. The primary objective of this conference was to garner "political support at the highest level for ending hidden hunger."[38] A similar acknowledgment took place one year later, in 1992, at the first FAO/WHO International Conference on Nutrition

[34] N. Kretchmer, J. L. Beard, and S. Carlson, 'The role of nutrition in the development of normal cognition', *The American Journal of Clinical Nutrition*, 63/6 (1996), 997S–1001S.

[35] A. Sommer, E. Djunaedi, A. A. Loeden, I. Tarwotjo, K. West, R. Tilden, and L. Mele, 'Impact of vitamin A supplementation on childhood mortality: a randomised controlled community trial', *The Lancet*, 327/8491 (1986), 1169–73.

[36] A. Sommer, *Vitamin A Deficiency and Its Consequences: A field Guide to Detection and Control*, (WHO, 1995).

[37] N. Dalmiya and W. Schultink, 'Combating hidden hunger: the role of international agencies', *Food and Nutrition Bulletin*, 24/4_suppl_1 (2003), S69–77.

[38] E. Messer, 'Conference report: ending hidden hunger – a policy conference on micronutrient malnutrition', *Food and Nutrition Bulletin*, 14/1 (1992), 1–3.

in Rome, where it was recognized that hidden hunger was a "matter of major public health concern."[39]

However, much more than a shift in discourse, the construction of hidden hunger as an object of governance entailed the deployment of tools, instruments, and technologies to make it actionable. In the context of increasing awareness and interest, IOs started to produce and assemble a significant body of knowledge that served to delineate the object as an incontrovertible scientific fact. "Accurate" knowledge of the vitamin content of foods, food consumption at the household level, and anthropometric indicators of nutritional deficiencies were fundamental in that regard.[40]

At the time, the WHO expressed concerns about the incommensurability of hidden hunger. The UN agency pointed to a "lack of consistency" of existing nutrition standards, in particular due to a lack of homogenization of "methods of analysis and presentation of survey results."[41] Up until that point, nutrition surveys often employed diverse methods, reporting systems, and reference values.[42] A similar issue of incommensurability existed regarding food consumption data, which is also crucial for making the object of hidden hunger actionable. As pointed out in a WHO Bulletin: "data on global patterns of dietary habits, as well as differences by population characteristics are not well established."[43] Such discrepancies and lack of homogeneity in measures and methods was largely seen by IOs as an obstacle to validating knowledge about hidden hunger across jurisdictions.

In response to the perceived lack of uniformization, IOs undertook different activities to universalize standards on diets and food intake. In 1949, the FAO/WHO Expert Committee on Nutrition was established

[39] WHO and FAO, *International Conference on Nutrition: Final Report of the Conference*, (1992).
[40] Barona, *From Hunger to Malnutrition.*
[41] M. De Onis and M. Blössner, 'The World Health Organization global database on child growth and malnutrition: methodology and applications', *International Journal of Epidemiology*, 32/4 (2003), 518–26, 519.
[42] WHO, '*WHO Global Database on Child Growth and Malnutrition 2022*', (2022).
[43] S. Khatibzadeh, M. Saheb Kashaf, R. Micha, S. Fahimi, P. Shi, I. Elmadfa, S. Kalantarian, P. Wirojratana, M. Ezzati, J. Powles, and D. Mozaffarian, 'A global database of food and nutrient consumption', *Bulletin of the World Health Organization*, 94/12 (2016), 931–34.

to set references for nutritional politics and health standards.[44] Although the committee was set up to provide technical advice to FAO/WHO secretariat, it also played a key role in insulating these two UN agencies from the politics of their member countries. From the very beginning the Joint Expert Committee expressed its wish to introduce an international codex of analytical methods that would assist scientists to ensure the generation of "uniform and comparable" data regarding the vitamin content of foods and diets.[45] Nowadays, the overarching framework governing FAO/WHO stipulates that all experts chosen must demonstrate impartiality and objectivity in their assessment.[46] Furthermore, a core tenet guiding joint WHO/FAO expert committees on nutrition is the principle of "neutrality," with their guidance mandated to be grounded solely in scientific evidence.[47]

During the same period, the WHO launched efforts to assemble a Global Database on Child Growth and Malnutrition with the aim of collecting, standardizing, and sharing child anthropometric data (indicators typically pertain to individuals' height and weight). The FAO also launched its Global Database on Food Consumption to standardize the number and proportion of people in each country who consume "insufficient" dietary energy.[48] Although FAO had been publishing "World Food Surveys" and "Food Balance Sheets," there was a need to further "strengthen micronutrient surveillance capabilities and activities by devising indicators to monitor strategies for achieving national goals related to coverage, compliance and effectiveness in targeted populations."[49] Among the efforts to quantify food consumption and nutrient intake was UNICEF's Multiple Indicator Cluster Surveys (MICS), a set of surveys that provided "internationally comparable and statistical data" compiled in more than 200 indicators on children and women.[50] According to UNICEF, MICS has become

[44] Barona, *From Hunger to Malnutrition.*

[45] Barona, *From Hunger to Malnutrition.*

[46] FAO and WHO, *FAO/WHO Framework for the Provision of Scientific Advice on Food Safety and Nutrition*, (2007), 15.

[47] FAO, 'FAO global database on food consumption', (2022).

[48] FAO, 'FAO global database on food consumption'.

[49] WHO and FAO, *International Conference on Nutrition: Final Report of the Conference.*

[50] D. Rose, B. Luckett, and A. Mundorf, 'Diet Matters: Approaches and Indicators to Assess the Role of Agriculture in Nutrition', ICN2 Second International Conference in Nutrition, Rome PTM-ICN2, (FAO and WHO, 2013).

the "largest source of statistically sound and international comparable data on children and women worldwide."[51] By standardizing data collection, providing internationally comparable statistics, and strengthening surveillance capabilities to monitor strategies aimed at addressing malnutrition and dietary deficiencies globally, these initiatives were crucial in problematizing hidden hunger as something detached from specific social contexts.

Efforts to delineate hidden hunger as a matter of fact also involved the deployment of a wide array of technologies as well as the provision of training assistance, particularly in laboratory capacity to measure the recommended indicators.[52] In order to collect biochemical data on nutritional deficiencies, infrastructures such as laboratories that allow for the storage of specimens were essential. Similarly, the availability of instruments such as rapid test kits, used during face-to-face interviews in different household surveys, were key for "testing" the bioavailability and food composition.[53] Additionally, analyzing vitamins in bodily fluids was another assessment method, which employed a spectrum of physical, chemical, and biological testing techniques to evaluate foodstuffs and ascertain their physiological effects and nutritional value of foods as sources of vitamins for human consumption.[54]

A final aspect that contributed to consolidating hidden hunger as a matter of fact involved its redefinition as a measurable economic concern. The link between economic competitiveness and hidden hunger was operated through the publication of studies that highlighted the impacts of hidden hunger on cognitive functioning, work capacity, and productivity, largely echoing dominant assumptions about development at the time.[55] For micronutrient malnutrition to be quantified

[51] UNICEF, 'About MICS', (2022).

[52] D. J. Alnwick, 'Combating micronutrient deficiencies: problems and perspectives', *Proceedings of the Nutrition Society*, 57/1 (1998), 137–47.

[53] FAO, 'Dietary assessment: a resource guide to method selection and application in low resource settings', (2018).

[54] Barona, *From Hunger to Malnutrition*.

[55] S. Brooks, *Rice Biofortification: Lessons for Global Science and Development*, (Earthscan, 2010); R. Martorell, 'The nature of child malnutrition and its long-term implications', *Food and Nutrition Bulletin*, 20/3 (1999), 288–92; Z. A. Bhutta, R. A. Salam, and J. K. Das, 'Meeting the challenges of micronutrient malnutrition in the developing world', *British Medical Bulletin*, 106/1 (2013), 7–17; J. Bagriansky, N. Champa, K. Pak, S. Whitney, and

in economic terms, it needed to be turned into indicators that could be specified numerically. The most tangible exemplification of this "economized" definition of hidden hunger is known as the WHO disability-adjusted life year (DALY).[56] DALY is a time-based statistical measure that combines years of life lost due to premature mortality and years of life lost due to time lived in states of less than full health, or years of healthy life lost due to disability.[57] The study identified malnutrition as "the risk factor responsible for the greatest loss of DALYs."[58]

Through the use of datasets, surveys, and numerical tools, IOs problematized hidden hunger in scientized and economized terms, or as an indisputable "matter of fact," that could be known through objective and universally applicable markers that could travel beyond nation states. Backed by estimates of validity and reliability, hidden hunger appeared thus as an objective reality.[59]

Omissions and Erasures

Problematizing hidden hunger as an exogenous object to be measured and apprehended through quantification is far from being a neutral exercise. As any "universalizing" attempt, it comes with its own erasures. A statistician working for UNICEF highlighted the significant challenges associated with collecting data on hidden hunger, especially in countries located in Africa, Asia, and certain parts of Latin America.[60] Due to the lack of available national surveys in these regions, statisticians tasked with modeling the data make inferences about these regions based on data from neighboring countries where such information is accessible. This is necessary to generate "reliable global estimates" that transcend national borders, despite the fact that

A. Laillou, 'The economic consequences of malnutrition in Cambodia, more than 400 million US dollar lost annually', *Asia Pacific Journal of Clinical Nutrition*, 23/4 (2014), 524–31.

56 C. J. Murray and A. D. Lopez, 'Global mortality, disability, and the contribution of risk factors: Global Burden of Disease Study', *The Lancet*, 349/9063 (1997), 1436–42.

57 'Disability-adjusted life years (DALYs)', (2024).

58 Murray and Lopez, 'Global mortality, disability, and the contribution of risk factors', 1440.

59 Ilcan and Phillips, 'Making food count'.

60 Interview with UNICEF statistician, November 2021.

data from Global South regions is excluded. On some other occasions, the problem does not come from the lack of data but from what IO staff refer to as "bad quality data" that countries, mainly from the Global South, provide to the IOs' secretariats.[61] As the UNICEF statistician added, in such scenarios, this data cannot be included in the statistical models as it does not fit the criteria for quality.[62] This statement shows that the numbers and data aggregated, mainly from the Global North, thus become the authoritative account of "the food problem" and of what the Global South "lacks." A peasant from a grassroots organization in Mexico also pointed out:

> They [international organizations] tell us that they are going to solve the problem of food and that we no longer need to think about what we are going to eat. I think the opposite: We need to think about what we want to eat and how to defend ourselves from what they want to impose on us. And it seems to me that this perpetuates this vision, about some "incapable" countries in which we must intervene, in Latin America, in Africa, in Asia, because in their countries these problems are supposedly solved. But then I tell them: you also created the idea that *you* have to help us and that it is only you who can "help" us.[63]

Additionally, defining hidden hunger as a matter of fact always entails drawing a sharp boundary between those with the capacity to diagnose, evaluate, and solve deficiencies and those who are the target of interventions. This echoes what Grotluschen and Buddeberg call "southering" – which means defining Global South countries in terms of what they lack while exposing them to a pronounced deficit perspective.[64] Within the dominant approach to hidden hunger people credentialed as experts such as IO staff and statisticians – and not the women who are responsible for feeding families or those who suffer from hunger – are the ones who "know" the problem and hence can prescribe solutions for the malnourished.[65] This narrow conception also evades a social view of hunger and malnutrition that would

[61] Ibid. [62] Ibid.

[63] Interview with member of a grassroots organization, September 2021.

[64] A. Grotlüschen and K. Buddeberg, 'PIAAC and the South: is southering the new othering? Global expansion of dominant discourses on adult literacy', *European Journal for Research on the Education and Learning of Adults*, 11/2 (2020), 167–81.

[65] Kimura, *Hidden Hunger*.

include macroeconomic and political issues of poverty, inequality, and marginality. For decades, agroecology movements, peasants, and grassroots organizations have emphasized the connections between industrial food production methods and the increasing levels of hunger worldwide.[66] While some of the most prominent multilateral institutions at the global level recognize the importance of such perspectives, they have largely remained at the margins.[67]

Therefore, addressing hidden hunger through a scientific account of "missing" nutrients evades a social view.[68] Hidden hunger, understood a matter of fact, de-roots food not only from its cultural richness and its sensual and practical dimensions but also from the broader contexts in which it is produced.[69]

Acting upon Hidden Hunger: Political Palliatives?

Nowadays hunger (including hidden hunger) is treated as a scientific matter, mainly concerned with diet quality and objectively measurable nutrient/caloric intake, a paradigm that historians have also referred to as "nutritionism".[70] When hunger is predominantly addressed by focusing on the nutrient content of food, only certain "magic bullet" solutions become viable.[71] Although there is a widespread consensus that acknowledges that interventions focusing on "food systems" could be long-term solutions to hidden hunger, those seems to have received the least attention in the past decades.[72] The rationale behind these asymmetries often stems from an argument about knowledge,

[66] J. Clapp, *Food*, (John Wiley & Sons, 2020); N. McKeon, *Food Security Governance: Empowering Communities, Regulating Corporations*, (Routledge, 2014); S. Prato and N. Bullard, 'Re-embedding Nutrition in Society, Nature and Politics', *Development*, 57/2 (2014), 129–34.

[67] M. Fakhri, H. Elver, and O. De Schutter, 'The UN Food Systems Summit: how not to respond to the urgency of reform', Inter Press Service (2021).

[68] Kimura, *Hidden Hunger*.

[69] G. Scrinis, 'On the ideology of nutritionism', *Gastronomica*, 8/1 (2008), 39–48.

[70] Scrinis, 'On the ideology of nutritionism'.

[71] Ruxin, 'Hunger, Science, and Politics: FAO, WHO, and UNICEF nutrition policies 1945–1978'.

[72] J. L. Villar, *Tackling Hidden Hunger: Putting Diet Diversification at the Centre*, (Third World Network, 2015). A. Littoz-Monnet and J. Uribe, 'Methods regimes in global health governance: the politics of evidence-making in global health', *International Political Sociology*, 2/17 (2023), 1–22.

attributing the marginalization of socio-economic interventions to the purported "lack" of data or evidence.[73]

Currently, food fortification or vitamin supplementation are the most celebrated way of addressing hidden hunger, despite the fact that many other longer-term strategies are also available.[74] For example, the World Bank has, in many iterations, emphasized the potential of food fortification, stating that "no other technology offers as large an opportunity to improve lives at such low cost and in such a short time."[75] Other influential actors of the global food and nutrition community, such as the Consultative Group for Agricultural Research and its "Micronutrients Project," have echoed the sentiment that such interventions are efficient as they have the advantage of treating "the symptoms rather than the underlying causes of micronutrient deficiencies."[76] Biofortification as a solution to the problem of hidden hunger, therefore, allows the international community to address malnutrition without having to completely rethink the real roots causes of hunger.

Over the past decades, IOs have undertaken numerous projects based on fortifying food with isolated nutrients. Under the "Brighter Futures" initiative, a program funded by the Gates Foundation, UNICEF has conducted large-scale fortification projects in several countries.[77] Similarly, the WHO has also provided extensive guidance to countries on the use of micronutrient powders, which are single-dose packets containing multiple vitamins and minerals that can be sprinkled onto semi-solid food. Such powders have been promoted as a "proven" strategy to combat this form of undernutrition.[78]

[73] M. T. Ruel and H. Alderman, 'Nutrition-sensitive interventions and programmes: how can they help to accelerate progress in improving maternal and child nutrition?', *The Lancet*, 382/9891 (2013), 536–51.

[74] R. Horton, 'Maternal and child undernutrition: an urgent opportunity', *The Lancet*, 371/9608 (2008), 179; Kimura, *Hidden Hunger*.

[75] The World Bank, *Enriching Lives: Overcoming Vitamin and Mineral Malnutrition in Developing Countries*, (1994).

[76] R. D. Graham, R. M. Welch, and H. E. Bouis, 'Addressing micronutrient malnutrition through enhancing the nutritional quality of staple foods: principles, perspectives and knowledge gaps', *Advances in Agronomy*, 70 (2001), 77–142.

[77] UNICEF, *Brighter Futures: Protecting Early Brain Development through Salt Iodization*, (2018).

[78] WHO, *WHO Guideline: Use of Multiple Micronutrient Powders for Point-of-Use Fortification of Foods Consumed by Infants and Young Children Aged 6–23 Months and Children Aged 2–12 Years*, (2016).

Other organizations working in close partnerships with IOs have also been established to conduct large-scale fortification programs in several countries. One of such initiative is the Micronutrient Initiative (later renamed Nutrition International), which since its inception in the 1992 Montreal Hidden Hunger summit has emphasized the provision of market-based interventions through the delivery of isolated nutrients such as vitamins and minerals.[79] According to its website, the organization works to "deliver the greatest nutrition impact at the lowest cost."[80] In 2008, Nutrition International supported the WHO Department of Nutrition for Health and Development in enhancing its capacity to provide "evidence-based" nutrition interventions.[81] For that purpose, Nutrition International facilitated the meetings of the WHO's Nutrition Guidance Expert Advisory Group and its activities related to fortification.[82] Similarly, Nutrition International was part of the "core group" that significantly influenced the policy-making process that resulted in the publication of one of the most important WHO/FAO fortification guidelines.[83]

While some of these programs have been key to addressing hunger and malnutrition, scholars argue that "top-down nutrient-specific" interventions alone do not "solve" the problem of hidden hunger, as they claim.[84] Some researchers have found that food fortification programs often tend to overestimate the magnitude of the problem in Global South countries. When such programs are implemented by IOs on a large scale, they also tend to ignore the eco-social specificities of countries as well as the socio-economic determinants of hunger and malnutrition.[85] In Colombia, for example, micronutrient powder supplementation was not the most adequate way of tackling

[79] Nutrition International, *Nutrition International Strategy 2018–2024*, (2018).
[80] Nutrition International, 'We make a difference because nutrition is the difference', (2023).
[81] WHO, 'First meeting of the WHO nutrition guidance expert advisory group (NUGAG)', (2010).
[82] WHO, 'First meeting of the WHO nutrition guidance expert advisory group (NUGAG)'.
[83] M. Lawrence, *Food Fortification: The Evidence, Ethics, and Politics of Adding Nutrients to Food*, (Oxford University Press, 2013).
[84] Lawrence, *Food fortification*.
[85] R. Priya, A. Kotwal, and I. Qadeer, 'Toward an ecosocial epidemiological approach to goiter and other iodine deficiency disorders: a case study of India's technocratic program for universal iodization of salt', *International Journal of Health Services*, 39/2 (2009), 343–62.

hidden hunger.[86] Another challenge is that, because fortified foods are more costly, they may be beyond the reach of people who are at the greatest risk of deficiencies and, instead, tend to most benefit the people who need them least.[87]

Despite the acknowledgment in recent years that food fortification and supplementation fail to address the root causes of hunger, the international community continues to portray them as some of the only "evidence-based" solutions. This was the case during the 2021 United Nations Foods Systems Summit, where "scaling up" biofortified crops was heralded as a "game-changing solution." The summit emphasized that, in order to deploy large-scale fortification programs, "market forces will be harnessed and leveraged" to ensure the success of this "cost-effective" intervention mostly in Africa, Asia, and Latin America.

The tendency to understand nutrition as a medical problem mainly stemming from a lack of nutrients consumption has several implications. On the one hand, when food is mainly seen as a chemical compound, it can easily be treated as a commodity that is sold and consumed, a frame that has largely served the commercial interests of industries based in Global North countries, which market food as a commodity delivering health promises.[88] At the global level, the agro-industrial and pharmaceutical complex have indeed largely benefited from this narrow meaning attributed to hunger and have used nutritional "deficits" as a goldmine offering ample market opportunities.[89]

More generally, such a reductive problematization of hidden hunger, and food in general, puts increasing pressure on individuals to take charge of their health.[90] Several programs are now being conducted in countries like Kenya, Ethiopia, or Bangladesh to address hidden hunger and malnutrition in children through the selling of

[86] A. Andrew, O. Attanasio, E. Fitzsimons, and M. Rubio-Codina, 'Why is multiple micronutrient powder ineffective at reducing anaemia among 12–24 month olds in Colombia? Evidence from a randomised controlled trial', *SSM-population Health*, 2 (2016), 95–104.

[87] M. Nestle, *Food Politics*, (University of California Press, 2013), 201.

[88] D. Stuckler and M. Nestle, 'Big food, food systems, and global health', *PLoS Medicine*, 9/6 (2012), e1001242.

[89] Prato and Bullard, 'Re-embedding Nutrition in Society, Nature and Politics'.

[90] M. Durocher, 'Biomedicalized food culture: a critical analysis at the intersection of "healthy" food, bodies and health', *Critical Dietetics*, 5/1 (2020), 23–33.

"Sprinkles," a manufactured package of micronutrients delivered through markets.[91] When hunger is construed as an individual concern, with all attention directed towards the consumer phase of the issue, the responsibility for "solving" it falls upon individuals. Through the purchase of nutrient-enriched food, or vitamins, individuals are tasked with bearing the responsibility of addressing unprecedented levels of global hunger.

Conclusion

In this chapter, I explored the ways in which different UN agencies, the WHO, the FAO, and UNICEF have problematized hidden hunger as an indisputable "matter of fact." By assembling a significant body of biochemical knowledge about malnutrition these institutions gave the object an aura of naturalness and objectivity. On the one hand, through data aggregation, surveys, and technologies, hidden hunger was defined as a problem stemming from a "deficit" in nutrient consumption in Global South countries. On the other hand, hidden hunger was defined by UN agencies in a highly economized way, placing emphasis on its measurable impact on economic competitiveness and the productivity of nations.

However, akin to any universalizing endeavor, this way of approaching hunger was not only exclusionary but also restricted the spectrum of possible responses and policy options. The chapter elucidated how the dominant problematization of hidden hunger as a problem of missing nutrients has largely authorized and validated short-term political actions, such as food fortification and vitamin supplementation. These responses functioned more as political palliatives than as transformative solutions addressing the root causes of hunger such as inequality, trade regimes, lack of access, environmental degradation, and industrial agriculture.

This chapter has highlighted that the ways in which IOs know and address problems is therefore never functional. Producing knowledge about a given issue and stressing how to "best" approach it is always

[91] R. Holla and L. Menon, 'Philanthrocapitalism and corporate social responsibility: do they really empower civil society?', in P. Maiti (ed.), *Corporate Social Responsibility: Critiques, Policies and Strategies*, (Sharada Publishing House, 2010).

an exclusionary practice that prioritizes certain voices at the expense of others. This brings a subtle but profound change in the ways in which we think about IOs' daily work and their power to shape governance practices. As this chapter has emphasized, it is by studying knowledge-making processes behind global problems that one can better understand who has authority to govern and why, and how boundaries and hierarchies are established, maintained, and potentially transformed.

Structures, Spaces, and Jurisdictions

7 *The Puzzle of Freedom*
Structure and Agency in International Adjudication

TOMMASO SOAVE

Introduction

For decades, critical scholars have debated the contours of agency and structure – or 'freedom and constraint'[1] – in the legal activities of international organisations.[2] According to some, the inherent indeterminacy and open-endedness of legal processes enable – indeed require – institutional actors to exercise political discretion in (re)definition of norms without reifying 'the ideas and attitudes that make the established order seem natural [and] necessary'.[3] Others, by contrast, highlight the structural 'limits and pressures, tendencies and orientations'[4] that shape normative possibilities, 'promote the expression of certain types of interests', and 'suppress that of others'.[5] Arguably, these are

[1] D. Kennedy, 'Freedom and Constraint in Adjudication: A Critical Phenomenology' (1986) 36 *Journal of Legal Education* 518.

[2] As used throughout the chapter, the word 'legal' is to be understood broadly and not limited to the formal sources of international law. Indeed, much of the output of international institutions takes the form not of general and binding rules but of 'soft law' instruments (resolutions, guidelines, recommendations, etc.) and *ad hoc* decisions (judgments, arbitral awards, etc.). That output has 'legal' force insofar as it shapes the conduct and stabilises the behavioural expectations of international actors. For discussion of this deformalised notion of legality, see e.g. J. Brunnée and S. J. Toope, *Legitimacy and Legality in International Law: An Interactional Account* (Cambridge University Press, 2010); J. d'Aspremont, *Formalism and the Sources of International Law: A Theory of the Ascertainment of Legal Rules* (Oxford University Press, 2011), 38–82.

[3] R. M. Unger, *False Necessity: Anti-Necessitarian Social Theory in the Service of Radical Democracy* (2nd edn., Verso, 2004), xx. See also e.g. D. W. Kennedy, 'One, Two, Three, Many Legal Orders: Legal Pluralism and the Cosmopolitan Dream' (2007) 31 *New York University Review of Law and Social Change* 641.

[4] S. Marks, 'False Contingency' (2009) 62 *Current Legal Problems* 1, 10.

[5] B. de Sousa Santos, 'Law: A Map of Misreading. Towards a Postmodern Conception of Law' (1987) 14 *Journal of Law and Society* 279, 297. See also e.g. G. Teubner and A. Fischer-Lescano, 'Cannibalizing Epistemes:

two sides of the same coin, and an emphasis on either position reflects the sensibilities and preoccupations of the observer.

In this chapter, I apply the agency/structure dichotomy to a specific subset of organisations, namely international courts and tribunals. Unlike other entities, judicial bodies do not possess the power of legal initiative: they are not supposed to create law from scratch, but to interpret and apply pre-existing rules to solve concrete cases. However, much like other institutions, courts and tribunals develop recursive – and often 'unwritten'[6] – practices, postures, and modes of world sensemaking that shape the meaning and evolution of international norms, with systemic effects that extend well beyond the parties to individual cases.

Indeed, the rise in prominence of international adjudicative mechanisms, like the International Court of Justice (ICJ), the European Court of Human Rights (ECtHR), the dispute settlement system of the World Trade Organisation (WTO), and investor-state arbitration (ISDS), has been the object of intense scrutiny by international lawyers, political scientists, and sociologists alike. Countless studies have appeared that seek to identify patterns and strategies in the jurisprudence of the various tribunals and reconstruct the ever-elusive *intention du juge*.[7] While those studies helpfully shed light on the external forces affecting the decision horizon of international adjudicators, they also tend to overplay systemic constraints and institutional biases.

Against this backdrop, it bears asking: what guides international courts in reaching their decisions? What structural limitations do they encounter? And what agency and discretion do judicial actors enjoy in the process? My main argument is that the legal production of the international judiciary reflects *the internal socio-professional dynamics of the community of professionals that run the machinery in its routine operations*. The ways those professionals interact, cooperate, and clash on a daily basis have a crucial impact on judicial outcomes – more

Will Modern Law Protect Traditional Cultural Expressions?', in C. Graber and M. Burri-Nenova (eds.), *Intellectual Property and Traditional Cultural Expressions in a Digital Environment* (Edward Elgar, 2008) 17, 20.

6 M. McDougal, H. Lasswell, and M. Reisman, 'The World Constitutive Process of Authoritative Decision' (1967) 19 *Journal of Legal Education* 253, 260.

7 See E. Jouannet, 'La Motivation ou le Mystère de la Boîte Noire', in H. Ruiz Fabri and J.-M. Sorel (eds.), *La Motivation des Décisions des Juridictions Internationales* (Pedone, 2008) 251, 271.

so than the substantive norms that courts are called upon to interpret and apply; and more so than the external political pressures to which they are subject. To illustrate this point, I unravel some of the everyday practices that occur inside international judicial institutions. My analysis reveals that those practices are at once *structured* – i.e. subject to social constraints and pressures – and *contingent* – i.e. open to change, contestation, and restructuring.

My argument proceeds as follows. In the section 'Determinism, Determinism Everywhere', I problematise the notion of institutional bias that has been expounded by several authors, and call for an anti-formalist and anti-determinist account of international judicial processes. In the section 'Sources of Constraint', I discuss the ways in which the inner circle of adjudication experts delimits and constrains the decision horizon of international courts. In the section 'Spaces of Freedom', I identify some residual spaces of freedom and discretion in the construction of international judicial 'truths'.

Determinism, Determinism Everywhere

In 1989, Martti Koskenniemi shook our disciplinary conscience by revealing the indeterminacy of the international legal argument. Because the body of international law doctrines can accommodate contrary outcomes and courses of action, expert argument enables 'the taking of any conceivable position in regard to a dispute',[8] thereby delegating the solution to 'an ultimately arbitrary choice'.[9] Some twenty years later, the same author offered a strikingly different account: 'in practice nothing is ever that random. Competent lawyers know that the world of legal practice is quite predictable.'[10]

This is intriguing. What has transpired in the meantime that has shifted the focus from indeterminacy to predictability? For Koskenniemi, the game-changer is 'the emergence and operation of *structural bias*'; more precisely, 'the creation of special regimes of knowledge and expertise' like human rights law, environmental law,

[8] M. Koskenniemi, *From Apology to Utopia: The Structure of International Legal Argument – Reissue with New Epilogue* (Cambridge University Press, 2005), 565.

[9] Ibid., 67.

[10] M. Koskenniemi, 'The Politics of International Law: 20 Years Later' (2009) 20 *European Journal of International Law* 7, 9.

trade law, investment law, and security law.[11] The consolidation of 'institutional projects [that] cater for special audiences with special interests and special ethos' has made it possible to predetermine the outcomes produced in the international world.[12]

This change of view neatly captures the existing narratives of international adjudication. Thanks to years of critical inquiry, we now know that international courts are more than 'apersonal'[13] bodies ascertaining the preordained meaning of rules and mechanistically applying it to facts.[14] We no longer expect the judicial interpreter to proceed in a scientific fashion, plodding through Articles 31 and 32 of the Vienna Convention on the Law of Treaties (VCLT), to 'deduce the meaning exactly of what has been consented to' and reach neutral and unassailable conclusions.[15] Our contemporary imagination is finally emancipated from the deterministic shackles of traditional legal formalism.

Yet, the notion of institutional bias, in its various permutations, still holds sway. To its proponents, judicial outcomes are determined by the sectoral mandate of each court, the backgrounds and entrenched ideologies of its adjudicators, and their quest for legitimacy in the eyes of political constituencies.[16] These 'external constraints'[17] reinforce

[11] Ibid., 9 (original emphasis). [12] Ibid., 9.

[13] G. Messenger, 'The Practice of Litigation at the ICJ: The Role of Counsel in the Development of International Law', in M. Hirsch and A. Lang (eds.), *Research Handbook on the Sociology of International Law* (Edward Elgar, 2018) 208, 210.

[14] J. Klabbers, 'Virtuous Interpretation', in M. Fitzmaurice, O. Elias, and P. Merkouris (eds.), *Treaty Interpretation and the Vienna Convention on the Law of Treaties: 30 Years On* (Martinus Nijhoff, 2010) 17, 23. See also I. Johnstone, *The Power of Deliberation: International Law, Politics and Organizations* (Oxford University Press, 2011), 35; I. Venzke, 'The Role of International Courts as Interpreters and Developers of the Law: Working Out the Jurisgenerative Practice of Interpretation' (2011) 34 *Loyola of Los Angeles International and Comparative Law Review* 99, 99–100.

[15] A. Orakhelashvili, *The Interpretation of Acts and Rules in Public International Law* (Oxford University Press, 2008), 286.

[16] See e.g. J. L. Gibson and G. A. Caldeira, 'The Legitimacy of Transnational Legal Institutions: Compliance, Support, and the European Court of Justice' (1995) 39 *American Journal of Political Science* 459; K. J. Alter, L. R. Helfer, and M. R. Madsen, 'How Context Shapes the Authority of International Courts' (2016) 79 *Law and Contemporary Problems* 1; N. Grossman et al., 'Legitimacy and International Courts: A Framework', in N. Grossman et al., *The Legitimacy of International Courts* (Cambridge University Press, 2018), 1.

[17] S. Dothan, *Reputation and Judicial Tactics: A Theory of National and International Courts* (Cambridge University Press, 2015), 87.

'institutionally ingrained problem definitions and strategies for solution',[18] thus framing the categories and vocabularies through which legal issues are addressed. Institutional bias is often depicted as irresistible. A human rights court will be 'programmed'[19] to prioritise fundamental freedoms over state interests; a WTO panel will invariably privilege trade liberalisation over, say, environmental protection; an international criminal tribunal will always be inclined to pierce through sovereign immunity and combat the culture of impunity; and so on.

Taken to an extreme, institutional bias is as deterministic as traditional formalism. Both tend to explain the decisions of international judges by reference to some *other* reality, invisible to their eyes, that guides their every action. For traditionalists, that reality is the law itself: a concrete entity with its own inherent logic and rationality, somehow independent of the human agents who routinely create, interpret, apply, resist, and are bound by it.[20] For institutional bias theorists, it is the context of 'deeper, impersonal forces' that exert their pressure and inexorably nudge courts in a set direction.[21] In either case, the *people* actually involved in the process possess little agency, squeezed as they are between the Scylla of legal determinacy and the Charybdis of ideological partiality.

This sombre picture leaves many questions unanswered. How, for one, do 'particular normative biases and preferences come to be embedded within an international regime at a particular point in its historical trajectory'?[22] And how, for another, can individuals exercise responsible freedom in the definition and evolution of judicial outcomes? In the pages that follow, I seek to provide tentative answers to these questions and offer an anti-formalist *yet* anti-determinist account of international adjudication.

[18] Teubner and Fischer-Lescano, 'Cannibalizing Epistemes', 20.

[19] *Fragmentation of International Law: Difficulties Arising from the Diversification and Expansion of International Law*, Report of the Study Group of the International Law Commission, A/CN.4/L.682 (13 April 2006), para. 488.

[20] For a critique of this view, see e.g. P. Schlag, *The Enchantment of Reason* (Duke University Press, 1998), 100–104.

[21] D. W. Kennedy, 'Challenging Expert Rule: The Politics of Global Governance' (2005) 27 *Sidney Law Review* 1, 4.

[22] A. Lang, 'Legal Regimes and Professional Knowledges: The Internal Politics of Regime Definition', in M. A. Young (ed.), *Regime Interaction in International Law: Facing Fragmentation* (Cambridge University Press, 2012) 113.

To do so, I deconstruct the notion of international courts as cohesive and monolithic entities and shed light on their micro-level practices. Seen from this angle, the ethos and the preoccupations of each court are not carved in stone, but are shaped by the evolving socio-professional dynamics of the club of legal experts that contribute to its routine functioning. This club, which I call the *international judicial community*,[23] comprises all the professionals that gravitate in the immediate proximity of a given judicial institution. International judges are just the tip of the iceberg. Other less visible players include the professional litigators (state agents, government lawyers, private counsel, NGOs, etc.) representing the parties in court; the legal bureaucracies (registries, secretariats, clerks, etc.) assisting the bench with the preparation, deliberation, and drafting of judgments; the specialised scholars developing the unified grammar and conceptual categories of each judicial field; and the like.

The relationships, interactions, and worldviews of the international judicial community are *both* constrained by existing social arrangements *and* open to renegotiation, contingency, and agency. As such, they are both the vehicle of reproduction of legal outcomes and the source from which legal changes originate. On the one hand, intersubjective socialisation and patterned repetition allow for shared assumptions and expectations to crystallise, thus ensuring predictability in adjudication. On the other hand, the endless struggles among community members, which in turn reflect their power relations and relative capital, enable the contestation of pre-established patterns, the opening of paths to resistance, and the creation of avenues for the gradual evolution of legal systems.

To fully understand these dynamics, we must stop treating international courts as 'reified collectives forming separate and self-standing units of analysis'.[24] Instead, we must open the 'black box' of judicial institutions[25] and engage in a micro-analysis of their inner workings.

[23] See T. Soave, *The Everyday Makers of International Law: From Great Halls to Back Rooms* (Cambridge University Press, 2022).

[24] A. Vauchez, 'Communities of International Litigators', in C. P. R. Romano, K. J. Alter, and Y. Shany (eds.), *The Oxford Handbook of International Adjudication* (Oxford University Press, 2014) 655, 655–656.

[25] J. L. Dunoff and M. A. Pollack, 'International Judicial Practices: Opening the Black Box of International Courts' (2018) 40 *Michigan Journal of International Law* 47.

This can be done through a variety of methods, including field sociology, practice theory, and ethnographic participant-observation. In the next sections, I sketch a tentative framework for this analysis and link it to the overarching theme of structure vs. agency. I begin by identifying the socio-professional sources of constraint in the production of judicial outcomes, after which I turn to the interstitial spaces of freedom where judicial actors can steer the course of proceedings in new and unexpected directions.

Sources of Constraint

If, as Koskenniemi posits, international norms are inherently indeterminate, then what limits the discretion of international courts in the definition of legal outcomes? Can adjudicators really take any conceivable position regarding a dispute? Of course not. The scope of what is 'legitimately assertable' in judicial discourse is subject to powerful constraints, stemming from the collective expectations and dispositions of the international judicial community.[26]

The community plays this constraining role in an active and a passive way. Throughout the adjudicative process, it pushes and forces adjudicators by expressing views as to how certain issues should be addressed, how certain legal terms should be read, and what bodies of rules should be considered to solve the case at hand. Once the judgment is rendered, it carefully tests its analytical rigour, ascribes (in)competence based on background knowledge, and acts as the ultimate arbiter of professional recognition. In short, the community constitutes the immediate audience of international courts. Adjudicators are keenly aware of these internal pressures, and their decisions often 'speak' more directly to the legal professionals gravitating around them than to broader political constituencies.[27]

The dispositions of the international judicial community are often un-reflexive, deeply entrenched, and stubbornly resistant to change, and hence the impression that institutional bias is inescapable. Yet, as I will argue in the section 'Spaces of Freedom', the socially constructed

[26] S. Kripke, *Wittgenstein on Rules and Private Language* (Blackwell, 1982), 78.

[27] See T. Soave, 'Who Controls WTO Dispute Settlement? Socio-professional Practices and the Crisis of the Appellate Body' (2020) 29 *Italian Yearbook of International Law* 13, 18–19.

nature of that bias means that it can be contested and overcome under certain conditions. For now, let me discuss how the community secures and maintains its grip on the routine activities of international courts and fosters the crystallisation of their ingrained preferences. In a nutshell, the pathways of control relate to: (a) the institutional design of each court; (b) the social structures governing the relationships among community experts; and (c) the patterned practices and competent performances that those experts carry out on a routine basis.

Institutional Design

To begin with, the community plays a pervasive, if often unacknowledged, role in shaping the institutional architecture of judicial mechanisms, with obvious repercussions on the manner in which cases are prepared, filed, pleaded, and deliberated. Courts endowed with compulsory jurisdiction, like the ECtHR or WTO panels, may interpret and discharge their mandate differently from those that require the consent of the responding party, such as the ICJ.[28] Likewise, the relevant rules of procedure, the applicable standard of review, the remedies available, and the delimitation of the body of rules falling within a court's purview bear on the conduct of proceedings. Less noticeably, but equally importantly, the internal organisation of a court's bureaucracy informs the interplay and the division of labour between adjudicators and their legal advisors, giving rise to a variety of power dynamics.[29]

Traditional functionalist narratives tend to treat these design features as an external given, dictated by the preferences of constituent states and immutable in time. After all, it is government delegates who, through protracted negotiations, define the core structure and characteristics of each court, debate its competence and powers, and eventually ratify its constituent treaty. Later, they periodically negotiate the

[28] See e.g. L. Gross, 'Compulsory Jurisdiction under the Optional Clause: History and Practice', in L. F. Damrosch (ed.), *The International Court of Justice at a Crossroads* (Transnational, 1987) 19.

[29] See e.g. D. Caron, 'Towards a Political Theory of International Courts and Tribunals' (2007) 24 *Berkeley Journal of International Law* 401; T. Soave, 'The Politics of Invisibility: Why Are International Judicial Bureaucrats Obscured from View?', in F. Baetens (ed.), *Legitimacy of Unseen Actors in International Adjudication* (Cambridge University Press, 2019) 323.

appointment of judges and, if needed, set the agenda for institutional reform. These forms of engagement ensure the continued goodwill of political stakeholders towards international courts[30] and make them the ultimate arbiters of the system's legitimacy.[31]

However, these narratives obscure the crucial contribution of professional litigators to the establishment and reform of international courts. Those litigators are not mere 'operators' of judicial systems, but rather 'entrepreneurs' who co-decide the shape those systems should take in the first place.[32] If many states have embraced international adjudication as a mode of governance, it is partly because of their exposure to a transnational network of experts, who forged alliances with government departments, academic circles, and civil society organisations to promote their views and foster their agendas.[33] Lawyers 'created' their clients as much as clients 'created' their lawyers.[34]

Take ISDS, for instance. There, in the 1980s and 1990s, a handful of pioneering practitioners developed the very legal doctrines that would later be used to consolidate the system and turn it into a core component of international economic law.[35] Or think of international criminal justice, where NGOs and advocacy groups played a key role in the negotiation of the Rome Statute.[36] More recent

[30] See e.g., A.-M. Slaughter and L. R. Helfer, 'Why States Create International Tribunals: A Response to Professors Posner and Yoo' (2005) 93 *California Law Review* 899, 946–949.

[31] See T. Soave, 'WTO Dispute Settlement', 16–17.

[32] Y. Dezalay and M. R. Madsen, 'The Force of Law and Lawyers: Pierre Bourdieu and the Reflexive Sociology of Law' (2012) 8 *Annual Review of Law and Social Science* 433, 444.

[33] See notably Y. Dezalay and B.G Garth, *Dealing in Virtue: International Commercial Arbitration and the Construction of a Transnational Legal Order* (University of Chicago Press, 1996).

[34] M. Shapiro, 'Judicialization of Politics in the United States' (1994) 15 *International Political Science Review* 101, 109. See also Vauchez, 'International Litigators', 657.

[35] A good case in point is Jan Paulsson's elaboration of the doctrine of 'arbitration without privity'. J. Paulsson, 'Arbitration without Privity' (1995) 10 *ICSID Review – Foreign Investment Law Journal* 232. For discussion, see e.g. S. Schill, 'W(h)ither Fragmentation? On the Literature and Sociology of International Investment Law' (2011) 22 *European Journal of International Law* 875, 876.

[36] See e.g. Z. Pearson, 'Non-governmental Organisations and the International Criminal Court: Changing Landscapes of International Law' (2006) 39 *Cornell International Law Journal* 243.

history is equally rich in examples. The Multi-Party Interim Appeal Arbitration Arrangement, adopted by several WTO members to compensate for the demise of the Appellate Body, was politically promoted by the EU delegation, but technically developed by a trade law firm based in Geneva.[37] Similarly, the ongoing UNCITRAL talks on ISDS reform see the participation of some élite arbitration practitioners and scholars, who infiltrated state delegations and secured a seat at the negotiating table.[38]

As these examples show, the international judicial community has constrained the institutional design of international courts since their very inception, thus leaving its initial imprint on the kind of judicial discourse those courts will later develop.

Social Closure

Past the moment of genesis, the community's control of judicial processes gets even tighter by virtue of its social closure. Community members form a close-knit network of habitués who walk the corridors of courts regularly, maintain first-name personal contacts, and cultivate friendly professional relationships.[39] Ostensibly, they occupy distinct and well-defined positions. However, the boundaries are blurrier than they first appear. Throughout their careers, legal professionals swap roles frequently, sometimes donning multiple hats at once. Prominent professors may take a break from their faculty chairs to serve on an international court;[40] arbitrators in an ISDS case may appear as counsel in another; registry or secretariat lawyers may later be recruited

37 See Soave, 'WTO Dispute Settlement', 30.

38 See Soave, *Everyday Makers*, chapter 2.

39 See J. H. H. Weiler, 'The Rule of Lawyers and the Ethos of Diplomats: Reflections on the Internal and External Legitimacy of WTO Dispute Settlement' (2001) 35 *Journal of World Trade* 191, 195; K. Hopewell, 'Multilateral Trade Governance as Social Field: Global Civil Society and the WTO', (2015) 22 *Review of International Political Economy* 1128, 1142–1143.

40 Some 40 per cent of the judges sitting on permanent international courts 'have significant academic credentials' (D. Terris, C. P. R. Romano, and L. Swigart, *The International Judge: An Introduction to the Men and Women Who Decide the World's Cases* (Oxford University Press, 2007), 20) and about one third of investment arbitrators are former or current scholars (J. A. Fontoura Costa, 'Comparing WTO Panelists and ICSID Arbitrators: The Creation of International Legal Fields', (2011) 1 *Oñati Socio-Legal Series* 1, 17).

by government departments or private law firms;[41] and so forth. All combinations are possible.[42] These revolving doors among the bench, the bureaucracy, the bar, and the academe help strengthen existing bonds and forge new ties.

The closure of the network consolidates trust among its participants and perpetuates its insulation from external interference.[43] Court proceedings gradually come to be characterised by an increasing sense of 'clubbiness' and familiarity. The same handful of counsel appear at most hearings alongside their clients. Their intimate knowledge of the intricacies of international adjudication grants them a competitive edge over new entrants in the litigation market. Meanwhile, registry and secretariat bureaucrats incessantly work behind the scenes to streamline adjudicative practices, ensure consistency in jurisprudence, and serve as the institutional memory of the court. Finally, scholarly production in the field is densely populated by authors who have direct or indirect stakes in the system.[44] Being an 'insider' in the game means being familiar with its rules, adopting strategies that resonate with other players, and ultimately shaping judicial outcomes to an extent that is usually precluded to 'outsiders'.

At the same time, social closure reinforces the epistemic bias of community participants,[45] each of whom becomes 'a fully instrumentalised cog in the respective machine'.[46] Over time, the circle of professionals orbiting around each court develops a set of assumptions as to which legal sources, categories, and modes of reasoning are 'in line with [its] philosophy' and which others should be 'kept largely at bay'.[47]

[41] For instance, it is customary for firms specialising in international trade to hire former WTO secretariat officials, panellists, and even, on occasion, Appellate Body members. See Soave, 'WTO Dispute Settlement', 24.

[42] See J. d'Aspremont et al., 'Introduction', in J. d'Aspremont et al. (eds.), *International Law as a Profession* (Cambridge University Press, 2017) 1, 8; Vauchez, 'International Litigators', 661.

[43] See R. S. Burt, *Brokerage and Closure: An Introduction to Social Capital* (Oxford University Press, 2005), 93–97.

[44] See e.g. S. Schill, 'W(h)ither Fragmentation', 894; H. Schepel and R. Wesseling, 'The Legal Community: Judges, Lawyers, Officials and Clerks in the Writing of Europe' (1997) 3 *European Law Journal* 165, 171.

[45] Burt, *Brokerage and Closure*, 168.

[46] M. Koskenniemi, 'The Fate of Public International Law: Between Technique and Politics' (2007) 70 *Modern Law Review* 1, 26.

[47] M. Waibel, 'Interpretive Communities in International Law', in A. Bianchi, D. Peat, and M. Windsor (eds.), *Interpretation in International Law* (Oxford University Press, 2015) 147, 163.

This, as Koskenniemi had foreseen, results in a turf war among different sub-fields of expertise, such as trade, human rights, investment, or environmental law, each striving to preserve its internal rationality from 'disturbing outside perspectives'.[48] Any attempt to export expertise, practices, and worldviews from one sub-field to another is considered a trespass that might shake the 'context-preserving routine'.[49]

Competent Practices

Besides structuring community relationships, this degree of social cohesiveness gives rise to the most powerful source of constraint in judicial activity: recursive practices. Emmanuel Adler and Vincent Pouliot have famously defined 'practices' as 'competent performances'.[50] More precisely, practices 'are socially meaningful patterns of action which, in being performed more or less competently, simultaneously embody, act out, and possibly reify background knowledge and discourse in and on the material world'.[51] This definition captures the characteristics of the myriad activities the community carries out on an everyday basis, and which have a pervasive impact on the outcomes of disputes.

First, practices are 'patterned', meaning that they exhibit 'certain regularities over time and space' and 'reproduce similar behaviors with regular meanings'.[52] Although every dispute is unique in content, the internal steps that mark its unfolding are standardised. Every case begins with the parties' submission of written memorials, often followed by rejoinders and counter-rejoinders. These filings are then processed by the court bureaucrats who circulate internal memoranda to summarise their analyses and help the adjudicators prepare for the next steps. After the written phase, most courts hold hearings. After that, the adjudicators convene for deliberations and cast their decisions on the issues at stake. Based on the adjudicators' instructions, the final judgment is drafted, reviewed, approved, and circulated. Recursiveness extends to the actors involved in the process who, as

48 I. Venzke, *How Interpretation Makes International Law: On Semantic Change and Normative Twists* (Oxford University Press, 2012), 157.
49 Unger, *False Necessity*, 32.
50 E. Adler and V. Pouliot, 'International Practices', (2011) 3 *International Theory* 1, 4.
51 Ibid. 52 Ibid., 6.

discussed, tend to know each other well, communicate regularly, and entertain long-term professional relationships. Hence, judicial practices occur within a 'highly organised context'.[53]

Second, practices can be performed more or less 'competently' depending on the shared 'background knowledge' of the actors carrying them out.[54] This means that the hallmarks of (in)competence in judicial processes are socially attributed by the community based on collectively held standards. Through education, training, and work experience, community members are initiated to the way things are done[55] – the doctrines, argumentative techniques, ethos, aesthetics, and mythologies of their peers and superiors[56] – and reproduce them through communication and transmission of knowledge. These channels of socialisation contribute to perpetuation of the structures that 'condense and are confirmed as a result of the system's own operations.[57] At the same time, being socialised in the game *enables* each player to make arguments and take positions that will be accepted as 'true' or 'valid' by other players.[58]

Background knowledge informs every aspect of the judicial process, including – and perhaps especially – the interpretation of norms. The consensus of the community determines, at any given moment, whether the reading of a given norm is (un)acceptable, whether an interpretive posture is (un)viable, whether a legal argument is (un) persuasive, and ultimately whether a judicial decision is (in)correct.[59] An interpretation that meets them will be recognised as legitimate and

[53] Dunoff and Pollack, 'International Judicial Practices', 62.

[54] Adler and Pouliot, 'International Practices', 6–7 (emphasis omitted).

[55] J. Gross Stein, 'Background Knowledge in the Foreground: Conversations about Competent Practice in "Sacred Space"', in E. Adler and V. Pouliot (eds.), *International Practices* (Cambridge University Press, 2011) 87, 89.

[56] See e.g. D. W. Kennedy 'The Disciplines of International Law and Policy' (1999) 12 *Leiden Journal of International Law* 9; P. Schlag, 'The Aesthetics of American Law' (2002) 115 *Harvard Law Review* 1047.

[57] N. Luhmann, 'Operational Closure and Structural Coupling: The Differentiation of the Legal System' (1992) 13 *Cardozo Law Review* 1419, 1424.

[58] See e.g. S. B. Ortner, *Anthropology and Social Theory: Culture, Power and the Acting Subject* (Duke University Press, 2006), 3; Dunoff and Pollack, 'International Judicial Practices', 54.

[59] See e.g. A. Bianchi, 'Textual Interpretation and (International) Law Reading: The Myth of (In)Determinacy and the Genealogy of Meaning', in P. Bekker, R. Dolzer, and M. Waibel (eds.), *Making Transnational Law Work in the Global Economy: Essays in Honour of Detlev Vagts* (Cambridge University Press, 2010) 34, 39–40.

authoritative, and might be tolerated even if it slightly departs from established canon. Conversely, an interpretation that radically breaks from accepted standards is likely to fail to 'find acceptance' by the community[60] and be dismissed as anomalous or aberrant.

This, no more and no less, is what we mean by *precedent* in international law – a system without formal *stare decisis*. The authority of an interpretation stems solely from its consistent use. Judicial decisions have no other force than their patterned reproduction. Yet, no serious practitioner would dare to ignore those decisions altogether: the community backs their fragile existence and consolidates them into *jurisprudence*.

Spaces of Freedom

As argued in the previous section, the international judicial community constrains the discretion of courts in many ways, including by participating in their institutional design, perpetuating their operational closure, and developing patterned practices and shared standards of legal argument. Yet, these constraints do not make judicial outcomes automatic or entirely predictable. After all, stability is only 'an illusion created by the recursive nature of practice', whereas change 'is the ordinary condition of social life'.[61] Indeed, amid the tight socio-professional structures of the community, there remain interstitial spaces for agency, responsibility, and freedom. It is there that new paradigms emerge – and legal evolution becomes possible.

In this section, I provide an initial mapping of these spaces of freedom and suggest ways to preserve them from the deterministic tendencies of the international judicial system. In particular, I focus on the possibilities offered by: (a) the creative interpretation of norms; (b) the competition among members of the international judicial community; and (c) the many contingent and accidental occurrences that punctuate proceedings. The term 'freedom', of course, should be handled with care: international adjudication being a collective endeavour, no single individual is, alone, in full control of the process. If any freedom is possible, it can only emerge from the interactions of multiple actors over time.

60 Venzke, *Interpretation*, 5.
61 Adler and Pouliot, 'International Practices', 18.

Creative Interpretation

First, the indeterminacy of international norms enables judicial actors to promote and defend interpretations of those norms that resonate with their ethical commitments or policy preferences. Faced with competing and equally viable rationalisations of legal constructs, courts must take sides. No pseudo-scientific exercise, no rigorous application of the VCLT rules of interpretation can relieve them from the inevitable duty of making choices. Hesitation, rather than certainty, is the essence of adjudication.[62] Why else would we speak of judicial *decisions*?

The moment of doubt is gleefully celebrated by the defenders of 'false necessity' as a tenet of moral psychology. David Kennedy, for instance, describes the exposure to the irreducible pluralism of possible solutions as a moment of supreme 'professional freedom', where we are 'open to persuasion', and we 'have lost control', precisely 'because *we do not know* what the law determines'.[63] Doubt provides us with an opportunity to unlearn our 'methodological predilections', transcend the 'widely shared commitments' of our profession, and bravely leap forward into the unknown.[64] Similarly, Duncan Kennedy imagines a left-leaning judge wishing to express their '"political" objection' and promote their vision of justice against a line of adverse precedent.[65]

To engage in judicial creativity is akin to Lévi-Strauss' *bricolage*. Unlike the 'engineer', who first comes up with an overarching plan and then selects the tools required to carry it through, the '*bricoleur*' is ready to use 'whatever is at hand' to get the job done.[66] A certain precedent bothers you – then paraphrase and dilute it. You struggle with the legal status of a rule – then simply 'take note' of that rule and move on. The parties' logical constructs give you a headache – no problem, just shift the emphasis from abstract reasoning to the factual context. Rigid textualism, open-ended reasoning, reliance on general principles, matter-of-factual analysis – anything goes, provided it sustains the flow of your narrative.

[62] See B. Latour, *The Making of Law: An Ethnography of the Conseil d'État* (Polity Press, 2010), 91.

[63] Kennedy, 'Many Legal Orders', 644 (original emphasis).

[64] Ibid., 645.

[65] Kennedy, 'Freedom and Constraint', 519–520.

[66] C. Lévi-Strauss, *The Savage Mind* (Weidenfeld and Nicolson, 1966), 16–17.

The problem with imbuing the law with your commitments is that, first, you need to know *what* your commitments are – at least in relation to the specifics of the case at hand. Duncan Kennedy's idealised judge is conveniently equipped with a coherent set of beliefs that guide their strategy and positioning throughout the case.[67] Whether *real-world* judicial professionals share such a deep understanding of means, ends, and consequences is open to debate. Focused as it is on technical mastery, international legal practice leaves relatively little time to consider the 'vivid odds and ends'[68] of distributive trade-offs. The 'ideals' moving the community can be as vague as the protection of human rights, generic support for economic development, or a 'broad renunciation of power politics, militarism, and the aspiration to empire'.[69] Not exactly the ideal ground for principled decision-making.

Despite these limitations, self-reflexivity and overt policy reasoning can play an important role here. Instead of dissimulating their choices behind the veneer of legal objectivity and technical jargon,[70] judicial actors should openly disclose the discretional and value-laden nature of their conclusions. This would enable the audience to grasp the real *intention du juge* and contest it in legal and political terms in subsequent cases.

Socio-professional Struggle

But freedom is not only a matter of individual agency. The very social structure of the international judicial community presents 'clusters and holes'[71] that open up avenues for dissent and renegotiation. In fact, despite its social cohesiveness, the community is neither homogenous nor internally peaceful. Instead, borrowing from Pierre Bourdieu, it is

67 That judge has – no less! – a 'general preference for transforming the current modes of American economic life in a direction of greater worker self-activity, worker control and management of enterprise, in a decentralized setting that blurs between "owner" and "worker", and "public" and "private" enterprise'. Kennedy 'Freedom and Constraint', 520.

68 T. Eagleton, *The English Novel* (Blackwell, 2005), 311.

69 Kennedy, 'Many Legal Orders', 645.

70 For an indictment of this tendency, see e.g. G. Shaffer and D. Pabian, 'Case Note: *European Communities – Measures Prohibiting the Importation and Marketing of Seal Products*, WT/DS400/AB/R, WT/DS401/AB/R' (2015) 109 *American Journal of International Law* 154.

71 Burt, *Brokerage and Closure*, 222.

'the site of a competition for monopoly of the right to determine the law', within which 'there occurs a confrontation among actors possessing a technical competence which is inevitably social' and which 'consists essentially in the socially recognised capacity to interpret a corpus of texts'.[72]

Disagreement and conflict pervade every corner of international courts from hearing rooms to backroom corridors. Case after case, community members strive against one another to assert their authority and impose their visions of the law as dominant – agents and counsel through their submissions, court bureaucrats through their memoranda, scholars through their articles, and adjudicators through their decisions.

Every step of the process sees the deployment of schemes, postures, and strategies that, depending on the circumstances, may be 'risky or cautious, subversive or conservative'.[73] Incumbents have a natural tendency to perpetuate their dominance. Challengers must come up with other plans, ranging from opportunistic deference to overt defiance, to get the upper hand. At every turn, old alliances break down and new ones emerge, in a continuous process of assertion, contestation, and restructuring.

It follows that the boundaries, priorities, and preoccupations of the community are 'never inherently fixed or stable', but are 'constantly being renegotiated' among its members.[74] The expert vocabularies in use in international courts are 'sites of controversy and compromise where prevailing "mainstreams" constantly clash against minority challengers'.[75] Each agent modifies the form taken by arguments and the salience of texts, and traces 'a set of divergent paths, mobilising clans who confront each other with facts, precedents, understandings, opportunities or public morality, all of which are used to stoke the fire of the debate'.[76]

Over time, these tensions open the door to new legal approaches, new interpretive postures, new ways of doing things. Innovations are

[72] P. Bourdieu, 'The Force of Law: Toward a Sociology of the Juridical Field' (1987) 38 *Hastings Law Journal* 805, 817 (emphasis omitted).

[73] P. Bourdieu and L. Vacquant, *An Invitation to Reflexive Sociology* (University of Chicago Press, 1992), 98.

[74] Adler and Pouliot, 'International Practices', 18.

[75] Koskenniemi, *From Apology to Utopia*, 12.

[76] Latour, *Making of Law*, 192.

seldom presented as radical, lest they be dismissed out of hand. They will usually creep in through the backdoor – discussed as a side point during a meeting, inserted in the paragraph of a party submission, etc. The most successful then slowly grow in the system – first as obscure footnotes buried in a judgment, then as *obiter dicta* in the main text, and finally as the new standard against which the community measures the persuasiveness of legal reasoning.

Ultimately, change occurs when the dominant assumptions embedded in a judicial regime are successfully challenged and replaced by new assumptions, as a result of the piecemeal evolution of the power relationships among competing actors. Whenever this happens, 'it is never because pure law has triumphed, but because of the internal properties of these relations of force or these conflicts between heterogeneous multiplicities'.[77]

Contingency

Finally, one should not underestimate the role that contingency and accident play in the unfolding of proceedings. While formalist accounts typically depict the judicial process as an orderly endeavour guided by an overarching rationality, things are often much, much messier. The construction of judicial 'truths' is akin to a meandering, uncertain, painstaking knitting process throughout which community actors 'grapple with a file';[78] assemble, disassemble, and reassemble claims and arguments; single out the salient facts among the plethora of evidence on record; assert, resist, and test their interpretive choices and moral instincts; until, eventually, the patchwork takes the form of a coherent whole.[79]

Along this 'developing drama',[80] countless 'amanuenses'[81] work tirelessly to reduce the amorphous factual context that gave rise to a dispute into a binary legal equation – the only form in which the case can be adjudicated. Along the way, the folders of relevant materials become thinner and thinner. The most salient information is gradually selected while the rest falls into the background. Eventually,

[77] Ibid. [78] Ibid.
[79] See C. Wells, 'Situated Decisionmaking' (1990) 63 *Southern California Law Review* 1727, 1734–1736.
[80] Ibid., 1734. [81] Latour, *Making of Law*, 77.

a judgment will emerge which obscures all intricacies, inconsistencies, and hesitations that marked every phase of the process.

This process of 'denial', 'abstraction', and 'essentialisation'[82] entails a mutual adaptiveness of positions, an incessant construction and deconstruction of discursive possibilities, and an iterative quest for meaning and persuasion. At every turn, 'a whole series of tensions, vectors, currents, pressures [are] slightly rearranged'.[83] Submission after submission, pleading after pleading, question after question, certain subjects gain or lose traction; lawyers and adjudicators acquire or forgo authority; stumble momentarily; overcome roadblocks; glide over new terrains; affirm or disavow precedents; and revise interpretations.

No litigator, not even the most prescient, can confidently forecast the exact trajectory of a case. Arguments that seemed dispositive at the early stages of the dispute may be progressively sidelined, whereas seemingly mundane elements may rise in prominence and eventually become the cornerstone of the final ruling.

These contingencies can be exploited to introduce novel approaches and unorthodox views into the gears of the judicial machinery. They go on to show that nothing is as predetermined and predictable as the proponents of institutional bias would have us believe. The challenge is to identify those critical junctures, those loopholes in the socio-professional fabric of the international judicial community, and harness their tremendous creative potential.[84] After all, as a poet once put it, it is through the cracks that the light gets in.[85]

Conclusion: Structured Contingency?

In this chapter, I have started to unravel the relationship between agency and structure in the legal production of international judicial institutions. Seen from a distance, international courts appear as

82 P. Schlag, 'Spam Jurisprudence, Air Law, and the Rank Anxiety of Nothing Happening: A Report on the State of the Art' (2009) 97 *Georgetown Law Journal* 803, 816.

83 Latour, *Making of Law*, 141.

84 See e.g. I. Venzke and K. J. Heller (eds.), *Contingency in International Law: On the Possibility of Different Legal Histories* (Oxford University Press, 2021).

85 Leonard Cohen, 'Anthem'.

subservient entities, pulled apart by the competing forces of metaphysical law and unscrupulous politics. At closer examination, however, they reveal themselves as a site of socio-professional struggles, competing positions, and clashing worldviews. These micro-level relationships and practices are the source of both systemic constraint and responsible freedom in the definition of international legal outcomes.

Therefore, I would conclude that international adjudication takes place in conditions of *structured contingency*.[86] 'Contingency', because the path that leads to the formation of an international judgment is not predetermined, but susceptible to contestation and unforeseen twists. Every step of the process contemplates purposeful choices and value-judgements on the part of the actors involved. Each actor has countless opportunities to voice their opinion, assert and resist claims, and consciously exercise their discrete portion of agency to steer the course of proceedings. 'Structured', because while existing arrangements can be changed, 'change unfolds within a context that includes systematic constraints and pressures'.[87] Departing too abruptly from the tacit rules of the game would lead to professional reprimand, public derision, or outright expulsion from the game. Perhaps, then, the puzzle of freedom can be solved by paraphrasing Karl Marx: international courts 'make their own history, but they do not make it just as they please in circumstances they choose for themselves; rather they make it in present circumstances, given and inherited'.[88]

[86] See Soave, *Everyday Makers*. [87] Marks, 'False Contingency', 2.

[88] K. Marx, 'The Eighteenth Brumaire of Louis Bonaparte', in T. Carver (ed.), *Marx: Later Political Writings* (Cambridge University Press, 1996) 31, 32.

8 Reassembling Transnational Legal Conflicts across Global Institutions

Ethnographic Perspectives on Claims of Authority over the Mediterranean Sea

KIRI OLIVIA SANTER

Introduction

Contemporary global governance is characterised by the deterritorialised production of law – a process in which International Organisations (IOs) play an increasingly important role.[1] Some scholars have understood this movement in lawmaking beyond the traditional sites of normative production ('beyond the state'[2]) as an instance of fragmentation. This, as Koskenniemi has argued, leads to deformalism and managerialism.[3] But this movement has material effects and outcomes that go beyond the normative and ideational, a fact that is often overlooked by legal scholars. Legal fragmentation within the transnational realm can lead to legal conflicts, where actors with differing power positions in the global order seek to shape particular apparatuses or issues of government in distinct ways and according to their interests,[4] within a legal landscape lacking clear hierarchy. These legal conflicts have material outcomes since they shape the social and political world and affect parties to the conflict in differentiated ways.

[1] J. Eckert and P. Dann, 'Norm-Creation beyond the State' in M.-C. Foblets, M. Goodale, M. Sapignoli, and O. Zenker (eds.), *The Oxford Handbook of Law and Anthropology*, (Oxford University Press, 2020), pp. 808–26.

[2] Eckert and Dann, 'Norm-Creation beyond the State', p. 816.

[3] M. Koskenniemi, 'Formalism, Fragmentation, Freedom: Kantian Themes in Today's International Law' (2007) 4 *No Foundations: Journal of Extreme Legal Positivism* 7–28; T. Broude, 'Keep Calm and Carry on: Martti Koskenniemi and the Fragmentation of International Law' (2013) 27 *Temple International & Comparative Law Journal* 279–92.

[4] International Law Commission, *Fragmentation of International Law: Difficulties Arising from the Diversification and Expansion of International Law: Report of the Study Group of the International Law Commission.* Finalized by Martti Koskenniemi (2006) p. 15.

In transnational law, the line between informal and formal norms is blurry and so the lack of hierarchy in the fragmented international legal sphere pushes the question of authority to the forefront of theories of global governance; understanding how authority is exercised helps to grasp which norm(s) takes precedence over another in situations of global legal pluralism. And, in turn, how certain orders or ways of governing are perpetuated in time.

In this chapter, I make the proposal that an ethnographic engagement with Transnational Legal Conflicts (TLCs) can help shed light on the ways in which authority and hierarchisation within TLCs manifest and shape the social and political world and the galaxy of IOs for that purpose. In the context of the conflict over the responsibility to rescue migrants at the contentious border zone in the Central Mediterranean, I examine the struggle for control over a large stretch of international waters, where migrants attempt to make the perilous crossing having departed from Libya and where NGO vessels carry out rescue activities of the former. Feldman has proposed 'non-local'[5] ethnography not just to describe the dots or sites linked to governance activities or to represent daily practice but rather to decode governance processes or regimes functioning to 'regulate large populations'.[6] This approach, he argues, is fitted to study 'historically particular apparatus',[7] which span several sites and involve many actors, overlapping policies, and different technologies. Apparatuses coalesce to produce historically contingent models and networks geared towards the management of populations or control the economy. In his words, the ethnography of global governance should 'uncover how discourses give an emerging regime its shape and direction',[8] as opposed to limiting itself to the description of the components of governance.

In the following, I apply such a non-local approach to the TLC over the responsibility for rescue in the Central Mediterranean. I excavate

[5] G. Feldman, 'If Ethnography Is More than Participant-Observation, then Relations Are More than Connections: The Case for Nonlocal Ethnography in a World of Apparatuses' (2011) 11 *Anthropological Theory* 375–95.

[6] G. Feldman, 'Illuminating the Apparatus: Steps toward a Nonlocal Ethnography of Global Governance' in C. Shore, S. Wright, and D. Però (eds.), *Policy Worlds: Anthropology and the Analysis of Contemporary Power*, (Berghahn, 2011), pp. 32–49 p. 32.

[7] Ibid., p. 33. [8] Ibid.

the power dynamics at stake that manifest at sea and beyond and show how operational hierarchies are set despite all actors referring to the lawfulness of their actions. In the Central Mediterranean, international borders – both physical and immaterial – have been redrawn by the actions of international institutions, situated far away from the dilemmas of those carrying out rescues. The emergence of the Libyan Search and Rescue Region (SRR) in the International Maritime Organization's (IMO) Global Search and Rescue (SAR) Plan in June 2018 legitimised European authorities' handing over of responsibility to Libyan authorities to coordinate the rescue of migrants and to thus disembark survivors in Libya. This clashes with the international principle of non-refoulement and the duty to disembark rescued people in a place of safety according to the 1979 SAR Convention. With this in mind, I analyse how the emergence of this new zone enables an extremely formal interpretation of the SAR convention, ultimately meaning that European authorities can delegate the responsibility for rescue to their Libyan counterparts. I start by outlining how an ethnographic approach to TLCs can help us understand the competing and fragmented jurisdictions in spaces of transnational governance. Then, I move to the setting of the Central Mediterranean Sea and depict the materiality and situatedness of TLCs, relating to conflicts over the responsibility to rescue migrants at sea. I show how different claims of authority manifest in these TLCs, and thus, how the EU has managed to shape the governance of a large stretch of international waters shot through by multiple jurisdictions, to meet its own interests of reducing irregular migration.

Ethnographies of Transnational Legal Conflicts

The de-formalisation induced by global legal pluralism[9] has been criticised for weakening formal rules of procedure and 'formalised limits of competence', and, perhaps counter-intuitively, privileging 'power over plurality'.[10] To delve deeper into the power dynamics of a TLC, it is necessary to pay close attention to time and space and empirically engage

[9] P. Schiff Berman, *Global Legal Pluralism: A Jurisprudence of Law beyond Borders* (Cambridge University Press, 2012).
[10] Eckert and Dann, 'Norm-Creation beyond the State', p. 815.

with instances in which 'law' is used and referred to.[11] An anthropological approach to 'the transnational' can help shed light on which 'chains of interdependence are deemed relevant'[12] and which can be disregarded, within situations of legal overlap. Such a situational approach enables the micro study of macro-relations within situations of structured contingency.[13] Hence, an ethnographic approach to TLCs leads to a path beyond legal formalism, helps understand the materiality and meaning of the context, and enables the excavation of power dynamics that might often be masked as references to 'neutral' international legal frameworks and the IOs upholding them. In the context of the externalisation of migration control in and around the Mediterranean for example containment policies, in which IOs such as the International Organisation for Migration (IOM) are often active partners,[14] are underpinned by the dominant paradigm both in international and domestic law of the nation-state's prerogative to exclude non-nationals.[15] Their legal architecture masks the racialised and neo-colonial nature of the contemporary migration governance at the borders of Europe.[16]

As mentioned earlier, legal conflicts can be summarised as arising due to actors' different pursuits and desires in a pluralistic global society.[17] Therefore, fragmentation is not just the result of a lack of formal integrity of international law; it is also fundamentally a question of politics. For Koskenniemi and Leino, fragmentation emerges because of the utopian disposition of international law: it is used by actors in ways that try and advance the political present that has been 'in some way or another' revealed to be 'unsatisfactory'.[18] In this chapter,

[11] This is similar to what Zumbansen proposes in his socio-legal approach to transnational law: P. Zumbansen, 'Transnational Law as Socio-legal Theory and Critique: Prospects for "Law and Society" in a Divided World' (2019) 67 *Buffalo Law Review* 909–60.

[12] J. Eckert, 'Beyond Agatha Christie: Relationality and Critique in Anthropological theory' (2016) 16 *Anthropological Theory* 241–48 at 244.

[13] Eckert, 'Beyond Agatha Christie'.

[14] J. Brachet, 'Policing the Desert: The IOM in Libya beyond War and Peace' (2016) 48 *Antipode* 272–92.

[15] T. E. Achiume, 'Migration as Decolonization' (2019) 71 *Stanford Law Review* 1509–74.

[16] T. E. Achiume and A. Bali, 'Race and Empire: Legal Theory within, through, and across National Borders' (2021) 67 *U.C.L.A. Law Review* 1386–431.

[17] International Law Commission, *Fragmentation of International Law*, p. 15.

[18] M. Koskenniemi and P. Leino, 'Fragmentation of International Law? Postmodern Anxieties' (2002) 15 *Leiden Journal of International Law* 553–79 at 578.

I am less interested in the worldviews and justifications of international lawmakers than I am interested in examining how to study the material and ideational outcomes of what happens when different (sometimes utopian) visions of law, or sets of international rules, come into collision with one another.

TLCs Over Responsibility for the Preservation of Life at Sea

Europe's 'obsession'[19] with clandestine migration by sea in the last decade has had to balance the securitisation of the external border with the issue of preserving life at sea. Walters coined the term 'humanitarian border'[20] to describe the rise of importance of borders for Western states, as sites concentrating a set of concerns and fears and therefore in need of being securitised. The counter-intuitive placing of 'humanitarian' next to 'border' is to signify how these sites have increasingly concentrated a variety of activities carried out by state and non-state actors, which mix dynamics of protection and control.[21] In the Mediterranean, policing, humanitarian action, and intelligence-gathering have all become entangled in a series of networks, including states, international organisations, and NGOs within a system designed to both intercept and rescue migrants in distress at sea.

In the face of these paradigmatic tensions, the responsibility for survivors of a distress situation at sea, or for their death, has taken on geopolitical dimensions in the Mediterranean with the increasingly securitised way in which migration and maritime migration has been dealt with in the EU since the early 2000s. In 2004 already, the German humanitarian ship *Cap Anamur* rescued thirty-seven people from an inflatable dinghy in the strait of Sicily and was subsequently denied the right to enter Italian territorial waters. For eleven days, the ship was made to wait in international waters, whilst Malta, Italy, and

19 R. Andersson, *Illegality, Inc.* (University of California Press, 2014), p. 12.

20 W. Walters, 'Foucault and Frontiers: Notes on the Birth of the Humanitarian Border' in U. Bröckling, S. Krasmann, and T. Lemke (eds.), *Governmentality: Current Issues and Future Challenges*, (Routledge, 2009), pp. 138–64.

21 see also P. Pallister-Wilkins, 'Humanitarian Rescue/Sovereign Capture and the Policing of Possible Responses to Violent Borders' (2017) 8 *Global Policy* 19–24.

Germany debated where the people should be allowed to disembark.[22] At the heart of the contention lies the SAR regime and associated 1979 International Convention on Maritime Search and Rescue[23] (hereinafter: SAR Convention), which splits the high seas (the waters beyond territorial waters) into zones and distributes coordination responsibility among coastal states for rescue operations. Whereas in territorial waters (12 nautical miles (NM) off the baseline of a state's coast) and the contiguous zone (up to 24 NM off the coast) states enjoy, respectively, quasi full and some limited policing power, on the high seas or international waters, they can exercise jurisdiction in only very limited ways.[24] On the one hand, the SAR regime was designed to precisely improve safety at sea by ensuring that coordination responsibilities are clear. On the other, in the Mediterranean, states like Malta have disputed the extension of their responsibility to such a large portion of international waters.[25]

The tensions around where to disembark survivors, depending on where they were rescued and by whom, has meant that states have often engaged in a responsibility ping-pong relating to whom should intervene, which has sometimes had deadly consequences. In October 2013 for example, a boat carrying over 400 people, most of them

[22] P. Cuttitta, 'From the Cap Anamur to Mare Nostrum. Humanitarianism and Migration Controls at the EU's Maritime Borders' in C. Matera and A. Taylor (eds.), *The Common European Asylum System and Human Rights: Enhancing Protection in Times of Emergencies*, (Asser Institute, 2014), pp. 21–37.

[23] International Convention on Maritime Search and Rescue, Hamburg, 27 April 1979, United Nations Treaty Series, vol. 1405, p. 119.

[24] V. Moreno-Lax, 'Protection at Sea and the Denial of Asylum' in C. Costello, M. Foster, and J. McAdam (eds.), *The Oxford Handbook of International Refugee Law*, (Oxford University Press, 2021), pp. 483–501 p. 487.

[25] Malta has been a party to the 1974 SOLAS Convention since 1986 and to the 1979 SAR Convention since 2002. Its SAR zone mirrors the state's Flight Information Region, which was inherited from the British Flight Identification Region. The country has long complained that the zone is too big for it to handle and carries too large a responsibility for the issue of migrant rescues. In 2004, Malta refused to sign the amended version of the SOLAS and SAR conventions, thereby not recognizing the principle of disembarkation of survivors to the closest port of safety. See: J. Coppens, 'The Essential Role of Malta in Drafting the New Regional Agreement on Migrants at Sea in the Mediterranean Basin' (2013) 44 *Journal of Maritime Law & Commerce* 89–111; V. Moreno-Lax, 'Seeking Asylum in the Mediterranean: Against a Fragmentary Reading of EU Members States' Obligations Accruing at Sea' (2011) 23 *International Journal of Refugee Law* 174–220 at 197.

Syrian refugees, sunk off the coast of Lampedusa, killing 200 people, about 60 of whom were children. An Italian navy ship, the *Libra*, was stationed a mere 19 miles aways from the distress case, in the Maltese SAR zone. The migrants had called the Italian coast guard for help, but the coast guard had repeatedly told them to call Malta instead. The Maltese eventually intervened, hours after the migrants had called and begged for support. And this even though the *Libra* was only about an hours' navigational time away from the scene.

Yet the law of the sea is very clear when it comes to the duty to rescue people who find themselves in distress. The 1982 UN Convention on the Law of the Sea (UNCLOS),[26] the 1974 Convention on Safety of Life at Sea (SOLAS Convention),[27] and the 1979 SAR Convention all require that life be preserved at sea at all costs, regardless of nationality. They set out the duties of the master of a ship to render assistance and to proceed with speed to conduct a rescue, upon receival of a distress signal. According to the text of the SAR Convention, an SRR[28] does not entail jurisdiction but assumes duties. However, in practice, this is not a clear-cut distinction. *De facto*, SAR zones extend a form of jurisdiction as states carry out patrol and surveillance activities.

Shaping a Maritime Control Cooperation Partner Anew: The Genesis of the Libyan SRR

Libya has been a partner to the EU and Italy for what concerns maritime migration control since the early 2000s.[29] The Treaty on Friendship, Partnership and Cooperation was signed between Italy and Libya in 2008, which provided the grounds for joint patrols and off-shore pushbacks.[30] The fall of the Gaddafi regime in 2011 after the NATO led intervention brought about the collapse of a stable

[26] United Nations Convention on the Law of the Sea, Montego Bay, 10 December 1982, United Nations Treaty Series, vol. 1833, p. 397.

[27] International Convention for the Safety of Life at Sea, London, 1 November 1974, United Nations Treaty Series, vol. 1184, p. 278.

[28] In this chapter, I use Libyan SAR zone and Libyan SRR interchangeably.

[29] see: L. Bialasiewicz, 'Off-shoring and Out-sourcing the Borders of Europe: Libya and EU Border Work in the Mediterranean' (2012) 17 *Geopolitics* 843–66.

[30] E. Paoletti, 'Historical Background on the Agreements between Italy and Libya' in *The Migration of Power and North-South Inequalities*, (Palgrave Macmillan, 2010), pp. 139, 157.

discussion and cooperation partner for the EU on migration matters. Libya has been in political turmoil since. The legitimacy of the General National Congress (GNC), established in 2012, came under threat by General Haftar calling for the GNC's dissolution in February 2014 and the Prime Minister, Ali Zeidan, being removed from office in March of the same year. Amidst the insecurity induced by the civil unrest and fall of the dictatorship, migrant crossings increased. This led to the EU changing its external approach to Libya in 2014, shifting from an approach that promoted democracy and institution-building, to one that framed the Libyan crisis as a migration and border crisis.[31] The increase in clandestine crossings also brought about an increase in migrant deaths at sea.

After hundreds of migrants lost their lives in a series of shipwrecks in 2013 off the coast of Lampedusa, the Italian government reacted by launching a national rescue operation *Mare Nostrum*. However, the operation rapidly came to an end a year later under pressure from both domestic critics and European policymakers more generally who blamed the operation for being a 'pull-factor' for immigration into Europe.[32] This narrative was soon to be shifted onto NGO vessels, the first of which began to operate in the Strait of Sicily at the end of 2014. In April 2015, another series of shipwrecks in the Central Mediterranean prompted a special EU Council meeting in which the EU reaffirmed its commitment to preserving life at sea in the face of this 'human emergency'.[33] Despite this, Frontex's area of operation under Joint-Operation Triton, which was launched after the end of *Mare Nostrum*, did not patrol the zone where most distress cases were declared, south of the Italian SAR.

When I interviewed a retired member of the Italian Coast Guard about this period, he clearly stated that these years after 2011 had constituted a great challenge for him and his team. The Italian Coast

[31] K. Ivashchenko-Stadnik, R. Petrov, P. Rieker, A. Russo, and L. Raineri, 'How the EU is facing crises in its neighborhood: Evidence from Libya and Ukraine', *EUNPACK Working Paper* (2018) p. 60.

[32] S. Carrera and L. den Hertog, 'Whose Mare? Rule of law challenges in the field of European border surveillance in the Mediterranean', *CEPS Paper in Liberty and Security in Europe* (2015) p. 5.

[33] EU Council, Special meeting of the European Council Statement: www.consilium.europa.eu/en/press/press-releases/2015/04/23/special-euco-statement/ (23 April 2015)

Guard often had to intervene in scenes of impending mass casualty, sometimes far outside of their own SAR zone, whilst the Maritime Rescue Coordination Centre in Rome (ITMRCC) was overwhelmed by calls from different sources signalling distress cases. What emerged from the point of view of the ITMRCC, he told me, was a need for an authority with whom they could have a regular dialogue as expected by the conventions.[34] In 2017, an agreement was signed between the Italian Coast Guard and the European Commission's DG Home to grant funds for the action 'Assessment of the Libyan Coast Guard legal framework and capability in terms of SAR Services'.[35] This was to be one of the first steps towards helping the Libyan Coast Guard gain capacity for rescue in the Central Mediterranean. The action was funded by the EU Internal Security Fund (ISF) and included a feasibility study, which was to define under which conditions the LMRCC (Libyan Maritime Rescue Coordination Centre) and an associated SAR zone could be established.

Despite not yet having their own SRR, the Libyan Coast Guard (LYCG) had already massively increased interceptions in 2017. In 2016, NGOs accounted for the highest number of rescues, whilst in 2017, the trend was inverted with the LYCG intercepting more migrants than any other actor.[36] In parallel to the feasibility study being carried out for the establishment of the Libyan SRR, Marco Minniti, Italian interior minister at the time, struck the infamous Memorandum of Understanding with then prime minister Fayez al-Sarraj.[37] Italy also then approached the European Commission in May 2017 with a 'major proposal for integrated border and migration management in Libya'[38] to be funded under the EU Emergency Trust Fund

[34] Interview, retired Italian Coast Guard official, Rome, 11 September 2020.

[35] The full text of the agreement can be found here: www.guardiacostiera.gov.it/stampa/Documents/progetti-finanziati/Grant%20Agreement%200051%20signed.pdf (accessed 25 October 2021)

[36] C. Heller and L. Pezzani, 'Mare Clausum: Italy and the EU's undeclared operation to stem migration across the Mediterranean', Report for Forensic Oceanography project (2018) p. 13. Available at: https://content.forensic-architecture.org/wp-content/uploads/2019/05/2018-05-07-FO-Mare-Clausum-full-EN.pdf

[37] Memorandum dintesa (…) tra lo Stato della Libia e la Repubblica Italiana, 02.02.2017: www.governo.it/sites/governo.it/files/Libia.pdf (accessed 2 May 2022)

[38] EUTF, Support to Integrated border and migration management in Libya – First Phase (T05-EUTF-NAO-LY-04) (2017).

for Africa (EUTF),[39] and to complement the ISF funding. The projects caught under the North Africa window of the EUTF to be implemented in Libya focused almost entirely on improving the Libyan authorities' ability to 'manage' migration and secure their borders.[40] On 10 July 2017, the Libyan Ports and Maritime Transport Authority (Ministry of Transport) communicated in a letter to the IMO the designation of the Libyan SRR. In the letter, the Libyan authorities mentioned the lack of resources and facilities of the coast guard and the air forces resulting from the destruction caused by the 2011 military operations. For some time before the actual declaration of the Libyan SRR, when the LYCG had already greatly increased their activity, the Italians were in fact acting as the coordination authority from Tripoli from a military ship.[41]

On 27 June 2018, the coordinates of a new Libyan SRR were uploaded to the IMO's Global Integrated Shipping Information System (GISIS). This banal act had juridical consequences: henceforth, the LYCG had coordination priority for SAR events over a vast area of international waters. It was a unilateral declaration with a constitutive effect, the authority of which was based on the structural dominance of states in their ability to grant powers to specific actors 'at the confluence of legal structures'.[42] Taken alone and distinct from

[39] The EUTF was established at the Valletta Summit on Migration in November 2015.

[40] As quoted from the Action Fiche of project T05-EUTF-NAO-LY-04: 'Activity 3: Assistance to the Libyan concerned Authorities with a view to enabling them to declare a Libyan SAR Region (as per assessment results). Detailed design for the setup of a full-fledged MRCC in Tripoli (or nearby), associated with proper communication facilities'. The Action Fiche is available here: https://ec.europa.eu/trustfundforafrica/sites/default/files/t05-eutf-noa-ly-04_modified.pdf

[41] As affirmed by numerous sources, including in a judgement on the confiscation of the ship of the NGO Open Arms in March 2018, which stated: 'the personnel on board the Italian military vessel (NAURAS operation), stationed in Tripoli informed Rome that a patrol boat belonging to the Libyan coastguard would shortly be leaving its moorings to head for the target and specified that the aforementioned coast guard would take responsibility for the rescue operation' (translation from Italian my own). Tribunale di Catania. 2018. *Decreto di convalida e di sequestro preventivo*. Tribunale di Catania: Sezione del giudice per le indagini preliminari. N. 3476/18 R.G.N.R. Available at: www.statewatch.org/media/documents/news/2018/apr/it-open-arms-sequestration-judicial-order-tribunale-catania.pdf (accessed 8 June 2022)

[42] Eckert and Dann, 'Norm-Creation beyond the State', p. 816.

the socio-legal context in which it came into being, the notification could seem straightforward: it simply defined which state would take coordination responsibility for rescues in this stretch of international waters. However, it did not emerge in a neutral space. In fact, it was declared in an already saturated legal landscape: the sea, although it has long been portrayed as a 'lawless space beyond sovereignty and justice',[43] is permeated by a complex (and expanding) regulatory system,[44] which prescribes the conduct of ships in fields ranging from trade to environmental protection and rescue. The emergence of the Libyan SRR was another layer adding to the legal sediments striating the justifications for different conduct of actors passing through the Central Mediterranean. It made the LYCG into a legitimate cooperation partner for the Italian coast guard to coordinate rescues, as set by the law of the sea. Simultaneously, it formalised a practice of systematic pull-backs of migrants to Libya in violation of the 1951 *non-refoulement* principle. In sum, it further entrenched the conflict between a securitised approach to maritime migration and a more humanitarian and rights-conforming approach.[45]

The Libyan SRR formalised the LYCG's authority to coordinate rescues in this region, giving Libyan authorities primary responsibility to ensure rescued people be disembarked in a 'place of safety'.[46] Although 'place of safety' (and the concept of 'safety' more broadly) has not been clearly defined in international legal frameworks, it is widely accepted that it must be interpreted in accordance with refugee law provisions where the principle of *non-refoulement* is guaranteed.[47]

[43] W. Walters, 'Bordering the Sea: Shipping Industries and the Policing of Stowaways' (2008) 7 *borderlands* 1–25 at 5.

[44] A. J. Dickson, 'Mobility Control in Ungovernable Spaces: Cultivating the Mediterranean's Fatal Materiality' (2021) 39 *Environment and Planning C: Politics and Space* 993–1010.

[45] See V. Moreno-Lax, D. Ghezelbash, and N. Klein, 'Between Life, Security and Rights: Framing the Interdiction of "Boat Migrants" in the Central Mediterranean and Australia' (2019) 32 *Leiden Journal of International Law* 715–40.

[46] SAR Convention, Annex, para. 1.3.2.

[47] A. Fischer-Lescano, T. Löhr, and T. Tohidipur, 'Border Controls at Sea: Requirements under International Human Rights and Refugee Law' (2009) 21 *International Journal of Refugee Law* 256–96. The 2004 IMO Guidelines on the Treatment of Persons Rescued at Sea (Resolution MSC.167(78), 20 May 2004) specify that survivors should not be disembarked to a place 'where their safety would be further jeopardized' (para. 5.6). Although 'place of safety'

There is an obligation of result that comes with the duties of the state responsible for the SAR zone to ensure that rescued people are effectively disembarked.[48] International law scholars and human rights organisations have argued that 'place of safety' *should* be interpreted in accordance with refugee law provisions. However, it is not my goal to go into the detail of the normative interpretation of these provisions. Rather, here I want to point out that *despite* the existence of this framework that prohibits the disembarkation of people in a place where their lives and safety are threatened, the enactment of the Libyan SRR enabled a fragmentary reading of these provisions and attributed authority to specific officials in acting out this reading.

As I will show in the following section, the TLC at hand was shaped and hierarchised in such a way that the LYCG were able to gain operational advantage over rescue NGOs and maintained this advantage over time. The way these overlapping jurisdictions could be hierarchised in a specific way was deeply dependent on the way they connected to the priorities and ideologies of the institutions involved in governing the maritime space. In the following section, I show how hierarchy was imposed in that conflict, thus shaping the outcome of political and social behaviours and operational patterns which persist to this day.

has no stable definition in the law of the sea, the IMO Guidelines give some precisions: a place of safety is where 'rescue operations are considered to terminate (...) where the survivors' safety of life is no longer threatened' (para. 6.12, also in SAR Convention 1979, Annex, para. 1.3.2). Another ship cannot be considered as a place of safety, only a temporary accommodation before alternative arrangements are met (ibid., para. 6.13). The Guidelines stress that each rescue case is unique (ibid., para. 6.15), and that provisions should be made to 'avoid disembarkation in territories where the lives and freedoms of those alleging a well-founded fear of persecution would be threatened is a consideration in the case of asylum-seekers and refugees recovered at sea' (ibid., para. 6.17). The responsibility to ensure that survivors are delivered to a place of safety lies with the coastal state that coordinates the SAR region in question. However, Moreno-Lax ('Seeking Asylum in the Mediterranean: Against a Fragmentary Reading of EU Members States' Obligations Accruing at Sea', p. 196) notes that 'the duty on the coastal state is limited to ensuring collaboration and does not include a commandment to allow for disembarkation onto its own territory, the amendments establish nonetheless an obligation of result', referencing the SAR Convention, Annex, para. 3.1.9 and the SOLAS Convention, ch. V, Regulation 33.

48 Moreno-Lax, 'Seeking Asylum in the Mediterranean: Against a Fragmentary Reading of EU Members States' Obligations Accruing at Sea', 196.

Authority in the Libyan SRR

To delve deeper into the question of how and which kinds of authority come to shape the governance of the EU's external maritime border in international waters, I take the following examples from fieldwork I carried out at sea onboard an NGO rescue ship in the autumn of 2018.[49] This was shortly after the Libyan SRR had been declared. At the time, NGOs and human rights organisations had already been critical of the role of the LYCG in the growing number of interceptions carried out by them.[50] Violent encounters between the LYCG and NGOs had also taken place, for example in November 2017.[51] In July 2017, the Italian Minitti government had tried to impose a Code of Conduct on rescue NGOs, which was widely criticised for being legally unclear and for imposing obligations on NGOs and leaving out the responsibilities of the Italian state.[52] The code emphasised, amongst other things, the obligation for a ship master to immediately notify the competent authorities of the flag State once a rescue had been conducted in a zone where there was no official SRR. It was a clear attempt by the Italian government to push other states to become involved in the contentious issue of disembarkation of rescued people by trying to establish responsibility through the flag state. Moreover, the wave of criminalisation

[49] I have described these same scenes of rescue in the article 'Governing the Central Mediterranean through Indirect Rule: Tracing the Effects of the Recognition of Joint Rescue Coordination Centre Tripoli' (2019) 21 *European Journal of Migration and Law* 141–65. There I make a different argument. Namely, that the creation of the Libyan SRR enabled the European Union and Italy to govern this stretch of international waters in an indirect manner.

[50] See for example Amnesty International, *Libya's Dark Web of Collusion: Abuses against Europe-Bound Refugees and Migrants* (2017).

[51] On the 6 of November 2017, the LYCG carried out an interception/rescue of a migrant dinghy of 150 people that capsized. The ITMRCC called all ships in the area to head to the distress scene to support the operation since the situation was critical. When the NGO vessel *Sea Watch* arrived on the scene there was an altercation between the LYCG and the NGO ship. At least 20 people died. For a detailed reconstruction of the case see Section B in V. Moreno-Lax, 'The Architecture of Functional Jurisdiction: Unpacking Contactless Control – On Public Powers, S.S. and Others v. Italy, and the "Operational Model"' (2020) 21 *German Law Journal* 385–416 at 388–90.

[52] I. Papanicolopulu, 'Immigrazione Irregolare via Mare, Tutela Della Vita Umana e Organizzazioni Non Governative' (2017) 3 *Diritto, Immigrazione e Cittadinanza* 1–29.

against rescue NGOs had started, drastically reducing their abilities to effectively operate in the Strait of Sicily. Then, in the summer of 2018, Italy, spearheaded by far-right interior minister Matteo Salvini, declared the country's ports shut to all foreign-flagged vessels that had rescued migrants off the coast of Libya. Thus, when I first arrived in Marseille to embark on the NGO ship *Aquarius*, operated by *SOS Méditeranée* and *Médecins sans frontières*, the tension, linked to the political climate in which SAR activities in the Central Mediterranean were unfolding, was palpable. Gibraltar had just announced that it would strip the *Aquarius* from its registers and so, after initially being told that we would leave the port on 1 September, the departure of the ship was delayed from week to week as the search for a new flag dragged on. The ship operator had made a request to the Panamanian authorities for a flag a few days before I arrived, which was finally approved.

We were finally able to leave the port of Marseille on 30 September 2018, in this jittery operational atmosphere. A few days into navigation, we encountered the first dinghy in need of rescue. It was a small fibreglass boat with eleven people on board, which had been spotted by local fishermen. The SAR coordinator on board the *Aquarius* tried calling Joint Rescue Coordination Centre (JRCC) Tripoli to request instruction, but his calls remained unanswered.[53] Since Tripoli was not picking up the phone, the captain reverted to contacting another RCC.[54] The Italian MRCC reacted to the call and the SAR coordinator informed them about the failed attempts to contact Tripoli. Once the rescue was completed, he wrote an email to the Italian Coast Guard again to inform them of the number of people who were now aboard the *Aquarius*, copying Malta and Tripoli in the process. By the end of the morning, JRCC Tripoli had emailed back to inform that it was taking coordination of the SAR event and gave a set of coordinates where they proposed to transfer the rescued people onto a Libyan asset. The *Aquarius* responded that it could not proceed to the transfer, referring to the

[53] According to the SAR Convention, section 2.3.3, any operational Rescue Coordination Centre (RCC) should be available on a 24-hour basis and be manned by trained staff with working knowledge of English.

[54] As outlined in the IMO Guidelines: 'in a case where the RCC responsible for the area where the survivors are recovered cannot be contacted, attempt to contact another RCC' (para. 5.1.4).

SAR conventions, which prevented them from taking survivors back to an unsafe place; by accepting to make the transfer, they would potentially be in violation of the *non-refoulement* principle. The LYCG then responded by saying that the *Aquarius* should contact another RCC or its flag state for coordination and for attribution to a place of safety.

Shortly after this event, the Panamanian Maritime Authority released a press communiqué stating it had initiated proceedings to remove the Panamanian flag from the *Aquarius*. The reason stated in the release was that the vessel had 'refused to deliver immigrants and refugees to their place of origin'.[55] The information that the *Aquarius* had disobeyed orders from the Libyan authorities had been delivered to Panama by the Italian authorities.[56] Panama had declared it was going to have to exclude the *Aquarius* from its register because not doing so would entail severe political difficulties for the many Panamanian ships operating in European ports.

A second rescue took place a couple of days later. This time, the *Aquarius* was alerted to a boat taking on water, which was said to have left from Zuwara, Libya. The boat was overcrowded and contained around fifty people, including women and children. After having informed the ITMRCC of the potential case – JRCC Tripoli was once again unreachable – the captain and SAR coordinator decided to head towards the area of the GPS coordinates. The Italian authorities were obviously in contact with the Libyans through other means than those that were available to the *Aquarius* because they knew that there was a LYCG patrol boat close by. On the phone, they gave the SAR coordinator the name of the Libyan patrol vessel (PV) and said that he should try to enter into contact with it. About an hour later and after several attempts, the bridge managed to establish contact with the PV in question, *al-Kifah*. *Al-Kifah* informed the NGO ship that it was going to be the on-scene 'commander'. The SAR conventions give provisions for the designation of an on-scene coordinator, to ensure

[55] Autoridad Maritima de Panama, 'Aquarius 2 ex Aquarius' (21 September 2018). Available at: https://amp.gob.pa/noticias/aquarius-2-ex-aquarius/ (accessed 4 July 2022).

[56] Médecins Sans Frontières, 'Le Panama révoque le pavillon de l'Aquarius sous la pression du gouvernement italien' (23 September 2018). Available at: www.msf.fr/communiques-presse/le-panama-revoque-le-pavillon-de-l-aquarius-sous-la-pression-du-gouvernement-italien (accessed 20 December 2018).

the smooth sequencing of events during a rescue.[57] The designation of 'commander' signalled the way in which roles would be distributed on the scene. This was not so much about collaboration as it was about operational hierarchy.

When, some hours later, the *Aquarius* reached the position of the boat in difficulty, the SAR coordinator informed the LYCG that the small inflatable rescue boats of the *Aquarius* had been launched and were ready to start transferring the survivors. The communication with PV *al-Kifah* became extremely tense and the LYCG demanded that the *Aquarius*' small rescue zodiacs stabilise the situation but then stay five miles away from it. The SAR coordinator explained calmly that this would not be possible, since the boat was in distress. Both zodiacs were made to station next to the boat in distress for close to an hour, with the rescue teams wondering why they were not being given the order to transfer – they were not aware of the difficult ongoing communications between the Libyans and the bridge of the *Aquarius*. In the early hours of the morning, the LYCG ordered them to move fifteen nautical miles away from the scene and threatened to arrest the rescue ship teams over the radio. Another hour of fraught and volatile communication ensued, with confusing back-and-forth instructions from PV *al-Kifah* and attempts from the bridge to de-escalate the situation. The final order to start transferring the people to the *Aquarius* was only given at 7:00am, after the Libyan patrol boat had drawn itself up very close to the wooden boat and the zodiacs and had then proceeded to circle the *Aquarius* menacingly. The last communication through the radio from the LYCG was an order for the *Aquarius* to leave the Libyan SRR and not to come back.

The SAR Convention states that when multiple facilities are about to engage in SAR operations, the RCC should designate 'the most capable person' to act as on-scene coordinator.[58] Details are not given

[57] SAR Convention, Annex, para. 4.7.2: 'When multiple facilities are about to engage in search and rescue operations, and the rescue co-ordination centre or rescue sub-centre considers it necessary, the most capable person should be designated as on-scene co-ordinator as early as practicable and preferably before the facilities arrive within the specified area of operation. Specific responsibilities shall be assigned to the on-scene co-ordinator, taking into account the apparent capabilities of the on-scene co-ordinator and operational requirements.'

[58] SAR Convention, Annex, para. 4.7.2.

as to what exactly 'most capable' might signify. The *Aquarius*, with its extensive experience of rescues and accumulated collective knowledge of how to deal with these kinds of flimsy boats, as well as its medical teams onboard, could certainly qualify for 'most capable'. UNCLOS and the SOLAS and SAR conventions all stress the duty of the master of the ship to proceed as fast as possible to the scene of distress and to offer their assistance.[59] What is clear from the earlier description of the altercation is that the LYCG took up its role as 'competent authority' to mean 'authority that all assets involved in rescues should obey'. The LYCG effectively became a policing force without the mandate to act as one. This clashed with the NGO boat's understanding of the 'spirit' of solidarity at sea, codified by international law and SAR procedures and which they emphasised their abidance by.

The examples I just outlined show how TLCs are not the product of a legal clash in relation to a set hierarchy, in which clearly defined legal levels conflict with one another. Rather, different actors shape the rescue situations, all the while claiming to be abiding by procedures set in legal regulations. The social and material field in which both the LYCG and the *Aquarius* were pitted against each other is the product of a wider conflict between frames of reference in the contested Central Mediterranean region. Beyond the situations of rescue themselves, the conflict is shaped by decisions, institutional cultures, and ideologies of institutions whose reach extends transnationally. In particular, the EU and Italy were able to institutionalise the 'right' procedure to adopt when conducting rescues of migrants in distress, which gave an operational advantage to the LYCG. The power to shape the legal conflict from afar was linked to coercive power (criminalisation of 'disobedient' NGOs) and privileged access to information and communication networks, as well as the material and financial support offered to the Libyan authorities. The legitimacy of the support given to the LYCG also came from a specific framing of the migration 'crisis' in the Mediterranean and the need to respond to it, which could be observed in the interviews I conducted with European officials and bureaucrats working on the Mediterranean and Libyan migration situation.

The justificatory framing discursively combined the need to act ('Europe cannot stand by whilst lives are being lost') with the need

[59] UNCLOS, Art. 98, SOLAS, Reg. 33–1, SAR Convention, Annex, para. 2.1.10, IMO Guidelines on the Treatment of Persons Rescued at Sea.

to secure the external border.[60] This duality could be traced down into the discourses of EU officials and civil servants. Senior officers and managers working on of the North Africa window of the EUTF whom I interviewed expressed the idea that 'something' had to be done to preserve life at sea in the Central Mediterranean, combined with the EU's commitment to combat irregular migration. One manager lauded the EUTF as a successful instrument for the Central Mediterranean because of its capacity to 'achieve results'. He brushed away the criticism of human rights and international organisations that migrants were being brought back to Libya: 'at least we are present', he scoffed, 'we know that the Libyan Coast Guard is corrupt. But our strategy works! If you look at the numbers, there are way less deaths at sea now, not in absolute but in relative terms'. As the official acknowledged, this way of managing the EU's external maritime border included risks and came with its load of controversies given the tensions. Another EU official, this time working for the External Action Service (EEAS), asserted to me that if migrants were rescued in the Libyan SRR, 'they should go back to Libya'. She complained that some NGOs were being disruptive when they did not follow the LYCG's instructions, adding 'sorry, but within the Libyan SRR they need to be brought back to Libya. Each country has to manage its borders.' NGOs, on the other hand, asserted that they were following international law by refusing to hand people over to the LYCG or step aside for the LYCG to conduct rescues.

So, what has enabled the operational advantage of the LYCG to prevail in time despite them acting within international waters which have been characterised as 'unmanageable'[61] and where freedom of navigation is a fundamental norm limiting sovereign power over the seas?[62] To answer this question, it helps to more closely examine the issue of authority in global governance. In his recent book, Michael Zürn notes that there is something puzzling about international relations and global governance when we start to look more closely at the issue of authority and obedience.[63] According to him, subordination without force in global governance should be a central issue for

[60] See for example European Commission, *A European Agenda on Migration* (2015).

[61] Dickson, 'Mobility Control in Ungovernable Spaces', 8. [62] Ibid., 10.

[63] M. Zürn, *A Theory of Global Governance: Authority, Legitimacy, and Contestation* (Oxford University Press, 2018).

scholarly enquiry for four reasons.[64] He says, firstly, that states rarely give up their sovereignty or only in very specific situations, then, that global governance institutions came after states in a historical perspective (so states are not 'born' into the authority of IOs) and states have developed many mechanisms to question obligations stemming from the international realm, and, finally, IOs (including the European Union) do not induce obedience or compliance because of a domination through resources since they do not employ large amounts of people. Moving away from rationalist and constructivist conceptions of global authority, he develops the notion of reflexive authority,[65] to revisit the concept of authority under conditions of global governance. Reflexive authorities 'depend on the epistemic constructions that identify the limits of subordinates and the realm of superiority of an authority'.[66] Because command and deference are not at the heart of this theory of authority, the social processes in which 'superior knowledge' or 'an impartial perspective'[67] is established become of utmost importance. Zürn then speaks of the objectivisation and institutionalisation of authority under global governance, which are necessary for operational hierarchy to be imposed.

With the Libyan SRR both of those processes are at play: they are essential for understanding how such a criticised, conflictual, and contested way[68] of governing the EU's external border can be maintained in time. The authority of the IMO plays an important role here. An authority relationship is objectivised when the 'knowledge order that underlies the relationship becomes a dominant worldview or ideology that reaches beyond the immediately involved actors to external audiences'.[69] Although the notification made by Libya to the IMO was voluntary and sovereign, the IMO participates in the process of objectivising the institutions relating to the control and coordination

[64] Ibid., pp. 37–40.
[65] Reflexive, public authority is based on epistemic foundations. It leads to deference through 'the recognition of the authority as worth observing', Ibid., p. 45.
[66] Ibid., p. 46. [67] Ibid., p. 47.
[68] Human Rights organisations such as Human Rights Watch and Amnesty International have heavily criticised the EU's delegated return of migrants to Libya over the past years, UN organisations UNHCR and IOM have also condemned the return of migrants and refugee to Libya.
[69] Zürn, *A Theory of Global Governance: Authority, Legitimacy, and Contestation*, p. 49.

of the area, including JRCC Tripoli. The coordinates of the zone are uploaded to the GISIS, a centralised database of shipping information containing everything from contact for authorities and authorised organisations relating to IMO questions, to relevant regulations and marine data. The EU and European coastal maritime states such as Italy and Malta then take part in the second part of the legitimation of the LYCG, through institutionalising it; according to Zürn still, the institutionalisation of authority takes place when decisions and interpretations can be delegated or pooled.[70] This is exactly what is enabled by the establishment of the Libyan SRR: neighbouring European RCCs can delegate rescue and the interpretation of whether a case constitutes a distress case or whether a rescue needs to be coordinated by the LYCG. It is important to point out that although there is proximity between authority and legitimacy, they cannot simply be merged by defining authority as legitimate power. There is a *process* of legitimation which participates in the hierarchisation of authority of the LYCG. Added to the fact they are backed up by coercive force, they can act as a policing force in international waters despite having no formal mandate to act as one.

The formalisation of the authority of the LYCG provided a basis for justification of measures I described in the rescue scenes earlier. For example, disobeying the orders of the so-described 'legitimate' coordination authority provided state authorities with the grounds to strip the *Aquarius* of its flag whilst it was still at sea. Similar other capillary effects are to be observed in the augmented capacity for states to argue against NGOs in cases of criminalisation. In June 2018, the NGO ship MV *Lifeline* entered the port of Valetta after having rescued 234 people in the Libyan SRR.[71] During the rescue operation, MRCC Rome had initially coordinated the rescue and allocated a SAR number to it but they had then informed the captain of the *Lifeline* that the LYCG had taken over the coordination. The captain, judging that Tripoli could not be considered a safe place of disembarkation for the survivors, had then sailed north, considering the port of Valetta as the next port of call. Malta had then not allowed the *Lifeline* to land. The captain

70 Ibid.

71 The description of the event is taken from Moreno-Lax, V., D. Ghezelbash, and N. Klein, 'Between Life, Security and Rights: Framing the Interdiction of "Boat Migrants" in the Central Mediterranean and Australia' (2019) 32 *Leiden Journal of International Law* 715–40 at 724–26.

had finally decided to enter the territorial water and port. Importantly, Malta accused the captain of 'reportedly ignor[ing] instructions of the responsible authority, i.e. the Libyan Coast Guard'.[72] The captain was subsequently arrested, and the ship was impounded.

Operating in the Libyan SRR meant having to collaborate with the recognised authority associated with the zone. However, if this given authority insisted that rescued individuals, migrants, or refugees be taken back to Libya, then NGOs or any other vessel having conducted a rescue faced a situation where they were stuck between a rock and a hard place: either they disobeyed orders and had to face the likely retaliation of European states, refusing or delaying the disembarkation of survivors on European shores. Or they obeyed the orders, and in doing so were in violation of the *non-refoulement* principle in international law. These frames of reference are themselves related to the 'institutionalised power embedded in scalar relations':[73] geopolitical stakes are at play in a moment of tense negotiations over the lives of those who have been turned into political chess pieces. This, to the extent that it is more than a simple clash of legal references, but a clash of who is given the right to act and operate in a newly governed zone.

Conclusive Remarks: The Power to Redraw Borders

In June 2020, over a hundred NGOs and individuals wrote to the IMO to request the revocation of the formal recognition of the Libyan SRR.[74] The signatories of the letter denounced the zone being used 'opportunistically' to create a 'fictional account' allowing states and the EU to abdicate their duties under international law. Evoking the

[72] Quoted in D. Ghezelbash, V. Moreno-Lax, N. Klein, and B. Opeskin, 'Securitization of Search and Rescue at Sea: The Response to Boat Migration in the Mediterranean and Offshore Australia' (2018) 67 *International and Comparative Law Quarterly* 315–51 at 317.

[73] A. Çağlar and N. Glick Schiller, *Migrants & City-Making: Dispossession, Displacement, and Urban Regeneration* (Duke University Press, 2018), p. 9.

[74] Statewatch, *Press Release: Hundreds of NGOs and Individuals Call for the Revocation of Libya's Maritime Search and Rescue Zone* (29 June 2020). Available at: www.statewatch.org/news/2020/june/press-release-hundreds-of-ngos-and-individuals-call-for-the-revocation-of-libya-s-maritime-search-and-rescue-zone/ (accessed 10 February 2022)

IMO's role as the 'guardian of the law of the sea', whose responsibility it was to uphold UNCLOS and the SOLAS and SAR conventions, they appealed to the IO's legitimising role in upholding the LYCG's authority.[75] The zone still exists today and pull-backs to Libya have increased every year since 2017,[76] despite the outcry.

An ethnographic and multi-scalar approach to the TLC over responsibility for rescue in the Central Mediterranean provides insights both into the manifestations of authority in the governance of the EU's external border, and into how this authority can be maintained in time. The IMO objectivises the LYCG's authority by continuing to recognise the Libyan SRR. The EU and its member states then participate in the institutionalisation of the LYCG by integrating JRCC Tripoli into the operational procedures that are adopted in case of a distress case being declared in the extensive section of international waters. The material translation of this institutionalisation is then experienced by NGOs having to negotiate or interact with the LYCG when they try to conduct rescues, but also by migrants who testify to being chased by the coast guard or intercepted repeatedly when they try to flee Libya by the sea. This institutionalisation justifies the technical and material support such as patrol boats and trainings offered by EU authorities to the LYCG since 2017.[77]

The externalisation of migration control, which has accompanied other processes of privatisation of migration control and securitisation since the end of the Cold War,[78] has rendered the departure and transit of migrants wanting to head for Europe increasingly difficult. Migration policies from states of the global North are dominated by the deterrence paradigm[79] in which policies and practices

[75] Ibid.

[76] FIDH, ECCHR, and Lawyers for Justice in Libya, *No Way Out: Migrants and Refugees Trapped in Libya Face Crimes against Humanity* (2021) p. 44.

[77] see Amnesty International, *Libya's Dark Web of Collusion: Abuses against Europe-Bound Refugees and Migrants*, pp. 45–47.

[78] T. Spijkerboer, 'The Global Mobility Infrastructure: Reconceptualising the Externalisation of Migration Control' (2018) 20 *European Journal of Migration and Law* 452–69.

[79] T. Gammeltoft-Hansen and N. Feith Tan, 'Beyond the Deterrence Paradigm in Global Refugee Policy' (2016) 39 *Suffolk Transnational Law Review* 637–50; N. Feith Tan and T. Gammeltoft-Hansen, 'A Topographical Approach to Accountability for Human Rights Violations in Migration Control' (2020) 21 *German Law Journal* 335–54; Spijkerboer, 'The Global Mobility Infrastructure: Reconceptualising the Externalisation of Migration Control';

of externalisation push the occurrences and manifestations of border enforcement and control, always further from the territorial borders of the states sponsoring these policies. In the Central Mediterranean, the imperative of securing the EU's external maritime border has been mixed with the duty posed by international regulations to preserve life at sea. The empowerment of the LYCG since 2017 has enabled a form of 'contactless control'[80] from the part of EU authorities, mixing these two imperatives of border control and 'rescue', whilst limiting their responsibility and accountability for the rights violations induced by these deterrence policies. In the Central Mediterranean, the policing competence of a specific actor – the LYCG – has been inflated under the discourse of increasing rescue capabilities. Simultaneously, overlapping protection regimes of international refugee and human rights law are disregarded or, as Moreno-Lax has claimed, 'deflate[d]'.[81]

The actions of IOs, such as the EU and the IMO redraw international borders both physically and immaterially. The emergence of the Libyan SRR, with the forms of authority associated with it, not only renders the maritime border more impassable for migrants fleeing across the Mediterranean Sea and attempting to reach Europe. It also trickles into the argumentation of states in their attempts to criminalise rescue NGOs. The methodological flexibility offered by more ethnographic approaches to global governance helps to highlight the processual dynamics involved in the formation of authority in spaces of jurisdictional overlaps. In the case of the governance of the EU's external border, I have shown how under the guise precisely of *increasing* the preservation of life at sea, the Libyan SRR has rather exacerbated a politics of irresponsibility for rescue and disembarkation in places of safety. TLCs are not just about legal fragmentation entailing dilemmas of interpretation for international lawyers longing for a long-lost single source of normative validity. They are dynamic

M. Casas-Cortes, S. Cobarrubias, and J. Pickles, '"Good Neighbours Make Good Fences": Seahorse Operations, Border Externalization and Extra-territoriality' (2016) 23 *European Urban and Regional Studies* 231–51.

80 V. Moreno-Lax and M. Giuffré, 'The Rise of Consensual Containment: From "Contactless Control" to "Contactless Responsibility" for Forced Migration Flows' in S. S. Juss (ed.), *Research Handbook on International Refugee Law*, (Edward Elgar Publishing, 2017), pp. 82–108.

81 Moreno-Lax, 'Protection at Sea and the Denial of Asylum', p. 484.

interactions in which particular hierarchies of power and exclusion get sedimented in and through legal orders. Paying close attention to the different types of manifestations of authority within TLCs provides an analytical framework for examining how these hierarchies are made to persist in time within the multi-polar landscape of global governance.

9 *Placeholders*

An Archival Journey into the Interim Histories of International Organizations

DANIEL R. QUIROGA-VILLAMARÍN

For all the great hopes placed in these organizations, Geneva in 1920 did not offer more than a disused hotel for the League of Nations (l'Hôtel National) and an old boarding school for the International Labor Organization. The first Assemblies of the League took place in the austere Salle de la Réformation, which was subject to all sorts of criticism by the international press.

G. Meyer, 'Genève et Les Organisations Internationales: une Histoire Locale de 'International'[1]

The delay in securing a permanent site of course increased the problems of organization [...] At first everything [in New York] was improvised. The Assembly that year had to take place in a converted skating rink at Flushing Meadows on Long Island, in buildings which had once been part of the World's Fair. From the end of 1946 both the Secretariat and the Assembly moved to Lake Success, outside New York, camping in the buildings of a disused gyroscope factory.

E. Luard, A History of the United Nations. Vol. 1: The Years of Western Domination, 1945–1955

Introduction

Almost exactly a century ago,[2] on April 26, 1921, the Establishment Officer of the League of Nations (LoN) Howard Huston alerted his

[1] My own translation. Thereafter, any material in French or Spanish will be translated in the same way.

[2] This chapter draws from, and expands, some of my previous work. See D. R. Quiroga Villamarín, '"Suitable Palaces": Navigating Layers of World Ordering at the Centre William Rappard (1923–2013)' (2023) 27 *Architectural Theory Review* 19–40; D. R. Quiroga-Villamarín, 'The Americas and the United Nations: Reimagining Good Neighborliness for a Global Era (1939–1973)' in

colleagues about an impending "housing crisis within the Secretariat."[3] In a memorandum directed to Herbert Ames – the first Financial Director of the LoN – Huston requested an immediate increase of funds to expand the working capacity of the then headquarters of the League: a building called the National Hotel (*l'Hôtel National*). In his request, Huston clarified that these measures were urgently needed due to the enlargement of the Economic Section of the League and the division between the Health and the Social Section. But above all, the creation of an Armaments Section – which was later renamed as the more fitting *Dis*armaments Section – demanded a spatial expansion without parallel in the early years of this nascent international organization (IO). Huston, in particular, demanded the approval of an additional expenditure of 1,000 gold francs per month. This would be destined for the renting of a neighboring property. Indeed, one of the reasons that had convinced League officials of acquiring the *Hôtel National* for the enormous price of 5,500,000 gold francs was that this property had nearby plots or venues that could be incorporated as the IO grew.[4] But above all, the dignified architecture and structure of the *Hôtel* had convinced the League to choose this site for its first permanent dwelling. In fact, Eric Drummond – first Secretary-General of the organization – considered that this was the only site in Geneva that could meet the expectations of the organization.[5] While local press outlets saw this as a lavish choice – as it gave the staff "a kind of high life in offices which had been hotel rooms overlooking [l]ake [Leman]"[6] – Drummond instead believed that the institution had finally settled in a building whose "dimensions, style, and architectural beauty are worthy of the great international task that lies before

J. M. Amaya-Castro, L. Betancur Restrepo, L. Obregón, and D. R. Quiroga-Villamarín (eds.), *The Oxford Handbook of International Law and the Americas* (Oxford University Press, forthcoming in 2025).

3 'Memorandum to Herbert Ames', April 26, 1921, in League of Nations Archives (LoNA) R1536. Thereafter, any archival materials are scanned on file with the author. I thank Jacques Oberson and his team at the LoNA for their guidance. I am also grateful to Anne Françoise Fraser and her team at the United Nations Archives and Record Management Section (UNARMS).

4 'Vente par la Société de l'Hôtel National et la Société de l'Industrie des Hôtels a la Société de Nations', September 28, 1920, in LoNA R1534.

5 'Mémorandum a l'égard de l'achat de l'Hôtel National à Genève', 1920, in LoNA R1536. 3.

6 M. Housden, *League of Nations and the Organisation of Peace* (Pearson Longman, 2012). 15.

the League."[7] Regardless of this lofty statement, by the early twenties, it was becoming evident to those toiling within the *Hôtel* that its walls were growing increasingly small for the League.[8]

If it was raining at the LoN, next door at the International Labor Organization (ILO) it was pouring. A year or so after Huston's memorandum, the ILO governing body adopted a similarly strongly phrased memorandum in relation to its own limitations of space.[9] With the French national Albert Thomas at its helm, the ILO had found its first permanent dwelling in the basement of the *Institut International d'Education la Châtelain* in 1920, often called the Thudichum school after its rector.[10] This edifice would eventually be refashioned as the Carlton Hotel, and later would become the site of the International Committee of the Red Cross – but that is a story for another occasion.[11] For our purposes, we must note that, by 1921, ILO officials were increasingly at odds with the basement of this boarding school. In their opinion, the limited space "does not r[e]ach even a reasonable standard from the hygienic point of view, to say nothing of it allowing the space necessary for really efficient work."[12] In fact, these ILO bureaucrats – not unlike myself – were toiling in a cramped space in the wake of a global pandemic. For that reason, we can easily sympathize with their concerns related to their hunch that the "high rate of sickness this winter has been partly due to the inadequacy of the present accommodation."[13] And even in the face of these limitations, this IO was constantly expected to grow. If for Huston the main problem before the League was the inauguration of the Armaments Section, for the ILO the rising

[7] Ibid, 3.

[8] Not to mention a scare related to a fire, which sapped the morale of many working in this pioneer institution. See 'Memorandum regarding the Indemnity of the Fire of December 12, 1920', January 14, 1921, in LoNA R1536.

[9] 'Installation du Bureau International du Travail: Extrait du Report du Comité du Budget Approuvé par le Conseil d'Administration et Mémoire Présenté par le Directeur', June 1, 1922, in LoNA R1536.

[10] M. Viple, 'Les singulières mais prodigieuses années du BIT' (2019) 65 *Message* 17–20. 17.

[11] E. M., 'Le nouveau siege du Comite international de la Croix-Rouge' (1946) 28/336 *Revue Internationale de la Croix-Rouge* 1026–27; J. Billaud, 'Masters of Disorder: Rituals of Communication and Monitoring at the International Committee of the Red Cross' (2020) 28 *Social Anthropology* 96–111. 96–7.

[12] 'Installation du Bureau International du Travail', 16 (in English). For French, see 3.

[13] Ibid.

tensions came from the ever-expanding library. And these preoccupations were only related to the edifices that served as the working places for the full-time staff of these institutions. The limitations of space also extended to the lack of proper infrastructures for parliamentary meetings. At this early stage of the history of IOs, the ILO and League assemblies were held awkwardly either at the Casino *Kursaal* (nowadays the Fairmont Grand Hotel) or the *Salle de la Réformation* – also called the *Calvinium*(!), demolished in 1969.[14] Both were fairly inconvenient in terms of logistics or acoustics.[15] The former was described by its contemporaries as a "barn-like structure situated at the other end of Geneva and intended for [...] Calvinist worship" while the latter was seen as "a sort of combined vaudeville show and dance hall."[16]

A careful reading of the traces and silences found in the archival collections of these early IOs shows that infrastructural and spatial anxieties were the bread and butter of the everyday operations of global governance. More often than not, the lofty goals of the pursuit of peace were punctuated by the routine malfunction of machinery, the occasional industrial fire, and the general displeasures of overcrowded offices. The men – and rarely but increasingly, women[17] – that served as the pioneering cohorts of international civil servants had (just like any contemporary reader) to muster the resources and navigate the constraints imposed upon them by their built environments – and often to their chagrin. This is especially true to those involved in the so-called first generation of IOs, which through luck and improvisation produced knowledge and practices that later came to define the operations of future international institutions.[18]

[14] R. B. Henig, *The League of Nations* (Haus Publishing, 2010). 72.

[15] 'Letter from Establishment Officer Huston to Secretary General Drummond on the offer of the Kursaal', November 5, 1921, in LoNA R1536. 1. See also A. Call, 'The Fifth Assembly of the League of Nations' (1924) 86 *Advocate of Peace through Justice* 600–606. 600.

[16] C. H. Ellis, *The Origin, Structure & Working of the League of Nations* (The Lawbook Exchange, 2003). 170.

[17] S. Pedersen, 'Women at Work in the League of Nations Secretariat' in H. Egginton and Z. Thomas (eds.), *Precarious Professionals* (University of London Press, 2021), pp. 181–204.

[18] T. Kahlert, K. Gram-Skjoldager, and H. A. Ikonomou, 'Introduction' in K. Gram-Skjoldager, H. A. Ikonomou, and T. Kahlert (eds.), *Organizing the 20th-century World: International Organizations and the Emergence of International Public Administration, 1920–1960s* (Bloomsbury Academic, 2020), pp. 1–12. 2.

And yet, the anxieties and promises that space and architecture posed for these networks of transnational governance are, by and large, absent from our scholarly accounts. Sinclair's recent monograph on the history of IOs in international law, for instance, tells us a nuanced and rich account of the intellectual history of Thomas's tenure and the context of the early ILO without mentioning the frustrations that the organization faced in the crowded basements of *La Châteleine* or its eventual displacement to the Bloch property in Geneva – a building that today hosts the World Trade Organization – also a story for another time.[19] In the neighboring fields of international and global history, the surge of interest in the study of internationalisms has not necessarily been accompanied by a careful interrogation of the spaces and venues of IOs. The *Hotêl National*, for example, only appears in two sentences of Sluga's (masterful, to be sure) history of internationalisms,[20] while Pedersen's groundbreaking monograph on the League's Mandate system tell us little about the material investments behind the so-called l'espirit de Genève.[21] Most accounts, in other words, divorce their analysis of actors, ideas, or norms from the seemingly banal histories of the "buildings, staffs, and letterheads."[22] While the "human component" of IOs has been submitted to an increased scrutiny in international history,[23] and in the aftermath of "biographical turn" to "people with projects" in international law,[24] the non-human and more-than-human elements of international institutions have remained largely unexplored. These elements, moreover, warrant study for it is within those very concrete

[19] On the early ILO, see G. F. Sinclair, *To Reform the World: International Organizations and the Making of Modern States* (Oxford University Press, 2017). 29–47. See also D. Maul, *The International Labour Organization: 100 Years of Global Social Policy* (De Gruyter, 2019). On this story, see Quiroga-Villamarín, 'Suitable Palaces'.

[20] G. Sluga, *Internationalism in the Age of Nationalism* (University of Pennsylvania Press, 2013). 54.

[21] S. Pedersen, *The Guardians: The League of Nations and the Crisis of Empire* (Oxford University Press, 2017). 7. The same is true for S. Ghervas, *Conquering Peace: From the Enlightenment to the European Union* (Harvard University Press, 2021). 148–219.

[22] K. Raustiala, 'Governing the Internet' (2016) 110 *American Journal of International Law* 491–503. 502.

[23] Kahlert, Gram-Skjoldager, and Ikonomou, 'Introduction'. 2.

[24] I. de la Rasilla, *International Law and History: Modern Interfaces* (Cambridge University Press, 2021). 308–338.

"rooms" in which international lawmaking operations take place – imposing constraints and providing resources for those engaged in this sort of work.[25]

What is more, "IOs are inclined to define their own histories by writing 'official histories' themselves [... and s]uch official histories maybe be written by insiders, who lack a scientific or critical regard," as Reinalda duly noted.[26] This fact is even more salient when it comes to the literature on edifices of IOs, which often follows the genre of coffee table literature – highlighting hagiographic narratives of progress and downplaying moments of tension and conflict.[27] The literature, if at all, might present us with a rosy picture of the grand palaces that eventually came to host IOs, but will remain stubbornly silent with regards to the rather precarious and improvised locales that actually came to serve the fledging system of IOs in their infancy. Conversely, in this chapter, I draw from, and contribute to, the recent or forthcoming works that bring the study of material culture, space, and art and architecture into the conversation on global governance.[28] In this vein, I trace a history of the interim dwellings of IOs, arguing that a study of the built environments that haphazardly nested these institutions might reveal much about the structural limitations and jurisdictional

[25] D. R. Quiroga-Villamarín, 'Staging Grounds: Dialectics of the Spectacular and the Infrastructural in International Conference-hosting' (2023) 11 *London Review of International Law* 349–377.

[26] B. Reinalda, 'Biographical Analysis: Insights and Perspectives from the IO BIO' in K. Gram-Skjoldager, H. A. Ikonomou, and T. Kahlert (eds.), *Organizing the 20th-century World: International Organizations and the Emergence of International Public Administration, 1920–1960s* (Bloomsbury Academic, 2020), pp. 15–32. 17.

[27] To paraphrase the history of design scholar Tania Messell, editor of the volume T. Messell, A. J. Clarke, and J. Aynsley (eds.), *International Design Organizations: Histories, Legacies, Values* (Bloomsbury, 2022). On hagiography in the history of internationalism and IOs, see D. Rodogno, 'Certainty, Compassion and the Ingrained Arrogance of Humanitarians', in N. Wylie, M. Oppenheimer, and J. Crossland (eds.), *The Red Cross Movement: Myths, Practices and Turning Points* (Manchester University Press, 2020), pp. 27–44. 29.

[28] C. Biltoft, 'Sundry Worlds within the World: Decentered Histories and Institutional Archives' (2020) 31 *Journal of World History* 729–760; C. N. Biltoft, *A Violent Peace: Media, Truth, and Power at the League of Nations* (The University of Chicago Press, 2021); R. Bavaj, K. Lawson, and B. Struck (eds.), *Doing Spatial History* (Routledge, 2021); A. Iriye and P. Goedde, *International History: A Cultural Approach* (Bloomsbury Academic, 2022).

boundaries of these "delicate machines" of world ordering.[29] To do so, after this short introduction, we return to (2) the ironically named *Hôtel National*. Then, (3) we cross the Atlantic to the early United Nations complex in Lake Success and Flushing Meadows in the state of New York. This will allow me to (4) conclude with some remarks on the relevance of primary sources and archival research in the theory and history of international law and IOs.

A Contradiction in Terms? The Hotel National, Home to the International Community

In an "irony of history," the first permanent dwellings of one of the pioneering twentieth-century IOs was the former *Hôtel National*.[30] From there, the League "overflowed into two or three surrounding buildings."[31] As I mentioned earlier, its acquisition had been partly prompted by Drummond's desire of finding a *dignified* site for the IO – and the *Hôtel*, for him, was the only serious option that Geneva offered.[32] But most dramatically, the acquisition of this edifice was also prompted by the attempt of other cities to dethrone Geneva as the foremost site of interwar internationalism.[33] As noted in the epigraph, spectators in both Switzerland and abroad were painfully cognizant of the fact that, "[f]or all the great hopes placed in these organisations, Geneva in 1920 did not offer more than a disused hotel for the [LoN] and an old boarding school for the [ILO]."[34] To be sure, Genevese and Swiss authorities were aware of this. William Rappard, who had served as the chief Swiss negotiator at the Paris

[29] To paraphrase the speech that the Unitedstatesean President Truman delivered at the 1945 San Francisco conference. *Public Papers of the Presidents of the United States – Harry S. Truman 1945* (United States Government Printing Office, 1961). 21.

[30] Ellis, *The Origin, Structure & Working of the League of Nations*. 170–1.

[31] Ibid.

[32] 'Mémorandum a l'égard de l'achat de l'Hôtel National à Genève', 1920, in LoNA R1536. 3. On the importance of "dignity and gravitas" in the history of English courtroom design, see L. Mulcahy, *Legal Architecture: Justice, Due Process and the Place of Law* (Routledge, 2010). 9.

[33] J. Kuntz, *Geneva and the Call of Internationalism: A History* (Editions Zoé, 2011). 48.

[34] Meyer, 'Genève et les organisations internationales: une histoire locale de l'international'. 91.

peace negotiations, knew that other European municipalities were competing to oust Geneva – something that would be unacceptable to his Swiss constituency. The mere fact the Viennese newspaper *Freien Presse* had published a call for furniture supply for the secretariat had angered local businessmen, as it made them doubt whether the League had "the restoration of Swiss industry from its present depression at heart."[35] In fact, Brussels had almost outbid Geneva when the League's Council recommended that the US President Wilson convene the first assembly in Belgium in 1920.[36] While Geneva was saved by Wilson's "friendly and spontaneous" gesture to prefer the neutrality of Switzerland over the *revanchisme* of the recently invaded Belgium,[37] this episode convinced Rappard and the President of the Swiss Confederation, Giuseppe Motta, that now it was their turn to reciprocate. Had it not been for the personal rapport between Wilson and Rappard, perhaps Geneva "might well be nothing more than a cantonal capital."[38]

The first Swiss overture to sway the League to stay in Geneva came in the form of a tax exemption in 1920. At that time, the Genevese *Conseil d'État* decided not to charge the LoN for the *droits de mutation et des transcription* (a tax related to the acquisition of property) of the *Hôtel National*, which amounted almost to 700,000 gold francs.[39] The majority of the council members favored the exoneration as a way to support the League and show their commitment to its historical mission – and pivotal role in warranting Swiss neutrality and

[35] 'Letter from Establish'ment Officer Huston to Mr. E. Koch, Président du Schweizwache Verband', July 25, 1922, in LoNA R1536. 1.

[36] Kuntz, *Geneva and the Call of Internationalism*. 56–57; R. de Groof, 'Promoting Brussels as a Political World Capital: From the National Jubilee of 1905 to Expo 58' in R. de Groof (ed.), *Brussels and Europe: Acta of the International Colloquium on Brussels and Europe* (ASP, 2009), pp. 97–126. 110–114.

[37] D. Hunter Miller, *The Drafting of the Covenant – Volume Two* (G.P. Putnam's Sons, 1928). 365–368; L. E. Ambrosius, *Woodrow Wilson and the American Diplomatic Tradition: The Treaty Fight in Perspective* (Cambridge University Press, 1990). 119; J.-C. Pallas, *Histoire et architecture du Palais des Nations (1924–2001): l' art déco au service des relations internationales* (Nations Unies, 2001). 21.

[38] J. Kuntz and E. Murray, *Centre William Rappard: Home of the World Trade Organization* (WTO, 2011). 12.

[39] 'Geneve Siege de la Societe des Nations' in *Journal de Genève du Mardi 21 Septembre 1920*. LoNA R1534. See further J. Kuntz, *Genève internationale: 100 ans d'architecture* (Éditions Slatkine, 2017). 17.

independence. And yet, a minority of socialists, led by M. Burklin, argued against the measure, claiming that the state could not afford to exonerate the payment of this tax amid the acute housing crisis which affected the local working class. Along these lines, M. Nicole stated that the League represented the interests of the international capitalist class, which is why the only stable peace could be built by the international workers' movement. In the end, the socialist faction remained adamant, tallying twenty-two votes against the majority's sixty-two votes to exonerate the tax. In the following weeks the Council, presided by Paul Pictet, published its official decision to exonerate, laying the first stone upon which "International Geneva" was erected.[40] Indeed, it was only after this that the Federal and local authorities began investing heavily in infrastructure "to live up to the privilege of being chosen."[41] In the years that followed, Geneva witnessed the opening of a new railway station (named *Cornavin*), an airport (named *Cointrin*), and a series of infrastructures for communications and transport technologies.

Despite this tax exemption, the League still paid a hefty amount to acquire the *Hôtel*. While it had been originally erected in the late 1870s to create a luxurious hotel on the right bank of the lake (*rive droite*), it failed to reach commercial success. Not only did its construction costs exceed the initial expectations (leading to the dramatic suicide by defenestration of one of its initial owners),[42] but its location in the then-outskirts of Geneva failed to attract wealthy clients. Even in the 1920s and 1930s, League officials were skeptical of the *Hôtel's* location "at the extremity of an industrial and working-class neighborhood, still in development."[43] After the Great War, the plans to reopen the edifice as a hotel were quickly scuttled after the League manifested its interest in the property, and it was instead renovated by the architects Marc and Jean Camoletti for a bureaucratic use (Figure 9.1). But even after these repairs, it was clear that "the old

[40] 'Arrété Législatif autorisant le Conseil d'État à exonérer la Société de Nations du paiement des droits de mutation et des inscriptions sur l'achat de l'Hôtel National', September 15, 1920, in LoNA R1534.

[41] Kuntz, *Geneva and the Call of Internationalism*. 67. See also 63.

[42] Kuntz, *Genève internationale*. 24–35.

[43] 'Quatorzieme Seance, tenue à Genève le mardi 19 Janvier à 15 h. 30' in *Procès-verbal de la deuxième session – Jury International d'Architects (Janvier 1926)*, in LoNA R1541/32/49424/28594, 52.

Figure 9.1 *Genève, Hôtel National.* Unknown author (1919). *Bibliothèque de Genève*, vg p 0140 ©.[44]

hotel was not particularly well-suited for administrative functions and as the League's work picked up pace, the leadership of the League Secretariat was struggling to fit the growing number of staff [and] meetings."[45] The spatial layout of the League, in fact, reflected its own internal hierarchies. Unsurprisingly, the top floors were reserved for the higher echelons of staff (Drummond, for instance, used a corner office that overlooked the lake, where former Habsburg aristocrats had spent their nights), with various Sections located in the middle floors of the edifice.[46] "Ancillary services" were relegated to the basement, attic, and the neighboring villas. In 1924, the hotel complex was suggestively renamed *Palais Wilson*, in an homage to the Unitedstatesean President who had strongly vouched for Geneva in the struggle to find a dignified location for the League.

[44] I thank Mr. Alexis Rivier and his team at the *Biliothèque de Genève* for their kind authorization to reproduce this image.

[45] K. Gram-Skjoldager, '"Utterly below Criticism" – Working Conditions in the Palais Wilson 1930' (July 2017) https://projects.au.dk/inventingbureaucracy/blog/show/artikel/utterly-below-criticism-working-conditions-in-the-palais-wilson-1930.

[46] D. Macfadyen, M. Davies, M. Norah Carr, and J. Burley, *Eric Drummond and His Legacies* (Springer, 2019). 90.

All in all, "the pattern that emerges [...] is one of an organisation that is clearly bursting at its seams."[47] The League officials were painfully aware of this, which is why they started to look for new alternatives to move out almost as soon as they moved in. Archival traces from 1925 note that the Secretary-General himself was "experiencing the utmost difficulty in finding office accommodation for the staff. All the available space in the *Hôtel National* has been utilised and further dividing and subdividing [...] is no longer possible."[48] The ILO – which, as seen earlier, was also in a dire place in terms of infrastructure – eventually built its own edifice in another lakeside property donated by the Genevese and Swiss authorities. The fact that they had managed to do so for much less (around 3,000,000 gold francs) was not lost on the League's secretariat. Eventually, after receiving some land donations from the Genevese and Swiss authorities, the League also moved to erect its own purpose-built *Palais des Nations*, the design of which was to be selected through an international competition of architects.[49]

In the meantime, the League tried unsuccessfully to sell the *Hôtel National* to increase the budget for the new edifice. Alas, despite the "untiring efforts which M. Motta [on behalf of the Swiss Confederacy] has made to bring these delicate negotiations to a satisfactory conclusion," the League failed to receive even a single offer for the *Hôtel*.[50] Motta and the Swiss Federation even wanted an assurance that the Helvetic state would complement any private bid so that the League at least received four million gold francs (which was still one and a half million less than it had spent in 1920 to buy the venue). And yet, no offers came. As the global economic situation worsened, it was easy for League officials to look back and conclude, "the acquisition of the *Hôtel National* had not been a brilliant operation but was justified by urgency."[51] The Belgian architect Victor

[47] Gram-Skjoldager, '"Utterly below Criticism" – Working Conditions in the Palais Wilson 1930'.

[48] 'Note by the Secretary General – Supervisory Commission – Construction of a Conference Hall' in LoNA R1540/32/43591/28594. 4–5.

[49] See generally, Pallas, *Histoire et architecture du Palais des Nations (1924–2001)*.

[50] 'Report submitted to the Special Assembly of the Second Committee – Erection of an Assembly Hall and of Annexes for the Use of the Secretariat', March 13, 1926, in LoNA R1542/32/50153/28594. 73.

[51] 'Première Séance tenue le vendredi 22 Janvier 1926, à 11 h. 15.' in *Commission Chargee d'Examiner l'Emplacement de la Future Salle*

Horta – President of the Jury of Architects elected to supervise the erection of the new *Palais* – was even more blunt in his assessment. In his view, the acquisition of the *Hôtel* proved that the League had, "in their efforts to buy a draught horse, mistakenly accepted to purchase an elephant."[52]

The early years of the League, in other words, were tied to this white elephant. Due to the delays and complications, the official *Palais* open its doors only in 1937. But at that time, the League was no longer expanding but was rather on the verge of collapse due to the worsening international climate. Aloft, the *Palais* remained "something of a pristine haunted house,"[53] while most of the technical staff of the League sought refuge in Princeton at the other side of the Atlantic during the second great war.[54] The League's lifetime, in other words, had been marked by its awkward tenure at the *Hôtel*. Indeed, once it became clear selling the *Hôtel* was not possible, the organization did its best to find respite in the limitations of this dwelling. The most salient example of this was the improvised modernist pavilion that was built by the local architect Adolphe Guyonnet in 1931, commissioned for the upcoming Conference for the Reduction and Limitation of Armaments.[55] It was there where the League witnessed one of its most remembered "failures"[56] – as the thirties witnessed a surge towards rearmament and the opening of a new chapter in the twentieth-century European civil war. In its wake, the nascent United Nations organization would also have to find a home to call its own – this time away from the shores of lake Leman. We turn to this now.

des Assemblees et des Nouveaux Batiments du Secretariat, in LoNA R1541/32/49123/28594. 12.

52 Cited in 'Deuxième Commission de l'Assemblee Extraordinaire, tenue à Genève le mercredi 10 mars 1926 a 15 heures' in LoNA R1542/32/50153/28594. 129.

53 C. N. Biltoft, 'Decoding the Balance Sheet: Gifts, Goodwill, and the Liquidation of the League of Nations' (2020) 1 *Capitalism: A Journal of History and Economics* 379–404. 381.

54 P. Clavin, *Securing the World Economy: The Reinvention of the League of Nations, 1920–1946* (Oxford University Press, 2015). 267–304.

55 Kuntz, *Genève internationale*. 30–1.

56 H. A. Ikonomou, 'The Administrative Anatomy of Failure: The League of Nations Disarmament Section, 1919–1925' (2021) 30 *Contemporary European History* 321–334.

Lake Failure: Commuting to the Early United Nations

With the utopian promise of exhibiting "the world of tomorrow," the 1939 World's Fair opened its doors in the Flushing Meadows complex in New York. Originally conceived to promote economic recovery after the sorrows of the Great Depression, the start of the second great war four months later gave its motto a new meaning.[57] "The world of tomorrow" entailed not only a globe changed by the innovations in technology or consumer goods,[58] but also the promise of a new planetary order forged during and after the "scourge of war." As the conflagration dawned in Europe, spectators roamed around the fair's Court of Peace to visit the adjacent national pavilions and the Hall of Nations. While the German Reich had conspicuously withdrawn its participation at the last minute, the Italian Pavilion reminded the fairgoers of the towering vision that the Axis powers wanted to impose on European soil.[59] Not far away, the pavilion of the Second Polish Republic survived exclusively on the private support from the Polish-Unitedstatesean benefactors, as its Government-in-Exile could no longer afford to run it.[60] Defiant – as if aware of the suffering to come – the Soviet and "Jewish Palestinian" pavilions remained not far, articulating their own visions of the world of tomorrow.[61] In the 1939 New York World's Fair, just like the many other international exhibitions that have sprouted in the North Atlantic world since the nineteenth century, the aesthetical, political, and socio-technical dimensions of the world ordering were seamlessly intertwined.[62]

[57] M. Duranti, 'Utopia, Nostalgia and World War at the 1939–40 New York World's Fair' (2006) 41 *Journal of Contemporary History* 663. See further Quiroga-Villamarín, 'The Americas and the United Nations'.

[58] R. W. Rydell, 'Selling the World of Tomorrow: New York's 1939 World's Fair' (1990) 77 *The Journal of American History* 966.

[59] J. J. Fortuna, 'Fascism, National Socialism, and the 1939 New York World's Fair' (2019) 8 *Fascism* 179. 214.

[60] M. S. Kopacz and A. Bajka-Kopacz, 'A Polish King at the World of Tomorrow: A Brief Social History' (2017) 62 *The Polish Review* 73. 80.

[61] See, respectively, A. Swift, 'The Soviet World of Tomorrow at the New York World's Fair, 1939' (1998) 57 *The Russian Review* 364; J. L. Gelvin, 'Zionism and the Representation of "Jewish Palestine" at the New York World's Fair, 1939–1940' (2000) 22 *The International History Review* 37.

[62] D. R. Quiroga-Villamarín, 'All's Fair in Love and War Imperial Gazes and Glaring Omissions at the Expositions Universelles (1851–1915)' (2021) 1 *Cognitio* 1.

After the end of the war, the infrastructure that once had heralded the coming of the "world of tomorrow" in 1939 came to serve a similar purpose in the years after 1945. Initially, the UN would come to use a variety of venues scattered in Long Island while the final headquarters were being erected in Manhattan.[63] The first of those was the Bronx campus of Hunter College (nowadays, CUNY's Lehman College).[64] During the war, the campus had been vacated of students and readapted as a training station for the US Navy WAVES ("women accepted for voluntary emergency service.") Again, improvisation marked the first steps of this new-born IO. The pool in the gym building was covered up with planks to create a makeshift press center – with the *New York Times* relegated to the "hairdrying room."[65] What is more, that same gym room would be the venue for the first strike of the UN personnel of the first (out of many) walkouts of the Soviet Delegation from the Security Council.[66] Later that year, the UN moved to a more "permanent" temporary venue (insofar as they would stay there three to five years): the Sperry Gyroscope Company in Lake Success.[67] Just like Hunter College, the new house of peace had formerly had a military function, as it housed "one of the biggest war plants in the New York area, and one of the most secret, closely guarded factories anywhere in the world."[68] While 118 residents of Lake Success voted in favor (with 70 against) of becoming "the world's capital city," the refurbished military factory was still far from perfect.[69] The *New York Times*, for instance, raised "violent objections [...] on the inadequacy of press facilities" of both the Lake Success and the Hunter College makeshift headquarters.[70] Perhaps as a revenge for its time in the College's "hairdrying" room, the *Times* complained that – unlike in

[63] R. Barreneche, *A Home to the World: The United Nations and New York City* (Oro Editions, 2020).

[64] *1946: The Early Days of the U.N. Inspire an International Legacy at Lehman College* (Lehman College of Media Relations and Publications, 2008). 2.

[65] *1946: The Early Days of the U.N.* 7.

[66] *1946: The Early Days of the U.N.* 11 and 3.

[67] 'Conference and General Services – Building and maintenance – lease – Sperry plant – Lake Success', January 12, 1948, in UNARMS S-0472-0050-0018-00001. 6.

[68] F. Wickware, 'Elmer Sperry and His Magic Top' (1943) 169 *Scientific American* 66–84. 67.

[69] 'Welcome to Lake Success' (1946) *Special to the New York Times* 19.

[70] 'Press Is Irritated by Seating in U.N.' (1946) *Special to the New York Times* 3.

the League's edifices – the UN's Long Island sites "have separated bar and lounge facilities" for delegates and the press. Moreover, the lack of space forced the UN to reject more than 2,500 requests for seats, as only 385 of the 732 places of the new Council Chamber were available for the public. The battle waged by the press for more space in the room was paralleled by a similar international dispute between the US and Soviet delegations in relation to the admission of new member states to the IO.[71] In sum, the walls of Hunter College ended up being too small to host "international society."

To resolve this, the UN turned towards the leftover infrastructure from the 1939 fair. From then on, the "New York City Building" (nowadays the Queens Museum) housed the UN General Assembly from 1946 to 1950 (Figure 9.2). This was initially confusing for the "delegates, visitors[,] and [journalists]" who were flabbergasted to arrive at an international building that had the words "[*The*] *City of New York* emblasoned in black letters across the façade."[72] Be that as it may, it was in the Flushing Meadows complex, in fact, that the UN's partition plan for Palestine was voted in 1947 – not far away from the "Jewish Palestinian" pavilion, which was situated roughly halfway between the New York building and the Court of Peace. Even the old fair's railroad service was reopened by the Long Island Rail Road system, allowing for a relatively straightforward commute from New York's Penn Station every half an hour or so to the newly renamed "United Nations station" in Flushing Meadows. The interim headquarters at Lake Success, however, were a bit more difficult to reach, as the route required delegates and staff to take a train to the Great Neck and then hail a bus.[73] Tired of these "intramural headaches," the Secretary-General Lie urged for the creation of a *national home* for "[t]he wandering United Nations, now shuttling between a fair building and a reconverted factory, [... desperate to] have a place to call its own."[74]

71 T. Hamilton, 'Russia Rebuffs US: Rejects Plan Offered for Admission of All the Applicants to U.N.' (1946) *Special to the New York Times* 1–2. See also 'United Nations Oral History Project. Interview with Ambassador W. Tapley Bennett by James S. Sutterlin on "The Founding of the United Nations"'. 3–4.

72 'Designation of Building Confuses U.N. Audience' (1946) *Special to the New York Times* 4.

73 ARRT'S Archives, 'United Nations Station and Service' (May 2015).

74 'Pleas for UN Home Moves Delegates', September 24, 1947, *the New York Times*, in UNARMS S-0593-0002-0003. The phrasing "national home" is mine, not Lie's.

Figure 9.2 United Nations Temporary Headquarters. Unknown author (1947). *UN Multimedia*, UN7720617 ©.[75]

In this sense, the 1939 fair's "Hall of Nations" was but an early dress rehearsal for the posterior negotiations related to the creation of a "United Nations Organisation." And yet – just like the *Hôtel National* in the case of the League – one finds little to no references in the literature in relation to the everyday geographies of the early days of these IOs.[76] This is unsurprising, given the hegemonic hold of the methodological benchmarks of intellectual history on the field of the theory and history of international law and international institutions.[77] But for the men and women who toiled within these IOs, spatial, architectural, and infrastructural considerations were anything but ancillary. The same was true, I suggest, for the leading state and non-state actors that were involved in the financing and erection of these sites.

[75] Permission granted by the UN Multimedia Resources Unit on April 18, 2024.

[76] To paraphrase R. E. Sullivan, *The Geography of the Everyday: Toward an Understanding of the Given* (University of Georgia Press, 2017).

[77] D. R. Quiroga-Villamarín, 'Beyond Texts? Towards a Material Turn in the Theory and History of International Law' (2021) 23 *Journal of the History of International Law* 466–500.

As we have seen, both in Geneva and in New York, the "location, location, location" of an IO was a hotly contested affair – intimately tangled with questions of national jealousy, international rivalries, and the "dignity" of international institutions. As we have seen, ideas – on their own – do not erect headquarters; establish bureaucracies; or cross frontiers.[78] To do so, they require land, capital, and labor. In this chapter, I offer but a modest example of how the stories of the political economies of two pioneer IOs can be rewritten into our histories of international institutional law.

Concluding Remarks: Archival Research for International Institutional Law

Given the fixation of international (institutional) lawyers with the history of our (sub)discipline and its "founding fathers,"[79] one can understand why some might believe that we already *know* everything about the history of our IOs.[80] Indeed, in a discipline where teleological narratives of progress are so pervasive,[81] it is easy to dismiss the early days of the League or the UN as times of inchoate experimentation, only relevant insofar as they pave the way for our own contemporary institutional arrangements.[82] Indeed, until very recently, the League was mostly remembered as a "failed" IO – relegated as a moment of "not yet" in the history of an increasingly sophisticated international order.[83]

But the collective memory of our discipline – just as the one of its individual members – is partial and fickle. To decide to see and

[78] S. Moyn, 'On the Nonglobalization of Ideas', in S. Moyn and A. Sartori (eds.), *Global Intellectual History* (New York: Columbia University Press, 2013), 187–204.

[79] D. R. Quiroga-Villamarín, 'Book Review: Adom Getachew, Worldmaking after Empire' (2022) 24 *Journal of the History of International Law* 589–595.

[80] For a survey of institutionalist approaches to the history of international law, see de la Rasilla, *International Law and History* 283–307.

[81] T. Altwicker and O. Diggelmann, 'How Is Progress Constructed in International Legal Scholarship?' (2014) 25 *European Journal of International Law* 425–444.

[82] See N. Mansouri and D. R. Quiroga-Villamarín, 'Seeing International Organizations Differently', editorial introduction in this volume.

[83] S. Pedersen, 'Back to the League of Nations' (2007) 112 *The American Historical Review* 1091–1117. 1092. See also Mazower, *Governing the World: The History of an Idea, 1815 to the Present.*

remember the League's history as one of failure was a particular disciplinary choice, with important distributive and political implications.[84] The same is true, of course, for the early UN, which quickly had to justify its mandate by contrasting its operations with those of its Geneva-based predecessor. Instead of this tired narrative of "failure," a growing trend of interventions in international law and global history are challenging the "historiographical amnesia" of our standard accounts of the development of IOs.[85] To "unlearn some common tropes,"[86] a new generation of scholars in both fields have delved into the "archives of universal history" of IOs.[87] Within them, as I've tried to show in this chapter, we have found "sundry worlds within the world" – a plethora of traces and silences that bear witness to the quotidian hopes and anxieties that surrounded the lofty project of world ordering through international norms and institutions.[88] This sobering encounter with primary sources and archival collections, I hope, can push international legal scholars to note that perhaps we do not *know* everything about the history of international institutions. In fact, an archival journey often pushes us as researchers to come to understand our "known unknowns" – and more dramatically, to discover we might still have many "unknown unknowns."

This is not to argue that we should take archival collections as pristine repositories of truth, nor that we should approach primary sources without a critical eye. We need not to succumb to the fever of the archive.[89] This is an important point, as some international lawyers have come to mistakenly read all primary source-based historical work as epistemologically modernist and politically conservative.[90] In fact,

[84] Clavin, *Securing the World Economy* 10.

[85] Aloni, *The League of Nations and the Protection of the Environment* 1.

[86] To paraphrase J. d'Aspremont, 'Unlearning Some Common Tropes' in S. Droubi and J. d'Aspremont (eds.), *International Organisations, Non-State Actors, and the Formation of Customary International Law* (Manchester University Press, 2020).

[87] E. Rothschild, 'The Archives of Universal History' (2008) 19 *Journal of World History* 375–401.

[88] Biltoft, 'Sundry Worlds within the World'. 729.

[89] J. Derrida, 'Archive Fever: A Freudian Impression' (1995) 25 *Diacritics* 9–63. 14.

[90] Orford, *International Law and the Politics of History*. See further D. R. Quiroga-Villamarín, 'Friendly Fire: The Politics & Elective Affinities of International Law and the Politics of History' (2023) 9 *Global Intellectual History* 729–744.

some of the leading interventions in the histories of internationalism precisely anchor their narrative in biases and limitations of their archival repositories.[91] This is particularly true for IOs. While their archives "are an extraordinarily fertile, undervalued, underutilised, and endangered source," they have been also compiled and curated following the geopolitical biases and pressures that these institutions faced in their day-to-day activities.[92] It is because of these pressures and biases – and not in spite of them – that the traces and silences found in these primary sources and archival collections have much to say about the ways in which "the international" was forged, negotiated, and contested within these institutions.[93] It is time we, as students and scholars of international institutional law, start listening.

91 G. Sluga, *The Invention of International Order: Remaking Europe after Napoleon* (Princeton University Press, 2021). 253–268.

92 G. Sluga, 'Editorial – The Transnational History of International Institutions' (2011) 6 *Journal of Global History* 219–222. 220.

93 S. Kott, *Organiser le monde: une autre histoire de la guerre froide* (Éditions du Seuil, 2021) 7–8.

People, Practices, and Performance

10 *The Micro-politics of International Commissions*
The Case of Telegraphic Standards

JAN EIJKING

If our aim is to pluralise the 'subjects, methods, and aims' of the academic study of international organisations,[1] then one fairly obvious route to follow is the route of historicisation. But what exactly does historicisation entail, and what added value can it bring to the study of international organisations? This is not always clear. Historians of international organisations have elected a variety of avenues to relate the creation and the design of international institutions to the industrial-capitalist functions they were intended to serve,[2] the diplomatic crises they were intended to solve,[3] the technocratic intellectual legacies of their emergence,[4] and their continuities with imperial forms of governance.[5] Methodologically, accounting for its breadth and strength, this work is characterised by eclecticism and diversity rather than uniformity.[6]

The present chapter aims in this context to illustrate the distinctive contribution of historicisation to our understanding of international organisations. I follow the overall impetus outlined by the editors in two ways. On the one hand, the chapter offers another tool to the methodological toolkit on display across the present volume; on

[1] Introduction to this volume.

[2] C. N. Murphy, *International Organization and Industrial Change: Global Governance Since 1850* (Oxford University Press, 1994).

[3] G. Sluga, *The Invention of International Order: Remaking Europe after Napoleon* (Princeton University Press, 2021).

[4] J. Steffek, *International Organization as Technocratic Utopia* (Oxford University Press, 2021).

[5] J. Morefield, *Covenants without Swords: Idealist Liberalism and the Spirit of Empire* (Princeton University Press, 2005).

[6] For an excellent discussion of this diversity see, E. J. Ravndal, 'Colonies, Semi-sovereigns, and Great Powers: IGO Membership Debates and the Transition of the International System' (2020) 46 *Review of International Studies* 278–98.

the other hand and more specifically, I want to think about what international organisations are from the point of view of their making. To do so, I zoom in on one important moment in the history of modern international organisations: the 1865 commission whose chief purpose it was to determine, at the International Telegraph Conference (ITC) in Paris, the scope and purpose of the first formal and permanent international organisation, the International Telegraph Union (ITU).

Building on previous histories of international organisations, I approach this case through the lens of *micro-politics*, combining biographical and sociological methods. Methodologically I study international organisations by means of biographical membership analysis; theoretically I argue that international organisations cannot be fully understood in separation from the situated political motives of their makers. Below I first outline what a lens of micro-politics entails, and what its methodological consequences are. Second, I sketch out the historical context of mid-nineteenth-century technical international cooperation. Third, I present a micro-political analysis of the 1865 commission. I conclude with some observations for the study of international organisations more broadly.

Micro-politics and Commissions

International commissions, if understood as prototypical international organisations, can be thought of as performances of global governance *avant la lettre*: their choices about membership, qualifications, and the output they generate all reflect certain historically specific understandings of what kinds of social capital are politically valuable, what symbols reflect status, and what acts and actions require special legitimation for whom. We can therefore study them in terms of who lays claim to what, who such a claim is addressed to, and what form of political action gets legitimised as a result. In order to study these inherently subjective influences upon the scope and authority of international organisations, however, extant approaches largely based on rationalist and critical varieties of functionalism are insufficient. Instead I wish to foreground the contingency involved in the making and situating of new organisations, in a space as indeterminate and contested as 'the international'. To do this I argue that we need to pay attention to and indeed follow the individual practitioners concretely invested in the institutionalisation of particular modes of governance.

Attention to practitioners is largely in line with relatively recent trends in the study of international organisations, in both international law and international relations. Scholars from both disciplines have participated in a 'practice turn', which emphasises the performative work at the heart of claims to authority within and between institutional contexts. Vincent Pouliot, for example, applies theoretical insights from the work of Pierre Bourdieu to the study of performed hierarchy and status behaviour in the context of international organisations.[7] Marieke Louis and Lucile Maertens develop a similarly sociological analytical framework for studying the depoliticising work of international organisations.[8] Annabelle Littoz-Monnet makes a strong case for zooming in on the concrete interventions of expert actors operating in delineated policy fields within international organisations.[9] All four scholars share reservations about functionalist conceptions of international organisations, their scope, and their political authority. I build on their work and characterise the underlying orientation as 'micro-political'. Micropolitics is a relatively under-conceptualised shorthand for small-scale political behaviour that gets overlooked for various reasons, whether methodological or theoretical.[10] In the case of international organisations, we may for instance overdetermine the functional purpose apparently fulfilled by an institution and therefore pay little attention to the political contestation involved in defining and prioritising this purpose.

[7] V. Pouliot, *International Pecking Orders: The Politics and Practice of Multilateral Diplomacy* (Cambridge University Press, 2016).

[8] M. Louis and L. Maertens, *Why International Organizations Hate Politics: Depoliticizing the World* (Routledge, 2021).

[9] A. Littoz-Monnet, 'Expert Knowledge as a Strategic Resource: International Bureaucrats and the Shaping of Bioethical Standards' (2017) 61 *International Studies Quarterly* 584–95; A. Littoz-Monnet, 'Exclusivity and Circularity in the Production of Global Governance Expertise: The Making of "Global Mental Health" Knowledge' (2022) 16 *International Political Sociology* olab035.

[10] P. S. Mann, *Micro-politics: Agency in a Postfeminist Era* (University of Minnesota Press, 1994), 1. C. Dörrenbächer, Christoph, and M. Geppert. 'Micro-politics and Conflicts in Multinational Corporations: Current Debates, Re-framing, and Contributions of This Special Issue' (2006) 12, no. 3 *Journal of International Management* 251–65; R. Willner, 'Micro-politics: An Underestimated Field of Qualitative Research in Political Science' (2011) 7 *German Policy Studies* 155–85.

For this chapter I define micro-politics as *interpersonal instances of contestation*, whether performed through speech, disruptive action, repetition, or otherwise. A micro-political study of international organisations demands that we zoom in on individual practitioners, their backgrounds, experiences, and preferences, as well as the social networks they are a part of. The key assumption of a micro-political lens is that identifying the characteristics and emphasising the conditional agency of practitioners working for international organisations allows for inferences about the character and scope of such organisations. Sociological analysis of practices and networks, but also biographical information about individual trajectories followed by practitioners, then provides significant clues about two central questions for non-functionalist work on international organisations: (a) what international organisations are, other than responses to functional need and (b) how international organisations produce authority relations.

Following the practitioners through a micro-political lens can go different ways; for purposes of clarity I distinguish three. First, sociological international-relations scholars have studied the intra-institutional activities, initiatives, and interventions of individual policy-makers, lawyers, civil servants, advisors, and others working for international organisations. Here we can trace, as Marieke Louis and Lucile Maertens have recently done, the distinct pathways and strategies followed by permanent and non-permanent staff dealing with problems of international cooperation.[11] This option is particularly well-geared towards contemporary research and works well with e.g. ethnographic methods such as participant observation. Second, we might want to look for the past socialisation that individual practitioners bring to the governance process: the extent to which, for instance, a practitioner's education affects their policy preferences and strategies they later adopt once working for an international organisation. This avenue is popular among sociological work deploying social network analysis, but for obvious reasons also works well for historically oriented scholarship.[12]

A third option is to apply the second approach to a separate moment in the life of an institution: its inception. Here we are able to connect

[11] Louis and Maertens, *Why International Organizations Hate Politics.*

[12] For an excellent application of this approach see A. Hoffmann, 'The Transnational and the International: From Critique of Statism to Transversal Lines' (2022) 35 *Cambridge Review of International Affairs* 796–810.

biographical backgrounds, intellectual formation, and political context in order to draw some – if limited – inferences about the contestation, political ambitions, and expectations involved in the establishment of a given organisation. Jens Steffek's recent intellectual history of modern international organisations is a good example here, and indeed there is much that students of international organisations can learn from intellectual-historical methods more generally. By tracing the careers of individual thinkers and practitioners, Steffek is able to tell us how the intellectual influences and previous practical engagements of individual pioneers in international organisations have shaped their technocratic preferences and as such significantly influenced modern conceptions of the scope and authority of international organisations more widely.[13]

The third avenue thus invites us to combine biographical and sociological intuitions about the micro-politics of international organisations. I pursue this avenue for two main reasons. On the one hand, empirically we simply know more about the inner life of a fully fledged international organisation than we do about those early founding moments. On the other, our conceptual, analytical, and theoretical horizons are affected by this empirical basis: currently a rational-functional understanding of institutional design and creation dominates scholarship. If we wish to historicise this literature we need to relax our assumptions – my approach, as I aim to show in the remainder of this chapter, is able to do so.

A micro-political approach also has consequences for how we conceptualise authority. While there is disagreement as to how exactly authority and legitimacy relate,[14] for present purposes I pragmatically define international authority as '*power taken to be legitimate*'.[15] This places emphasis on recognition and audiences and takes no stance on how successful a given claim to legitimacy may be. I adopt a relational position that sees authority as an ever-contested relationship arising from interaction.[16] On this view authority needs to be *produced* in the

[13] Steffek, *International Organization as Technocratic Utopia.*

[14] See, M. Zürn, *A Theory of Global Governance. Authority, Legitimacy, and Contestation* (Oxford University Press, 2018).

[15] J. Kustermans and R. Horemans, 'Four Conceptions of Authority in International Relations' (2021) 76 *International Organisation* 204–28, 3; emphasis original.

[16] J. Costa Lopez, 'Political Authority in International Relations: Revisiting the Medieval Debate' (2020) 74 *International Organization* 222–52, 226–28.

first place, meaning it is historically contingent.[17] Julia Costa Lopez notes the central role of 'constant (re)authorization' in this context. On her view, authority relies on semantic fields that get deployed to 'reauthorize authority' – 'these categories and their variability are central to understand the production and evolution of authority itself'.[18] A relational view is a useful starting point for thinking about how authority relations are produced.

Zooming in on the micro-politics of historical international commissions – of their composition and of their interventions – puts processes of legitimation centre-stage. Methodologically, to foreground the social production of authority relations inherent in decisions about institutional design, rather than study design at an abstract level I combine biographical and sociological methods. This allows me to zoom in on membership composition as a particular aspect of institutional design.

Telegraphs in the Nineteenth Century

Building upon recent work on nineteenth-century international organisations[19] I examine how, and in response to what historical currents, the ITC assumed the specific shape it did. The nineteenth century is crucial here as a period during which technical international institutions proliferated in parallel to the acceleration of industrial capitalism, imperial expansion, and technocratic conceptions of political institutions. Let me briefly outline this historical context in more detail before I turn to the ITC as a key example of that context.

In 1837, the first overland electric telegraph line was laid from London to Birmingham, replacing the optical telegraph system of semaphores with a more efficient and less easily sabotaged means of

[17] See, O. J. Sending, *The Politics of Expertise: Competing for Authority in Global Governance* (University of Michigan Press, 2015).

[18] Costa Lopez, 'Revisiting the Medieval Debate', 229. Consider the authorisation of great powers by naming them, E. Keene, 'The Naming of Powers' (2013) 48 *Cooperation and Conflict* 268–82.

[19] D. Howland, 'An Alternative Mode of International Order: The International Administrative Union in the Nineteenth Century' (2014) 41 *Review of International Studies* 161–83; J. Yao, *The Ideal River: How Control of Nature Shaped the International Order* (Manchester University Press, 2021); Ravndal, *Colonies, semi-sovereigns, and Great Power*; Sluga, *The Invention of the International Order*.

communication. During the second half of the 1840s, lines proliferated and interconnected at dizzying speeds. The demand for administrative integration grew: in 1848, Prussia alone had to conclude a total of fifteen conventions with other German states just to link Berlin's cables to its own borders. Telegraph standards were multilaterally negotiated at the Austro-German Telegraph Union (AGTU), created in 1849, and the French-led Western European Telegraph Union (WETU), created in 1855. In 1864 the French Imperial Government invited all countries with a telegraph administration (excluding those, like Britain, where telegraphs were in private hands) to settle international telegraphic standards. Twenty countries confirmed their attendance, including the Austrian, Ottoman, and Russian Empires. Representatives gathered in Paris to vote on a proposal, put forth by a Commission of Special Delegates, for a single ITU. The conference set technical standards for telegraphs including Morse code, uniform instructions for cable operation, common tariff rates, accounting rules, pricing units, or the maximum length of a word. The convention came into effect on 1 January 1866; two years later, a permanent International Bureau in Bern completed the creation of an international telegraph regime. The world's first formal international organisation, still in existence today, provided a blueprint that many others followed.[20]

The ITU is a significant case for two main reasons: first, it was the first-ever formal international organisation, and thus marked a formative stage in the institutionalisation of global governance practices. Second, the technical management of international telegraphy was a striking pathway in parallel to the proliferating capitalist and imperial competition for its control. The 1860s international telegraph regime thus seemed to endow telegraph cooperation with substantial autonomy and independence from political interference, effectively reinforcing the hierarchies this arrangement denied – a surface appearance that rested on the 'universal but not global' scaffolding of a world structured by empire and capitalism.[21]

[20] B. Reinalda, *The Routledge History of International Organisations: From 1815 to the Present Day* (Routledge, 2009), 85–89.

[21] W. Vrasti, 'Universal but Not Truly "Global": Governmentality, Economic Liberalism, and the International' (2013) 39 *Review of International Studies* 49–69.

The 1865 Commission

Against the historical background sketched out in the previous section, let me now zoom in on the practitioners involved in the micro-political thick of telegraph cooperation. My analysis proceeds in two steps, asking *how and for whose benefit the international telegraph regime assumed the shape that it did.* In each subsection I highlight the agency of practitioners and their motives, and the resulting legitimation of cable-laying as a political intervention. To do so, I first contextualise the political undercurrents of the diplomatic and technical negotiations prior to 1865: Austro-Prussian competition, French imperial expansion, and the question of who should be invited to Paris were, contrary to functionalist portrayals, controversies with which architects of the ITU had to deal. Second, I present my biographical membership analysis to draw inferences based on individual members' backgrounds, socialisation, and political preferences.

Political Tensions and Micro-political Management

Fundamentally unequal and exploitative dynamics characterised the global telegraph enterprise: cables fuelled a highly profitable globalised market, triggering aggressive competition and cartel formation, exacerbated by the imperial demand for cable communication. One of the first messages on the 1858 transatlantic cable was a cancellation of 'an order for two regiments of troops to be sent from Canada to India', the British government saving £50,000 as a result.[22] Such potential, evidenced by the role of telegraphs in deploying British troops to the 1857 Indian Revolt as well as the laying of French cables to Algiers in 1861, whetted the appetite of investors and entrepreneurs. Innovations such as curb transmission, duplex telegraphy, and the siphon recorder invigorated the industry further.

Though telegraphs never became the 'Victorian internet' they are sometimes caricatured as,[23] prices dropped significantly. The 1870s

[22] D. R. Headrick, *The Tools of Empire: Technology and European Imperialism in the Nineteenth Century* (Oxford University Press, 1981), 158.

[23] Indeed *non*-use of the telegraph reflected the extent to which telegraphy was a primarily commercial and elite means of communication throughout the second half of the century. S. M. Müller, *Wiring the World: The Social and Cultural Creation of Global Telegraph Networks* (Columbia University Press, 2016), 11. For the 'Victorian internet' thesis see, T. Standage,

consequently saw an expansion of international lines from imperial cores to the periphery, with the infamous British All-Red Line as its New Imperial pinnacle. Despite self-portrayals to the contrary, the ITU was not an innocent forum altogether immune against this predatory world of capital and empire. Its creation is therefore best understood as a political intervention.[24] The ITU's format, membership, and structure ultimately were responses to three mid-century developments in particular: intra-European imperial rivalry; extra-European imperial expansion; and financial interests in tariff revenues.

First, the shape of the ITU was in part a response to intra-European imperial rivalry between Prussia and Austria. Rivalry revolved around what was known as the German question, which had emerged in the wake of 1848 as a choice between Greater Germany, unified under Austrian patronage, and Little Germany unified under Prussia. Prussia's ambitions within the German Confederation had been newly growing, and telegraphs gave territorial unification special urgency. Given the kingdom's division into East and West, telegraphic connections between Prussia's main cities required that 'the telegraph wires had per force to cross foreign states'. By the early 1860s the idea that became the ITU was for the most part based on stipulations and agreements already in place under AGTU or WETU provisions.[25] The merger of the two was far from unproblematic, as it required a stance by all parties involved, particularly France, on the German question – even if by proxy of technicalities. The Prussian *Zollverein* was an administrative and legal precedent for the cross-border administration of telegraphs, thus a potential Prussian-leaning choice for the ITU. On the other hand, from the French point of view Austria was an important conduit to Russia and by extension to the Asian colonies. The ITU's regulations, however, circumvented politicisation by firmly staying in the technical terrain of international cables, tariff rates, taxes, rules. Such a rules-based international order, as it were,

The Victorian Internet: The Remarkable Story of the Telegraph and the Nineteenth Century's On-line Pioneers (Bloomsbury, 1998).

24 See in particular, G. Balbi, S. Fari, G. Richeri, and S. Calvo, *Network Neutrality: Switzerland's Role in the Genesis of the Telegraph Union, 1855–1875* (Peter Lang, 2014); G. Balbi and A. Fickers (eds.), *History of the International Telecommunication Union (ITU). Transnational Techno-diplomacy from the Telegraph to the Internet* (De Gruyter, 2020).

25 See Fari in Balbi et al., *Network Neutrality.*

did not need to take a stance on national-imperial matters so long as it promoted telegraph communication in general.

Second, extra-European imperial expansion contributed to the shape the ITU later assumed. This was the case for the French, Austrian, Ottoman, and Russian Empires. French access to Russian telegraph lines on the way to its new colonies in South East Asia was pivotal for the effective expansion of Napoleon III's newly ambitious empire. Inaugurating nearly one hundred years of French colonial rule in Indochina, Cochinchina (present-day South Vietnam) was placed under French rule in 1864; in 1867, Cambodia would become a French protectorate. In light of this gradual expansion of French imperial rule in Asia, uniform and standardised telegraphy would facilitate communication between Paris and the colonies.[26] To illustrate, the French initially wanted to keep Austria out and did not extend an invitation to Austria for the planned 1865 conference. The Swiss urged the French to reconsider (and ultimately managed to persuade them) inviting Austria, primarily by pointing to the Austrian telegraph network as a doorway to the East. Cable access via the Ottoman and Russian Empires to possessions in Asia would have had to cross Austria.

Third, the globalisation of industrial capitalism supports an interpretation of the ITU as a political intervention. Creating the conditions under which the telegraphic market could expand and prosper was a political choice, and so the ITU was an 'expression of a capitalistic compromise between national states [sic] and big business to defend the acquired market position with an implicit cartel and their consequent entry barriers'.[27] Less obviously, the ITU did not merely make the lives of cable companies and rubber manufacturers easier, but also required decisions about tariff revenues in transit countries. For example, the Swiss Federal Council gave its delegates at the 1865 Paris conference clear instructions on its telegraphic national interest: to promote an arrangement whereby 'the highest possible number of international telegraphs crossed Swiss territory and drew in a hefty

[26] On Napoleon III's foreign affairs activism in the 1860s see Balbi et al., *Network Neutrality*, 87–88.

[27] Fari in Balbi et al., *Network Neutrality*, 188. On gutta-percha see J. Tully, 'A Victorian Ecological Disaster: Imperialism, the Telegraph, and Gutta-Percha' (2009) 20 *Journal of World History* 559–79; H. Godfrey, *Submarine Telegraphy and the Hunt for Gutta Percha: Challenge and Opportunity in a Global Trade* (Brill, 2018).

income from transit tariffs'.[28] Indeed the Federal Council unmistakably stressed that the Paris delegates were to promote 'the most liberal and favourable dispositions for traffic in general' yet never to lose 'sight however of the interests of revenue'.[29] Overall the ITU spurred 'considerable growth in communications between governments and private sectors in Europe and the world at large',[30] as a result 'enabling the spread of telecommunications and, in turn, the international flow of goods and services' and promoting 'the principles of a free market, open trade and comparative advantage'.[31]

International telegraphs thus expanded under conditions of economic and imperial competition on the one hand, and international standard-setting and regulation on the other. These conditions could be presented as separate projects, but in fact they were mutually reinforcing: the gradual sophistication of imperial power through technology was helped by setting international industrial standards. Existing international relations accounts of the ITU emphasise its significance as the first formal international organisation and blueprint for later institutions such as the Universal Postal Union. Craig Murphy aptly characterises these as the fruits of nineteenth-century functionalist efforts to institutionalise technical cooperation in a world of growing transnational interdependence. On his account, the first international organisations both responded to and facilitated industrial change as they helped extend European and imperial markets. By the turn of the twentieth century, the 'trading area that was partly regulated by the Public International Unions extended the continental market to the overseas dependencies of the European empires'. The telegraph regime features here not simply as a response to functional needs, but as creator of particular sites of regulatory action.[32]

[28] Balbi et al., *Network Neutrality*, 98.

[29] Swiss Federal Council 1865, SFA, E52, 503.

[30] Reinalda, *The Routledge History of International Organisation*, 87.

[31] K. Lee, *Global Telecommunications Regulation: A Political Economy Perspective* (Pinter, 1996), 59.

[32] Murphy, *International Organization and Industrial Change*, 17, 8, 42–43. See also J. Boli and G. M. Thomas, *Constructing World Culture: International Nongovernmental Organizations since 1875* (Stanford University Press, 1999); A. Iriye, *Global Community: The Role of International Organizations in the Making of the Contemporary World* (University of California Press, 2004); M. Krajewski, *World Projects: Global Information before World War I* (University of Minnesota Press, 2014).

This aligns closely with existing interpretations of mid-nineteenth-century international relations. Douglas Howland has argued that the ITU inaugurated a 'novel form of international order' based on an 'administrative internationalism' that offered a 'striking alternative to the international society of great powers, sovereignty, and forms of imperial domination'.[33] Ellen Ravndal in turn has shown that the ITU's distinctive membership criteria reflected international norms in contrast with imperial or diplomatic norms.[34] The ITU was not alone in this: on Joanne Yao's account, for example, the 1856 Danube Commission too had presented itself as a functional-executive body while carrying out a 'deeply political' and 'ideological' project.[35]

Existing work thus suggests, in various ways, that international organisations are political interventions in and of themselves – even, or perhaps especially, where they engage in the supposedly 'low' politics of regulation and standards: 'these activities are often referred to as "technical" or apolitical, they were related to direct government involvement and national interests'.[36] The case of the ITU shows this logic at work. Excavating its micro-politics in this context allows us to make crucial background conditions visible – not least imperial reach and the exploitative harvesting of gutta-percha – that have escaped the self-conception of, and with it the functionalist approach to, modern global governance.

International Commissioners as Parochial Agents

Let me now unpack the micro-politics of actor authorisation at the 1865 Commission of Special Delegates. Table 10.1 presents the full picture with individual backgrounds of each member, compiled from biographical dictionaries, obituaries, and other archival data. What we can glean from this is, of course, limited, but if considered alongside the earlier sketch of political context, it adds an important level of granularity to our analysis.

The ITC was drawn, contrary to its self-portrayal as a cohesive epistemic unit, from a diverse array of aristocrats, military officers, and entrepreneurs. What united them was political favour,

33 Howland, 'An Alternative Mode of International Order', 161–62.
34 Ibid; Ravndal, *Colonies, Semi-sovereigns, and Great Powers.*
35 Yao, *The Ideal River*, 6–7.
36 Reinalda, *The Routledge History of International Organisations*, 91.

Table 10.1 *1865 Special Delegates*

Special Delegate	Delegation	Background
Baron von Weber, Max Maria (1822–1881)	Kingdom of Saxony	Director of Railways of the State of Saxony; railway engineer who trained with Brunel and Stephenson; 1876 author of *Nationality and Railway Politics*.
Brändström, Per (1803–1874)	United Kingdoms of Sweden and Norway	Director-General of Swedish Telegraphs; civil servant; 1831 chancellor at the Chamber of Commerce; 1839 support to Swedish minister in Berlin to conclude new postal accord with Prussia; 1846 the same with Russia; 1855 Swedish commissioner at the Paris World's Fair; 1862 head of Swedish Telegraphs.
Brunner von Wattenwyl, Karl Friedrich (1823–1914)	Austrian Empire	Director of Telegraphs; Swiss postmaster and entomologist; known for orthopterology.
Curchod, Louis (1826–1889)	Swiss Confederation	Central Director of Telegraphs; engineer and diplomat; 1849 graduate École Centrale des Arts et Manufactures; 1870–73 Head of Board of Directors of *French Submarine Telegraph Company*.
Damasio, José Vitorino (1807–1875)	Kingdom of Portugal	Colonel of Artillery, Director-General of Telegraphs; previously director of the Lisbon Industrial Institute.
de Hakar	Kingdom of Spain	District Inspector.
Effendi, Krikor Agathon (1823–1868)	Ottoman Empire	First non-Muslim minister of Ottoman government; studied agriculture in France; worked in Belgium, England; trained at Ottoman Translation Bureau; recruited into Ottoman Telegraph Administration for language skills; General Director of Ottoman Telegraphs 1864–68.

Table 10.1 (*cont.*)

Special Delegate	Delegation	Background
Faber, Peter (1810–1877)	Kingdom of Denmark	Director-General of Telegraph Lines; telegraph engineer and songwriter, remembered primarily for Danish folk songs and amateur photography.
Fassiaux	Kingdom of Belgium	Director-General of Railways, Posts and Telegraphs; Railway Union advocate.
Gauß, Joseph (1806–1873)	Kingdom of Hannover	Counsellor; engineer in chief of the Hannover railway administration.
Herbet, Charles F. E.	French Empire	State Councillor, Director of Commerce in the Ministry of Foreign Affairs.
Jagerschmidt, Charles (1820–1894)	French Empire	Under-Director for Consulates and Commercial Affairs, Ministry of Foreign Affairs; diplomat, 1850–55 French *chargé d'affaires* in Tangiers, Morocco; 1852 initiative for Cape Spartel Lighthouse; 1853 Gibraltar Strait Hydrographic Expedition.
Manos	Kingdom of Greece	Head of Section, Ministry of the Interior.
Minotto, Giovanni (1803–1869)	Kingdom of Italy	Head of Department, Ministry of Public Works; engineer widely noted in Italy for developing the Minotto apparatus (telegraph equipment), rise to fame as first director of national telegraph administration in 1860s.
Nielsen	United Kingdoms of Sweden and Norway	Director-General of Norwegian Telegraphs.
Poppen	Grand Duchy Baden	Counsellor of the Ministry.
Sanz	Kingdom of Spain	Director of Telegraphs.
Schwerd, Ludwig Emil	Grand Duchy Baden	Inspector of Telegraphs; electrical engineer, patent holder for a lamp (1882) and a telegraph apparatus, later director of *L. E. Schwerd of Carlsruhe.*

Table 10.1 (*cont.*)

Special Delegate	Delegation	Background
Staring	Kingdom of the Netherlands	Counsellor, Department of the Interior; military career, First Lieutenant, as which involved in construction of Maastricht-Liège canal, thereafter appointed referendary to the Thorbecke government, as which later promoted to first director of the first Dutch telegraph administration. Delegate to Austro-Prussian Telegraph Union and all subsequent ITU conferences.
van Dyck	Kingdom of Bavaria	Director of Telegraph Lines.
Vinchent, Julien	Kingdom of Belgium	Engineer in Chief, Director of Telegraphs; published on international telegraph tariffs.
Viscount de Vougy, Henri Michon (1807–1891)	French Empire	Director-General of Telegraph Lines; former Military Officer.
von Chauvin, Franz (1812–1898)	Kingdom of Prussia	Lieutenant-Colonel, Director of Telegraphs; military career, First Lieutenant. Signed 1857 Austro-Prussian Telegraph Union Treaty on behalf of Prussia. Head of Battlefield Telegraphy in 1864 Danish-Prussian and 1866 Austro-Prussian War; head of Prussian military telegraph administration; author of 1884 volume on military uses of telegraphy.
von Guerhard	Russian Empire	Major General, Engineer and Director of Telegraphs.
von Klein, Ludwig (1813–1881)	Kingdom of Württemberg	Director of Telegraphs of the Kingdom of Württemberg; railway engineer.
von Weber	Kingdom of Bavaria	Counsellor of the Ministry of Foreign Affairs.

not pure epistemic superiority. Each country brought one or several Plenipotentiary Delegates, distinguished diplomats with Ambassador-Extraordinary status, and one or several Special Delegates, usually the heads of each country's telegraph administration. Significantly, both were endowed with diplomatic credential for the time of the conference. As French Minister of Foreign Affairs and patron of the conference Edouard Drouyn de Lhuys pointed out, 'the nature of the questions attached to a telegraphic treaty demand a detailed examination, as well as technical knowledge' such that 'to prepare the solution of these questions the various Governments would surely want to send special delegates'. On that basis he proposed that 'a commission be formed, composed of special delegates, charged with submitting to the Conference a general treaty proposal'.[37] The proposal received unanimous approval.

This arrangement in itself – and here the chapter speaks to previous sections in this volume on the role of experts in international organisations – represented a remarkable elevation of telegraph officials to international expert status, and a significant enlargement of the expert mandate. Paris witnessed 'the coming together of the European "technical elite"'.[38] The Special Delegates, not diplomats, carried out 'the actual work on the final convention and regulations'. Chaired by French Telegraph Director the Viscount de Vougy, this group convened to work out a common framework for tariffs and technical standards. Despite varying numbers of members per delegation, each was given a single vote to pass the convention by a simple majority. Over the course of sixteen sessions between 4 March and 11 April, the Committee drafted a convention which was approved and signed by all twenty participant countries after extensive negotiations lasting until 17 May. The ITU was born.[39] The draft convention emphasised throughout the international – autonomous – interest of shared telegraphic standards. The document thus consistently referred to 'la télégraphie internationale', prefacing the need for an international telegraph regime as follows:

> [The Special Delegates,] animated by the desire to secure for all telegraph correspondence, exchanged between their respective States, the advantages

[37] Swiss Federal Archives 1865, no. 109.
[38] Balbi et al., *Network Neutrality*, 101.
[39] ITU, *L'Union Télégraphique Internationale (1865–1915)* (Bureau International de l'Union Télégraphique, 1915).

of a simple and reduced rate, to improve the present conditions of international telegraphy, and to establish a permanent understanding between their States, while retaining their freedom of action for measures which do not concern the whole of the service, have resolved to conclude an Agreement to this effect.[40]

The agreement thus also left leeway to signatories for their own regulations under exceptional circumstances such as warfare. It took over AGTU and WETU articles distinguishing between State, Service, and Private Dispatches, with different limitations and conditions applying to each. Only State and Service Dispatches were permitted, as per Articles 7–9, to be written in code or secret language, 'whether in its totality or in parts'. Whether private correspondence, in other words, could use code or secret language depended on each telegraph administration's own rules.

But who were these newly minted protagonists of international order? The common credential, as can be seen in Table 10.1, was an international portfolio of experiences, from cable-laying to canal-digging. All of them firmly believed in the natural necessity of technical cooperation, but their views differed on the question of how pacifying such cooperation would eventually be. Consider, for example, French Special Delegate Henri Michon Viscount de Vougy (1807–1891), who also presided over the Special Commission and was the person who urged Napoleon III to call for an international telegraphic conference. Vougy had been trained as a military officer of distinction, serving from 1827 to 1848, at one time as aide-de-camp to the Minister of War. He had also served as prefect of the Haute Loire and Nièvre and in 1853 was named head of the Telegraph Service by his cousin Jean Gilbert Victor Fialin, Duc de Persigny; 'nepotism', as one scholar put it, 'undoubtedly played a role in his selection'.[41] From June 1854 he was Director-General of Telegraph Lines of the French Empire.[42] In 1861, Vougy also oversaw the laying of three international cables to England (Dieppe–New Haven), to Algeria (Port Vendres–Alger), and to Corsica

[40] ITU, *Convention télégraphique internationale* (Historical Archives of the International Telecommunication Union, 1865); author's translation.

[41] A. J. Butrica, *From Inspecteur to Ingénieur: Telegraphy and the Genesis of Electrical Engineering in France, 1845-1881* (PhD thesis, Iowa State University, 1986), 43–44.

[42] A. Belloc, *La télégraphie historique: Depuis les temps les plus reculés jusqu'à nos jours* (Firmin-Didot, 1894), 199.

(Toulon–Ajaccio) and signed a convention with the Regency of Tunis for the 'exploitation, by French agents, of the Tunisian network and its linkage with the Algerian telegraphic network'.[43]

Under Vougy's direction, the French telegraph network expanded from 22,919 km to 40,992 km; wires from 59,976 km to 116,437 km; submarine cables starting in 1865 grew to 571 km by 1870; telegraphic bureaux from 364 (1860) to 2,003 (1871); domestic dispatches from 568,365 (1860) to 5,042,302 (1870); international dispatches from 151,885 (1860) to 590,794 (1871). Vougy thus possessed a mix of military distinction, political and imperial esteem and influence, and a record in promoting international telegraphy. He was not merely an apolitical bureaucrat, which not least his perception by contemporaries attests to: major newspaper outlets at the time either glorified or demonised him. The *Figaro* wrote that 'for the most part, the developments and improvements of the telegraphic service are due to the intelligence and activity of M. de Vougy'.[44] By contrast, a rather scathing critic writing for the *Gaulois* claimed that 'M. de Vougy understands nothing, but absolutely nothing, of the telegraphy he directs. He would not be capable of maneuvring an apparatus, nor of explaining what purpose exactly it serves. That, at least, is the current opinion within his administration'.[45] Commissioners' credential, in other words, was not just unstable across different delegations but also contested.

Likewise, the Special Delegate of Austria, Karl Friedrich Brunner von Wattenwyl (1823–1914), was Director of Telegraphs in his country at the time – but had earned his reputation primarily as an entomologist. A pioneer in the field of orthopterology and Professor of Physics in Bern, he went on to be remembered as 'one of the two greatest Orthopterists of his day', his work being 'an indispensable necessity in the library of the general Orthopterist'. His obituary noted that he was 'the organizer of the telegraph service of Austria' but made no mention of his contribution to the 1865 Paris Convention.[46] The Prussian delegate in turn, Franz von Chauvin (1812–1898), First Lieutenant and later Major of the Prussian Army, had served as Colonel of the

[43] Cited in Belloc, *Télégraphie historique*, 228.

[44] P. Dauriac, No title, *Figaro* (1863) 915, 4.

[45] F. Sarcey, 'Qu'on le nomme au sénat', *Le Gaulois* (1869) 420, 1.

[46] J. A. G. Rehn, 'Obituary. Carl Brunner von Wattenwyl' (1915) 26 *Entomological News and Proceedings of the Entomological Section of the Academy of Natural Sciences of Philadelphia* 285–86.

Engineering Corps and Head of Battlefield Telegraphy in the Prussian-Danish War just one year prior to the Paris conference, a service that earned him the Prussian noble title 'von'.[47] In 1866 he served as Head of Battlefield Telegraphy in the Austro-Prussian War, and in 1884 he even published a book titled *Organisation of Electric Telegraphy in Germany for the Purposes of War* in which he described how 'The telegraph network, with its countries-spanning iron meshes and stations, functions like the nervous system of the human body and even surpasses it in terms of speed and diversity'.[48]

It may ultimately seem quite straightforward to get together each country's diplomatic and telegraphic representatives, and this may simply seem an effective way of reaching politically robust, technically well-informed conventions to regulate international telegraph communication. Yet we need to remember that telegraphs were never politically neutral: in the background there were powerful corporations vying for their share in the globalising telegraph markets, the imperial weight of France and Britain, and not least the fact that apart from an Ottoman and a Russian delegation this was a very European conference.

In the closing remarks of Drouyn de Lhuys, this was 'the meeting together of men of the highest rank ... who could pool the results of their experience and form a sort of supranational instruction centre'. Drouyn de Lhuys explicitly framed the exercise as one in which hurdles to communication could be overcome – a choice that pushed economic matters of cable production, legal issues surrounding cable routes, and normative questions about the legitimacy of not consulting opposed parties, outside the remit of international cooperation.

Conclusion

After the 1865 Paris conference, the ITU went on to convene on a regular basis in the capitals of its member countries. What characterised its activity during the last three decades of the nineteenth century was a resolute refusal to become a forum where the intense military and economic rivalries surrounding the technology would be on

[47] B. von Poten, 'Chauvin, Franz von' (1903) 47 *Allgemeine Deutsche Biographie* 469.

[48] F. von Chauvin, *Organisation der elektrischen Telegraphie in Deutschland für die Zwecke des Krieges* (Berlin, 1884), 20.

display. Instead, the institution managed to refine its standards and regulations, and its delegates managed to reach agreements and make compromises despite the considerable tensions between its member governments. This was tied to the ITU's emerging self-understanding, on the one hand, and shifts in its institutional design, on the other. The ITU's self-understanding that I have examined here later turned into an inalienable global governance standard. The 1875 St Petersburg conference determined that henceforth ITU conventions would be held by Special Delegates only. What resulted was 'a more precise definition of the conference as "meetings of experts"', now explicitly defined as 'intelligent men, ready to be enlightened by discussion and to modify their opinion according to the considerations that they hear being developed'.[49]

The case of the ITC, I have argued, illustrates the consequences of adopting a micro-political approach in the historical study of international organisations. So, to return to the initial question of this chapter: what then is the distinct value that historicisation can bring to the scholarly aims of this volume? The approach followed in this chapter invites us to think, through a micro-political lens, about what international organisations are from the point of view of their making. Empirically I zoomed in on one important moment in the history of modern international organisations: the 1865 commission whose chief purpose it was to determine, at the ITC in Paris, the scope and purpose of the first formal and permanent international organisation, the ITU.

In the introduction to this chapter I defined micro-politics as *interpersonal instances of contestation*, whether performed through speech, disruptive action, repetition, or otherwise. The key assumption of this approach, I argued, is that identifying the characteristics and emphasising the conditional agency of practitioners working for international organisations allows for inferences about the character and scope of such organisations. Sociological and biographical analysis of individual trajectories then provides clues about two central questions: (a) what international organisations are, other than responses to functional need and (b) how international organisations produce authority relations. Let me return to each of these aspects.

49 Fari in Balbi et al., *Network Neutrality*, 184; ITU, *Conférence Télégraphique Internationale de St Petersburg* (Bureau International de l'Union Télégraphique, 1875), 295. Author's translation.

Unpacking instances of contestation requires that we know about individual commissioners' backgrounds, experiences, and preferences, as well as the social networks they are a part of. Of course this is limited: as can be seen in the biographical table presented in the previous section, information is incomplete where archival data is not available. This real practical limitation is further complicated by an analytical limitation: from a historical point of view we will never know actors' real preferences or private reasons for joining a particular enterprise or undertaking. Yet if we consider individual backgrounds of ITC members – the 'international' portfolio they share in common, and the technical knowledge they do not – alongside the political tensions to which the ITU had to respond *by design*, then we actually gain important insights about the making of international organisations.

First, we get to say something new about what international organisations are, if not straightforward responses to naturally arising functional needs. Rather than a mechanism to overcome obstacles to international cooperation, by telegraph standardisation say, the ITU in this chapter appears much more as a focal point of contestation about political orders. ITC negotiations granted countries such as Switzerland and Belgium 'middling' status on the important issue of tariff revenue. This has had repercussions for the general position of both countries in the European international order, both at the time and for decades to come. Further, at the ITC negotiations, national standards as such collided and had to be reconciled. Nationhood was perhaps the greatest European political concern at the time, and so the ITU was an expression of a particular understanding of national autonomy and its limits. In sum then, identifying commissioners as individuals with particular loyalties and interests, rather than servants of a predetermined common cooperative goal, puts the resulting international organisation into perspective as a political intervention.

Second, we get to say something new about how international organisations produce authority relations. Specifically in this case, I started from a conception of authority as the inchoate and reiterative process of authorisation: authority is never entirely there as an analytical given but rather requires constant performance and relational production. On this understanding, the ITC as a unit can be understood as a political performance whereby actors are authorised as 'international commissioners' by virtue of *cohering in and representing* something that gets labelled and then institutionalised as an international organisation. This was, in the middle decades of the nineteenth century, revolutionary – the label of 'internationality' was still in its infancy at the time, and attaching it to institutional entities was a novelty. As we have seen in my discussion in this chapter, this label had powerful effects where it was invoked to signal autonomy from the political currents 'outside' of the world of telegraphs. Authorisation then, in this context, extended from a move of separating telegraph standards from political purpose.

This chapter zoomed in on the micro-politics of the creation of the first formal, modern international organisation: the ITU. In so doing I have on the one hand tried to make the case for a biographical-sociological approach to examining the role of individual commissioners; on the other hand, I have presented a non-functionalist case study of institutional design. If historicisation is a promising avenue for the study of international organisations, it is especially so because it allows us to trace them back to their beginnings. This helps us learn something about their character, shape, and scope from the political context they responded to. In conclusion, the micro-politics of international organisations can be studied with a potent combination of biographical and sociological analysis, allowing us to gain some distance from functionalist overdetermination. Rather than see international organisations through the lens of foregone conclusions – the functions they are to serve – historicisation leaves the 'point' of international organisations open. Instead we can then look for the aims, partial interests, and political preferences that the makers of these institutions bring to the drafting table: when institutional design actually happens, we can then ask, what non-technical, non-functional considerations play a role? Social networks, loyalties, allegiances, and past performances on vaguely connected matters, as discussed in this chapter, all play into the process.

11 Keeping Up Standards for a Better World

Anthropological Alternatives to the Study of International Organisations

MIIA HALME-TUOMISAARI

'*You should let William* [*the footman*] *do that!*' Mrs Hughes, the housekeeper, exclaims upon entering the room. '*He's got enough on his hands getting the uniforms out of mothballs*', responds Mr Carson, the butler. Sweat is running down his customarily calm forehead as he rushes around the room, carrying heaps of silverware for polishing. '*You have to ease up a bit or you'll give yourself a heart attack. There's a war on! Things cannot be the same when there's a war on!*' blurts Mrs Hughes. '*I do not agree. Keeping up standards is the only way to show the Germans that they will not beat us in the end*', the steadfast Mr Carson rebuts as he proceeds to polish the silver. '*Well, give me some warning the next time we're expecting Germans at Downton and I'll see what I can do*', Mrs Hughes notes wryly before exiting the room.

Downton Abbey, Series 2, Episode 2[1]

In the post-World War II era, international lawyers have occupied the front seat in studying not only international organisations (IOs) but human rights as well. Thus, it is both understandable and sensible to frame insights from international law as dominant, and those from other disciplines as offering alternative, perhaps somewhat subordinate viewpoints. During the past decade, this disciplinary hierarchy has grown to feel increasingly unsatisfying, including to an increasing number of international lawyers who are 'losing faith' in their discipline, both as an analytical framework and as a tool for

[1] This chapter is based on the plenary paper held at the conference 'Alternative Approaches to International Organizations in International Law: Potentials, Complexities and Pitfalls', Geneva Graduate Institute in International and Development Studies, 14 October 2021.

world improvement.[2] From the perspective of empirical reality, this disciplinary hierarchy has likewise outlived its usefulness: in the continued proliferation of IOs accompanied by various regulative frameworks, mandates, and normative orders, what exactly makes them 'legal' has grown increasingly unclear.

In this chapter, I enter the debate using perspectives from my ethnographic fieldsite, namely, the UN Human Rights Committee,[3] embedding my discussion in a decade of anthropological work on IOs.[4] One of ten treaty bodies monitoring state compliance with the main UN human rights covenants, the Human Rights Committee monitors how states comply with the obligations they have assumed by becoming parties to the International Covenant on Civil and Political Rights (ICCPR). In the continued – and perhaps permanent – absence of an international human rights court operating under the UN, the committee is often called the most 'lawlike' and authoritative of all the UN human rights monitoring mechanisms.[5] At the same time, the Human

[2] A. Riles, 'Outputs: The Promises and Perils of Ethnographic Engagement after the Loss of Faith in Transnational Dialogue' (2017) 23 *Journal of the Royal Anthropological Society* 182–197; S. V. Scott, 'The Decline of International Law as a Normative Ideal' (2018) 49 *Victoria University of Wellington Law Review* 627–644; D. Guilfoyle, 'The Future of International Law in an Authoritarian World' (2019) *European Journal of International Law: TALK!*; M. Halme-Tuomisaari, 'Toward Rejuvenated Inspiration with the Unbearable Lightness of Anthropology' (2021) 115 *American Journal of International Law Unbound* 283–288.

[3] M. Halme-Tuomisaari, 'Embodied Universalism at the UN Human Rights Committee: Meeting the World at the Palais Wilson' in R. Niezen and M. Sapignoli (eds.), *Palaces of Hope: The Anthropology of Global Organizations* (Cambridge: Cambridge University Press, 2017), pp. 127–151; M. Halme-Tuomisaari, 'Methodologically Blonde at the UN in a Tactical Quest for Inclusion' (2018) 26 *Social Anthropology/Anthropologie Sociale* 4, 456–470; M. Halme-Tuomisaari, 'Guarding Utopia: Law, Vulnerability and Frustration at the UN Human Rights Committee' (2020) 28 *Social Anthropology/ Anthropologie Sociale* 1, 35–49.

[4] See B. Müller (ed.), *Gloss of Harmony: The Politics of Policy Making in Multilateral Organizations* (London: Pluto Press 2013); R. Niezen and M. Sapignoli, (eds.) *Palaces of Hope: The Anthropology of Global Organizations* (Cambridge: Cambridge University Press, 2017).

[5] For recent scholarship on the UN Human Rights Committee and the other UN treaty bodies, see D. Moeckli and H. Keller (eds.), *The Human Rights Covenants at 50* (Oxford: Oxford University Press, 2018); G. Neuman, 'Human Rights, Treaties, and International Legitimacy' in S. Voeneky and G. L. Neuman (eds.), *Human Rights, Democracy, and Legitimacy in a World of Disorder* (Cambridge: Cambridge University Press, 2018), pp. 51; L. Oette,

Rights Committee, similarly to other UN treaty bodies, suffers from under-reporting and lacks influence, raising concerns over whether the committee's work really matters.[6]

This chapter anchors its inquiry in an ethnographic glimpse from 2013 when the committee first held a Constructive Dialogue session 'with itself' concerning the state report of Belize, a small state bordering Mexico. Belize's initial report to the committee was due circa fifteen years before Belize finally submitted it in 2013, but then it did not send a state delegation to the committee's session as is the usual practice. The committee has since examined a great number of reports *in abstentia*. These sessions form a noted contrast to the expectation that processing state reports constitutes an active verbal exchange between members of the international community, that is, Human Rights Committee members and state representatives. These sessions offer an illuminating vantage point for reflecting on the diverse ways in which IOs' forms and practices 'keep up standards' for a better world.

Klabbers notes the dominant idea is that 'international organisations are apolitical and cost-effective, doing things states cannot do on their own (or are reluctant to do on their own)'.[7] Further, 'while apolitical, they nonetheless contribute to world peace or, at the very least, the "salvation of mankind"'.[8] Hence, IOs are widely perceived as 'inherently good and benign, and their functioning should accordingly be facilitated – they form the benevolent alternatives to nasty states'.[9] Particularly in the past decade, questions have increasingly

'The UN Human Rights Treaty Bodies: Impact and Future' in G. Oberleitner (ed.), *International Human Rights Institutions, Tribunals, and Courts* (New York: Springer, 2018), pp. 95; A. Seibert-Fohr, 'The UN Human Rights Committee', in G. Oberleitner (ed.), *International Human Rights Institutions, Tribunals, and Courts* (New York: Springer, 2018), p. 117.

6 J. Krommendijk, 'The Domestic Effectiveness of International Human Rights Monitoring in Established Democracies. The Case of the UN Human Rights Treaty Bodies' (2015) 10 *Review of International Organizations* 4, pp. 489–512; Halme-Tuomisaari, 'Guarding Utopia'.

7 J. Klabbers, 'Theorizing International Organizations' in A. Orford and F. Hoffman (eds.), *The Oxford Handbook of the Theory of International Law* (Oxford: Oxford University Press, 2016), pp. 625–626; see also M. Louis and L. Maertens (eds.), *Why International Organizations Hate Politics: Depoliticizing the World* (London: Routledge, 2021).

8 Klabbers *ibid*.

9 Klabbers *ibid*.

arisen as to whether IOs are realising these expectations and whether international law is actually effective.[10]

One recurring source of criticism is that, instead of actually acting in the world, IOs 'generate documents that heighten obscurity, while producing ideas and policies behind closed doors'.[11] Frequently, the generation of 'obscure' documents seems to 'hinder' IOs doing things that actually matter and which IOs *should* be doing. In part, these accusations can arise from IOs leading a 'life of their own, distinct from that of their member states'.[12] In this 'life of their own', *talking* appears to have replaced doing, and meetings have increasingly become a substitute for action. What were supposed to be the means to an end seem to have become the end in itself.

People working in IOs take these criticisms seriously. Many actively question the direction and continued legitimacy of their operations and invite anthropologists to conduct ethnographic studies of their organisational cultures.[13] Some IOs revisit their foundational visions and significantly revise them to remain relevant in a rapidly changing world. One example of this is Amnesty International's increasing shift towards 'sustainability', a new concern in the field of human rights.[14]

In this chapter, I engage with these criticisms and ask: can we find another perspective from which to assess effectiveness? What happens if we stop investing our analytical attention in what we think IO operations and their desired 'impacts' *should* be? What kind of insights can we gain from non-normative inquiries into what IOs *actually* do? I reflect on these questions by asking: What can we learn about IOs' visions if we focus on the legal technicalities and practical materialities that define their operations and the 'mundane forms through which these work',[15]

10 A. Bianchi, 'The Unbearable Lightness of International Law' (2018) 6 *London Review of International Law* 335.

11 Niezen and Sapignoli, *Palaces of Hope*, 1.

12 J. Klabbers and G. Fiti Sinclair, 'On Theorizing International Organizations Law: Editors' Introduction' (2020) 31 *European Journal of International Law* 2, 489–496, 490.

13 M. Halme-Tuomisaari, 'Consultancy, Confidentiality and Scholarly Responsibility: Glimpses from the UN OHCHR', (2019) Humanity Journal's Blog, http://humanityjournal.org/blog/consultancy-confidentiality/.

14 Amnesty International, *Sustainable Development Goals: A Practical Guide for National Action and Accountability* (2016), www.amnesty.org/en/documents/act10/4699/2016/en/

15 H. Brown, A. Reed, and T. Yarrow, 'Special Issue: Meetings: Ethnographies of Organisational Process, Bureaucracy, and Assembly' (2017) 23 *Journal of the Royal Anthropological Institute* 1, 5–207, 10.

the seemingly 'thin' documents and the 'boringly, even achingly, familiar routines'?[16] I link these questions to ethnography by asking: According to what kind of logic does it make sense for a high-profile UN human rights monitoring body to have a '*dialogue with itself*'?

The Flourishing Anthropology of IOs

Since 2010, the anthropology of IOs has grown into a vibrant field of research. Anthropology was once characterised by geographically distant, elusive fieldsites and the study of exotic tribal customs. This created an inevitable division between those who did the studying and those who were studied, a distinction graphically captured by the still-circulating images of Bronislaw Malinowski, often called the founder of ethnography, clad in impeccably white attire amongst his 'natives', inhabitants of Trobriand Island.[17] Much of early anthropological work was embedded in the kind of evolutionary thinking likewise characteristic of international law: for example, many early works in legal anthropology were premised on 'advancement' from informal modes of dispute resolution to formal law.[18] The distinction between the western 'civilised' ethnographer and the 'savage' subjects of inquiry created a legacy that the discipline has attempted to reckon with, even if not with completely satisfactory results.[19]

Simultaneously anthropology has a long tradition of 'studying up',[20] generating ethnographies of organisations. The result is a rapidly growing body of research analysing different UN entities[21] and

[16] Brown et al, 'Meetings'.

[17] B. Malinowski, *Argonauts of the Western Pacific* (London: Routledge 2014 (1922)); images at K. Fletcher, 'Bronislaw Malinowski – LSE Pioneer of Social Anthropology' (2017) https://blogs.lse.ac.uk/lsehistory/2017/06/13/bronislaw-malinowski-lse-pioneer-of-social-anthropology/.

[18] See, for example, E. Durkheim, *De la division du travail social* (Paris: Ancienne librairie Germer Baillier et Cie, 1893); H. Maine, *Ancient Law* (London: John Murrey, 1861).

[19] For ongoing discussions on the need to decolonise the curriculum and anthropology, see H. Mogstad and L.-S. Tse, 'Decolonizing Anthropology' (2018) 36 *The Cambridge Journal of Anthropology* 2, 53–72.

[20] L. Nader, 'Up the Anthropologist – Perspectives Gained from Studying up' in Dell Hymes (ed.), *Reinventing Anthropology* (New York: Vintage Books, 1974), pp. 284–311.

[21] M. Abélès, *Des anthropologues à l'OMC: scènes de la gouvernance mondiale* (Paris: CNRS Editions, 2011); H. Deeb and G. E. Marcus, 'In the Green

international law.[22] These include ethnographies of international courts,[23] including the European Court of Human Rights[24] and the International Criminal Court,[25] and of truth-and-reconciliation commissions.[26] Anthropological work focuses on the UN Human Rights Council's Universal Periodical Reviews[27] and treaty bodies, including the Committee on the Elimination of Discrimination against Women,[28] and the Convention against Torture[29] and the Human Rights Committees.[30] Studies of the World Bank[31] complement ethnographies of human rights activities, including failures in diverse local settings[32] and their links to global networks, and research on expert techniques,[33] transnational activist and expert networks.[34] Together

Room: An Experiment in Ethnographic Method at the WTO' (2011) 34 *PoLAR: Political and Legal Anthropology Review* 1, 51–76.

22 A. Riles, 'Introduction to the Symposium on the Anthropology of International Law' (2021) 115 *AJIL Unbound* 283–272.

23 A. Cubucku, *For the Love of Humanity: The World Tribunal on Iraq* (Pennsylvania: University of Pennsylvania Press, 2018).

24 M.-B. Dembour, *Who Believes in Human Rights? Reflections on the European Convention*, 1 ed. (Cambridge: Cambridge University Press, 2006); J. Greenberg, 'Law, Politics, and Efficacy at the European Court of Human Rights' (2020) 47 *American Ethnologist* 4, 417–431.

25 K. Clark, *Affective Justice: The International Criminal Court and the Pan-Africanist Pushback* (Durham: Duke University Press, 2019).

26 R. Wilson, *The Politics of Truth and Reconciliation in South Africa* (Cambridge: Cambridge University Press, 2001).

27 J. Cowan, 'The Universal Periodic Review as Public Audit Ritual,' in H. Charlesworth and E. Larkin (eds.), *Human Rights and the Universal Periodic Review* (Cambridge: Cambridge University Press, 2014), pp. 42–62.

28 S.E. Merry, *Human Rights & Gender Violence: Translating International Law into Local Justice* (Chicago: University of Chicago Press, 2006).

29 T. Kelly, *This Side of Silence: Human Rights, Torture, and the Recognition of Cruelty* (Philadelphia: University of Pennsylvania Press, 2011).

30 Halme-Tuomisaari, 'Guarding Utopia'; M. Halme-Tuomisaari, 'Contested Representation: Exploring China's State Report' (2013) 1 *Journal of Legal Anthropology* 3, 333–359.

31 G. Sarfaty, *Values in Translation: Human Rights and the Culture of the World Bank* (Stanford: Stanford University Press, 2012).

32 L. Allen, *Rise and Fall of Human Rights: Cynism and Politics in the Occupied Palestine* (Stanford: Standford University Press, 2012).

33 S. E. Merry, *The Seductions of Quantification: Measuring Human Rights, Gender Violence, and Sex Trafficking* (Chicago: University of Chicago Press, 2016).

34 A. Littoz-Monet, *Governing through Expertise* (Cambridge: Cambridge University Press, 2021); M. Keck and K. Sikkink, *Activists beyond Borders: Advocacy Networks in International Politics* (Ithaca: Cornell University Press, 1998).

this scholarship documents the growing influence of independent experts[35] and their influence on transnational legislation,[36] EU policy-making,[37] and informal law-making.[38]

In fact, it may be easier for anthropologists to study and theorise IOs than it is for international lawyers, for whom the multiplicity of IOs presents a significant hurdle. How does one arrive at satisfactory legal definitions or theorisations when the concrete incarnations, criteria for membership, and scopes of operations differ so greatly?[39] Yet, where international lawyers perceive troubling differences, anthropologists see significant sameness. First, there is IOs' community of practice, the (permanent) staff of which share great similarities. With rare exceptions, they all belong to the same transnational elite possessing similar educational backgrounds and work experiences.[40]

Sameness likewise characterises their professional endeavours. When IO staff produce and process human rights reports, they generally do so using similar knowledge practices and legal technicalities, no matter where in the world they are located.[41] Thus, sameness unites the international human rights and humanitarian sector: it matters little whether the documents are processed by the UN Human Rights Council, the Human Rights Committee, or a regional human rights monitoring body, or whether the individuals processing documents are UN secretariat members, state delegates, or NGO staff.

An inductive field of research characterised by 'pre-theoretical commitments',[42] anthropology has a proclivity for theorising from the ground up, in stark contrast to law, which is both deductive and normative. For example, when examining IO operations, a legal inquiry commonly commences with a distinct fiction regarding what

[35] T. Piccone, *Catalysts for Change: How the U.N.'s Independent Experts Promote Human Rights* (Washington, DC: Brookings Institution Press, 2012).

[36] N. Reiners, *Transnational Law-Making Coalitions for Human Rights* (Cambridge: Cambridge University Press, 2021).

[37] P. Leino-Sandberg, *The Politics of Legal Expertise in EU Policy-Making* (Cambridge: Cambridge University Press, 2021).

[38] J. Pauwelyn, R. Wessel, and J. Wouters, *Informal International Lawmaking* (Oxford: Oxford University Press, 2012).

[39] Klabbers & Sinclair, 'On Theorizing International Organizations Law'.

[40] Halme-Tuomisaari, 'Guarding Utopia'; Niezen & Sapignoli, *Palaces of Hope*, 2.

[41] Riles, 'Outputs'.

[42] H. Moore, 'Global Anxieties: Concept-Metaphors and Pre-theoretical Commitments in Anthropology' (2004) 4 *Anthropological Theory* 1, 71–88.

constitutes an IO and its mandate, followed by assumptions about the impacts IOs *should* have.

Inductive theorisation, however, begins with IOs' inner logic and operations, which anthropologists observe, participate in, and hear our interlocutors describe. It portrays IOs as 'social worlds with distinct characters, influenced by their connections with civil society, states, transnational corporations, and publics'.[43] It reveals how 'international organisations involve collective and individual actors in their policy-making, absorb critique, attempt to neutralise political conflict, and create new political fields in competition and collusion with local actors and national governments'.[44] It further highlights the 'affective lives of bureaucracies', and 'how actors maintain a sense of purpose and agency in spite of the tedious and burdensome nature of the administrative procedures in which they take part'.[45]

After sufficient analysis, an ethnographically grounded, theoretical understanding emerges that transcends the borders of formality and legal fiction, encompassing the informal, the improvised, the unexpected, and the irrational. In my own work, inductive theorising generated a description of the UN human rights monitoring framework as a formidable 'apparatus'. This conception borrows from Foucault, who describes the apparatus, aka, the dispositive, as a 'heterogenous ensemble consisting of discourses, institutions, architectural forms, regulatory decisions, laws, administrative measures, scientific statements, philosophical, moral, and philanthropic propositions – in short, the said and the unsaid'.[46]

I complement this description with ice as a metaphor for describing the complexity of organisational inner contours.[47] Ice is likewise an apt metaphor for illustrating the 'fuzzy logic' of the UN human rights apparatus. 'Fuzzy logic' is borrowed from Bourdieu, who used

43 Niezen and Sapignoli, *Palaces of Hope*, 3. 44 Müller, *Gloss of Harmony*, 2.

45 J. Billaud and J. Cowan, 'The Bureaucratisation of Utopia: Ethics, Affects and Subjectivities in International Governance Processes' (2020) 28 *Special Issue, Social Anthropology/Anthropologie Sociale* 1, 10.

46 M. Foucault, 'The Confessions of the Flesh' in C. Gordon (ed.), *Power/ Knowledge: Selected Interviews and Other Writings* (New York: Pantheon Books. 1980 [1977]), pp. 194–228; see also G. Feldman, 'If Ethnography Is More than Participant-Observation, Then Relations Are More than Connections: The Case for Nonlocal Ethnography in a World of Apparatuses' (2011) 11 *Anthropological Theory* 375–395, 380.

47 Halme-Tuomisaari, 'Guarding Utopia'.

it to underline the exaggeratedly rigid nature of 'system' or 'structure' as analytical concepts, by emphasising the indeterminacy of the rules diverse agents mobilise in practice, as well as to highlight the creative gap between 'habitus and institutional structure'.[48]

Examining UN operations using inductive fuzzy logic captures an interesting paradox that evades deductive inquiries. One of IOs' cardinal values is that their operations should be transparent. Yet, the very documents such organisations produce may in fact create confusion and obfuscation. This outcome may partly be due to specialised jargon and procedural complexity. Indeed, rather than constituting a problem or shortcoming, fuzziness or partial opacity may be a desired element for seasoned insiders. A UN treaty bodies example clarifies this. The mandate of human rights treaty bodies is based on covenant provisions. For example, the basis of the Human Rights Committee's operations is stated in Article 36 of the ICCPR.[49] Yet, these provisions leave the scope of operations for the treaty bodies themselves to define.

Over the past decades, the committees and the UN have determined many elements of what the treaty bodies do and how. One example of this is the role NGOs play in Human Rights Committee sessions. Although formally only states and treaty bodies participate in Constructive Dialogues about state reports, NGOs have extensive opportunities to voice their views by submitting ancillary reports, contributing to the Lists of Issues on the basis of which Constructive Dialogue takes place. In addition they are able to share their views immediately before the Constructive Dialogue in the lunch-time briefing sessions open only to NGO delegates and committee members.

Moreover, the scope of treaty body operations has expanded, as illustrated by the UN Human Rights Committee processing state reports in the absence of state parties. The expansion does not please all states, giving rise to aspirations to curb treaty body operations.[50] Expansion has been largely made possible by the UN human rights

[48] P. Bourdieu, *In Other Words: Essays toward a Reflexive Sociology* (Stanford: Stanford University Press, 1990), 62–63, see also P. Bourdieu, *Outline of a Theory of Practice* (Cambridge: Cambridge University Press, 1977), 81–82.

[49] International Covenant on Civil and Political Rights, www.ohchr.org/en/instruments-mechanisms/instruments/international-covenant-civil-and-political-rights

[50] Halme-Tuomisaari, 'Guarding Utopia'.

apparatus's 'fuzzy logic', which allows seasoned insiders to manoeuvre in diverse, subtle ways. Yet, both the manoeuvring and its consequences would be lost in accounts emerging from deductive, formal, normative theorising about IOs.

Anthropologising Impact

Chimni notes how '[i]n the corpus of literature which constitutes international legal studies, there is little reflection on the role of international institutions in sustaining a particular vision of world order'.[51] Billaud and Cowan echo this when they point out how seldom bureaucracies, national or international, are viewed as the site of visions, let alone utopias. Instead, they note, 'classic representations tend to describe bureaucratic formations as "rationality machines", administrations as homogeneous black boxes and bureaucrats as individuals working "without hatred or passion" to implement a broader vision of which they remain largely ignorant'.[52]

International legal scholarship, particularly human rights scholarship, may be illuminative when it comes to grasping underlying visions, for instance, in Paul Lauren's *The Evolution of International Human Rights: Visions Seen.*[53] In his sweeping exploration of the origins of human rights thinking in various global regions, Lauren also depicts a world on a steady march away from superstition and moving toward rationality, human rights, and rule of law.[54]

In legal scholarship, the most common criticism of UN treaty bodies realising their underlying vision to improve human rights in the world is that their efforts are legally non-binding, and hence, ineffective. Indeed, the Human Rights Committee can only produce documents with authoritative significance, and some scholarship suggests minimal impact, when assessed via criteria such as including Committee

[51] B. S. Chimni, 'Marxism and International Law: A Contemporary Analysis' (1999) 34 *Economic and Political Weekly* 6, 337–349, 343.

[52] Billaud and Cowan, 'The Bureaucratisation of Utopia', 6.

[53] P. Lauren, *The Evolution of International Human Rights: Visions Seen* (Pennsylvania: Pennsylvania University Press, 1998).

[54] M. Halme-Tuomisaari and P. Slotte, 'Revisiting the Origins of Human Rights: Introduction' in P. Slotte and M. Halme-Tuomisaari (eds.), *Revisiting the Origins of Human Rights* (Cambridge: Cambridge University Press, 2015), pp. 1–36.

Concluding Observations in legislative debates, court proceedings, or parliamentary debates.[55]

Yet, anthropological insights reveal alternative paths of influence. Riles examines how individual documents and sessions can form a seamless cycle to constitute human rights dialogue. The significance of such dialogue originates in its capacity to link seemingly disparate events – such as processing an individual state report by a UN treaty body – into meaningful continuities. Together, these continuities form trajectories that apparently embody progress, as illustrated by changing the language in UN documents from 'sex' to 'gender' in the early 1990s.[56] Another avenue explores the informal influence that treaty body proceedings have. This may happen when a state civil servant picks up a UN treaty body report condemning the state's practices towards minorities. The civil servant may use the report to argue for increased resources, thus ideally improving the position of minorities, while also advancing human rights.[57]

There is a third avenue, which directs an analytical gaze on the 'mundane forms through which (IOs) work',[58] the 'boringly, even achingly, familiar routines'.[59] Helpful here is Riles' work on legal technicalities, 'those aspects of legal practice that cannot be reduced to norms, trust or other sociological concepts'.[60] One tangible example is the 'routinised pathways of thought' via which lawyers approach legal documents. This manner of approaching documents constitutes 'a profoundly aesthetic practice' 'of fidelity to proper form'. The 'legitimacy of law inheres in its aesthetic dimensions and practices',[61] which becomes 'a script for a particular kind of collaboration'.[62] In the following ethnographic vignette, I elaborate upon the significance these insights offer for understanding the role of 'lawlike' organs like UN treaty bodies, including the values that they uphold in their operations.

55 Krommendijk, 'The Domestic Effectiveness'.

56 A. Riles, 'Infinity within the Brackets' (1998) 25 *American Ethnologist* 3, 378–398, 380.

57 M. Halme-Tuomisaari, 'New Paradoxes in Human Rights' in L. Pedersen and L. Cligget (eds.), *The SAGE Handbook in Cultural Anthropology* (London: SAGE Publications, 2021), pp. 604–611.

58 Brown et al, 'Meetings', 10. 59 *Ibid.*

60 A. Riles, 'Afterword: A Method More than a Subject' in D. Cowan and D. Wincott (eds.), *Exploring the 'Legal' in Socio-legal Studies* (London: Palgrave Macmillan, 2015), 257, 259.

61 *Ibid*, 259. 62 *Ibid.*

Dialogue with Ourselves

> We're going to have a hearing on Belize in the absence of a report .... Essentially, the role of the committee is to review states' periodic reports. Because for a number of countries there were no reports at all, the committee adopted a rule of procedure whereby it is permitted to consider a situation in the absence of a report...(This)... it is hoped, will lead to the production of a report. In fact, as often as not it does, but sometimes it doesn't, and then the committee has to deal with whether or not the state sends a response to the list of issues and/or a delegation. As often as not, we get both. But this time, we have the responses but not the delegation, which is why we're going to be having the constructive dialogue with ourselves.[63]

It was an irregular UN Human Rights Committee session in Geneva at the Palais Wilson, the headquarters of the UN High Commissioner for Human Rights. For the first time, the seats state representatives customarily occupied at the front of the spacious conference room were empty. In all other respects, the stage was set for the undoubted culmination point of this high-profile, international gathering, the Constructive Dialogue, which is UN treaty body work's most treasured component. Committee members were seated in their places and ready for action; the interpreters were in their glass booths; members of the UN Secretariat were there, as were UN Conference services members and several NGO representatives, interns, and other observers. Press secretaries were ready to record the events, and the webcam a Geneva-based NGO operated was prepared to start transmitting 'to the world'. Only the lead character in this scene – the state – remained conspicuous by its absence.

The session that followed testified that the situation was novel for everyone involved. Committee members asked numerous times why there was no delegation from Belize. UN secretariat member responses suggested the reason might be financial, or as one committee member candidly stated, the state was 'broke'. Another committee member noted, had the session occurred at UN headquarters in New York – as one in every three Human Rights Committee sessions had prior to 2013 – Belize could simply have sent a staff member from its permanent mission. As committee sessions are now held exclusively in Geneva, where Belize has no permanent mission, this was not an

[63] Opening remarks of Sir Nigel Rodley, Human Rights Committee Chair, Constructive Dialogue on Belize, 107th session of the Human Rights Committee, Palais Wilson, Geneva, 15 March 2013, 3:00pm.

option. Other committee members questioned this reasoning: '*Just because a state says something does not mean you should believe it.*'

As the session wore on, the committee members' frustrations became palpable: several said it was a shame there was no delegation from Belize to respond to the numerous questions the committee had regarding implementation of the ICCPR. However, the committee members did not slack off: despite the absence of a respondent, they followed the usual session choreography by posing pointed questions regarding Belize's inaction regarding the ICCPR. The longest monologue by an individual committee member lasted almost forty minutes.

Constructive dialogue is a curious phrase. *Dialogue* is a staple of the UN treaty body operations and draws from the rhetoric of 'dialogue' prevalent in international collaboration. Yet, neither *constructive dialogue* nor *dialogue* have clear-cut definitions or distinct statuses in international law. In pragmatic terms, UN committees' Constructive Dialogues are highly orchestrated exchanges that usually last six working hours per state, consisting of formal opening statements read out by the heads of state delegations, followed by questions posed by committee members, mostly concerning compliance with the ICCPR, a round of answers by state representatives usually after brief preparation time, then follow-up questions by the committee, and, time permitting, a final round of answers by states.

Although accompanied by an air of spontaneity, in reality, all the elements of dialogues are carefully prepared in advance, requiring jointly months of labour. The questions committee members pose are based on extensive background research, as are the answers state representatives offer. More often than not, both questions and potential answers have been written down prior to sessions.[64] Significant labour accompanies the most important 'shadow actions' of the public performance, namely, the ancillary reports national and international NGOs prepare, submit, and present to the committee in sessions closed to state representatives.

From Savage to Civilised via Human Rights Reports

What is the relevance of Constructive Dialogues? What really happens during them and according to what logic does it make sense to have

[64] Halme-Tuomisaari, 'Contested Representation'.

one *with oneself*? Officially, Constructive Dialogues are moments for sharing factual information. Elsewhere, I challenge this, arguing that, in addition to, or perhaps instead of, exchanges of factual information, they entail significant hidden communications connected to tensions over who is a legitimate representative when it comes to providing information on behalf of a population.[65] In this chapter, I want to propose another answer by focusing on the importance of the seemingly insignificant and even banal: the forms and practices of Constructive Dialogues; in other words, the fact of their occurrence.

I thus ask the following: What if part of UN treaty bodies' relevance hinges on the very fact that UN expert bodies process documents called 'state reports' in elaborate, ritual sessions called 'Constructive Dialogues'? What if, by extension, the legitimacy of IOs and the means for them to realise their visions lie in 'aesthetic practices' embedded in 'fidelity to proper form',[66] which bestow upon these documents and practices – in the words of Jessie Allen – 'legal magic'.[67] To unpack these assertions, it is useful to take a momentary detour to explore the notion of the 'standard of civilisation', a notion for which, despite inspiring vast scholarship,[68] we lack agreed-upon definitions. However, the link between civilisation and international law appears uncontested: as Obregon summarises, 'international law carries the weight of being pronounced as the ultimate product of civilisation, making it into an utopian ideal of a transnational organised legal system that would bring progress and peace to the world'.[69]

Obregon connects this assertion to Kant's *Perpetual Peace*, in which he states that the difference between 'savage' and 'civilised' rests on insistence on a constitution and a preference for 'rational liberty' as opposed to a 'savage state of lawlessness'.[70] Tzouvala echoes this characterisation, arguing that the civilised standard became 'a way of

65 *Ibid.* 66 Riles, 'Afterword'.

67 J. Allen, 'A Theory of Adjudication: Law as Magic' (2008) 41 *Suffolk University Law Review* 773–831.

68 See L. Obregon, 'The Civilized and the Uncivilized' in B. Fassbender and A. Peters (eds.), *The Oxford Handbook of the History of International Law* (Oxford: Oxford University Press, 2012), 917. See also D. P. Fidler, 'Return of the Standard of Civilization, the International Human Rights Law in Practice' (2001) 2 *Chicago Journal of International Law* 137–157.

69 Obregon *ibid.*

70 *Ibid.* I. Kant 'Perpetual Peace' in H. Reiss (ed.), *Kant's Political Writings* (Cambridge: Cambridge University Press, 1996).

systematising and legitimising a wide range of juridical practices'.[71] These practices were 'justified with highly moralising references to civilisation',[72] amounting to a 'logic of improvement'.[73] Parfitt echoes these thoughts, noting that 'only those political communities that had been successfully interpellated as modern, bureaucratic and juridically separate from society and economy, were deemed to be civilised and, therefore, full subjects of international law'.[74] As Koskenniemi and Anghie, among others, illustrate, the standard of civilisation formed grounds for exclusion, conquest, and colonisation of peoples and states by 'those who thought themselves civilised or at least "more civilised"'.[75] Thus, the standard of civilisation creates 'a conundrum between exclusion and conditional inclusion'.[76]

Today, the standard of civilisation is increasingly seen as synonymous with 'metrics, indexes and "best practices" that give contemporary iterations'.[77] It is moreover embodied by the human rights system's expansion,[78] with the consequence that states which do not conform to this standard risk being 'exiled from the inner core of international society'.[79] The idea of meeting a standard of civilisation depends on fulfilling metrics determined by human rights reporting

[71] N. Tzouvala, *Capitalism as Civilisation: A History of International Law* (Cambridge: Cambridge University Press, 2020), 59–60.

[72] *Ibid*, 59–60.

[73] Tzouvala adds: 'the universalisation of institutions historically associated with the emergence, diffusion and reproduction of the capitalist mode of production becomes clearer if we examine the different reforms that were commonly associated with the achievement of civilised status.' *Ibid*, 59–60.

[74] R. Parfitt, *The Process of International Legal Reproduction: Inequality, Historiography, Resistance* (Cambridge: Cambridge University Press 2019), 146.

[75] Obregon, 'The Civilized and the Uncivilized, 92, A. Anghie, *Imperialism, Sovereignty and the Making of International Law* (Cambridge: Cambridge University Press, 2005); B. Bowden, *The Empire of Civilization: The Evolution of an Imperial Idea* (Chicago: The University of Chicago Press, 2009); M. Koskenniemi, *The Gentle Civilizer of Nations: The Rise and Fall of International Law, 1870–1960* (Cambridge: Cambridge University Press, 2002), 134–135, see also Tzouvala, *Capitalism as Civilisation*, 2.

[76] Tzouvala *ibid*, 2. [77] Tzouvala *ibid*, 45.

[78] G. Simpson, *Great Powers and Outlaw States: Unequal Sovereigns in the International Legal Order*. (Cambridge: Cambridge University Press, 2004), 281; J. Donnelly, 'Human Rights: A New Standard of Civilization?' (1998) 74 *International Affairs* 1–23.

[79] Simpson *ibid*, 343.

obligations, accompanied by quantified indicators.[80] This resonates with Mbembe's observations regarding postcolonial relations, according to which power works 'in its minute details', on 'the principles of assemblage which give rise to its efficacy' together with 'types of institutions, knowledges, norms, and practices that issue from it ... as well as the light that the use of visual imagery and discourse throws on the nature of domination and subordination'.[81]

Adhering to human rights reporting obligations often suffices for acceptance into the international community, or at least it is the only remaining, uniformly expected – or promised – action that the contemporary human rights regime offers. As Donnelly notes, '(t)he international community still refuses to act before ethnic conflict erupts into widespread bloodshed, or even to develop early warning systems'.[82] This inaction is problematic: as many noted regarding the Bosnian War, among others, military action justified in the name of human rights often causes as many problems as it solves. There is an indisputable sense of disappointment when confronted with this reality: just as with Belize's state report, the UN Human Rights Committee, like other UN treaty bodies, usually continues its diligent examination of documents accompanied by carefully choreographed Constructive Dialogues, even when, for example, military actions or terrorist attacks have taken place.

Sitting in the calm conference room of the Palais Wilson, the voices of children playing in the adjacent schoolyard entering through the windows, this situation may seem downright ludicrous. Proceeding with the calm processing of documents through 'UN reality' may feel like the last thing that should happen in the face of severe wrongdoings. Yet, this is what the committee does, and further, what it has been mandated to do by the covenant it monitors. With these observations, we return to *Downton Abbey*'s grand mansion. This time, we find ourselves at the upstairs dinner table – for which location Mr Carson, the butler, fervently polished the silverware. The crystal glassware and porcelain serving dishes are matched by the elaborate detail on the ladies' dresses. The men are impeccably dressed in white

[80] Merry, *Human Rights and Gender Violence.*
[81] A. Mbembe, 'African Modes of Self-Writing' (2002) 14 *Public Culture* 1, 239–273.
[82] Donnelly, 'Human Rights', 17.

ties. After some polite chitchat, an exchange ensues. Participating are Mr Branson, the chauffeur who became Lord Grantham's son-in-law, and Lord Grantham's mother, Lady Grantham, a true specimen of old British noblesse.

Mr Branson asks, as a continuation of an earlier conversation: '*But why do the rituals, the clothes and the customs matter so much?*' to which the elderly Lady Grantham responds: '*Because without them we would be like the wild men of Borneo.*'[83]

With this statement, our circle is complete. We find ourselves, quite unexpectedly, drawn back to the remote and exotic, both the islands of the Pacific and the small coastal states of Central America. Yet, in this instance, it is not the anthropologist's whites that separate the civilised from the savages. Nor is it the silverware that, via feverish polishing according to vigilant standards, communicates to the brute Germans that they have not conquered civilised Britain. Instead, the separation between 'civilised' and 'savage' is created and maintained by aesthetic practices concerning documents and meetings that demonstrate 'fidelity to proper form' – just as the vigorously examined documents and carefully choreographed rituals in the main conference room of the Palais Wilson do.

In all simplicity, this means that part of the 'civilising mission' is embedded in the very fact that IOs exist. By extension, a core part of their importance is embedded in the very materiality of their work. In the field of human rights, 'fidelity to proper form' refers to the continuous proliferation of different 'units', 'policies', 'programmes', 'committees', and 'rules'. Thus, in 2018, when Belize sent a state delegation to participate in the proceedings, the Human Rights Committee framed the matter in praise of progress, which it included in its finally adopted Concluding Observations.[84] Indeed, the significance of such forms and practices is not determined by their impact or effectiveness, but rather by their mere existence.

This example elucidates that, in the human rights field, the very production of infinite numbers of 'lawlike' documents, as well as

[83] *Downton Abbey*, Series 5, Episode 5.
[84] UN Human Rights Committee: Concluding Observations on the Initial Report of Belize, *CPR/C/BLZ/CO/1/Add.1*, 11 Dec 2018, https://documents-dds-ny.un.org/doc/UNDOC/GEN/G18/361/75/PDF/G1836175.pdf?OpenElement.

the elaborate practices according to which these documents are processed, form the civilised standards for a better world. When examined from this perspective, more important than whether or not such documents have binding legal force, or even what they contain, is that they convey their messages *by means of appropriate organisational aesthetics*, including covenant-like paragraphs and sub-paragraphs that rely extensively on individual pieces of legislation, court rulings, policies and action plans, and ritualised meetings. It is the *legal technicalities* that give these forms and practices their 'legal magic' and by extension their legitimacy. Their existence comes to embody a vision of a better world characterised by technicalities and proper aesthetic practices, and by extension, the values of rationality, transparency, and the rule of law.

Conclusion

In this chapter, I highlighted the alternative approaches that anthropology may offer to the study of IOs in international law. These include insights into the effects that IOs may exert on today's world order and the mechanisms via which this occurs. Focusing on legal technicalities and materiality offers new analytical avenues for reflecting on the relevance and consequences of IOs' operations. Such a focus also offers insights into the historical continuities characterising both IOs and international law. To date, such continuities have been largely overlooked in scholarship on IOs.

This approach opens fresh avenues for considering the future of IOs and their visions, allowing us to ask whether IOs still have utility. The world depicted in *Downton Abbey* started to vanish soon after the historical moment described at the beginning of this chapter – although not because of the war with the Germans and definitely not due to lacking standards where polishing silverware was concerned. Since the start of the COVID-19 pandemic in early 2020 we have seen again how quickly and unexpectedly the world can change. We have experienced how fast the life that seemed normal to us to can be turned upside down.

We have likewise experienced how quickly new standards for a better world can be introduced, whether they are the face masks we began to wear or the COVID-19 vaccination certificates we became accustomed to showing to enter airplanes, hotels, and restaurants – all things that just a few years prior would have felt impossible to imagine. We do not yet know how permanent these new standards will be or when the subsequent waves of pandemics or other world crises will occur that will upend what we know as proper procedures. These changes, however, make apparent how much the world has changed since the inception of IOs decades ago, when global concerns were very different from those we face today. What will happen to IOs in the future, and whether they will be able to adapt to everchanging world situations, we do not yet know. What remains certain is that to understand this future – the impacts and effects of IOs operations, as well as the diverse roles legal technicalities, materialities, and aesthetics play – sustained interdisciplinary debate remains essential.

Thus, anthropology offers to the study of IOs insights into the effects that IOs may exert in today's world order, as well as the mechanisms via which they do so. It also provides alternative means for considering the legitimacy of IOs and the historical continuities that accompany the 'civilising mission' that they embody.

12 'The Critic Is Not the One Who Debunks, but the One Who Assembles'

On Professional Performances and Material Practices

DIMITRI VAN DEN MEERSSCHE

Introduction

When Roberto Dañino, former General Counsel at the World Bank, arrived in the institution, he found a department perceived to be at the verge of 'marginalisation' – a dire state he diagnosed and soon attributed to the rigid 'culture' of legal practice. In tracing Dañino's efforts to 'make the department relevant again', we get a glimpse of the situated, material, embodied institutional life of international law: the changes Dañino instilled were manifested not in formal legal sources but in the introduction of new cultural codes, professional prototypes (the 'how to' lawyer), and technical routines of risk management. In the domain of international institutional law – often oriented towards abstraction, comparison, or aspiration – such prosaic legal practices tend to be underplayed. If we want to perceive or evaluate changes in the cultural technique of international law(yering) such as those sparked by Dañino, I argue, we need to redirect our attention to 'that which lies at the edges of conventional international legal sightlines', as Johns argued – to focus not on 'grand designs' but on 'lived practices and techniques', in the words of Riles. This chapter signals two productive entry points for such a turn to practice: (i) a focus on the shared and contingent criteria of competence – the 'social grammar' – that mark professional postures and performances and (ii) a heightened attention for the practices of relationality, translation, and materiality through which law is composed – the string of 'people and things' that it assembles. This methodological orientation to professional scripts and material routines also offers a perspective on 'critique' that differs from the familiar structuralist modes of analysis and intervention. What might legal 'critique' become if, with Levi and Valverde, we were to trade the 'abstracted view of "structure" [for] the empirical work of studying action, actors, communication, imitation and translation, networks, knowledge flows and the continual process that constructs society itself'? If we associated the 'critical' gesture, in Latour's terms, with 'multiplication, not subtraction' – with more, not less? If the direction of 'critique' were not away from its objects (a flight into their social or political conditions of possibility) but 'toward the gathering'? If the 'critic' were not 'the one who debunks, but the one who assembles'? Perhaps it is in tracking and tracing, mapping and multiplying, and not in the stylized posture of scepticism that 'critique' might regain potential?

'I Wanted to Make the Legal Department Relevant Again'

When Roberto Dañino – former Peruvian Prime Minister and ambassador to the United States – was appointed as the World Bank's General Counsel in 2003, he felt he arrived at a department in disarray. Only a few years after Ibrahim Shihata's departure – Dañino's illustrious predecessor whose presence still lingered in the organization and who, according to Dañino, had 'very much exercised the power of the office' – he perceived that the legal department had now become 'marginalised'.[1] There was a decline in requests by the World Bank's Board of Executive Directors for formal legal opinions, and lawyers present at that time expressed that they were increasingly kept at a certain distance from the organization's transactional process. Experiencing an expanding distrust of the institution's political Board,

[1] Interview with Former General Counsel Roberto Dañino, October 2016 ('Dañino Interview'). This interview material is drawn from and contextualized in D. Van Den Meerssche, *The World Bank's Lawyers: The Life of International Law as Institutional Practice* (Oxford University Press, 2022). This crisis narrative and trope of 'marginalisation' was, in fact, a recurring one. When Shihata, General Counsel from 1983 to 2000, was appointed in the World Bank he, in his words, 'discovered that the Legal Department was very demoralized [and] marginalised'. In response, his first act as General Counsel was the physical relocation of its department back to the main building, across the street from where it had been (on his request, the department was moved back across H street from the N building to the E building – the main building). The diagnosis of marginalisation, in this sense, also provided a platform for heroic interventions of revival and renewal to take place.

a lingering discontent of its operational branches, and a diminishing esteem for the department, Dañino framed this dire state as the result of a particular 'culture' in the legal department.[2] The issue, as he construed it, was that too many lawyers displayed their power by saying 'you cannot do this ... this is wrong'.[3] While the institution's senior management demanded ambition and agility in the face of new global challenges, a close ally of Dañino lamented, the law had become 'fossilized'.

In articulating his strategy to instil a new 'paradigm' of legal practice in the Bank, Dañino categorized this 'old type' of lawyer as the 'why not' lawyer.[4] 'My strategy for making the LEGAL VPU [Vice Presidency] more relevant and better positioned to meet the needs of the Bank', he stated early in his tenure, is to 'change our attitude from "why not" to "how to". We cannot just be policemen, blindly enforcing the rules. We need to go beyond that and provide ... value-added to our clients'.[5] This was the time of the Millennium Development Goals and the Comprehensive Development Framework. A time of radical expansion, moral reinvigoration, and institutional growth led by James Wolfensohn – probably the most ambitious Bank president since McNamara.[6] This was not the time to slow down the grinding mills of global liberal reform by adopting a principled posture of legal formalism.[7]

To make the department 'relevant again', Dañino perceived that it was necessary to rewrite the script of legal practice in the Bank and articulate a new ideal-type for the international institutional lawyer: the creative and client-oriented 'how to' lawyer. The 'cultural' clash caused by this new professional prototype escalated in a discussion over the legality of the Bank's engagement with criminal justice and

[2] Dañino Interview. [3] *Ibid.* [4] *Ibid.*

[5] R. Dañino, 'The World Bank: A Lawyer's Perspective', Talk at Harvard Law School, 1 November 2004.

[6] On the extensive reformist ambitions of Wolfensohn, see G. Sinclair, *To Reform the World: International Organizations and the Making of Modern States* (Oxford University Press, 2017).

[7] On the principled posture that Shihata cultivated and how it was frustrating those with an ambitious vision of reform, see Van Den Meerssche, *The World Bank's Lawyers*. I have also elaborated on this in D. Van Den Meerssche, 'Performing the Rule of Law in International Organizations: Ibrahim Shihata and the World Bank's Turn to Governance Reform' (2019) 32 *Leiden Journal of International Law* 47–69.

security sector reform in developing countries. For Shihata – and the conservative lawyers still clinging to his scriptures – this area was categorically off-limits. Several years before Dañino arrived, a legal memorandum had been drafted that argued that police power was an expression of the sovereign power of a state, and that, consequently, the financing of police expenditures would not be consistent with the organization's Articles of Agreement.[8] The World Bank, it underlined, should not be seen as a 'world government' with an unlimited mandate and should only engage with those tasks specifically included in its constituent charter.[9] This position epitomizes the 'old approach': its methodology is formalistic, its principled logic produces clear legal boundaries, and its legal conclusion urges rigidity and restraint. In this 'old approach', 'sovereignty' figures as a central pivot: since the World Bank is not a 'world government', as Shihata would consistently reiterate, its legal competences are both constituted and constrained by the codified exercise and expression of state consent.[10] This mode of legal practice reflects a familiar functionalist imaginary: the idea that the mandate and competences of the organization resulted from an act of attribution from a collective principal (the member states) to an agent (the World Bank) in the form of a multilateral treaty – the Articles of Agreement. In this sense, the principled policing of legal boundaries and the World Bank's prohibition to engage with 'politics',

[8] This opinion is cited as the conservative position to questions on criminal justice reform in A.-M. Leroy, *Legal Note on Bank Involvement in the Criminal Justice Sector*, 9 February 2012, para. 22 ('one traditional view in the Bank has it that criminal justice is ... essentially an exercise of sovereign power, akin to the military, support for which will inevitably involve the Bank in making political judgments and therefore not a proper subject for Bank intervention'). Leroy's legal opinion, which explicitly draws on and incorporates the change in legal paradigm developed by Roberto Dañino, is available at https://documents.worldbank.org/en/publication/documents-reports/documentdetail/138001468136794111/legal-note-on-bank-involvement-in-the-criminal-justice-sector (accessed 7 November 2024).

[9] The trope of the 'world government' was recurrent in the writings of Ibrahim Shihata, who consistently invoked it to point out the functionalist limits of the organization's purposes and mandate.

[10] In prior writing, Geoff Gordon and I have qualified this as the international law's *oedipal* manifestation – its presence as prohibitive, principled constraint on behaviour. D. Van Den Meerssche and G. Gordon, 'A New Normative Architecture' – Risk and Resilience as Routines of Un-governance' (2020) 11 *Transnational Legal Theory* 267–299.

for Shihata, ultimately echoed the principle of state sovereignty and sovereign equality.[11]

This imaginary had limited not only the organization's engagement with criminal justice reform but also its involvement in situations of conflict and its interventions in the sphere of governance reform more generally. In the former case, Shihata had made an appearance before the Board, where he articulated a number of central legal principles, described as 'either self-evident or dictated by the Articles'.[12] 'The first principle', he stated, is that the World Bank 'is not a world government ... with an unlimited mandate. It is an international organization with a mandate defined in its Articles of Agreement'.[13] In the latter case, the 'world government' trope returns: 'it is perfectly clear that the Bank's purpose is not to substitute itself for the peoples and governments of its borrowing member countries in deciding how these countries are to be governed. This might be a task for a world government, not the World Bank'.[14] Furthering the vision that the institution has limited competences, attributed in the Articles, Shihata argued that it 'cannot venture to act beyond its purposes and statutory obligations without the risk of acting *ultra vires*'.[15] The *ultra vires* concept is tied to 'the basic principle of *pacta sunt servanda*, the cooperative nature of the Bank and the consensual basis of its actions'.[16]

Importantly, however, Dañino ascribed the dire state of the legal department not to the application of particular theories or doctrines, but to the prevalence of a specific professional 'culture'. Shihata had,

[11] The political prohibitions clause, Shihata argued, linked with 'principles of equality of states and non- intervention in domestic affairs, enshrined in the UN Charter (Article 2(1) and (7)) and high in the minds of the original drafters of the Articles who envisaged universal membership' in the Bank. I. Shihata, 'The World Bank and "Governance" Issues in its Borrowing Members', in I. Shihata (ed.), *The World Bank in a Changing World – Selected Essays*, Vol. I (Martinus Nijhoff Publishers, 1991), 66–67.

[12] IBRD, *A Framework for World Bank Involvement in Situations of Conflict*, Transcripts of Board Meeting, 18 February 1997, http://documents1.worldbank.org/curated/en/225911521016631337/pdf/124249-TSCP-PUBLIC-03-Transcript-of-IBRD-IDA-Board-Meeting-of-February-18-1997-Redacted.pdf (cleared upon request) (accessed 7 November 2024), 35.

[13] *Ibid.* [14] Shihata, *The World Bank in a Changing World*, 80.

[15] *Ibid.*, 96.

[16] I. Shihata, 'Introductory Chapter: Interpretation as Practiced at the World Bank', in I. Shihata (ed.), *The World Bank Legal Papers* (Martinus Nijhoff Publishers, 2000), lvi.

indeed, consciously cultivated an 'attitude' or 'posture' of liberal legalism inside the department and the institution more generally. 'I believe in discipline', he noted in an interview at the turn of the millennium, '[a]nd, you have to respect the rule of law because you cannot advocate it and not respect it, internally'.[17] This was tied to a specific vision of the role of the lawyer in safeguarding the thriving and survival of the World Bank (and the system of global governance more broadly): '[i]gnoring [the limitations of the Articles] can work only to the detriment of the Bank and, in the long run, of all its members', Shihata responded to his critics at American Society of International Law in 1988.[18] This principled posture was not only instrumental in nature but also related to a specific social trusteeship ideal of the legal profession. Even as Director General at the OPEC Fund, Shihata noted: 'I did a great deal of the technical legal work myself, mainly out of concern for my own profession. I don't consider management a profession'.[19] This 'concern' for the international legal profession expressed itself in performances of detachment and an iconology of constraint: 'I have not acted simply as the spokesman for Management', he later recalled, 'I have acted as the spokesman for the law'.[20] This liberal promise of speaking truth to power, for Shihata, reflected varying 'cultures' in the 'attitude of lawyers depending on [their] background': the 'typical practicing lawyer in a law firm [who] is driven by the interest of the client', he argued, acts 'very different [to] a law professor who cares for what he thinks is legally correct'.[21] This 'care' and 'commitment' was portrayed to verge on heroism: 'not everyone has it in himself to [take these positions]', Shihata observed,

17 Interview with I. Shihata, World Bank Oral History Program, 23 and 24 May 2000, 82.

18 ASIL, *Proceedings of the 82nd Annual Meeting*, American Society of International Law, Washington D.C., 1988, 42.

19 Interview with I. Shihata, World Bank Oral History Program, 11 May 1994, 13. On Shihata's professional path prior to joining the World Bank, see the marvellous account in U. Özsu, 'Hydrocarbon Humanitarianism: Ibrahim Shihata, "Oil Aid", and Resource Sovereignty' (2020) 23 *Journal of the History of International Law* 137–160.

20 Interview with I. Shihata, World Bank Oral History Program, 23 and 24 May 2000, 15. *Cf.* D. Kennedy, *A Critique of Adjudication (fin de siècle)* (Harvard University Press, 1997), 3 (pointing to the 'iconology of constraint' at the heart of a particular strand of liberal legal culture).

21 *Ibid.*, 31. In this sense, Shihata consciously operated as a 'counterweight to management'.

'because many people want to continue in their job and feed their children which is legitimate, and I am not blaming them. Other people [referring to himself] are not like that, however ... [T] hey feel strongly about principles and they act accordingly no matter what happens to them'.[22] This cultivated posture was, of course, not idiosyncratic but aligned with a particular ideal of international liberal legalism shared by many in Shihata's personal and professional milieu. It is reflected, for example, in Bedjaoui's identification of the 'frustrating tyranny of a certain praetorian subjectivism' at the 'margin of indeterminacy' – a 'crushing responsibility' he faced 'anxiously' and 'humbly'.[23] These specific professional ideals were reflected inside the World Bank not only in the restrictive reading of the Articles of Agreement, as pointed out earlier, but also in how the department was organized. There was a hierarchical culture where only Shihata formally published legal opinions or academic writings. These opinions entail thick webs of references (to *travaux préparatoires*, judicial precedents, VCLT provisions, or classic constitutional authorities) assembled in a dense textual form and legalist style. Management often lamented that Shihata drafted not legal opinions but constitutional edicts. When he was asked about his views on demands for decentralization, he cautioned that a 'lawyer in the field is not like a lawyer here because he doesn't have the same institutional support, and he may tend to become overwhelmed by the context of where he is'.[24] This, he feared, would promote a 'culture in the attitude of lawyers driven by the interest of the client', which was antithetical to his 'commitment' to the 'rule of law'.[25]

Upon Dañino's arrival, he (and those close to him) quickly recognized this professional culture – with its centralized structure,

[22] Interview with I. Shihata, World Bank Oral History Program, 23 and 24 May 2000, 15.

[23] See M. Bedjaoui, 'Expediency in the Decisions of the International Court of Justice' (2001) 71 *British Yearbook of International Law*, 3–4. Haskell sharply describes this cultivation of an internal posture of constraint as essential in neutralizing the political implications of legal discretion. Political choice, he observed, is hereby masked by a cultivated cosmopolitan sensibility of 'prudence'. See J. Haskell, 'A Case in the Politics of Form: Yearbooks of International Law' (2020) 50 *Netherlands Yearbook of International Law* 21–35.

[24] Interview with I. Shihata, World Bank Oral History Program, 23 and 24 May 2000, 31.

[25] *Ibid.*

principles borderlines, legalist style, and outdated social trusteeship ideals – as a 'conservative course' that was preventing the institution from being an innovator or pioneer, and from playing a leading role in non-traditional domains of development practice (such as criminal justice or security sector reform). 'I didn't want lawyers', Dañino later observed, 'who always said: "you cannot do this", but lawyers who could tell you how to do things in a legal way'.[26] Aware of the need for a professional change in the department, he recalls: 'I came up with a motto ... going from the "why not" to the "how to" lawyer'.[27] The introduction of the 'how to' lawyer entailed a change in both the purpose and the instruments of legal practice. On the first level, the 'how to' lawyer, for Dañino, had to be a profoundly pragmatic and goal-oriented professional with the capacity to 'fix' problems and, in doing so, provide a 'value added' to the organization's mission.[28] This lawyer would be a welcome actor in the day-to-day operational processes of the Bank (as opposed to the 'why not' lawyer, who frustrates the operational process by producing rigidity and formal barriers). In order to achieve these goals, lawyers need to display 'creative thinking' and an ability to design 'tailor-made' solutions for problems at particular levels. On the second level, this change in the practice of lawyering demanded a new set of material tools of legal practice. In

[26] Dañino Interview. [27] *Ibid.*

[28] We see a resonance with Kratochwil's diagnosis of cultural changes in the international legal profession: 'Meanwhile [lawyers] claiming special expertise seem equally distanced from the ideal of the "moral politician" for whom Kant had rooted as they are from the professional or the *spoudaios* who was the ideal of the social trusteeship professionalism. As the new expertocratic professionals are caught up in an interminable slew of meetings and deadlines, they have little left for reflection and critical assessment ... [C]omfort and confidence come from frantic activity ... being part of "the team", and from reliance on routinized and deeply engrained techniques. Props like graphs, PowerPoints and best practices have then increasingly to substitute for reflective judgment, as work becomes more and more reified and subject to "scientific" (mostly quantitative) assessment ... [T]he modern [legal] professional becomes a Macher (both in the sense of the homo faber and the Yiddish "fixer" who gets things done), since even in "third sector" organizations s/he has to be a "go-getter" and mission junkie rather than the helper of yore who lived his "calling".' F. Kratochwil, 'Spoudaios, Professional, Expert or "Macher"? Reflections on the Changing Nature of an Occupation', in W. Werner, M. De Hoon, and A. Galan (eds.), *The Law of International Lawyers: Reading Martti* (Cambridge University Press, 2017), 256.

this context, Dañino introduced a 'doctrine' for legal practice that would replace formal 'judgments' with a 'risk-analysis approach'. This transformation was associated with the introduction of a set of novel bureaucratic techniques, (visual) heuristics, and managerial expert committees geared towards a more efficient measurable evaluation and assessment of operational needs. Ingrained in the shift from the 'why not' to the 'how to' lawyer, in short, was the introduction of a deeply deformalized and multidisciplinary language of legality.

Capturing this shift in the 'culture', 'philosophy', and 'mindset' of lawyering, Dañino's legal opinion on criminal justice applied the 'risk-analysis approach' to matters of operational expansion.[29] Rather than a 'blanket prohibition' on engagement in this sector, the opinion argued, that for many of those projects of criminal justice reform that pose some risk of political interference, that risk could be 'managed'.[30] This 'risk management' approach relied on managerial processes of 'consultation' and 'systemwide diagnostic analysis' as well as the creation of an *ad hoc* 'special review mechanism'.[31] This departure from the Shihata doctrine demanded a completely different professional orientation and a new set of decision-making tools. The shift to 'risk management' implied a mode of evaluation that did not need to be 'binary' (legal/illegal): by adopting a new range of managerial heuristics – case-by-case diagnostics, tailored involvement, risk mitigation measures, and compliance tools built around indicators, safeguards, or monitoring devices developed by *ad hoc* task teams – the prohibitive binary approach that had marked Shihata's tenure would be traded for an enabling framework of contextual, non-binary risk assessment. The new policy was to identify the 'green lights, yellow lights and red lights' within those operational domains that Shihata had previously considered as part of the sovereignty function of the state and beyond the legal mandate of the Bank. The 'risk management approach' was

29 R. Dañino, 'Legal Opinion on Bank Activities in the Criminal Justice Sector', 31 January 2006. This legal opinion is referenced and reproduced in Leroy, *Legal Note on Bank Involvement in the Criminal Justice Sector*. Leroy later noted that '[t]he 2012 Legal Note built on a 2006 Legal Opinion which, for various reasons, did not find full institutional acceptance, but which encapsulated the evolution in thinking, perhaps a bit too far "before its time"'. World Bank Legal Vice Presidency, *Annual Report FY 2013: The World Bank's Engagement in the Criminal Justice Sector and the Role of Lawyers in the 'Solutions Bank'* (Washington, DC: World Bank, 2013), 95.

30 Dañino, *Legal Opinion on the Ibid. Justice Sector*.

31 *Ibid.*

framed as a 'process-based solution' instead of one that would categorize specific activities as permissible or impermissible. This radical change in approach expressed in this process-based solution would evolve into a new set of heuristics and bureaucratic techniques for legal practice: 'risk assessment templates', an online 'risk portal' for adaptation at the project level, 'rules-of-thumb', 'roadmaps', and 'colour codes' for risk evaluation and mitigation, as well as the reallocation of roles and responsibilities in 'special review mechanisms' built for 'dynamic' forms of 'risk management'.[32]

The heuristic of the 'how to' lawyer hereby appears as rationalization for a thoroughly deformalized mode of legal practice inscribed within bureaucratic processes of decision-making operating on the basis of risk scores, indicators, managerial mechanisms, informal guidelines, and exogenous forms of expertise (indeed, lawyers would not need to play a central part in the committee in charge of the risk management process). None of the aims sought to be achieved through these processes are immanent to the 'rule of law' itself: the teleology of the 'how to' lawyer is client satisfaction, the reduction of transaction costs, and managerial effectiveness. Yet, it is important to note that this transformation occurred in conjunction with a more 'holistic' approach to development issues – as expressed in the Comprehensive Development Framework of Wolfensohn and the diagnostic instruments this entailed – as well as the embrace of risk analysis in public governance more widely.[33] The shift in 'doing law' from the 'why not' to the 'how to' lawyer thus entailed a move away from the coordinates of public international law thinking (with the associated functionalist constraints of intergovernmental consent) to a mode of lawyering fine-tuned to the exigencies and ambitions of a growing global bureaucracy.

In trading practices of formal treaty interpretation and the policing of boundaries for such adaptive, creative, and client-oriented forms of risk management, Dañino asserted that lawyers could become 'agents of change', which would make 'the legal department relevant again' in

[32] On the introduction and effects of these decision-making tools, see Van Den Meerssche, *The World Bank's Lawyers*.

[33] See, for example, J. Black, 'The Emergence of Risk-Based Regulation and the New Public Risk Management in the United Kingdom' (2005) *Public Law* 512–549.

an institution marked by rapid operational expansion.[34] This ideal of change – and the deformalizing drift that it entailed – was inspired by a cosmopolitan vision of global governance no longer constrained by the shackles of sovereignty – a vision inspired by those reformers who, Dañino felt, 'really make a difference in the world'.[35] Cosmopolitan commitments were attuned to corporate scripts of legal practice in an effort to counteract the lingering constitutional sensibilities and prohibitive interventions by the remaining 'conservative' lawyers in the Bank.[36] As formal treaty interpretation was displaced by routines of risk assessment, some in the legal department protested and qualified these new standards as unlawyerly. While Dañino wanted 'jurisprudence' to be made 'at the level of the lawyers' in a decentralized and deformalized fashion, he experienced 'a lot of pushback inside the legal department itself': 'changing culture', a former lawyer close to Dañino observed, 'is just the most difficult thing in an institution like this'.[37] In navigating these tensions, Dañino immediately saw the need for internal administrative reform: he launched an 'aggressive decentralization strategy', created the 'legal and judicial reform unit' with an explicit operational mandate, put forward a 'simplification and streamlining' of 'legal services', changed the department's recruitment policies (targeting young lawyers who still 'wanted to change the world'), and distributed working papers, guidance notes, and brainstorming memos aimed at rewriting the scripts of legal practice, and persuading those still committed to old routines.[38]

By the time Dañino left the Bank, the standards of professional practice had significantly shifted. A new legal imagination had gained ground – a *bricolage* of reformist ambitions, managerial modes of public sector governance, corporate ideals of lawyering, and tropes of

[34] Dañino Interview ('lawyers can be agents of change or agents of stopping that change').

[35] *Ibid.* In the interview, Dañino referred to Kofi Annan (who just published his manifesto *In Larger Freedom*) as well as Mary Robinson and Louise Arbour. Yet, the leading example for Dañino was President James Wolfensohn himself.

[36] Referring to the 'very conservative lawyers' in the World Bank, Dañino observed: 'I'm just not that kind of lawyer. I don't believe in natural law ... I think laws are made by humans and they always need to be adapted to changing circumstances ... as things evolve in the world'. *Ibid.*

[37] *Ibid.*

[38] He already laid out many of these plans early in his tenure. See Dañino, 'The World Bank: A Lawyer's Perspective'.

moral universalism that were drawn from Dañino's prior professional life as politician, entrepreneur, and investment banker.[39] This new way of 'doing legal knowledge' had profound political effects: the role of the 'how to' lawyer was no longer to draw legal boundaries but to enable a smooth operational expansion, safeguard 'client satisfaction', and contribute to Dañino's ambitious agenda of global legal and judicial reform.[40]

How does change in international law occur? How does international law obtain meaning and political substance? How does it channel and mediate social and institutional relations? This account displayed that international law's politics and pathways to change are not (only) expressed in grand legislative interventions, not (only) in its semantic twists and turns or in its deeply embedded 'structural biases', not (only) in its theoretical reconfigurations, (neo)colonial codes, or the capricious choices of solitary giants. It is in the mundane and material – the risk-based colour code, the new professional prototype, the habits and routines, the tools and templates, the cultural criteria of competence – that we see the life of international law change course (a change, of course, interwoven with and interweaving broader patterns of socio-political transformation). As a skilled 'navigator', Dañino changed the course of law in the World Bank in precisely this manner; not as a doctrinal architect of international (institutional) law but through the gradual cultivation of a new material practice and professional performance.

Pluralizing Our Ways of Seeing International Organizations (Law)

This brief vignette, I believe, signals several challenges of methodological and political significance to the discipline of international organizations law. While it shows salient changes in the orientation

[39] On the notion of law as *bricolage*, an experimental use of tools that are 'lying around', see M. Koskenniemi, *To the Uttermost Parts of the Earth Legal Imagination and International Power 1300–1870* (Cambridge University Press, 2021).

[40] This reference to Riles signals the importance of focusing on the material 'technicalities' of this change. See A. Riles, 'A New Agenda for the Cultural Study of Law: Taking on the Technicalities' (2005) 53 *Buffalo Law Review* 973–1033. This resonates in the changing technical registers of lawyering as it transmuted into a managerial routine of risk analysis.

and organizational effects of legal labour, these changes prove difficult to articulate with reference to the doctrines, archives, and sources that shape this field of literature.[41] Oriented towards abstraction, comparison, or aspiration, intellectual interventions in international institutional law tend to underplay (or ignore) the importance of prosaic legal practices and the performative effects that they engender in concrete institutional spaces. I therefore subscribe wholeheartedly to this volume's aim of studying international organizations at 'sites of socio-technical struggles', and to pluralize and politicize the subjects, methods, and aims of international institutional law in a non-doctrinal fashion.[42] If we want to perceive and possibly problematize shifts in the 'cultural technique' of international law(yering) of the type sketched out earlier,[43] we need to redirect our attention to 'that which lies at the edges of conventional international legal sightlines',[44] as Johns has argued – to focus not on 'grand designs' but on 'lived practices and techniques'.[45] The brief empirical exploration in the previous section shows two particularly productive socio-legal entry points, I believe, for what such a 'turn to practice' could entail.

First, as Dañino's efforts clearly testify, I see a need to focus on the changing 'role of the lawyer' and the professional scripts that shape how legal norms are being enacted.[46] Koskenniemi's indeterminacy

[41] *Cf.* Sinclair, *To Reform the World* (on the limited selection of materials in international organization law). This archive is described as 'the treaty constituting a particular IO, the rules of procedure of individual organs [and] a number of decisions and opinions of the ICJ' in J. Von Bernstorff, 'Procedures of Decision-Making and the Role of Law in International Organizations' (2008) 9 *German Law Journal* 1939–1964.

[42] *Cf.* N. Mansouri and D. R. Quiroga-Villamarín, 'Editorial Introduction: Seeing International Organizations Differently' in this volume.

[43] *Cf.* C. Vismann, *Files – Law and Media Technology* (Stanford University Press, 2008) (on law as a 'cultural technique').

[44] F. Johns, *Non-Legality in International Law: Unruly Law* (Cambridge University Press, 2012), 187.

[45] A. Riles, *Collateral Knowledge: Legal Reasoning in the Global Financial Markets* (University of Chicago Press, 2011), 246. *Cf.* G. Sullivan, '"Taking on the Technicalities" of International Law – Practice, Description, Critique: A Response to Fleur Johns' (2017) 111 *AJIL Unbound* 181–186.

[46] The need to devote critical attention to the 'changing role of the legal "professional"' is signalled also in Kratochwil, *Spoudaios, Professional, Expert or "Macher"?* This changing role of the lawyer within the World Bank would later be consolidated by General Counsel Anne-Marie Leroy. D. Van Den Meerssche, Deformalising International Organizations Law: The Risk

thesis, which strongly influenced the trajectory of 'critical' international law, points to the 'gap' between 'legal materials (rules, principles, precedents, doctrines) and the legal decision'.[47] It is in this 'gap' – and not in the substance of the (inherently indeterminate) legal institution – that the 'politics' of international law is purportedly performed.[48] For Koskenniemi, this indeterminacy 'gap' is a space of freedom and responsibility: if every opposing political position can plausibly be articulated in the language of international law, he argues, any legal 'choice will be just that – a "choice" that is "grounded" in nothing grander than a history of how we came to have the preferences that we have'.[49] Yet, while this view of the 'law-applier' as the final site of normative agency, imaginative possibility, and political responsibility might be suitable for the 'solitary giants' on which Koskenniemi's historical writings tend to focus, it misses out on the shared social practices that constitute and condition the meaning of these interventions.[50] If we want to situate the 'politics' of law(yering) in international institutions, it is necessary to focus on the 'social grammar' of legal practice – on the professional roles, institutional scripts, and 'feel for the game' that shape 'the conditions of ... law's production and existence',[51] and determine what can be qualified as a 'competent performance'.[52] This is reflected in the 'culture' that Dañino encountered upon his arrival and which he sought and struggled to change – understanding that

Appetite of Anne-Marie Leroy (2023) 34 *European Journal of International Law* 141.

[47] I am referring to what Koskenniemi has himself described as his 'weak' critical thesis. M. Koskenniemi, *From Apology to Utopia: The Structure of International Legal Argument (Re-issue)* (Cambridge University Press, 2005), 600ff.

[48] *Ibid.*, 601. [49] *Ibid.*, 615.

[50] *Cf.* F. Megret, 'Thinking about What International Humanitarian Lawyers 'Do' – An Examination of the Laws of War as a Field of Professional Practice', in W. Werner, M. De Hoon, and A. Galan (eds.), *The Law of International Lawyers: Reading Martti* (Cambridge University Press, 2017), 267ff (on Koskenniemi's focus on 'solitary giants').

[51] *Ibid.*, 274–275.

[52] F. Kratochwil, *The Status of Law in World Society: Meditations on the Role and the Rule of Law* (Cambridge University Press, 2014), 53 (on how the study of 'competent [legal] performance[s]' avoids 'endless rounds of deconstruction'). This argument gives sociological substance to the notion of 'structural bias' invoked by Koskenniemi as the 'strong critical thesis'.

any 'choice' that he would make in defiance of these professional standards would lack traction.[53]

In short, if the life of international law is not exhausted by its formal grammar (but shaped by a much thicker 'social grammar'), critical interventions should focus not only on the biases of solitary 'people with projects' but also on how their professional postures and routines – their modes of 'doing' legal knowledge – are shaped by shared criteria of competence.[54] At the pivotal juncture in legal practice described earlier, we observe precisely this struggle between competing actors to assert proper social criteria of competence in the practice of lawyering. The contestation voiced by the 'conservative' lawyers in the department was not that the legal claims in Dañino's opinion were flawed (according to internal standards of legal validity), but that the adopted way of reasoning was 'unlawyerly' – that it contradicted the immanent 'rules of the game' that structured their professional activity. What we witness at this juncture is not a clash of particular legal interpretations or a set of attempts to alter the legal norms through which the institution is governed, but a contentious encounter between diverging 'communities of practice' who compete over the culture of norm-use in an institutional setting.[55] It is in these

[53] The notion of 'culture' employed here can be perceived as a set of criteria on what constitutes a competent performance. This can be theorized as a common 'social grammar' (along Bourdieusan lines) or a *Lebensform* – a shared 'feel for the game' (along the lines of Wittgenstein's pragmatism). These various strands of theorizing resonate with Mégret and Kratochwil. *Cf.* Kratochwil, *Status of Law*, 58: 'Against the theoretical ideal that looks for external factors causing actions, Wittgenstein stresses practice; against the notion of concepts fitting objects, he emphasizes their "use" in language. But "use" depends on a "form of life" and on publicly shared criteria or grammars [that] establish our proper use of the terms.'

[54] *Cf.* T. Aalberts and I. Venzke, 'Moving Beyond Interdisciplinary Turf Wars – Towards an Understanding of International Law as Practices', in J. d'Aspremont, T. Gazzini, A. Nollkaemper, and W. Werner (eds), *International Law as a Profession* (Cambridge University Press, 2017), 307 ('[w]e suggest thinking of international law as a practice that contains within itself the yardstick of what counts as ... a "competent performance"').

[55] I am referring here to the argument of Brunnée and Toope, who define 'communities of practice' as a collective of individuals who, 'through engagement in a shared domain, develop a shared repertoire of resources, including cases, stories, tools, vocabularies, and ways of addressing recurring problems'. See J. Brunnée and S. Toope, 'Interactional International Law and the Practice of Legality', in E. Adler and V. Pouliot (eds.), *International Practices* (Cambridge University Press, 2011).

shifts in the logic of practice and the social grammar shaping the professional performance of international law, that we can observe and critically evaluate changes in international organizations law. The account provided earlier, in this sense, ties in with wider professional transformations at the intersection of cosmopolitan enthusiasm and corporate dynamism that demand critical scrutiny. It is precisely in these professional shifts, I argue, that we see the advent of a neoliberal legal practice – a disenchanted register of expertise (as expressed in forms of 'risk analysis') attuned to the exigencies of competitive market behaviour.[56]

Second, inspired by Science and Technology Studies (STS) and Actor-Network Theory (ANT), the 'turn to practice' can be enriched by exploring the technical and material qualities of lawyering, and showing how objects, rules-of-thumb, textual references, and templates of analysis or documentation mark and mediate the politics of international law.[57] In tracing the messy practices of relationality, translation, and materiality through which law is composed – the string of 'people and things' that it assembles – we can find new pathways for analysis and critique.[58] Recent writing by Riles, Johns, Hohmann, and others displays the rewards of a relational, materialist approach to the

[56] I have elaborated more on this in D. Van Den Meerssche, 'Governmentalities of Disorder' (2024) *Völkerrechtsblog*, https://voelkerrechtsblog.org/governmentalities-of-disorder/ (last accessed 7 November 2024). This observation aligns with the argument made in A. Lang, '"Global Disordering": Practices of Reflexivity in Global Economic Governance' (2024) 35 *European Journal of International Law* 93.

[57] I see this orientation towards non-human agency – beyond the image of international law as a discursive formation (a 'grammar') – to be at the vanguard of critical writing. Various strands of theory enable this disruption of the mind/matter, culture/nature divide that shapes the modernist terrain of international legal thinking – from Foucauldian *dispositifs* or Latourian assemblages to new materialist perspectives on 'vibrant matter'. What could critique look like if we started not with Kant and Hegel but Whitehead and Spinoza? For a radical account on matter/meaning as (re)configuring of the 'human' itself, see Z. I. Jackson, *Becoming Human – Matter and Meaning in an Antiblack World* (New York University Press, 2020).

[58] I am inspired here by Barad's 'agential realist elaboration of performativity', which 'allows matter its due as an active participant in the world's becoming'. In K. Barad, *Meeting the Universe Halfway: Quantum Physics and the Entanglement of Matter and Meaning* (Duke University Press, 2007), 136 and 334 ('relata do not pre-exist relations'). See also J. Hohmann, 'Diffuse Subjects and Dispersed Power: New Materialist Insights and Cautionary Lessons for International Law' (2021) 34 *Leiden Journal of International Law* 585;

study of legal expertise and authority as outcomes of 'how heterogeneous practices and techniques are woven together in ways that produce new relations, actors, and forms of power'.[59] If we want to grasp the changing politics of law in the brief vignette set out earlier, for example, we should appreciate how the material templates of risk management shape what matters and what is excluded from mattering.[60] How does the material shift from the textual templates of legal judgment to the adaptive managerial metrics and colour codes of 'risk analysis' alter the law's promise as a form of constraint or contestation?

'Toward the Gathering'

These methodological invitations reflect a radical approach to what a 'turn to practice' could entail – an approach where practices are not studied as specific instantiations of the law (subject to positivist empirics) but as performative enactments where law's boundaries are drawn and its politics enacted. Yet, the invitation to study professional scripts and material routines is aimed not only at enriching our methodological approach to international law as a specific cultural technique, but also at offering different entry points into the vexed question of what constitutes 'critique'. I expect this point to be somewhat polemical. If anything, would the endless tracing of networks and translations not erode the potential for a 'critical' intervention?[61] Is Latour's flat relational ontology – his scathing take on 'structuralism' and 'critical' sociology – not the epitome of postmodern delight and depoliticized drift?[62] Where do we find sites of political agency or intervention in these layered networks of material entanglement?

D. Van Den Meerssche, 'The Multiple Materialisms of International Law' (2023) 11 *London Review of International Law* 197.

59 Sullivan, *Practice, Description, Critique*, 183. *Cf.* Riles, *A New Agenda for the Cultural Study of Law*; Riles, *Collateral Knowledge*; M. Valverde, 'Jurisdiction and Scale: Legal "Technicalities" as Resources for Theory' (2009) 18 *Social & Legal Studies* 139–157; F. Johns, 'Data, Detection, and the Redistribution of the Sensible in International Law' (2017) 111 *AJIL* 57–103.

60 *Cf.* D. Gandorfer, *Matterphorics: On the Laws of Theory* (Princeton University PhD Thesis, 2020).

61 Yet, in her plea for more descriptive work – to study 'surfaces' rather than 'depths' – Orford finds 'critical' potential precisely in such 'descriptive' work. See A. Orford, 'In Praise of Description' (2012) 25 *LJIL* 609–625.

62 Some Marxists certainly think so, though, as Haraway noted, often by misconstruing his interventions. See R. H. Lossin, 'Neoliberalism for Polite

One particularly salient strand of 'critique', especially in work on the law of international institutions, situates the politics of the 'international' in the 'structural bias' – the 'deeply embedded preferences' – of specific regimes.[63] Such 'biases' would explain the consistency in law's distributive outcomes despite the inherent indeterminacy of its grammar. The role of the 'critic', from this vantage point, is both to detect the tectonic 'structural' forces that determine law's direction, and to diagnose their historical origins and political pathologies. In this vein – and to a great effect – scholars have identified the 'deeply embedded' neo-colonial hierarchies and innate logics of 'liberal reform' that are inscribed in the law of international organizations.[64] Yet, as the 'old nemeses' of critical international law have 'learned some new steps',[65] as Johns observed, perhaps we might revisit Latour's polemical question: 'has critique run out of steam?'[66] What would it mean to describe Dañino's efforts in terms of 'deeply embedded' causal forces hidden 'behind' or 'underneath' his expressed motives?[67] What do we learn about law's changing composition and performative politics by 'rel[ying] on players or phenomena somehow already present in the interstices of history' – do we thereby not 'end up assuming exactly what needs to be explained'?[68] Would we not subtract from the

Company: Bruno Latour's Pseudo-Materialist Coup', *Salvage #7 – Towards the Proletarocene*, 2020 ('[i]f neoliberalism were a Platonic Republic, Latour would likely be its philosopher-king'); The Dig Radio, 'Cyborg Revolution with Donna Haraway', 2 May 2019, www.thedigradio.com/podcast/cyborg-revolution-with-donna-haraway/ (last accessed 22 September 2021).

63 *Cf.* Koskenniemi, *From Apology to Utopia*, 607ff.

64 *Cf.* S. Pahuja, *Decolonising International Law: Development, Economic Growth and the Politics of Universality* (Cambridge University Press, 2011); Sinclair, *To Reform the World*.

65 F. Johns, 'From Planning to Prototypes: New Ways of Seeing Like a State' (2019) 82 *Modern Law Review* 834 ([t]hose old nemeses ... of international legal scholarship ... have learned some new steps, And in so doing ... may quite possibly have blunted or outrun the standard tools of critical, progressive, and reform-minded international lawyers').

66 B. Latour, 'Why Has Critique Run out of Steam? From Matters of Fact to Matters of Concern' (2004) 30 *Critical Inquiry*, 247 (aiming to 'associate the word *criticism* with a whole new set of positive metaphors, gestures, attitudes').

67 *Ibid*, 229 (describing this critical gesture as the 'wheeling of causal explanations coming out of the deep dark below').

68 J. Haskell, 'The Choice of the Subject in Writing Histories of International Law', in J. D'Aspremont, T. Gazzini, A. Nollkaemper, and W. Werner, *International Law as a Profession* (Cambridge University Press, 2017),

multiplicity of agential elements in law's emergence – from the effects it engenders and the networks that it ties together – if we portray the legal form merely as the passive carrier for forces emanating elsewhere?[69] If we, yet again, reduce law's institutional role to being the bearer of static neoliberal projects? Can law be more than merely a clumsy disguise? The critic more than an archaeologist of powerful pre-existing social, structural, deeply embedded forces?

What might 'critique' become if, in the words of Levi and Valverde, we were to trade the 'abstracted view of "structure" [for] the empirical work of studying action, actors, communication, imitation and translation, networks, knowledge flows and the continual process that constructs society itself'?[70] If we associated the 'critical' gesture with 'multiplication, not subtraction' – with more, not with less?[71] If the 'critic' were not 'the one who debunks, but the one who assembles' – 'not the one who lifts the rugs from under the feet of the naïve believers', but who offers 'arenas in which to gather'?[72] If the direction of 'critique' were not away from its objects (a flight into their 'social' or 'political' conditions of possibility) but 'toward the gathering'?[73] What might we see and what might become possible if salient forces (empire, capitalism, patriarchy, etc.) were not wielded as causal explanations lingering in the deep down below – as 'social' explanations wielded in the practice of 'critique' – but traced as material assemblages that are entangled with and extended by varying forms of legal labour (which are themselves relationally enacted through evolving cultural scripts, institutional forms, and mundane bureaucratic techniques)?[74] Perhaps it is in tracking and tracing, in mapping and multiplying, and not in

264–265. This can also be expressed as privileging inductive over deductive thinking, as argued in M. Halme-Tuomisaari, 'Keeping Up Standards for a Better World: Anthropological Alternatives to the Study of International Organisations', in this volume.

69 B. Latour, *Reassembling the Social: An Introduction to Actor-Network Theory* (Oxford University Press, 2005), 7 ('[i]n such a view, law ... should not be seen as what should be explained by "social structure" in addition to its inner logic; on the contrary, its inner logic may explain some features of what makes an association last longer and extend wider').

70 R. Levi and M. Valverde, 'Studying Law by Association: Bruno Latour Goes to the Conseil d'Etat' (2008) 33 *Law and Social Inquiry* 807.

71 Latour, *Why Has Critique Run Out of Steam*, 248. 72 *Ibid.*, 246.

73 *Ibid.*

74 Such a relational, materialist approach aligns with splendid work on the infrastructural mediation of global capitalism. L. Khalili, *Sinews of War and Trade Shipping and Capitalism in the Arabian Peninsula* (Verso, 2021).

the stylized posture of scepticism that spaces of action and resistance open and that 'critique' might regain potential?[75]

This call to dwell on relational entanglement – to 'stay with the trouble' in Haraway's terms – might trouble not only structuralist modes of 'critique' but also our commitments to the concept of 'law' as a stable social category. Perhaps to some disciplinary dismay, inquiries starting from materiality itself, as Pottage argued, might very well 'lead to the dissolution of law as a social instance'.[76] The aim is not to materialize law but to see how legal forms are made, displaced, or metabolized in emergent *dispositifs*.

[75] Perspectives on new materialism and relational ontology in feminist science studies, critical black theory, Anthropocene studies, and the digital humanities provides inspiring insights into the problem and potential of 'critique' along these lines. *Cf.* Barad, *Meeting the Universe Halfway*; D. Chandler, *Ontopolitics in the Anthropocene: An Introduction to Mapping, Sensing and Hacking* (Routledge, 2018); L. Amoore, *Clouds Ethics* (Duke University Press, 2020).

[76] A. Pottage, 'The Materiality of What?' (2012) 39 *Journal of Law and Society* 179–180.

Capital, Class, and Political Economy

13 *Laissez-Faire, State Capitalism, and the Making of International Organizations*

The Dynamics of a Struggle

NEGAR MANSOURI

Introduction

In *International Organization and Industrial Change: Global Governance Since 1850*, Craig Murphy offers a *longue durée* view of world institutions as emerging and evolving not from the changing phases of multilateralism – as mainstream social sciences and humanities tend to think – but from the changing scales of industrial capitalism and the impersonal pressure to improve the conditions of life on the margins of private property relations.[1] From this perspective, international organizations (IOs) have not only been crucial to the integration of markets and infrastructures, but they have also 'helped mitigate conflicts that go along with the expansion of the industrial systems [....] Their history is part of the dialectic between capitalism and alternative ways of organizing economic and political life'.[2] Indeed, a historical materialist approach to IOs as evolving from the co-constitutive functioning of capitalism's laws of motion and agents' politics unfolds new pathways for understanding stability and change in the world order.

Unsurprisingly, the law's place in capitalist social relations have been at the core of the Marxist literature in international law. Two main camps have emerged: the 'form camp' and the 'content camp'. The former argues that liberal (international) law *by form* abstracts from historical social relations by treating groups in different relations to the means of production (in terms of ownership, access, and accumulation of surplus value) as juridically equal and as such enables the

[1] C. N. Murphy, *International Organization and Industrial Change: Global Governance since 1850* (Oxford University Press, 1994). 34–35.

[2] C. N. Murphy, *Global Institutions, Marginalization, and Development* (Routledge, 2005). 34.

reproduction of the capitalist relations of production.[3] Those in the 'content camp' take issue not with the 'form' of law but with the ways in which the content of law comes to embed the interests of the capital and the ruling class.[4]

While the literature produced within both camps has greatly contributed to the study of capitalist social relations, the discipline of international law would benefit from going beyond the narrow realm of 'law' and engaging with the broader landscape of production relations, and elements such as the structure of the world order, processes of capitalist expansion, and hegemony, amongst others. Most notably, international lawyers have historically viewed the capitalist state as a homogenous category, losing sight of different trajectories of Anglo-American capitalism (laissez-faire capitalism) and the mainland European, Asian, and African capitalism (state capitalism) and what such variations in socio-political ordering mean for the form and content of international law.

This chapter borrows from historical materialist International Relations (IR), and particularly the works of the Dutch IR scholar Kees van der Pijl, to argue that capitalist social relations reproduce on the ground through not only commodification but also socialization or mitigating the dislocating effects of the capitalist mode of production. Across territories, capitalism expands through the struggles between two modes of organizing production relations: laissez-faire and state capitalism. The history of IOs since the mid-nineteenth century should, indeed, be seen in the context of such struggles. More specifically, the organization of production relations by the market in laissez-faire capitalism tends to peripheralize non-capitalist territories leading to the organization of production relations by emerging ethno-national bureaucratic vanguards (state capitalism) and geared towards territorially confined accumulation. After discussing these premises,

[3] C. Miéville, *Between Equal Rights: A Marxist Theory of International Law* (Brill, 2005). 111. See also, R. Knox, 'Marxism, International Law, and Political Strategy' (2009) 22 *Leiden Journal of International Law* 413–36; N. Tzouvala, *Capitalism As Civilisation: A History of International Law* (Cambridge University Press, 2020).

[4] See, S. Marks, 'International Judicial Activism and the Commodity-Form Theory of International Law' (2007) 18 *The European Journal of International Law* 199–211. B. S. Chimni, 'Capitalism, Imperialism, and International Law in the Twenty-First Century' (2012) 14 *Oregon Review of International Law* 17–44.

the piece empirically engages with them in the context of three historical developments in the post-1945 period, capturing the flow of manufactured commodities and raw materials as well as the machinery of such flows, i.e. marine logistics. The three histories are: liberalization of global telecommunications, the rise of open shipping registries in the transport of raw material, and the mass logging of tropical forests. The idea is not to offer full historical accounts, but rather to reconstruct the three histories through the proposed framework.

Capitalism's Laws of Motion and the Making of the International Relations

For IR historical materialism, the history of the modern international relations has been a history of political and impersonal struggles between two developmental variations of state/society complexes: Lockean and Hobbesian, as referring to two rather distinct political theories prescribing different modes of organization of production relations. The term 'Lockean' refers to John Locke's *Two Treatise of Government* and 'Hobbesian' to Thomas Hobbes's *Leviathan* or *The Matter, Forme and Power of a Commonwealth Ecclesiasticall and Civil.*

As the famous story goes, modern international relations emerged at the end of the Early Modern times or the late seventeenth century, and was marked by a transition from kin-based papal-monarch authority-territory towards impersonal administrative-juridical state apparatus exercising exclusive authority over certain territory.[5] The rise of petty commodity production and the decline of feudal regimes of accumulation in England was followed by the 1688 Glorious Revolution, the establishment of a constitutional monarchy, and the maturing of a capitalist class out of the aristocracy who went on to invest in commercialized lands and domestic production. These material and social transformations gave birth to a Lockean state/society, marked by a

[5] On capitalism and geopolitics see, J. Rosenberg, 'Social Structures and Geopolitical Systems: A Critique of the Realist Theory of International Relations' (September 1992). B. Teschke, *The Myth of 1648: Class, Geopolitics and the Making of Modern International Relations* (Verso, 2003). K. Van Der Pijl, *Transnational Classes and International Relations* (Routledge, 1998). K. Van der Pijl, *Nomads, Empires, States Modes of Foreign Relations and Political Economy* (Pluto Press, 2007), vol. I&II. M. Pal, *Jurisdictional Accumulation: An Early Modern History of Law, Empires, and Capital* (Cambridge University Press, 2020).

small government, a self-regulating market, and an entrepreneurial individual.[6] In the Lockean mode, 'production is organized organically and without interference from public authority'; state is subordinated to the bourgeoisie society, and its primary role is to protect 'the independence of relations of production'.[7] Mass immigration from England and colonization of the New World extended the English historic bloc to other territories.[8] In parallel, British foreign policy moved away from territorial expansion towards maintaining a certain configuration of power in the pre-capitalist Europe to enable the creation of new spheres of production and exchange by English capitalism.

To tackle peripheralization caused by the de-territorializing nature of Lockean capitalism, a series of from-above or bourgeoisie revolutions gave birth to another form of state/civil society complex in contender states such as France in the aftermath of the 1789 French Revolution and throughout the 1800s. France transformed from a pre-capitalist agrarian society with disparate and overlapping territorial claims into an absolutist regime pursuing territorially confined capitalist accumulation, before the 1848 Revolution paved the way for a republic. Similar transformations materialized in Prussia/Germany, Japan, Russia/USSR, and China, amongst others.[9] In the Hobbesian state/society complex, a strong state is put in place, and it is the sovereign rather than the capital that commands the organization of production relations in line with ethno-nationalist objectives. Territorially confined accumulation in the Hobbesian periphery is intended to overcome the temporally delayed capitalist advancement while ensuring survival in a 'transnational space dominated by the Anglo-Saxon ruling class'.[10] Yet, after the Second World War, mainland Europe underwent transformation again. As the US-led IOs such as the Organisation for European Economic Co-operation dismantled the Hobbesian mode of capitalism in mainland Europe in favour of laissez-faire capitalism, the rise of ethno-national states in Asia, Africa, South America and the rest of the developing world became the harbinger of a new wave of Hobbesian state/society complexes.[11]

[6] Van Der Pijl, *Transnational Classes*. 66. [7] Ibid. [8] Ibid, part III.
[9] Ibid, 79–84. [10] Van der Pijl, *Transnational Classes*, 81.
[11] On the changing direction of mainland Europe, see, K. Van Der Pijl, 'A Lockean Europe' (2006) 37 *New Left Review* 9–37. S. Sakellaropoulos and P. Sotiris, 'European Union as Class Project and Imperialist Strategy' (2018).

While different in socio-political organization, Lockean and Hobbesian state/society complexes are both formed around centralized ownership and control of means of production and similar processes of capitalist advancement. How does capitalism develop?

Capitalism moves across time and space and transforms social relations around means of production through commodification and socialization. Commodification involves *subjugating* the use value of things to an exchange value, through a 'constantly in the making' social activity that detaches the thing from the natural and historical condition.[12] Commodification and the dislocating effects it generates necessitates socialization (*Vergesellschaftung*). Socialization involves creating social coherence on the margins of the dominant mode of production, for example, by managing labour antagonism, ecological externalities of industrial production, and creating a shared image of production relations.[13] The need for socialization lies in the fact that '[u]nder the discipline of capital and the commodity form, the real subjects cannot execute the planning/normative function for themselves [which has] evolved into a special task of a special category of *functionaries subordinate to the ruling class – the cadres*'.[14] The post-1945 histories of liberalization of telecommunication networks and services, the rise of open shipping registries in the transport of raw materials, and the expansion of the global tropical timber trade are histories of not only continuous commodification and socialization but also broader struggles between the Lockean and Hobbesian state/society complexes, shaped by episodes of resistance against the de-territorializing nature of laissez-faire capitalism, followed by its ultimate victory.

Liberalization of the Global Telecommunications: The Defeat of the Hobbesian Mode

The post-World War II history of liberalization of the global telecommunication regime as developed in and beyond the International Telecommunication Union (ITU) has been a history of the defeat of

[12] See, C. Hermann, *Critique of Commodification: Contours of a Post-Capitalist Society* (Oxford University Press, 2021). Xi.

[13] S. Mau, *Mute Compulsion: A Marxist Theory of the Economic Power of Capital* (Verso Books, 2023). 144.

[14] Van der Pijl, *Transnational Classes and International Relations*, 16.

the statist telecommunication in mainland Europe and most of the developing world by the Lockean end-to-end telecommunications, where the laying of networks and delivery of services followed supply and demand and not national strategies set by the state. Liberalization of telecommunication networks and services in the last quarter of the twentieth century involved a decade-long process of commodification of what used to be characterized as 'utilities', followed by new rules and institutions to integrate nationally organized telecommunication sectors into the privatized global telecommunication regime, while also managing privatization anxieties amongst the masses in and beyond the developing world.[15]

Since the mid-nineteenth century, when the first transboundary telegraph networks were laid, all the way through to the mid-twentieth century, telephone and telegraph services were delivered by state-owned telecommunication enterprises. The International Telegraph Union (IT), the predecessor of the ITU, was established by the initiative of the nephew of Napoleon, Bonaparte III of France, in 1865 to institutionalize the reign of national telecommunication administrations, and as part of the broader European project for a transition to industrial capitalism.[16] The Union was intended to act as an 'international cartel of national telegraph agencies'.[17] For almost a century, the organization of networks was viewed as a sovereign choice, and under the ITU's operational norms, members states were protected against competition by each other's telecommunications administrations, equipment manufacturers, or operators based in their territories.[18] Crucial to nation-building, telecommunication infrastructures

15 See, S. Rhodes, *Social Movements and Free-Market Capitalism in Latin America Telecommunications Privatization and the Rise of Consumer Protest* (State University of New York Press, 2006).

16 The founding instrument of the IT, the International Telegraph Convention, was adopted by twenty mainland European countries in 1865: France, Austria, Baden, Denmark, Greece, Hanover, Italy, Saxony, Russia, Prussia, Sweden-Norway, Spain, Denmark, Belgium, Bavaria, Portugal, the Netherlands, Switzerland, Turkey, and Württemberg.

17 J. Hills, *The Struggle for Control of Global Communication: The Formative Century* (University of Illinois Press, 2010). 59.

18 For example, a 1927 CCIF Recommendation had mandated that '[i] nternational telephone communication circuits should not be lent for a given relation unless the number of circuits serving this relation makes it feasible; that ... it should not be possible for [central bureaus] to have the technical possibility of controlling the calls exchanged; [t]he stations so linked cannot

also became one of the first assets to be nationalized in post-colonial Asia and Africa.

While the ITU institutionalized the material capability of public-owned telecommunications in mainland Europe, the organization of telephony and telegraphy was different in the Lockean state/society complexes, most notably the United States and the United Kingdom. They relied on telephone monopolies at home (AT&T and British Telecom) while maintaining different models of international telephone services abroad. Due to the private ownership of their telegraph networks, neither of the two countries became founding members of the IT. The UK, however, joined the Union in 1868 when it nationalized its domestic telegraph, and to represent its interests in India.[19] The 1868 Convention adopted by the Vienna Plenipotentiary Conference also made it possible for companies to accede to the convention without being able to take part in standard setting.

The pace of technological advancement in the post-1945 US telecommunications, caused partly by the country's recent war effort but also by the Cold War, introduced a new level of political and impersonal pressure against the Hobbesian global telecommunication order and the normative infrastructure underpinning it. To respond to companies' telecommunication needs, the ITU's 1949 Telephone and Telegraph Regulations allowed the lease of telegraph circuits to one company from another.[20] However, inter-company resale of the telephone circuits remained prohibited. In a few years, the 1956 Recommendations allowed a 'multiple-user lease' by different private entities engaging in the same activity or in the same business. Yet, the Recommendation banned connection to public networks, imposed a surcharge on the leased traffic, and mandated that calls using leased

in any case be stations normally made available to the public', Comité Consultatif International des Communications Téléphoniques à grande distance [International Telephone Consultative Committee](CCIF), *Assemblée Plénière de Côme, 5–12 septembre 1927* (CCIF, 1927), pp. 117–19. Recommendation No. 13 on 'Rental of international communications circuits for the private service not including submarine sections'.

19 Telegraph Act 1870 (33 & 34 Vict c 88).

20 International Telecommunication Convention 1947, Annex, Telegraph Regulations 1949: Final Protocol to the Telegraph Regulations (signed 5 August 1949, entered into force 1 July 1950), Resolution No 9, 'Lease of Telegraph Circuits'.

circuits 'must be concerned exclusively with the personal affairs of the subscribers or those of their firms'.[21]

All these developments materialized as the newly independent states in Africa and Asia in the 1950s and 1960s had begun to pose a challenge to the status quo in the ITU. They contested the historical position of the ITU as a mere forum for industrialized countries' public telecommunications administrations or private telecommunications operators to compete for favourable rules and standards – what the US delegate once called 'the old boys club'.[22] They called for restructuring the ITU to allow the development of an overarching telecommunications policy and a strong secretariat to assist the Global South in developing their national telecommunications sectors along the Hobbesian lines.[23] In other words, they sought to tackle the threat of a Lockean global telecommunication order through intergovernmental intervention geared towards promoting and protecting statist telecommunication. The upcoming neoliberal turn in global telecommunications, however, soon rendered their visions of self-sufficiency obsolete.

What triggered privatization and deregulation of networks and services was the advent of the satellite and digital telecommunication technologies in the Lockean heartland, the growing pressure from the US administration for liberalization of global telecommunication, but also the de-territorializing nature of laissez-faire capitalism as travelling across networks and services. The commercial use of satellites for telecommunications was made possible by the positioning of satellite systems in the geostationary orbit (GEO). The first satellite to transmit voice signals was launched from the US in December 1958. With the establishment of the National Aeronautics and Space Administration the same year, a series of projects to develop satellite

[21] CCIF, XVIIIth Plenary Assembly (3–14 December 1956), Recommendation 21, 'Lease of International Communication Channels for Private Service', cited in J. Hills, *Telecommunications and Empire* (University of Illinois Press, 2007). 93. The provision was formalised into CCITT Recommendation D.1 in 1965.

[22] G. O. Robinson, 'Regulating International Airwaves: The 1979 WARC' (1981) 21 *Virginia Journal of International Law* 1–54. 34.

[23] See, J. Hills, 'Dependency Theory and Its Relevance Today: International Institutions in Telecommunications and Structural Power' (1994) 20 *Review of International Studies* 169–86.

technology started.[24] The potential for mass commercial use created a strong incentive for the US administrations to shape the path. In 1962, the US Congress set up the Communication Satellite Corporation (COMSAT) as a private corporation. However, in 1962, the Kennedy administration turned COMSAT into an intergovernmental organization with weighted voting called INTELSAT. Seventy-four nations joined. Circumventing the one-nation-one-vote ITU, INTELSAT soon became an exclusive club of existing and rising satellite powers, where investment shares determined the voting power.[25] The organization of the space regime around private capital had implications beyond space. It generated new geographies of accumulation for large firms and multinationals.

In parallel, the marriage of digital technologies with telecommunications, commercialized in the 1960s, became an important source of change.[26] The change from 'analogue' to 'digital' transformed both switching and transmission in telecommunication networks, allowing cheaper operation of networks and growing user base in the long term. Scrambling for the vast opportunities generated by digitalization, large American firms and multinationals lobbied for liberal telecommunications networks on an end-to-end basis so they could access networks on their own terms but also circumvent the surcharge they paid to subsidize national telecommunications. Starting in the mid-1970s, some mainland European public telecommunications operators unsuccessfully sought to contain the pressure of liberalization by upgrading their networks.[27]

The first salvo against the *ancien régime* was finally fired by the US Federal Communications Commission in 1980, when it unilaterally extended the US' rules on resale and sharing of networks with private firms to international services, in violation of the consensus built into the Recommendations of the Consultative Committee for International Telephony and Telegraphy (CCITT) for almost

[24] 'Development of Satellite Communication' in *Britannica*, 17 July 2020, www.britannica.com/technology/satellite-communication. Accessed 31 August 2021.

[25] J. Hills, 'The Telecommunications Rich and Poor' (1990) 12 *Third World Quarterly* 71–90, 71.

[26] See, R. Mansell, *The New Telecommunications: A Political Economy of Network Evolution* (SAGE Publications, 1994).

[27] See, G. Natalicchi, *Wiring Europe: Reshaping the European Telecommunications Regime* (Rowman & Littlefield, 2001).

a century.[28] The AT&T was also broken up into multiple firms by the US court, triggering a search for global markets by the US manufacturers and service providers.[29] The UK followed suit and so did Japan and gradually mainland Europe. With changing material capability, ideas and institutions had to also change. The same year, the US requested the Organisation for Economic Cooperation and Development (OECD) Trade Committee to study trade barriers in services. The US Coalition of Service Industries, represented by Citibank, played a substantial role in the process.[30] The final OECD report, as well as another study carried out by GATT, demonstrated good prospects for negotiation on liberalization of trade in services.[31] Four years later, twenty-five OECD member states expressed their resolve to include trade in services in the upcoming Uruguay Round and negotiate the expansion of such trade 'under conditions of transparency and progressive liberalisation',[32] against the wish of twenty-three developing countries.

This essentially meant a decline in relevance of the ITU and its Hobbesian logic, in favour of GATT and the Lockean end-to-end telecommunication order, underpinned by a de-territorializing entrepreneurism. To catch up with the pressure, the Union opted for change.[33] The 1982 Plenipotentiary Conference in Nairobi reproduced a 1932 provision from the Union's Constitution into the ITU Convention, requiring a change also in the operational rules such as Telephone and Telegraph Regulations and Recommendations. The 'special arrangements' clause had stipulated, '[t]he High Contracting Parties respectively reserve the right of making separately, between them, special arrangements of all kinds, on service points that are not of interest to

28 W. J. Drake, 'Global Private Networks and International Public Institutions: Leased Circuits and the International Telecommunications Regime' Private Networks and Public Objectives, Columbia Institute for Tele-Information Working Paper No. 513, (Columbia University, 1992).

29 See, J. Ratto-Nielsen, *The International Telecommunications Regime: Domestic Preferences and Regime Change* (Lulu, 2006). Chapter 3.

30 Hills, *Telecommunications and Empire*. 180.

31 T. L. McLarty, 'Liberalized Telecommunications Trade in the WTO: Implications for Universal Service Policy' (1998) 15 *Federal Communications Law Journal*.

32 Ministerial Declaration on the Uruguay Round (20 December 1986) GATT MIN.DEC, Part II.

33 P. Cowhey and J. D. Aronson, 'The ITU in Transition' (1991) 15 *Telecommunications Journal* 298–310. 301.

the generality of States …'.[34] As liberalization of telecommunications was being discussed by the GATT Uruguay Round, the 1988 ITU World Administrative Telegraph and Telephone Conference in Melbourne revised the International Telephone and Telegraph Regulations to recognize the right of the member states to retreat from the collective and open their networks to foreign capital, and providers to choose to deliver services to the public. The new regulations also made international rates 'cost-based'.[35]

Breaking away from its century-old function to coordinate the work of national telecommunication administrations, the Union's Secretariat also began not only to assist developing countries in revising their national laws to allow access and foreign direct investment (commodifying public-owned networks and services), but also to manage broader anxieties around liberalization of infrastructure by promoting narratives of entrepreneurship and competition as inducive to development.[36]

As ITU revised its rules in Melbourne, the Uruguay Round negotiations in Marrakech adopted the 1994 GATS Agreement along with an Annex on Telecommunications. The annex targeted value-added services such as data, image, and video. It committed Member States to give access to 'any service supplier of any other Member' for the 'use of public telecommunications transport networks and services on reasonable and non-discriminatory terms and conditions'.[37] Foreign service providers were given the right to 'establish, construct, acquire, lease, operate, or supply telecommunications transport networks or services' in a member state's territory should they agree.[38] Restrictions were allowed only to ensure the 'technical integrity of network', *only if they were necessary and not just a disguise to influence the competition.*[39] Basic telecommunication, i.e. voice telephony, was kept out of the agreement. But not for long! The impersonal pressure of Lockean organization travelled across not only geographies but also technologies. The Marrakech meeting adopted a document titled 'Decision on Negotiations on Basic Telecommunications' with a timeline for

[34] International Communication Convention, Madrid 1932, Article 13.
[35] Article 4 (3).
[36] K. Lee, *Global Telecommunications Regulation: A Political Economy Perspective* (Pinter, 1996).
[37] WTO, Annex on Telecommunication 1994, para. 5(a). [38] ibid para. 2.
[39] ibid para. (d).

negotiation of liberalization of telecommunications. In a sharp move, fifty-seven governments acceded to a reference paper that committed them to putting in place competitive safeguards and providing access to markets 'with interconnection at any technically feasible point in the network'.[40] Forty-seven of these countries also committed themselves to offering immediate access to their basic telecommunications.[41] On 15 February 1997, the WTO Agreement on Basic Telecommunications opened 'the biggest chunk of the global market', accounting for 93 per cent of the telecommunication networks across the globe.[42]

Rise of Open Shipping Registries: The Reign of the Lockean Mode

Unlike the global telecommunication regime, norms and processes of world shipping have emerged and evolved around laissez-faire capitalism since the rise of modern long-haul shipping in the nineteenth century. In the post-1945 era, open shipping registries in the transport of raw materials (bulk shipping) became a vivid manifestation of the organization of production relations by supply and demand, destabilizing what was historically known as national shipping. Although the system came to be challenged in the 1950s through to the 1970s by the proponents of the Hobbesian shipping order who favoured a national link between vessels and flags (and the crews and trade they carried), the 1980s neoliberal turn rendered aspirations for nationally organized marine logistics obsolete, culminating in the victory of open shipping registries.

The growth of the world shipping into a modern and rationalized industry in the nineteenth century (as opposed to the pre-modern shipping carried out by state-sponsored monopoly trading companies and dominated by piracy and mercantilist under-pricing) was the product of revolutionary technological developments in England.[43]

[40] WTO *Reference Paper: Negotiating Group on Basic Telecommunications* (30 April 1996) WTO Doc S/NGBT/18 para 2.2.

[41] S. K. Black, *Telecommunications Law in the Internet Age* (Morgan Kaufmann Publishers, 2002). 189.

[42] W. J. Drake, 'The Rise and Decline of the International Telecommunications Regime' in C. Marsden (ed.), *Regulating the Global Information Society*, (Routledge, 2000), pp. 125–75. 156.

[43] S. G. Sturmey, *British Shipping and World Competition* (The Athlone Press, 1962).

The construction of steam-powered vessels running on coal-generated steam engines and propellers enabled long-haul trips, followed by the adoption of standardized practices, tariffs, and rules within the European economic system. Although the normative foundation for 'freedom of the sea and navigation' was laid three centuries prior,[44] the material infrastructure for a liberal shipping order, underpinned by self-regulation and rationalized norms and practices, was concretely laid following the defeat of Napoleon in 1815 and the challenge of mercantilism in the Hobbesian mainland Europe. Britain's naval hegemony between the mid-nineteenth century and the Second World War meant norms, institutions, and practices governing long-haul shipping formed around Lockean self-regulation, mostly in London insurance and indemnity clubs, and without much interference from states.[45] One of the earliest maritime institutions, *Comité Maritime International* (CMI), was set up by European lawyers in 1897 to integrate commercial and maritime law to bring 'stability and security in the relations between the men who commit themselves and their belongings to the capricious and indomitable sea'.[46] CMI developed authoritative rules on bills of lading, liens, mortgages, and tort cases arising from collisions or stowaways – all forming the corpus of admiralty law – which were automatically accepted by governments.

In the post-WWII era, the transport of raw materials or 'bulk shipping' – as opposed to 'cargo shipping' concerned with carriage of packaged and manufactured commodities – became an emblem of organization of production relations by the market, competition, and comparative advantage. Bulk vessels carry unpackaged materials with low value to weight ratio (crude oil, refined oil, liquid natural gas, iron ore, timber, and grains, amongst others), shipped from a specific producer to specific buyers. While the cargo sector has historically been dominated by European shipping firms that formed cartels (shipping conferences), the sea transport of raw materials for most of the twentieth century materialized in a free market and was reigned over by American oil majors and other multinationals that integrated

44 R. P. Anand, *Origin and Development of the Law of the Sea: History of International Law Revisited* (Springer, 1983).

45 See, S. G. Sturmey, *British Shipping and World Competition* (The Athlone Press, 1962).

46 See, F. Berlingieri, 'Work of the Comite Maritime International: Past, Present, and Future' (1982) 57 *Tulane Law Review* 1260–73.

extraction, processing, transport, and marketing of raw materials. As marine wages and industry standards increased the costs of shipping in the Atlantic area, a large portion of the bulk vessels including oil tankers flagged out to Panama, Liberia, Honduras, and Costa Rica, amongst others.[47] In times of good business, the cheapest tankers and crews and relaxed flags helped bulk firms gain an upper hand in the market, and in times of bad business (for example in the aftermath of the 1973 oil crisis), they became crucial to compensating the financial loss.[48] Flags of convenience, however, became the object of contestation between, on the one hand, the US, American firms, and open registry states, and, on the other hand, traditional maritime states in Europe witnessing the decline of their national shipping and the new and developing world facing major hurdles in developing national maritime sectors to carry their trade.

Although the self-regulatory underpinning of world shipping could pose structural hurdles to intergovernmental intervention, the range of international shipping bodies set up by allies to coordinate merchant shipping during the war years created an amicable atmosphere for the creation of an IO on the margins of the private shipping enterprise. More importantly, the US-led campaign for trans-nationalization of production and exchange and the explosive rise in marine traffic for that purpose required socialization and managing externalities such as oil pollution on the seas. Moore called this 'maintaining a modicum of security and mopping up the mess around the enclaves of wealth extraction'.[49] It was in this context that the Intergovernmental Maritime Consultative Organization (IMCO) was set up with an altered mandate. Article 1 on 'purposes of the organization' carefully delineated the tasks of the IMCO on the margins of Lockean shipping. Paragraph (a) read 'to provide machinery for co-operation among, Governments in the field of governmental regulation and practices

[47] On the origin and history of open shipping registries see, R. Carlise, *Sovereignty for Sale: The Origins and Evolution of the Panamanian and Liberian Flags of Convenience* (Naval Institute Press, 1981). R. P. Carlise, '"American Century" Implemented: Stettinius and the Liberian Flag of Convenience' (1980) 54, no. 2 *The Business History Review* 175–91.

[48] B. N. Metaxas, *Flags of Convenience: A Study of Internationalisation* (Gower Publishing Company, 1985).

[49] D. Moore, 'The Second Age of the Third World: From Primitive Accumulation to Global Public Goods?' (2004) 25 *Third World Quarterly* 101.

relating to *technical matters* of all kinds affecting shipping engaged in international trade and to encourage the general adoption of the highest practicable standards in matters concerning maritime safety and efficiency of navigation'. As the oil spills such as the 1967 Torrey Canyon came to reshape the fate of the oceans in the Golden Age of Capitalism, the IMCO's gained an even higher relevance in restoring social coherence to the oceans. The organization helped develop the 1973 International Convention for the Prevention of the Pollution from Ships (MARPOL) and the International Convention for the Safety of Life at Sea, which set new safety standards for bulk shipping, without undermining its transnational modus operandi.[50]

Outside the IMCO, however, the very organization of open shipping registries came under attack by mainland European and later developing states in international courts and institutions, but also on the shores of the industrialized world by labour strikes.[51] The challenge was initially posed by a bloc of traditional maritime states such as the Netherlands and Norway but also the UK whose national shipping industry and labour were losing to the laissez-faire modus operandi of flags of convenience shipping. Earlier in the 1950s, the International Law Commission became a battleground for the definition of 'genuine link between the vessel and flag'. The output was the 1958 UN Convention on the High Seas, which recognized the right of states to fix the conditions of their shipping registries on their own, but required 'a genuine link between the State and the ship' by way of effective exercise of jurisdiction and administrative control.[52] As the IMCO was beginning its work in 1959, another legal conflict arose: should states with open shipping registries be considered among the 'largest ship-owning nations' for the purpose of membership in one of the organization's most important bodies, the Maritime Safety Committee. A request for advisory opinion was made to the International Court of Justice in 1960, in response to which the court stood by the laissez-faire spirit of freedom of navigation and the right

[50] See, M. W. Zacher and R. M. M'Gonigle, *Pollution, Politics, and International Law: Tankers at Sea* (University of California Press, 1979).

[51] See, B. A. Boczek, *Flags of Convenience: An International Legal Study* (Harvard University Press, 1962). See, N. Lille, 'Bringing the Offshore Ashore: Transnational Production, Industrial Relations and the Reconfiguration of Sovereignty' (2010) 54 *International Studies Quarterly* 683–704.

[52] Article 5.

of states to decide conditions of their shipping registries.[53] By the end of 1960s, Liberian and Panamanian flagged vessels had grown from 15 million gross tonnage to 32 million.[54] Soon enough, the recession of the late 1960s and oil crisis of 1973 resulted in rapid flight to the flags of convenience to save the profitability rate.[55]

While traditional maritime states in Europe were gradually moving in the direction of improving the operation of flags of convenience vessels as opposed to phasing them out, antagonism was growing amongst the new and developing countries.[56] Although they accounted for 90 per cent of the raw materials carried by tankers in the post-1945 era, they owned only 6 per cent of the bulk market.[57] To promote national shipping and a world shipping order in that direction, in the early months of the UN Conference on Trade and Development (UNCTAD), a shipping committee was set up in a coup-like move by the Secretariat and developing countries, with a mandate to conduct studies on world shipping and potentially develop regulatory frameworks in support of the Global South's national shipping.[58] This was part of the broader efforts within UNCTAD to tackle laissez-faire capitalism underpinning the work of Bretton Woods institutions through promoting state developmentalism.[59] From the late 1970s through to the early 1980s, the Group 77 in UNCTAD advocated for an international treaty that could phase out open registries in the bulk sector through a gradual transfer of ownership or employment of national crews. Yet, as the North–South negotiations over terms of global economy collapsed in the early

[53] Constitution of the Maritime Safety Committee of the Inter-Governmental Maritime Consultative Organization, Advisory Opinion of 8 June 1960: I.C.J. Reports 1960, p. 150.

[54] E. Gold, *Maritime Transport: The Evolution of International Marine Policy and Shipping Law* (Lexington Books, 1981). 271.

[55] T. Volscho, 'The Revenge of the Capitalist Class: Crisis, the Legitimacy of Capitalism and the Restoration of Finance from the 1970s to Present' (2015) 43 *Critical Sociology* 249–66.

[56] See, B. Gosovic, *UNCTAD: Conflict and Compromise. The Third World's Quest for an Equitable World Economic Order through the United Nations* (A. W. Sijthoff, 1972).

[57] UNCTAD, Merchant & Fleet Development, TD/222 (May 1979). 3.

[58] D. Tresselt, *The Controversy over the Division of Labour in International Seaborne Transport* (Institute for Shipping Research Bergen, 1970).

[59] Q. Slobodian, *Globalists: The End of Empire and the Birth of Neoliberalism* (Harvard University Press, 2018).

1980s, the efforts for an anti-flag of convenience treaty resulted in a feeble instrument that sufficed to improve the link between open shipping registries and flagged out vessels, while promoting the increasing share of the rest of the developing world in bulk transport.[60] Titled the '1986 UN Convention on Conditions of Registry of Ships', the convention sought to combine the right of states to decide the conditions of their shipping registries and neoliberal principles of efficiency in world shipping,[61] with interventionist measures such as the '*strengthening the genuine link* between a State and ships flying its flag'.[62] In that direction, the convention required the recruitment of a satisfactory portion of crews from the nationals of the flag states and increased ownership and management of bulk firms by nationals of the flag states, and as such the document came to accept the foundation of open shipping registries.[63] By the time the convention was opened for ratification, the opposition from UNCTAD's Secretariat and Global South governments to flags of convenience had declined, as open registries were becoming the norm in transport of raw materials and the Global South itself was being integrated into neoliberal narratives of entrepreneurism.[64] The convention has yet to enter into force.[65] The momentary Hobbesian challenge to the Lockean world of shipping and the efforts to restore national shipping failed to disrupt the centuries-old foundations of laissez-faire on the global ocean.

[60] M. Franczak, *Global Inequality and American Foreign: Policy in the 1970s* (Cornell University Press, 2022); H. Rowen, 'Reagan's Success at Cancun', *Washington Post* (19 October 1981).

[61] 'United Nations Convention on Conditions for Registration of Ships, Adopted by the United Nations Conference on Conditions for Registration of Ships on 7 February 1986, TD/RS/CONF/23'. Preamble &Article 4.

[62] Article 1. [63] Articles 7, 8, & 9.

[64] On the changing ideology of the UNCTAD Secretariat on the topic, see, S. R. Tolofari, *Open Registry Shipping: A Comparative Study of Costs and Freight Rates* (Gordon and Breach Science Publishers, 1989).

[65] Currently the number stands at fifteen countries, falling short of the requirement for entry into force. Countries that have ratified or acceded to the 1986 convention are: Albania, Bulgaria, Côte d'Ivoire, Egypt, Georgia, Ghana, Haiti, Hungary, Iraq, Liberia, Libya, Mexico, Morocco, Oman, and Syria). Countries that have only signed the convention subject to further actions are: Algeria, Bolivia, Cameroon, Czech Republic, Indonesia, Poland, Russian Federation, Senegal, and Slovakia. See, https://treaties.un.org/Pages/ViewDetails.aspx?src=IND&mtdsg_no=XII-7&chapter=12&clang=_en

Mass Logging of Tropical Forests: The Rise of the Hobbesian Mode

Just as mainland Europe created the ITU to institutionalize the state's control over infrastructures in the mid-nineteenth century, the creation of the International Tropical Timber Organization (ITTO) from the mid-1960s through to the mid-1980s, amidst the rise of the global tropical timber trade, was the product of post-colonial states in the tropics seeking to institutionalize their reign over resources and encase mass extraction through aid and trade. As GATT, alongside other Bretton Woods institutions, came to promote the supremacy of the market and price in socio-political ordering, so UNCTAD and the international commodity agreements developed under its auspices and as part of the broader movement for a New International Economic Order were intended to tackle laissez-faire capitalism through state developmentalism. The struggle for 'permanent sovereignty over natural resources' and growth for that purpose were ultimately premised on commodification.[66] Yet, while those gathering around the NIEO agenda opposed any retreat from economic growth and environmentalism without the reform of the international economic order in the 1970s and 1980s, the growing anxieties around tropical deforestation but also the ascent of neoliberalism in the 1990s came to render the Global South's militancy against liberal environmentalism obsolete, making way for the 'sustainable forest management' in and beyond the ITTO and the 1992 UN Conference on Environment and Development (UNCED). But where did the ITTO come from?

Soon after its creation in 1964, UNCTAD occupied itself with the development of international commodity agreements in response to the ongoing fall of commodity prices and the deepening laissez-faire underpinning of the global economic ordering as organized by the Bretton Woods institutions. UNCTAD's approach to the South's commodity challenge was famously shaped by the theory of commodity prices developed separately by the Argentinian economist and the first executive director general of UNCTAD Raul Prebisch and the German economist and future UN staff Hans Singer.[67] The theory argued that

[66] S. Pahuja, *Decolonising International Law Development, Economic Growth and the Politics of Universality* (Cambridge University Press, 2011), 128.

[67] See, H. Singer, *Relative Prices of Exports and Imports of Under-Developed Countries: A Study of Post-War Terms of Trade between Under-Developed*

the price of commodities since the 1940s, and in general, tends to decline faster than the manufactured products; that specialization in primary commodities were not conducive to industrialization – as claimed by many industrialized countries in the broader global division of labour. The way to break free from the unequal exchange between the two worlds was to undergo an episode of state-assisted extractivism and intergovernmental intervention to finance import-substitution industrialization.[68]

In 1966, UNCTAD's Integrated Programme for Commodities (IPC) was set up 'with a view to improving the terms of trade of developing countries and ... eliminate the economic imbalance between developed and developing countries'.[69] The IPC was intended to increase the capacity of the developing world in producing and marketing their raw materials, increase the prices, and enable processing at home countries for that purpose. Timber was the last item on the 18-item agenda and was added at the request of Congo Basin countries, which had been unsuccessful in establishing timber industries at home. As the process was becoming slow, Japan – the biggest consumer of tropical timber – tabled a resolution at the UN General Assembly for an international tropical timber agreement in 1983.[70] Two preparatory meetings were held in Geneva and the International Tropical Timber Agreement (ITTA) came into being.[71] Reflecting a vivid Hobbesian logic, Article 1 of the ITTA read, 'for the benefit of both producing and consuming members and *bearing in mind the sovereignty of producing members over their natural resources*'. Reflecting a pure logic of commodification, Article 2 restricted the work of the organization to 'tropical timber' and 'promoting the expansion and diversification

and Industrialized Countries (H.M.S.O. for United Nations, 1949). J. Toye and R. Toye, 'The Origins and Interpretation of the Prebisch-Singer Thesis' (2003) 35 *History of Political Economy* 437–67.

[68] Towards a New Trade Policy for Development, Report by the Secretary General of the United Nations Conference on Trade and Development (1964), E/CONF.46/3'.

[69] UNCTAD, Report of the 145th Plenary Meeting, Part One: 'Action taken by the Conference' (Resolution 93 (IV), 30 May 1976), Annex V(I). 7.

[70] See, D. Poore, *Changing Landscape: The Development of the International Tropical Timber Organization and Its Influence on Tropical Forest Management* (Earthscan Publications Ltd, 2003); F. Gale, *The Tropical Timber Trade Regime* (Springer, 1998).

[71] International Tropical Timber Agreement, 1983 (with annexes).

of tropical timber trade'. The provision created a material and ideological structure whereby 'forests' could only be dealt with in the form of 'extracted timber' destined for global markets, and questions of forest ecologies or forest-dwelling communities were excluded. ITTO was established as a commodity organization with weighted voting, which meant the largest timber producing and consumer countries had the highest vote in deciding not only the terms of the global tropical timber trade but also the extent of sustainable production.[72] In Colchester's words, 'the more a country destroyed tropical forests, the more votes it got'.[73]

The ITTO's early years revolved around tapping into new forests and lesser-known species, based on pre-project and project proposals developed by the producing countries or the Secretariat. Forty-two projects for promotion of tropical timber were already approved during the negotiations within UNCTAD. Sawmills were funded, wood villages were built, and loggers were trained in sawing difficult species and seasoning mixed species, amongst others.[74] Headquartered in a business skyscraper in Yokohama, Japan, and directed by the former deputy director of Malaysian forest department Freezailah Che Yeom, the ITTO functioned as a hub for a diffusion of Japanese and Southeast Asian entrepreneurism and state developmentalism – embedding what Cumings called a 'Bureaucratic Authoritarian Industrializing Regime' – to tropical Africa and South America.[75] The Secretariat embarked on a path of producing knowledge on marketable breeds, available timber reserves, and production capacity.

Yet, as the 1990s drew close, the commodification logic of the organization had to be accompanied with some degree of conservationism. Deforestation in Southeast Asia and South America, particularly the Amazon forests, and the impact of the ongoing debt of tropical countries on their forests had created global anxieties. Just in the 1980s, the global annual rate of logging had increased from 11 to 17 million hectares. To contain the fears, the ITTO began commissioning

[72] 1983 ITTA, Annex B.

[73] M. Colchester, 'The International Tropical Timber Organization: Kill or Cure for the Rainforests' (1990) 20 *The Ecologist* 167.

[74] For a list of projects funded by the ITTO, see, www.itto.int/project_search/

[75] B. Cumings, 'The Origins and Development of the Northeast Asian Political Economy: Industrial Sectors, Product Cycles, and Political Consequences' (1984) 38 *International Organization* 1–40.

several expert reports on ways to manage the ecological externalities of logging without undermining the logic and scale of industrial logging,[76] and as preparations for the 1992 UNCED took off the ground, the ITTO's Council adopted a declaration that committed the organization in a non-binding manner to ensuring that 'the total exports of tropical timber products should come from sustainably managed resources by the Year 2000'.[77]

UNCED became a battleground between developing countries, led by Malaysia and Brazil, insisting on old rhetorics of 'permanent sovereignty over natural resources' and proponents of liberal environmentalism in the North, calling for 'sustainable forest management' and an international treaty on tropical forests. The Bush administration, specifically, viewed a forest convention as a low hanging fruit to catch up with the pressure of environmentalism at home, while using tropical forest conservation as an alternative to carbon emission education.[78] More specifically, the initiatives around UNCED reflected a shift from the 1970s narratives of 'limits to growth' towards 'managing ecological crises' on the margin of the market and without retreat from the growth. It was ultimately the spirit of free trade and the ongoing GATT Uruguay Round that set the limit to environmentalism. Instead of an international treaty, the summit finally opted for a weaker instrument titled *the Non-Legally Binding Authoritative Statement of Principles for a Global Consensus on the Management, Conservation and Sustainable Development of All Types of Forests* (known as Forest Principles), which blended tropical states' extractivism with some degrees of liberal environmentalism in tropical forests. The adoption of the declaration was followed by renegotiation of the ITTA, the

[76] D. Poore, P. Burgess, J. Palmer, S. Rietbergen, and T. Synnott, *No Timber without Trees: Sustainability in the Tropical Forest (a study for ITTO)* (Earthscan Publications Ltd, 1989). Oxford Forestry Institute, 'Incentives in Producer and Consumer Countries to Promote Sustainable Development of Tropical Forests, Pre-Project Report Commissioned by the International Tropical Timber Organization' (Oxford Forestry Institute, February 1991).'The Case for Multiple-Use Management of Tropical Hardwood Forests – A Study Prepared by the Harvard Institute for International Development [HIID] – January 1988' (World Bank, records of the Agriculture and Rural Development Sector, 1988).

[77] ITTC(XXVIII)/28, 30 May 2000.

[78] D. S. Davenport, 'An Alternative Explanation for the Failure of the UNCED Forest Negotiations' (2005) 5 *Global Environmental Politics* 105–30; R. Weissman, 'Summit Games: Bush Busts UNCED' (August 1992).

founding instrument of the ITTO, in 1994 to recognize 'sustainable forest management' and with the objective to ensure sustainability of globally traded timber, a lousy goal that the organization continued to grapple with in the years that followed.[79]

The retreat from 'absolute sovereignty' was part of a broader neoliberal shift in the South's politics within UNCTAD following the Eighth Conference in Cartagena, Colombia in February 1992. The Conference adopted the 'New Partnership for Development' which acknowledged the role of private enterprise and free market in the South's economic growth,[80] what Lemoine characterized as 'the offering by the developing countries of the olive branch and its acceptance by the developed countries'.[81] UNCTAD's move away from the NIEO militancy was followed by the summit of the Non-Aligned Movement in Jakarta in September 1992, where, in the shadow of the breakdown of Yugoslavia and the debt problem, a collective decision was made to move towards 'a constructive North/South dialogue based on interdependence, mutual interest and shared responsibility'.[82] With juridification of global free trade in the 1990s, one can argue that both developing states' demands for a New International Economic Order and the industrialized world's compromised environmentalism were ultimately subsumed into neoliberal entrepreneurism and crisis management.[83]

Conclusion

While historical materialist approaches to international law have long unblackboxed the nature and function of 'law' in capitalist social relations and the 'Rule of Law' at the core of the liberal politics for that purpose, the 'state' as a socio-material structure has yet to become

79 See, Poore, *Changing Landscape*, chapter 9.

80 UNCTAD, 'A New Partnership for Development: The Cartagena Commitment', 8th session, Cartagena de Indias, Colombia, 22 February 1992

81 J. Lemoine, 'International Trade Regimes in Retrospect' in E. M. Chossudovsky, J. Lemoine, and M. A. Boisard (eds.), *Multilateral Diplomacy: The United Nations System at Geneva: A Working Guide*, (Brill, 1998), 410.

82 Conference of Heads of State or Government of Non-Aligned Countries, 10th session, NAC 10/Doc.12/Rev.1, 'The Jakarta Message: A Call for Collective Action and the Democratization of International Relations', Jakarta, Indonesia, 6 September 1992.

83 V. Menotti, 'Globalization and the Acceleration of Forest Destruction since Rio' (1998) 28 *Ecologist* 354–62.

a central problematique in Marxist international law. IR historical materialism and historical sociology from the works of the proponents of the Uneven and Combined Development and the Amsterdam School on European integration to the neo-Gramscian IR all offer rich ways of reconceptualizing IOs and the international law by essentially reasoning from local relations of production up to the world order and IOs.[84] This chapter sought to introduce, rather briefly, such ways of thinking into international institutional law by arguing that capitalism moves in times and space, transforming social relations around means of production through constant commodification and socialization. Beyond the ground-level, the world order and IOs for that purpose have been and continue to be shaped by struggles between two modes of capitalist social relations: one grounded in the organization of such relations by the market (and embedding a de-territorializing logic of advancement) and the other rooted in the organization of production relations by bureaucratic vanguards, along ethno-national lines and geared towards territorial regimes of accumulation.

I sought to demonstrate these dynamics by scrabbling around three histories from post-WWII regimes of flow of manufactured products, raw commodities, and marine logistics. I argued that liberalization of telecommunications, the rise of flags of convenience in world shipping, and the mass logging of tropical forests in the post-WWII era reflected not only the continuous oscillation between commodification and restoring social coherence through standard setting, but also the struggles between laissez-faire and state capitalism, ending in the gradual yet ultimate victory of the former as underpinned by the supremacy of the market in socio-political organization since the last quarter of the twentieth century.

[84] B. Jessop and H. Overbreek (eds.), *Transnational Capital and Class Fractions: The Amsterdam School Perspective Reconsidered* (Routledge, 2019); A. Budd, *Class, States and International Relations: A Critical Appraisal of Robert Cox and neo-Gramscian Theory* (Routledge, 2013); J. Rosenberg, '*Social Structures and Geopolitical Systems: A Critique of the Realist Theory of International Relations*' (September 1992); B. Teschke, *The Myth of 1648: Class, Geopolitics and the Making of Modern International Relations* (Verso, 2003); J. Rosenberg, 'Uneven and Combined Development' in K. Matin and A. Anievas (eds.), *Historical Sociology and World History: Uneven and Combined Development over the Long Durée* (Rowman & Littlefield, 2016), pp. 17–30.

14 Deconstructing 'Resilience Talk' in Global Governance

Toward a Critical Political Economy Approach

A. CLAIRE CUTLER

Introduction

A recent Special Issue on resilience in the EU and international institutions observes that '[r]esilience is one of those terms that seems to have appeared out of nowhere to be present everywhere: from billboards advertising "resilient skincare" to think tank policy talks about the need for more resilient critical infrastructures, and environmentalist calls for resilient planetary eco-systems'.[1] Indeed, resilience has become the buzzword or mantra of World Bank sustainable development policies; OECD recommendations for economic development and disaster management; international organisational approaches to supply chain governance; World Health Organization approaches to physical and mental health; the approaches to urban development of the International Committee of the Red Cross and United Nations; and development and disaster management strategies and national security policies in the UK, USA, EU, and elsewhere. This chapter begins from the premise that vocabularies matter in international law, as 'ideologies' in the 'technical sense of reifying, making seem necessary or neutral something that is partial and contested',[2] and in international relations, as disciplinary mechanisms of control and often structurally biased means of governance.[3] Accepting the view that 'resilience sits

[1] E. Korostelva, and T. Flockhart, 'Resilience in EU and International Institutions: Redefining Local Ownership in a New Global Governance Agenda,' (2020) 41 (2) *Contemporary Security Policy* 153–175, 153.

[2] M. Koskenniemi, 'The Politics of International Law – 20 Years Later,' (2009) 20 (1) *European Journal of International Law* 7–19 at p. 12.

[3] S. Smith, 'Singing Our World into Existence: International Relations Theory and September 11,' (2004) 48 (3) *International Studies Quarterly* 499–515.

precisely at the crux of governmentality and political economy',[4] it is possible to analyse 'resilience talk' as an essential element in the movement away from multilateral, institutional governance, towards the self-help system of self-regulating subjects under neoliberalism.[5] This chapter submits that resilience talk is often a hegemonic force that depoliticises and naturalises deep structural inequalities in the governance activities of international organisations and law. The language of resilience both instantiates and reflects the language, logic, and inherent crises of capitalism. By asking the critical political economy questions of 'who gets what' from resilience talk and just 'whose resilience' are we talking about, the chapter explores resilience as both an ideology and a material force in new constitutional governance.[6] The language of resilience has become the legal and governance common sense of the day, obscuring the underlying conflicting social forces created and advanced by new constitutionalism.

New constitutionalism differs in many ways from the old constitutionalism, but the most salient characteristic of contemporary new constitutional governance is the commitment of global leaders to the expansion of capitalism and the privileging of private, market-based means of capitalist appropriation as the *grundnorms* of global governance.[7] New constitutionalism, like the old or traditional understandings of constitutionalism, associated with the rule of law, limitations on governmental power, and equality before the law, is committed to the rule of law. However, this commitment is to law of a specific form: it is capital's law that can blow both hot and cold, hard and soft, depending upon the needs of capital.[8] As a mechanism of new

[4] A. Howell, 'Resilience as Enhancement: Governmentality and Political Economy beyond "Responsibilisation",' (2015) 35 (1) *Politics* 67–71.

[5] D. Chandler and J. Reid, *The Neoliberal Subject: Resilience, Adaptation, and Vulnerability* (London: Rowman & Littlefield, 2016).

[6] S. Gill and A. C. Cutler (eds.) *New Constitutionalism and World Order* (Cambridge: Cambridge University Press, 2014).

[7] For discussion of the differences between old and new constitutionalism see Gill and Cutler, *New Constitutionalism and World Order*, 1–14 and A. C. Cutler, 'The Rule of Law, Constitutionalism, and Transnational Legality' in C. May and A. Winchester (eds.) *Handbook on the Rule of Law* (Cheltenham, UK: Edward Elgar Publishing, 2018) pp. 307–321, 311–314. See S. Gill (ed.) *Global Crises and the Crisis of Global Leadership* (Cambridge: Cambridge University Press, 2012) for discussion of global leadership.

[8] See A. C. Cutler, *Private Power and Public Authority: Transnational Merchant Law in the Global Political Economy* (Cambridge: Cambridge University Press,

constitutional discipline, the language of resilience deepens global capitalism, both intensively and extensively, through the hegemony of neoliberalism, the privatisation and the individualisation of responsibility, and the preservation of hierarchies of power and domination as the common-sense foundations for law and good governance. The chapter makes the case for destabilising and disrupting this discourse and practice as a necessary move in revealing the class, gender, racial, and intersectional operations of resilience talk in order to humanise important institutions of global governance.

The chapter begins with a discussion of new constitutional governance, outlining the contours of a critical political economy approach to international organisations and law.[9] Analysis then shifts to document the various and multiple illustrations of the promotion of resilience by various actors, institutions, and legal texts engaged and implicated in global governance. The final section addresses what critical political economy has to offer to our understanding of the interests and purposes served by 'resilience talk' in global governance and makes the case for disrupting and challenging its hegemonic significance as 'common sense' by an appeal to transformative 'good sense'.

Critical Political Economy and New Constitutionalism

Adopting a critical political economy approach, the relationship between law and capitalism is here analysed as a new constitutionalism that often operates by subordinating the public domain to the disciplines of the private sphere of transnational capital accumulation. By definition, new constitutionalism refers to a combination of processes involving: the emergence of a *de facto* constitutional governance structure for the world market; the neoliberal restructuring of states

2003); A. C. Cutler, 'The Judicialization of Private Transnational Power and Authority,' (2018) 25 (1) *Indiana Journal of Global Legal Studies* 61–95.

9 I use the term critical political economy to capture a form of historical materialist analysis that goes beyond class distinctions to incorporate a more complex understanding of the sites and sorts of struggles that characterize global governance. I conceive of historical materialism as a philosophy of praxis and as a method of critical analysis and immanent critique that has unavoidable transformative and emancipatory potential. See A. C. Cutler, 'Toward a Radical Political Economy Critique of Transnational Economic Law' in S. Marks (ed.), *International Law on the Left: Re-examining Marxist Legacies* (New York: Cambridge University Press, 2008), pp. 199–219.

according to the juridical demands of market civilisation;[10] locking-in mechanisms, such as trade, investment, and financial laws, which support neoliberal accumulation; informality and flexibility in non-binding legal regulation; and the interpellation of the neoliberal subject in the development of the commodity form of law as the template of global governance.[11] While each process will be addressed in turn, critical political economy asks 'who gets what?' and 'whose interests and purposes are served?' through law under a new constitutionalism that obscures and shields foreign and transnational corporations from accountability, while locking states into legal commitments that continue to advance private transnational capital accumulation.[12]

As mentioned earlier, the new constitutionalism refers to the uneven emergence of a *de facto* constitutional structure for the global political economy. This development has largely coincided with the global expansion of capitalism since the 1980s and the pursuit over the past few decades by many states and associations of neoliberal policies and constitutional reforms, both domestically and globally. The new constitutionalism is further reflected in a proliferation of neoliberal trade and investment frameworks, such as the US, Mexico, Canada Free Trade Agreement, the World Trade Organization (WTO), the international investment regime, and in legal and institutional changes in macroeconomic policy, exemplified by politically independent central banks and currency boards. Changes in public service provision involving the privatisation of education, healthcare, and many other aspects of life are linked to neoliberal trade and investment frameworks and treaties, such as the General Agreement on Trade in Services (GATS)[13]

[10] Market civilization refers to a social order associated with late twentieth- and early twenty-first-century capitalism that is geared to the preservation and expansion of capitalist markets, locally and globally; nationally and transnationally. See Gill and Cutler, *New Constitutionalism and World Order*, p. 319.

[11] Gill and Cutler, *New Constitutionalism and World Order*.

[12] R. Cox, 'Social Forces, States and World Orders: Beyond International Relations Theory,' 10 *Millennium: Journal of International Studies* (1981) 126. See Negar Mansouri, this volume and A. C. Cutler, *Private Power and Public Authority* for elucidation of Cox's critical political theory.

[13] See Cutler, 'Toward a Radical Political Economy Critique of Transnational Economic Law' and A. C. Cutler, 'Unthinking the GATS: A Radical Political Economy Critique of Private Transnational Governance' in. M. Ougaard and A. Leander (eds.) *Business and Governance* (New York and London: Routledge, 2010), pp. 78–96.

and the global intellectual property regime,[14] and are subordinated to the demands and regulatory power of transnational business corporations. The new constitutionalism increasingly informs bilateral and multilateral trade and investment agreements, and other economic, social, and environmental policy frameworks.[15] It is redefining politics and governance globally and, in the terminology of the World Bank, involves locking in states to neoliberal frameworks of capital accumulation.[16] Neoliberalism is a 'theory of political economic practices proposing that human well-being can best be advanced by the maximisation of entrepreneurial freedoms within an institutional framework characterised by private property rights, individual liberty, unencumbered markets, and free trade'.[17]

The new constitutionalism is increasingly significant in shaping global public policy, in ways that may have long-term effects on the ontological and epistemological bases of constitutionalism, as well as more broadly on institutions of social reproduction associated with public services, care, and education.[18] In this regard, it provides the template for contemporary economic, social, and political regulation and entails the acceptance by society of the expansion of commodification through legal protection of private property rights as natural, rational, and common-sense modes of governance that serve the common interests of all, both the governors and governed.[19] Private appropriation becomes constitutionalised through law and state as a public good. Through new constitutionalism, the communal protection of

[14] S. Sell, *Private Power, Public Law: The Globalization of Intellectual Property Rights* (Cambridge: Cambridge University Press, 2003).

[15] D. Schneiderman, *Constitutionalizing Economic Globalization: Investment Rules and Democracy's Promise* (Cambridge: Cambridge University Press, 2008); A. C. Cutler, 'Transformations in Statehood, the Investor-State Regime, and the New Constitutionalism,' (2016) 23 (1) *Indiana Journal of Global Legal Studies* 95–126.

[16] World Bank, *Building Institutions for Markets* (Oxford: Oxford University Press, 2002).

[17] D. Harvey, 'Neoliberalism as Creative Destruction,' 610 (1) (2007) *The Annals of the American Academy of Political and Social Science* 22–44, 22.

[18] I. Bakker and S. Gill, *Power, Production and Social Reproduction: Human In/Security in the Global Political Economy* (Basingstoke, Hants and New York: Palgrave Macmillan, 2003).

[19] A. C. Cutler, 'New Constitutionalism and the Commodity Form of Global Capitalism,' in Gill and Cutler, *New Constitutionalism and World Order*, 45–62.

private property rights becomes a natural and organic accompaniment of global production and exchange.[20]

The commodity form of law is central to new constitutional governance. Evgeni Pashukanis,[21] building upon Karl Marx's critique of political economy, believed that law is inextricably linked to capitalism and is in fact itself a product of capitalism, functioning as an integral part of the commodity system: the commodity form of law is homologous with the commodity form of capitalism and mediates political interests.[22] The commodity form of law reinforces capital and is legitimated through the misrecognition of law as impartial, just, rational, and operating between juridically equal subjects. Law is therefore deeply imbricated in capitalism and its resulting relationships of power. To Pashukanis, this imbrication is predicated on the formation of the legal subject as the holder of legal rights as an abstract, impersonal, and, ultimately, juridical person. In fact, in recognising the juridical subject, capitalism assumes its legal character through the legitimation of exchanges of commodities as formally equal commodity owners: one party the owner of labour and the other the owner of surplus value, engaged in free exchange.[23] But to Marx and Pashukanis, this assumption of juridical equality masks the profound inequality that inheres in the very fabric of capitalist relations between owners and producers. Importantly, it is the role of new constitutionalism to obscure this inequality and render it invisible in the formation of common sense.

Indeed, critical political economy offers important insights into the constitution of common-sense meanings. It recognises that capitalism does not simply reproduce itself of its own accord, but requires certain attitudes, institutions, and apparatuses to enable its continuing

[20] A. C. Cutler, 'Gramsci, Law, and the Culture of Global Capitalism' (2005) 8 (4) *Critical Review of International Social and Political Philosophy* 527–542.

[21] E. Pashukanis, 'International Law' in. B. Piers and R. Sharlet (eds.) *Pashukanis: Selected Writings on Marxism and Law* (London: Academic Press, 1980) pp. 168–190 and E. Pashukanis, *Law and Marxism: A General Theory* (London: Pluto Press, 1978).

[22] See I. Balbus, 'Commodity Form and Legal Form: An Essay on the "Relative Autonomy" of the Law' (1976–1977) 11 (3) *Law & Society Review* 571–588 and T. Krever, 'The Rule of Law and the Rise of Capitalism' in C. May and A. Winchester (eds.) *Handbook on the Rule of Law* (Cheltenham: Edward Elgar Publishing, 2018) pp. 184–200, 197.

[23] Pashukanis, *Law and Marxism*.

reproduction and expansion.[24] Theories of the State recognise the analytical distinction between functions of accumulation and legitimation, recording the need of capitalist states for material, institutional, and normative or ideological reproduction. Robert Jessop, for example, differentiates between the 'accumulation strategies' of a state and its 'hegemonic project', suggesting that achieving the material conditions for capitalism is insufficient, for these conditions must be generally accepted by society.[25] Jessop articulates understandings of hegemony inspired by Antonio Gramsci and the idea that the dominant class achieves dominance or 'hegemony' through the combined influence of coercion and consent. Gramsci believed that hegemony, the process by which the ruling class establishes the conditions necessary for achieving leadership, could not be secured solely through coercion, but required the ideological capture of popular support. This involves the acceptance and internalisation by the masses of the interests and values of the ruling class as their own. Indeed, as Adam Morton observes, 'hegemony is the articulation and justification of a particular set of interests as general interests. It appears as an expression of broadly based consent, manifested in the acceptance of ideas and supported by material resources and institutions.'[26]

The acceptance by civil society of relations of dominance is thus a crucial dimension of hegemony. So too is the work of the 'organic intellectuals' who facilitate the internalisation of the interests of the ruling class as the common interest and, indeed, as the 'common sense' of the time. Antonio Gramsci observes that the acceptance by the masses of the dominant ethos as 'common sense' is not a result of 'self-deception [*malafede*]' but 'the expression of profounder contrasts of a social historical order' associated with its subjugation as a group.[27] It is organic intellectuals of the day who are able to generate the acceptance by the

[24] K. Marx, *Capital: A Critique of Political Economy*, vol. 1. trans B. Fowkes. (London: Penguin, 1976. [1867]); L. Althusser, 'Ideology and Ideological State Apparatuses: Notes towards an Investigation,' in *Lenin and Philosophy and Other Essays* (New York: Monthly Review Press, 1971), pp. 127–186.

[25] R. Jessop, *State Theory: Putting the Capitalist State in its Place* (Pennsylvania: Pennsylvania State Press, 1990), p. 216.

[26] A. Morton, *Unravelling Gramsci: Hegemony and Passive Revolution in the Global Political Economy* (London: Pluto Press, 2007), p. 113.

[27] A. Gramsci, Q. Hoare, and G. Smith (eds.) *Selections from Prison Notebooks of Antonio Gramsci* (New York: International Publishers, 1971), pp. 326–327.

masses of the interests of the ruling class as 'common sense'. Moreover, law is the 'instrument for this purpose'.[28] Indeed, organic intellectuals are able to garner both the 'spontaneous' consent of the masses and the legal enforcement of coercive discipline. In this latter respect, Gramsci regarded the law and legal institutions as playing a particular role in producing common-sense understandings under-girding hegemony.[29] Law becomes the mechanism for authorising the framing of private interests as public interests and as common sense. Although Gramsci wrote very little about law, his fragmentary analysis of law coupled with his understanding of hegemony inspires a *praxis conception of law* of great relevance to this analysis.[30] This conception derives from Gramsci's theorisation of Marxism as a philosophy of *praxis:* as a unity resulting from the dialectical development of contradictions between theoretical and practical activity. Gramsci contemplated this unity as 'immanent' in capitalist society and as realisable through practices informed by critical inquiry.[31] The role of the organic intellectual is linked to the processes of establishing the hegemony or leadership of the dominant social forces. The process of achieving hegemony and 'colonising the internal world of the dominated classes' involves three related developments in which organic intellectuals and law play leading roles: universalisation, naturalisation, and rationalisation.[32] Universalisation involves the representation by the dominant group of its private interests as common and public in nature, while naturalisation and rationalisation concern processes of reification that present the existing order as fully consistent with the natural and rational order of things. Law facilitates these processes by interpellating individuals as equal legal subjects, obscuring their actual subordination and inequality, and rationalising this appearance as part of the universal and natural order of things.[33] These processes may be achieved through *trasformismo*, being the absorption of opposition into the

[28] Ibid., p. 246.

[29] M. Benney, 'Gramsci on Law, Morality and Power' (1983) 11 *International Journal of the Sociology of the Law* 191–208.

[30] Cutler, 'Gramsci, Law, and the Culture of Global Capitalism'.

[31] Gramsci, *Selection from Prison Notebooks of Antonio Gramsci*, pp. 400, 450.

[32] D. Litowitz, 'Gramsci, Hegemony, and the Law,' (2000) 2 (2) *Brigham Young University Law Review* 515–551, 525.

[33] Althusser, in *Ideology and Ideological State Apparatuses*, developed the theory of interpellation to capture the role that ideology plays in constituting individuals as legal subjects who are aware of and identify with their own subjectivity, thereby participating consensually in the reproduction of capitalism.

dominant group,[34] which involves the work of organic intellectuals who 'perpetuate the existing way of life at the level of theory' as the rational and natural order of things.[35]

Resilience talk and the experts who cultivate and advance it through the work of international organisations and law are the organic intellectuals who naturalise and rationalise resilience as the best practice in global governance. They facilitate the interpellation of the subjects of resilience planning as 'neoliberal subjects' and active participants in the reproduction of capitalism and many of the conditions causing severe crises in capitalism in the first place.[36] In doing so, expert international lawyers are instrumental in the construction of hegemony, perhaps unwitting participants in the creation and maintenance of neoliberal hegemony. For example, international intellectual property lawyers who are advancing climate resistant seeds as the solution to climate change may be regarded as promoting the resilience paradigm and the common sense of adapting to, rather than resisting or trying to abate, the climate crisis. They are thus enabling climate capitalism to proceed as business as usual and possibly contributing to corporate concentration in the seed industry, which is threatening global food security.[37] The discussion will turn to consider how resilience is becoming the common sense in global governance of the climate change crisis, sustainable development, and disaster and refugee management strategies. These crises and disruptions are all interlinked in various ways to a deeper crisis in the production and reproduction of global capitalism.

Resilience Talk in Global Governance

Notable common tendencies in each of the resilience strategies adopted by international organisations considered here are the trends toward

[34] Gramsci, *Selections from Prison Notebooks of Antonio Gramsci*, pp. 57, 58–59.

[35] Litowitz, 'Gramsci, Hegemony, and the Law', p. 526. See also Cutler, 'Unthinking the GATS' for an Althusserian reading of the interpellation of transnational corporations as neoliberal subjects under global capitalism.

[36] B. Evans and J. Reid, 'Dangerously Exposed: The Life and Death of the Resilient Subject,' (2013) 1 (2) *Resilience: International Policies, Practices and Discourses* 83–98.

[37] S. Mahoney, 'Owning the World's Seed Supply: How Seed Industry Mergers Threaten Global Food Security' (2019) 31 (3) *The Georgetown Environmental Law Review* 563–79.

the enhanced role of technical experts in global governance, the deformalisation of law through the predominance of 'soft law',[38] and the management of crises in capitalism through the application of what Robert Cox refers to as 'problem-solving theory'.[39] Problem-solving theory is differentiated from 'critical theory' in that the former takes the world as it is with its existing power structures, while the latter seeks to transform the world and challenges existing hierarchies of power and authority. Resilience theory has its origins in multiple disciplines in the attempt to deal with risk management. It is 'concerned fundamentally with how a system, community or individual can deal with disturbance, surprise and change'.[40] Ecosystem stability, engineering infrastructure, psychology, the behavioural sciences, disaster reduction, supply chain regulation, and multilateral aid organisations are just some of the areas adopting resilience theory into their programming. The goal is to 'ensure that shocks and stresses, whether individually or in combination, do not lead to a downturn in development progress' and economic growth.[41] The focus on risk management and reduction and ensuring the continuity of economic expansion and growth is consistent with what Henk Overbeek refers to as the 'reformist' turn in global governance from a 'transformist rallying cry' in the late 1970s, to rule by technocratic experts and 'the global rule of capital' geared to 'the management of neo-liberal globalisation'.[42] Today global governance is 'increasingly informalised', 'based on self-regulation by private forces' and 'predicated on a constitutionally anchored legal basis':[43] the new constitutionalism. As we turn to examine examples of resilience governance it becomes apparent that they are connected in different ways to a deeper crisis of capitalism on a planetary scale.

[38] E. Ferris and J. Bergmann, 'Soft Law, Migration and Climate Change Governance,' (2017) 8 (1) *Journal of Human Rights and the Environment*, 6–29.

[39] Cox, 'Social Forces, States and World Orders.'

[40] T. Mitchell and K. Harris, 'Resilience: A Risk Management Approach,' *ODI Background Note* (January 2012) (The Overseas Development Institute, UK) 1. J. Walker and M. Cooper, 'Genealogies of Resilience: From Systems Ecology to the Political Economy of Crisis Adaptation,' (2011) 42 (2) *Security Dialogue* 143–160.

[41] Mitchell and Harris, 'Resilience,' 1.

[42] H. Overbeek, 'Global Governance: From Radical Transformation to Neo-Liberal Management,' in K. Dingwerth, P. Pattberg, and D. Compagnon, 'Forum: Global Governance: Decline or Maturation of an Academic Concept?' (2010) 12 (4) *International Studies Review* 696–719, 697.

[43] Ibid., p. 700.

Phillipe Bourbeau provides an excellent overview of the adoption in the social sciences of the resilience framework and notes that '[t]he United Nations, together with several international organisations and non-governmental organisations, has invoked resilience as a new organising principle' to address human suffering and reduce the costs of emergency responses.[44] The World Bank identifies building resilience as essential to achieving the goals of 'ending extreme poverty and promoting shared prosperity' by integrating the risks of climate change and disaster relief into development initiatives.[45] The World Health Organization similarly regards resilience building as at the 'core' of its *Health 2020* vision, while resilience building is integrated as well in United Nations Sustainable Development Goals.[46] In fact, adaptation to climate change,[47] sustainable development,[48] disaster relief,[49] climate migration management,[50] and the management

[44] P. Bourbeau, 'Resilience and International Politics: Premises, Debates, Agenda,' (2015) 17 (3) *International Studies Review* 374–395, 377.

[45] World Bank, *Building Resilience: Integrating Climate and Disaster Risk into Development* (Washington, DC: World Bank, 2013), viii.

[46] World Health Organization, *Strengthening Resilience: A Priority Shared by Health 2020 and the Sustainable Development Goals* (Copenhagen: WHO Regional Office for Europe, 2017).

[47] World Bank, *Building Resilience.*

[48] The United Nations Development Program, *Towards Human Resilience: Sustaining MDG Progress in an Age of Economic Uncertainty* (New York: United National Development Programme, 2011) www.preventionweb.net/files/24163workshopbuildingresiliencecasestudi.pdf; Swiss Agency for Development and Cooperation, *Building Resilience: Bridging Food Security, Climate Change Adaptation and Disaster Risk Reduction* (Rome: Swiss Agency for Development and Cooperation, 2011) www.preventionweb.net/files/24163_workshopbuildingresiliencecasestudi.pdf; the Swedish International Development Cooperation Agency, *Resilience, Risk and Vulnerability* (Stockholm: Swedish International Development Cooperation Agency, 2012).

[49] IPCC, *Managing the Risks of Extreme Events and Disasters to Climate Change Adaptation* (Cambridge: Cambridge University Press, 2012); the Intergovernmental Authority on Development Platform for Drought Disaster Resilience 2013 https://igad.int/about-us; the Global Alliance for Resilience Partnership National Resilience Template 2013 www.food-security.net/en/topic/global-alliance-for-resilience-agir/; UK Department of International Development, *Defining Disaster Resilience: A DFID Approach Paper* (London: UK Department of International Development, 2011); USAID, *The Resilience Agenda: Helping Vulnerable Communities Emerge from Cycles of Crisis onto a Pathway toward Development* (Washington, DC: USAID, 2011). Swiss Agency for Development and Cooperation, *Building Resilience*; The United Nations Development Program, *Towards Human Resilience*; the Swedish International Development Cooperation Agency, *Resilience, Risk and Vulnerability.*

[50] UNICEF, *Resilient migration* (Mexico: UNICEF, 2017).

of crisis-related supply chain disruptions[51] provide the most notable and growing imbrications of resilience-oriented global governance strategies and mechanisms into the foundations of capitalism, in both local and global political economies. As Julian Reid observes, the 'resilient subject is one which presupposes the disastrousness of the world, and likewise one which interpellates a subject that is permanently called upon to bear the disaster'.[52] The grafting of resilience strategies onto sustainable development policies by the United Nations Development Program (UNDP) and the United Nations Environment Program (UNEP)[53] integrated neoliberal rationalities into sustainable development projects and was a complicated process that is beyond the scope of this chapter.[54] However, the upshot of the process is the framing of sustainable development, not as a question relating to the *security* of the individual, but rather one relating to the *adaptability* of the individual. The resilient subject is thus 'not a secure but an adaptive subject;'[55] a subject that accommodates itself to the existing order and its existing power structures and 'not a subject which can conceive of changing the world, its structure and conditions of possibility'.[56] Indeed, the resilient subject is considered the 'new ethic of responsibility' for disaster management and championed by the Intergovernmental Panel on Climate Change (IPCC).[57] But critics question the suitability of a theory developed in addressing

[51] UNCTAD, *Review of MaritimeTransport* (New York, NY: United Nations Publications, 2020).

[52] J. Reid, 'Interrogating the Neoliberal Biopolitics of the Sustainable Development-Resilience Nexus,' (2013) 7 *International Political Sociology* 353–367, 355.

[53] See United Nations Development Programme, United Nations Environment Programme, World Bank, World Resources Institute, *World Resources 2008: Roots of Resilience – Growing the Wealth of the Poor* (Washington, DC: World Resources Institute, 2008).

[54] See Reid, 'Interrogating the Neoliberal Biopolitics of the Sustainable Development-Resilience Nexus' and M. Duffield, *Development, Security and Unending War: The Governing of the Worlds Peoples* (Cambridge: Polity, 2008) for a full account of these developments.

[55] Reid, 'Interrogating the Neoliberal Biopolitics of the Sustainable Development-Resilience Nexus,' p. 362.

[56] B. Evans and J. Reid, 'Dangerously Exposed: The Life and Death of the Resilient Subject,' (2013) 1 (2) *Resilience: International Policies, Practices and Discourses* 83–98.

[57] Evans and Reid, 'Dangerously Exposed,' p. 85; IPCC, *Managing the Risks of Extreme Events and Disasters*, pp. 32–38.

natural systems to social systems and highlight how resilience theory, rooted as it is in neoliberal, market-based, technical managerialism, erases 'the role that large scale social, economic and political processes play in shaping resilience', depoliticises solutions, and ignores gendered and intersectional dimensions of existing power structures in the communities subject to resilience policies.[58] In law, resilience talk forecloses the development of alternate possibilities. In the context of the climate resistant seeds discussed earlier, the resilience adaptation model forecloses legislation regulating corporate concentration in the seed industry or regulations limiting the sorts of seeds that can be patented and, ultimately, fails to address the underlying problems and risks to the environment and to global food security.[59]

Michael Mikulewicz illustrates how resilience-based development in Liberdade, a community on a small island in the Gulf of Guinea that is subject to impacts of climate change droughts, floods, and rising sea levels, is promoting resilience amongst the new leaseholder farmers. However, the resilience strategy developed by the UNDP rested upon the privatisation of agriculture and failed to provide the necessary agricultural support for the farmers as well as adequate investment in the project. As a result, there was complete failure to address the specific development needs of the people and the underlying structural inequalities relating to social, gender, and racial inequalities. As the state retreated from the countryside, the farmers were left to UNDP managers who excised these structural problems 'from the resilience formula'.[60]

Stephanie Wakefield, in a study of efforts to address rising sea levels in Miami Beach, emphasises the conservative nature of climate change resilience policies in urban environments that 'do not counter or transform existing social or economic urban relations. Instead, they attempt to extend and maintain existing relations into the future.'[61] They thereby 'secure and manage an unchanging urban order' dedicated to 'maintaining Miami Beach's current socio-economic order' premised upon tourism, high-end real estate markets, and luxurious lifestyles.[62]

[58] M. Mikulewicz, 'Thwarting Adaptation's Potential? A Critique of Resilience,' (2019) 104 *Geoforum* 267–282, 273.

[59] Mahoney, 'Owning the World's Seed Supply,' p. 579. [60] Ibid., p. 273.

[61] S. Wakefield, 'Miami Beach Forever? Urbanism in the Back Loop,' (2019) 107 (2) *Geoforum* 34–44, 40.

[62] Ibid.

Margherita Pieraccini shows how resilient legal strategies, involving customary, property, and environmental laws enacted to protect the common property area of Regole d'Ampezzo, Italy, in fact obscure underlying gendered power relations.[63] These laws sustained gender inequality by preventing women from inheriting rights and participating in management of the region, prompting the author to call for a politicised understanding of the legal regime.

The political economy dimension of resilience talk is vividly illustrated by its impact on climate migrants. The *United Nations Framework Convention on Climate Change* 2010 recognises mobility as an adaptive strategy for climate change and the Paris Agreement echoed this recognition and called for concrete recommendations. The result was the *Guidance on Protecting People through Planned Relocations from Disasters and Environmental Changes* and *Operational Guidelines*, both soft law initiatives developed by legal experts and representatives from international organisations and states to assist states and organisations in addressing displaced persons.[64] However, the treatment of displaced persons through the adaptation and resilience framework has reconceptualised migration as a solution to the problems of disaster and climate change, rather than as a result and consequence of the failure to mitigate these very problems in the first place. This reconceptualisation shifts the terrain of legal discourse, lenses, and solutions from one concerning threats of harm that need to be addressed and solved in the context of mitigating climate change, to one of adaptation to and management of climate change. Indeed, this treatment reflects a 'turn from a discourse of "climate refugees", in which the organisations perceive migration as a failure of both mitigation and adaptation to climate change, to one of "climate migration", in which organisations promote mitigation as a strategy of adaptation'.[65] Moreover, 'the growing mantra of resilience in climate policy and politics' and 'the more recent narrative on "migration as adaptation" appears to displace justice claims and inherent rights in favour of a depoliticised

[63] M. Pieraccini, 'A Politicized, Legal Pluralist Analysis of the Commons' Resilience: The Case of the Regole d'Ampezzo,' (2013) 18 (1) *Ecology and Society* 4.

[64] Ibid. See Ferris and Bergmann, 'Soft Law, Migration and Climate Change Governance,' p. 17.

[65] R. Felli, 'Managing Climate Insecurity by Ensuring Continuous Capital Accumulation: "Climate Refugees" and "Climate Migrants",' (2013) 18 (3) *New Political Economy* 337–363, 337.

idea of adaptation that relies on the individual migrant's ability to compete in and benefit from labour markets'.[66] The concept of 'climate refugee' has been displaced by the concept of 'climate migrant', signalling the ascendance of neoliberal reconfigurations of the problems of climate change and disaster management.[67] Once a refugee subject to the catastrophic effects of failures to mitigate climate change and possessing rights to security and (reparative) justice, the migrant is reconfigured as a resilient subject/worker with a duty to self-actualise the potential to manage and adapt to the crisis by integration as a migrant into the work force of the receiving state and contribute to the development of the home state by sending regular remittances home. The climate migrant is thus inserted into the global circuit of capital as a valuable source of remittance income through an expert policy discourse conducted in global governance circles.[68]

Indeed, international organisations have been very active in promoting the climate migrant/worker concept. The UNEP, the International Organisation of Migration, the United Nations University, and the Munich Re Foundation created an alliance – the Climate Change, Environment and Migration Alliance – in 2008 to 'mainstream environmental and climate change initiatives into migration management policies and practices, and to bring migration issues into global environmental and climate change discourse'.[69] In fact, the promotion of climate migration by the International Organisation for Migration (IOM) is 'a defining feature of this organisation'[70] and a central site for the development of expert discourses on climate migration resilience.[71]

The shift from climate refugee to climate migrant was accompanied by another subtle shift away from hard treaty law to soft laws and domestic policies. As Romain Felli observes, '[n]o longer should the

[66] G. Bettini, S. Nash, and G. Gioli, 'One Step Forward, Two Steps Back? The Fading Contours of (in)Justice in Competing Discourses on Climate Migration,' (2017) 183 (4) *The Geographical Journal* 348–358, 348.
[67] Felli, 'Managing Climate Insecurity by Ensuring Continuous Capital Accumulation,' p. 337.
[68] Ibid.
[69] A. Morton, P. Boncour, and F. Laczko 'Human Security Policy Challenges,' (2009) 31 *Forced Migration Review* 5–7, 7.
[70] Felli, 'Managing Climate Insecurity by Ensuring Continuous Capital Accumulation,' p. 342.
[71] See A. Pécoud, 'What Do We Know about the International Organization for Migration?' (2018) 4 (10) *Journal of Ethnic and Migration Studies* 1621–1638.

environmental migrant be located conceptually within the realm of international law and legal categories, as he comes to be surrounded by an ensemble of deformalised norms, and practices, such as "soft laws", advice, capacity-building practices, etc.'[72] In fact, international migration law is characterised by the predominance of soft law arrangements at the bilateral, regional, and international levels, although there are a few international treaties.[73] Felli associates this shift to deformalised norms with a shift away from 'the language of international law' and 'reparative justice' to a language of 'strategic individuals with an entrepreneurial ethos'.[74] Felli also regards the shift as part of a deeper process of primitive accumulation[75] that reconfigures the political economies of predominantly Southern states, dispossesses their climate migrants from the means of production, and subjects labour to precarious conditions of employment. It is important to note that this shift and these processes are instantiated through law and have profound legal consequences for those dispossessed through climate change.

In my view this shift is an example of the commodity form of law at work. Migrants are reconfigured and interpellated by soft law initiatives as resilient neoliberal subjects as they are injected into the global political economy of migrant labour. Indeed, the World Bank presents migration as adaptation through remittances of goods or money to a migrant worker's home state as a positive consequence of climate migration, while the IOM promotes temporary, circular labour migration and 'income diversification through remittances'.[76] The World Bank estimates that global remittances for 2020 were US$651 billion,[77]

[72] Felli, 'Managing Climate Insecurity by Ensuring Continuous Capital Accumulation,' p. 346.

[73] See Ferris and Bergmann, 'Soft Law, Migration and Climate Change Governance'.

[74] Felli, 'Managing Climate Insecurity by Ensuring Continuous Capital Accumulation,' p. 346.

[75] Felli (ibid., p. 349) defines primitive accumulation as an ongoing process within capitalist relations of production that keep the worker a 'dispossessed individual, separated from the means of production… who must constantly reproduce himself through the market by selling his labour power in exchange for a wage, making him productive for capital accumulation'.

[76] IOM, *IOM Policy Brief: Migration, Climate Change and the Environment* (Geneva: IOM, 2009), 2; IOM, *Compendium of IOM's Activities in Migration, Climate Change and the Environment* (Geneva: IOM, 2009), 53.

[77] World Bank Data, https://data.worldbank.org/indicator/BX.TRF.PWKR.CD.DT.

while the IOM 2020 Annual Report details the funding of over sixty-two countries in the development of migrant worker schemes.[78] Problematically, circular labour migration introduces 'extreme flexibilisation' into migrant labour and as a consequence labour unions worldwide and even the International Labour Organization have denounced migrant worker schemes, which Felli argues 'turns these migrants into an activity productive for the accumulation of capital. Climate change is thus harnessed toward the reconfiguration of social relations in a capitalist form.'[79]

Nicola Phillips identifies the promotion of migration as a development strategy and a form of accumulation by dispossession that inserts migrant workers from the South into transnational supply chains through the provision of labour. This strategy creates conflict between migrant workers and national workers by putting downward pressure on wages and leads to the extreme flexibilisation of labour.[80] As noted by others, this form of migration management 'is fundamentally about making migration economically beneficial, notably by connecting the supply of labour in the less-developed South with the migrant workers in the North'.[81] Felli calls for a reconsideration of how the conception of the climate migrant naturalises and depoliticises the politics of climate change, the dispossession it works, and the legal forms involved, to which attention turns.

Disrupting 'Common Sense' in Global Governance

Critics of resilience talk argue that resilience strategies are essentially reactive and function to shift development assistance responsibilities (as well as responsibilities for climate change mitigation, disaster relief, and so forth) away from states, international organisations, and business corporations and onto individuals, who are expected to achieve development as resilient neoliberal subjects. A study of the

78 IOM, *Annual Report 2020* (Geneva: IOM, 2020), 27.

79 Felli, 'Managing Climate Insecurity by Ensuring Continuous Capital Accumulation,' p. 356.

80 N. Phillips, 'Migration as Development Strategy? The New Political Economy of Dispossession and Inequality in the Americas,' (2009) 16 (2) *Review of International Political Economy* 231–259.

81 M. Geiger and A. Pécoud, 'The Politics of International Migration Management' in M. Geiger and A. Pécoud (eds.) *The Politics of Migration Management* (Basingstoke, Hants: Palgrave Macmillan, 2010), pp. 1–20, 14.

reception of Syrian refugees into Jordan and Lebanon under the guise of resilience frameworks reveals that very little development resulted for either the refugees or the host states and the framework is better regarded as a strategy to keep migrants out of the European Union.[82] Sarah Sharma notes that 'resilience is a reactive neoliberal policy tool implemented by the World Bank in urban spaces of the global South in both the transition from the Washington and post-Washington Consensuses and the rise of the climate crisis on the international development agenda'.[83] She further notes that '[r]esilience policies call for individuals to brace themselves, build up strength, and bounce-back from so-called exogenous shocks and stresses'.[84]

Resilience strategies are a form of neoliberal discipline and new constitutionalism. They deliver significant power and authority to technocratic experts and obscure underlying socio-political-economic causes of poverty, insecurity, and inequality. Attention is shifted away from providing solutions to the underlying causes of insecurity and inequality, such as the failure to achieve climate change mitigation, toward technocratic adaptation, management, acceptance, and normalisation of crises as something that requires adaptation. Resilience talk is, in the end, a form of post-politics that has evacuated the 'political' in favour of technical, economic, and managerial reason with profound implications for local and global political economies. Indeed, Mark Neocleous argues that resilience has colonised 'the political imagination': 'resilience is by definition *against resistance*. Resilience wants acquiescence, not resistance. Not a passive acquiescence, for sure, in fact quite the opposite. But it does demand that we use our actions to accommodate ourselves to capital and the state, and the secure future of both, rather than to resist them.'[85]

[82] R. Anholt and G. Sinatti, 'Under the Guise of Resilience: The EU Approach to Migration and Forced Displacement in Jordan and Lebanon,' (2020) 41 (2) *Contemporary Security Policy* 311–335.

[83] S. Sharma, 'Reactive, Individualistic and Disciplinary: The Urban Resilience Project in Dhaka,' 12 (6) (2021) *New Political Economy* 1078–1091, 1081.

[84] Ibid., 1082.

[85] M. Neocleous, 'Resisting Resilience' (2013) 178 *Radical Philosophy* 2–7, 7. Many question the emancipatory potential of international law, while 'resistance' is an increasingly contested concept in international law. Both concepts are beyond the scope of this paper. For the contested status of resistance see B. Rajagopal, 'International Law and the Challenges of Theorizing Resistance,' 41 (2) (2003) *Columbia Journal of Transnational Law*

How might we destabilise and dislodge resilience talk in global governance laws and institutions? The first step is to problematise the relationship between law and resilience thinking. Problematisation involves recognising that '[l]egal structures, principles, and processes, as well as core concepts of the rule of law, impinge on the capacity of societies to manage ecosystems, withstand environmental degradation as well as economic shocks'.[86] The next steps involve ascertaining *how* law affects these systems and identifying its positive or negative effects.

I believe that scholars of international law and organisation have a particular role to play in problematising the resilience paradigm of governance, as what Antonio Gramsci would call the 'organic intellectuals' of global governance. International lawyers, as legal experts, give shape to the norms and practices that articulate and, indeed, constitute the 'common-sense' foundations of global governance. Located at the intersection of national and transnational capitalist systems, they function to represent their disciplinary consensus as 'normal', transmitting it through society, consensually, as 'common sense'. But as David Kennedy has noted, in doing so they believe that they 'advise, they interpret, but they do not rule' and they 'sustain their self-image [as neutral experts] by locating the "political" elsewhere'.[87] As experts they are engaged in technical management, not governance. However, as Kennedy argues 'we need to relativise our idea of "international governance" more radically', because there is 'very little' in political life that is not better understood 'as the work of experts and the product of expertise'.[88]

We might begin by contesting the work of legal experts of resilience talk by first recognising that 'common sense' is precisely that: common opinion as framed by legal expert opinion makers. It is not 'good sense'

399–434 and A. Orford (ed.) *International Law and Its Others* (Cambridge: Cambridge University Press, 2006). For analysis of resistance against law, resistance through law, and resistance that redefines law, see A. C. Cutler, 'Reclaiming Sovereignty: Resistance to Transnational Authority and the Investor-State Regime' in P. Zumbansen (ed.) *The Oxford Handbook of Transnational Law* (Oxford: Oxford University Press, 2021), pp. 810–820.

[86] J. Ebbesson and E. Hey, 'Introduction: Where Is Law in Socio-Ecological Resilience?' (2013) 18 (3) *Ecology and Society* 25.

[87] D. Kennedy, 'Challenging Expert Rule: The Politics of Global Governance,' (2005) 27 (1) *Sydney Law Review* 5–28, 15.

[88] Ibid.

as Gramsci conceived of it in terms of understandings accompanying transformative political praxis. Governance through good sense contemplates self-reflexivity as well as conscious recognition of and moral and ethical engagement with contesting social forces. It begins, as Kennedy notes, with asking 'who wins and who loses' in resilience policies and programmes.[89] This directs attention to the political economy of resilience, the 'who gets what' in resilience politics, and the class, gender, and intersectional power relations embedded in the legal norms and structures. It also involves delving into the 'politics of consciousness' by examining the underlying 'shared assumptions', 'blind spots and biases' of resilience experts.[90] Contestation involves going beyond problem-solving theory in approaching crises, like those of climate change and climate refugee/migrants, to engage in critical theory by focusing on the purposes and interests served by resilience talk. Crucially, this involves a recognition that the politics of resilience does not lie elsewhere. The challenge is not about discovering cracks or openings in resilience talk, but recognising as critical theory reveals, that the cracks and openings are always already there, because dominant understandings require continuous articulation in order to remain dominant and there is always opening for contestation in this process.

Hegemony is a process and one that requires continuous reinforcement, justification, and legitimation. International lawyers must acknowledge their crucial role in the construction of hegemony and not acquiesce in assumptions that are taken for granted as the legal common sense of the day. The challenge is to critically examine the assumptions upon which law operates; to interrogate the relationships between law, capitalism, and humanity. They/we cannot, and, indeed, must not, seek shelter behind distinctions between law and politics, public and private, here and there. The investigation must interrogate the political, economic, and social consequences of the dominant legal forms of our time.

[89] Ibid. [90] Ibid., 22.

15 A White Knight in Shining Armour? Ethiopia, International Organisations, and the Global Colour Line

DANIEL R. QUIROGA-VILLAMARÍN

[...] Gentle Reader; for the problem of the Twentieth Century is the problem of the color-line.

W.E.B Du Bois, *The Souls of Black Folk: Essays and Sketches*[1]

The Japanese Pan-Asianists and the Young Ethiopians had similar ideas about how their respective governments should position themselves globally. They both perceptively understood that the universalism professed by international law and international organisation was a façade to defend Western colonial interests [...] The international space was constituted according to racist principles that made any Western talk of sovereign equality empty [...] As we have seen, however, [their...] political vision [...] was not a remaking of the world under more egalitarian principles of horizontal solidarity.

Sara Marzagora, 'Political Thought and the Struggle for Sovereignty in Ethiopian-Japanese Relations (1927–1936)'

Introduction: Or Else What?

Where can one find the United Nations (UN) and its sister international institutions? As an international organisation (IO) with a 'universal' reach,[2] the UN – just like international law – seems to be

[1] See further W. E. B. Du Bois and Adom Getachew, *W.E.B. Du Bois: International Thought* (New York: Cambridge University Press, 2022).
[2] Pitman B. Potter, 'Universalism versus Regionalism in International Organization', *American Political Science Review* 37, no. 5 (October 1943): 850–62.

both 'everywhere' and 'nowhere'.[3] Elsewhere in this volume, I have tried to answer this question by highlighting that IOs always have to function *somewhere* – and, as such, issued a plea for the study of their geographically situated and materially embedded sites in international institutional law.[4] Departing from this premise, in what follows I want to take this a step further to think about the entanglements of these institutions with what, following Du Bois, one could call the 'global colour line'.[5] With this, I make reference to the ways in which the institutions of international order pivoted on notions of racial hierarchy and white supremacy, including some peoples (while excluding others) within the bounds of the 'international community'.[6] As Obregón and others have shown, the quest of international order has long been haunted by the echoes of a nineteenth-century conception of 'civilised peoples' that has served to exclude and constrain non-European participation in the 'family of nations'.[7]

Indeed, given that the UN and its sister institutions were forged in the ideological crucible of what Hobsbawm has called the 'Age of Empire',[8] it would be easy to assume that they were unable to play a role in challenging the global colour line. And yet, as Mazower has shown, the fact that the UN had been created in the image and likeness of 'imperial internationalism' did not prevent a cast of generations of non-European and racialised international lawyers to flock to its hall to attempt to

[3] Annelise Riles, 'The View from the International Plane: Perspective and Scale in the Architecture of Colonial International Law', *Law and Critique* 6, no. 1 (1995): 39–54.

[4] Daniel R. Quiroga-Villamarín, 'Placeholders: An Archival Journey into the Interim Histories of International Organisations' in this volume (Chapter 9). See also Juan M. Amaya-Castro, 'Teaching International Law: Both Everywhere and Somewhere', in *Liber Amicorum in Honour of a Modern Renaissance Man: Gudmundur Eiríksson*, ed. Juan Carlos Sainz Borgo et al. (New Delhi: Universal Law Publishing, 2017), 521–36.

[5] Samuel Moyn, *The Last Utopia: Human Rights in History* (Cambridge: Harvard University Press, 2010). 100–1. See also Alexander Anievas, Nivi Manchanda, and Robbie Shilliam, eds., *Race and Racism in International Relations: Confronting the Global Colour Line*, Interventions (London: Routledge, 2015); William Schabas, *The International Legal Order's Colour Line: Racism, Racial Discrimination, and the Making of International Law* (New York: Oxford University Press, 2023).

[6] Kseniya Oksamytna and Sarah von Billerbeck, 'Race and International Organizations', *International Studies Quarterly* 68, no. 2 (2024).

[7] Liliana Obregón, 'The Civilized and the Uncivilized', in *The Oxford Handbook of the History of International Law*, ed. Bardo Fassbender and Anne Peters (Oxford: Oxford University Press, 2012), 917–39.

[8] E. J. Hobsbawm, *The Age of Empire, 1875–1914* (New York: Vintage, 1989).

create a post-colonial international order from within the very belly of Empire.[9] This is what Sayward has called the UN's 'Nehruvian moment';[10] or what Moyn has understood as the 'high tide of anti-colonial legalism'.[11] For some readers, the label of the first generation of Third World Approaches to International Law (TWAIL I) lawyer-diplomats might a be more familiar monicker.[12] What matters is that, in all of these attempts to rethink and challenge the global colour line, the UN played a salient role: either as an actor to ally with, as a source of (material and ideological) resources, or as a forum to dispute in.[13]

In this chapter, I show this by focusing on the relations between the polity of Ethiopia and the institutions of international ordering – the UN and its predecessor, the League of Nations ('the League'), chief among them.[14] For, if we look closely at one of the sites where the UN fashioned a shell for itself in the city of Addis Ababa,[15] we can see that the Ethiopian elites understood that the UN (with all of its flaws) had to play a protagonist role in the struggles to come. Let us turn, then,

9 Mark Mazower, *No Enchanted Palace: The End of Empire and the Ideological Origins of the United Nations* (Princeton: Princeton University Press, 2009). See also Mark Mazower, *Governing the World: The History of an Idea, 1815 to the Present* (London: Penguin Books, 2013).

10 Amy L. Sayward, *United Nations in International History* (London: Bloomsbury Academic, 2017). 21.

11 Samuel Moyn, 'The High Tide of Anticolonial Legalism', *Journal of the History of International Law* 23, no. 1 (2020): 5–31. Elsewhere, Negar Mansouri and I have tried to trace this by studying the life and careers of non-European international civil servants within these IOs. See Negar Mansouri and Daniel R. Quiroga-Villamarín, '"Third Worlding" International Organization: The Parallel Quests of Santa-Cruz and Aga Khan for a New International Institutional Order (1946–2002)' *Humanity* 15 (2) (in press).

12 Antony Anghie, 'Rethinking International Law: A TWAIL Retrospective', *European Journal of International Law* 34, no. 1 (2023): 7–112. 8. Pahuja and Eslava, in turn, use the expression 'midnight's lawyers'. See Luis Eslava and Sundhya Pahuja, 'Between Resistance and Reform: TWAIL and the Universality of International Law', *Trade, Law and Development* 3, no. 1 (2011): 103–30. 115–16.

13 Ian Hurd, *International Organizations Politics, Law, Practice*, 5th ed. (Cambridge: Cambridge University Press, 2024). 17–43.

14 Seeing that the name of the polity itself has its origins in a racial categorization (ancient Greek for 'burnt faces'), it offers a promising vantage point to reflect on the global colour line. See Ayele Bekerie, 'Ethiopica: Some Historical Reflections on the Origin of the Word Ethiopia', *International Journal of Ethiopian Studies* 1, no. 2 (2004): 110–21. 114.

15 Daniel R. Quiroga-Villamarín, '*Endroits* of Planetary Ordering: Violence, Law, Space, & Capital in the Diplomatic History of 19th Century Europe', *German Law Journal* 24, no. 7 (2023): 1169–83.

Figure 15.1 A White Knight in Shining Armour?[16]

to the central panel of the stained-glass tryptic *The Total Liberation of Africa*, of 1959 (Figure 15.1).

Designed by the Ethiopian artist Afewerk Tekle after winning a competition and under the supervision of Emperor Haile Selassie I, this three-part stained-glass window constituted the central artwork of the new building 'Africa Hall'.[17] As the edifice was erected to host the new UN Economic Commission for Africa and to provide the continent with a proper site for high-level diplomatic encounters, its design and construction was carefully supervised by the Ethiopian establishment with the purpose of dazzling local, regional, and international audiences alike. Here, tucked in the corner of the panel, we can *find*

[16] Middle panel of Afewerk Tekle's *Total Liberation of Africa* (1959). Photo by: Gunter Fischer © Education Images/Universal Images Group via Getty Images.

[17] Ministry of Information of the Imperial Ethiopian Government, *Africa Hall Addis Ababa* (Asmara: Il Poligrafico, 1963). As consulted in the UNECA repository https://hdl.handle.net/10855/24318. 46–47. I have explored the making of this building in more detail in Daniel R. Quiroga-Villamarín, '"At Long Last": Gifting Africa a True Continental Capital in Addis Ababa (1955–1974)' in *'Architects of the Better World': Democracy, Law, and the Construction of International Order 1919–1998*, PhD thesis (Geneva: Graduate Institute of International and Development Studies, 2024).

the UN. But the portrayal is quite particular: this IO appears as a white knight, clad in European armour and a daunting longsword. All the other figures are dark-skinned and 'wear traditional Ethiopian costumes, because it is felt by the Artist that Ethiopia should occupy this leading place' in the decolonisation of Africa.[18] But the White Knight, the sole European of the composition, with the UN's blue emblem in *his* chest, appears as a symbol 'of what the United Nations stands for and of Africa believing and appreciating its justice and willing[ness] to cooperate in the support of its ideals and aspirations'.[19]

This chapter traces the lofty promises, and resounding disappointments, that the UN (as a proverbial *White*, and *male*, Knight) offered the racialised peoples of the world – and Ethiopia, in particular – in their attempt to challenge the global colour line. The result is neither a blind celebration of the UN's anticolonial potential, nor a resolute condemnation of its imperial lineage.[20] Instead, I want to embrace the ambiguities offered by the metaphor of this racialised and gendered *saviour* trope – especially in relation to the racialised *savage* non-European other.[21] For in any attempt to overturn the global colour line, the UN will prove to be both utterly indispensable *and* insufficient. To argue this, I show how the Ethiopian polity engaged with the treacherous figure of the White Knight of international ordering, (2) from the pre-modern era all the way to the so-called (3) interwar period, and (4) the post-war age of the UN. This allows me to (5) conclude with some remarks on the limits of taking Ethiopia as a representative polity of the racialised peoples of the world.

In Lewis Carroll's rendition of this trope, Alice finds herself hostage to an unwanted session of poetry-reading by a towering White

[18] Afewerk Tekle, 'No title', in *Africa Hall Addis Ababa* (Asmara: Il Poligrafico, 1963), 47.

[19] Ibid. Years later, Tekle delivered a retrospective speech in which he stressed again that the Knight represented the promise 'that all those who are becoming free and independent have the right to enter the United Nations'. See Afewerk Tekle, 'The State of Art of Ethiopia', 27 July 2009. As consulted in www.loc.gov/item/2021688283/

[20] Compare, respectively, Evan Luard, *A History of the United Nations. Vol. 2: The Age of Decolonization, 1955–1965* (London: Macmillan, 2002); Margot Tudor, *Blue Helmet Bureaucrats: United Nations Peacekeeping and the Reinvention of Colonialism, 1945–1971*, Human Rights in History (Cambridge: Cambridge University Press, 2023).

[21] Makau Mutua, 'Savages, Victims, and Saviors: The Metaphor of Human Rights', *Harvard International Law Journal*, 42, no. 1 (2001): 201–46.

Knight.[22] After he appears to rescue her from (another equally unwanted) Red Knight, Alice falls under his 'protection' until she is ready to emerge as an independent queen – that is, a 'sovereign'.[23] In the meantime, she is exposed to his technological inventions and mavericks – including a poem that is 'very, *very*, beautiful'.[24] The White Knight proudly claims that '[e]verybody that hears me sing it – either it brings the *tears* into their eyes, or else'.[25] 'Or else what?' retorts Alice. 'Or else it doesn't, you know' replies the Knight.[26] Either way, Alice was about to hear it! The Ethiopian polity, like Alice, quickly realised that once one falls under the White Knight's 'protection', one might as well enjoy his poetry – what else? But like Alice, Ethiopia did not remain passive through its encounter with the White Knight. She remained always with one eye fixed towards the imaginary border that separated her from her sovereign crown.[27] With this metaphor in mind, we now turn to the story of Ethiopia's encounter with the 'World of White Knights' and their international institutions.[28]

The Kingdom of 'Prester John': Early Modern Fluidity in Interpolity Ordering

'Before the West', as Zarakol reminds us, notions of interpolity order looked quite different.[29] During the Early Modern era, the self-identification of the elites of the Ethiopian Solomonic Empire as 'an isle of Christians surrounded by a sea of pagans' made religion, rather than *race*, the key marker of their approach to foreign

[22] Lewis Carroll, *Through the Looking-Glass: And What Alice Found There* (New York: Harper & Brothers, 1902). 165–73.

[23] And indeed, relations of 'protection' have long structured imperial oversight of European over non-European peoples (and *mutatis mutandis*, patriarchal family constellations) in interpolity relations. See Lauren A. Benton, Adam Clulow, and Bain Attwood, eds., *Protection and Empire: A Global History* (New York, NY: Cambridge University Press, 2018).

[24] Carroll, *Through the Looking-Glass: And What Alice Found There*. 166. Italics in the original.

[25] Ibid. [26] Ibid. [27] In the story, this is a little brook. See Ibid. 172.

[28] With apologies to Martti Koskenniemi, *To the Uttermost Parts of the Earth: Legal Imagination and International Power, 1300–1870* (Cambridge: Cambridge University Press, 2021).

[29] Ayşe Zarakol, *Before the West: The Rise and Fall of Eastern World Orders* (Cambridge: Cambridge University Press, 2022).

affairs.[30] As early as the thirteenth century, Ethiopian pilgrims and merchants have found their way to the courts of the leading European polities, especially those with ports on the Mediterranean sea.[31] The first properly documented diplomatic visit sent by an Ethiopian emperor to the Venetian court happened in 1402, opening the door to the 'first age of Ethiopian-European diplomacy'.[32] Animated by the myth of a remote eastern kingdom that had been created by a lost Christian Priest-judge ('Prester John'), the Early Modern Europeans were generally friendly towards the Ethiopian overtures and treated them as 'peers'.[33] Indeed, they both shared an 'interest in military alliance against Muslim powers' and an ecumenical desire for religious dialogue.[34] By the sixteenth century, this reproachment reached its climax as Portuguese forces intervened in favour of the Ethiopian sovereigns in its war against Adalite and Ottoman Muslim forces – leading to a period of sharp Jesuit influence in the region.[35]

What matters for the purposes of this chapter is that, before the 'modern' era, Ethiopians were not seen as beyond the pale of the European family of nations, but rather as long-lost Christian cousins

[30] Serge Dewel, *Addis-Abeba (Éthiopie): Construction d'une Nouvelle Capitale Pour Une Ancienne Nation Souveraine – Tome 1* (Paris: L'Harmattan, 2018). 74. My own translation. Thereafter, any material in French or Amharic will be translated in the same way.

[31] Andrew Kurt, 'The Search for Prester John, a Projected Crusade and the Eroding Prestige of Ethiopian Kings, c .1200–c .1540', *Journal of Medieval History* 39, no. 3 (2013): 297–320.

[32] Samantha Kelly, 'Ewosṭateans at the Council of Florence (1441): Diplomatic Implications between Ethiopia, Europe, Jerusalem and Cairo', *Afriques* [Online] (2016), https://journals.openedition.org/afriques/1858?lang=en. See also Matteo Salvadore, 'Encounters between Ethiopia and Europe, 1400–1660', in *Oxford Research Encyclopedia of African History*, by Matteo Salvadore (Oxford University Press, 2018), https://doi.org/10.1093/acrefore/9780190277734.013.187.

[33] Matteo Salvadore, *The African Prester John and the Birth of Ethiopian-European Relations, 1402–1555* (London: Routledge, 2017).

[34] Kelly, 'Ewosṭateans at the Council of Florence (1441)'. The opposite was also true. See, for instance, Francisco Alvarez, *Narrative of the Portuguese Embassy to Abyssinia during the Years 1520–1527*, trans. Lord Stanley of Alderley (London: Hakluyt Society, 1881).

[35] Harold G. Marcus, *A History of Ethiopia*, Updated ed. (Berkeley: University of California Press, 2002). 33–34.

awaiting to be brought back into its fold.[36] Records of the arrival of an Ethiopian delegation in Lisbon in 1514 show that their hosts asked a slew of questions related to their 'written laws, law courts and magistrates [...] written history, [...] taxes [...] and proper styles of clothing and social distinction' as the Europeans sought to make sense of the shared practices of their Christian equals.[37] But as Pagden has shown, the 'discovery' and conquest of the Americas increasingly complicated (and racialised) the terms of encounter between Europe and its others.[38] As Salvadore notes in relation to the story of an Ethiopian noble who sought refuge and was welcomed in the highest echelons of European secular and religious society in the seventeenth century, 'race defined him in death, but not in life'.[39] With this, he makes reference that it was only later (in tandem to the introduction of racialised African slavery in the Americas) that an increasingly fixed notion of race began to trump Christian brotherhood in the European imagination.[40] By the late Renaissance, Korhonen notes that the proverb 'to wash an Ethiopian white is to labour in vain' was 'repeated so frequently [...] that it was understandable even when either half of the sentence was omitted'.[41] Indeed, on the eve of the Age of Revolutions and 'Modernity proper', the 'rather exceptional European attitude

[36] Siba N'Zatioula Grovogui, *Sovereigns, Quasi Sovereigns, and Africans: Race and Self-Determination in International Law* (Minneapolis: University of Minnesota Press, 1996). 16–28.

[37] Jeremy Lawrance, 'The Middle Indies: Damião de Góis on Prester John and the Ethiopians', *Renaissance Studies* 6, no. 3/4 (1992): 306–24. 322. In this same vein, Lauren Benton has long argued that very different polities shared a similar vocabulary to make sense of legal practices that she has called interpolity (or 'big') law. See Lauren Benton, *They Called It Peace: Worlds of Imperial Violence* (Princeton: Princeton University Press, 2024). 12–13.

[38] Anthony Pagden, *The Fall of Natural Man: The American Indian and the Origins of Comparative Ethnology* (Cambridge: Cambridge University Press, 1987). See also Anthony Pagden, *Lords of All the World: Ideologies of Empire in Spain, Britain and France, 1492–1830* (New Haven London: Yale University Press, 1998).

[39] Matteo Salvadore, '"I Was Not Born to Obey, but Rather to Command": The Self-Fashioning of Ṣägga Krəstos, an Ethiopian Traveler in Seventeenth-Century Europe', *Journal of Early Modern History* 25, no. 3 (2021): 194–226. 226.

[40] David Eltis, 'Europeans and the Rise and Fall of African Slavery in the Americas: An Interpretation', *The American Historical Review* 98, no. 5 (1993): 1399–423.

[41] Anu Korhonen, 'Washing the Ethiopian White: Conceptualising Black Skin in Renaissance England', in *Black Africans in Renaissance Europe*, ed. T. F. Earle and K. J. P. Lowe (Cambridge: Cambridge University Press, 2010), 94–112. 94.

toward slavery […] – specifically, its association with the concept of race' had now fully consolidated.[42]

This had important consequences for interpolity diplomatic relations. As Sluga has shown, the 'invention' of international order that occurred in 1815 (in the wake of the post-Napoleonic restoration) tended to ossify conceptual borders – at least in comparison to a 'relatively diverse aristocratic cosmopolitan brotherhood'.[43] While the Ethiopian establishment continued to pursue diplomatic relations abroad across the Mediterranean, this was 'only grudgingly conceded by Europe [… and this same right] was denied to powerful African states of the time like the Asanthi and the Zulu'.[44] By the late nineteenth century, Ethiopia had gone from Christian peer polity to a potentially conquerable 'savage' entity – and it increasingly found itself 'between the jaws of hyenas' of its former Christian cousins.[45] Shortly after the European great powers formalised the rules for the partition of Africa,[46] the Ethiopian polity inflicted a resounding blow on the encroaching Italian colonial army at the battle of Adwa of 1896.[47] Like the rising Japanese Empire (which, in turn, defeated the Russian Empire militarily in 1905), the Ethiopian elites understood that to be a 'sovereign' in the Modern era military and industrial might were indispensable.[48] While Ethiopia could have been recognised as an equal, even if 'black', Knight in the fifteenth century because of its common faith, on the eve of the Great War in the twentieth century it was clear unless it was ready to brandish its sword it would fall under European 'protection'. The nineteenth century, in this sense, constitutes a turning point in the relations between Europe and the Christian, but

42 Eltis, 'Europeans and the Rise and Fall of African Slavery in the Americas: An Interpretation'. 1415.

43 Glenda Sluga, *The Invention of International Order: Remaking Europe after Napoleon* (Princeton: Princeton University Press, 2021). 21.

44 K. V. Ram, 'Diplomatic Practices of Ethiopia in the Nineteenth Century', *Transafrican Journal of History* 15 (1986): 127–43. 140.

45 Richard Alan Caulk, *Between the Jaws of Hyenas: A Diplomatic History of Ethiopia (1876–1896)* (Wiesbaden: Harrassowitz, 2002).

46 Mathew Craven, 'Between Law and History: The Berlin Conference of 1884–1885 and the Logic of Free Trade', *London Review of International Law* 3, no. 1 (2015): 31–59.

47 Raymond Jonas, *The Battle of Adwa: African Victory in the Age of Empire* (Cambridge: Harvard University Press, 2011).

48 Marzagora, 'Political Thought and the Struggle for Sovereignty in Ethiopian-Japanese Relations (1927–1936)'. 100.

non-European, world.[49] The same, as the secondary literature has shown, was true of the Ottoman Empire and other polities that suddenly found themselves to be 'quasi-sovereign' after centuries of (at least nominal) equality with European rulers.[50]

The Great(er) War: Ethiopia and the League of Nations

Indeed, as an Ethiopian 'quasi-sovereign', *Lij* Iyasu was an unlikely victim of the upheavals of the Great War of 1914.[51] The prefix *Lij* is used in Ethiopian Amharic to denote a child of royal blood, which was fitting because Iyasu was never crowned, as such, due to his young age. He had been appointed as successor to Menelik II (the emperor who had defeated the Italians at Adwa) in 1909, and in that capacity attempted to rule amidst the palace wars of the period. But the declaration of an actual war in Europe, kilometres away, eventually led to the coup that deposed the young Iyasu in 1916. Given that he had been trained by a German tutor and was widely rumoured to sympathise with the Central Powers, a pro-Allied faction of local notables deposed him (arguing that it was a just a matter of time until the Crown Prince converted to Islam as an apostate and joined the Central Powers in their war effort).[52] He was replaced by an ambitious Crown Prince, who would eventually be crowned in 1930 as the Emperor Haile Selassie I.[53] Given that his rise to power was directly related to interpolity intrigues, it is not surprising that the new emperor would 'concentrate on Addis Abeba [his capital ...] and foreign affairs,

49 Charles Henry Alexandrowicz, *The European-African Confrontation. A Study in Treaty Making* (Leiden: Sijthoff, 1973). See also Charles Henry Alexandrowicz, *The Law of Nations in Global History*, ed. David Armitage and Jennifer Pitts, *The History and Theory of International Law* (Oxford: Oxford University Press, 2017). 223–302.

50 Antony Anghie, *Imperialism, Sovereignty and the Making of International Law* (Cambridge: Cambridge University Press, 2005).

51 In Amharic, ልጅ ኢያሱ. See further Marcus, *A History of Ethiopia*. 114–18.

52 Jakob Zollmann, 'Ethiopia, International Law and the First World War. Considerations of Neutrality and Foreign Policy by the European Powers, 1840–1919', in *The First World War from Tripoli to Addis Ababa (1911–1924)*, ed. Shiferaw Bekele et al. (Addis Abeba: Centre français des études éthiopiennes, 2019), 107–40. See also Ahmed Hassen Omer, 'The "Coup d'État" of September 26, 1916: Different Perceptions', *Journal of Ethiopian Studies* 46 (2013): 99–120.

53 Harold G. Marcus, *Haile Sellassie I: The Formative Years, 1892–1936* (Lawrenceville: Red Sea Press, 1995).

around which he would build his authority'.[54] This led him to undertake a European 'grand tour' in 1924, which culminated with the troubled accession of his polity to the new IO created in the wake of the war and international law's move to institutions: the League.[55]

And yet, Ethiopia's membership of the League was always tenuous – Getachew understands this as a 'burdened and racialised' membership.[56] Famously, the Japanese had been unsuccessful in their attempt to enshrine a racial equality provision in the Versailles peace settlement, with important consequences for the institutions created there.[57] As I have noted elsewhere reviewing some of the literature on non-European participation in the family of nations, 'territorial statehood is always precarious and unstable, constrained to the fulfilment of imperial standards of race; civilization; development; alien/human rights'.[58] In this particular context, it imposed a series of institutional obligations on Ethiopia *vis-à-vis* the League in relation to slavery and the slave trade.[59] With the establishment of the League in 1919, one of its tasks had been to supervise the management of conquered colonial territories, which were given as 'mandates' to the victorious allies.[60] Due to Ethiopia's racialised membership, its situation was almost closer to the non-self-governing mandates than to its peers among the European and Latin American polities, as the system offered 'little more than

[54] Marcus, *A History of Ethiopia*. 118.

[55] Boris Monin, 'The Visit of Rās Tafari in Europe (1924): Between Hopes of Independence and Colonial Realities', *Annales d'Ethiopie* 28, no. 1 (2013): 383–89. See also David Kennedy, 'The Move to Institutions', *Cardozo Law Review* 8, no. 5 (1987): 841–988.

[56] Adom Getachew, *Worldmaking after Empire: The Rise and Fall of Self-Determination* (Princeton: Princeton University Press, 2019). 37–70. See also Rose Parfitt, '*Empire Des Nègres Blancs*: The Hybridity of International Personality and the Abyssinia Crisis of 1935–36', *Leiden Journal of International Law* 24, no. 4 (2011): 849–72; Megan Donaldson, 'The League of Nations, Ethiopia, and the Making of States', *Humanity* 11, no. 1 (2020): 6–31.

[57] Thomas W. Burkman, *Japan and the League of Nations: Empire and World Order, 1914–1938* (Honolulu: University of Hawai'i Press, 2008). 60–103.

[58] Daniel R. Quiroga-Villamarín, 'Vicarius Christi: Extraterritoriality, Pastoral Power, and the Critique of Secular International Law', *Leiden Journal of International Law* 34, no. 3 (2021): 629–52. 637–38.

[59] Jean Allain, 'Slavery and the League of Nations: Ethiopia as a Civilised Nation', *Journal of the History of International Law* 8, no. 2 (2006): 213–44.

[60] Susan Pedersen, *The Guardians: The League of Nations and the Crisis of Empire* (Oxford: Oxford University Press, 2017).

colonialism by another name'.[61] Most famously, Ethiopia's member status did not prevent its brutal invasion by another 'peer' (Italy) in 1935 – an event that, for Du Bois, proved that despite the League's lofty promises, the world was run by those who pinned 'their faith on European civilization, the Christian religion and the superiority of the white race'.[62]

And yet, the institutional set-up of the League (both for the mandates and for Ethiopia as a quasi-sovereign member) offered opportunities for those who sought to challenge racial hierarchy in international order *through* international order. Du Bois, who had participated in the League's first General Assembly in 1920, believed that it could play a central role for anti-racist activism on behalf of both African-Unitedstateseans and colonised Africans.[63] Indeed, even Haile Selassie I never lost his faith in the League. As the Italian armies encroached his homeland, he departed towards exile in the UK. But not before he went to Geneva to personally address the League in 1936.[64] While he was ultimately unsuccessful,[65] the League 'provided a formal stage' where the emperor performed the dances of (quasi)sovereignty.[66] Even if the White Knight's 'protection' was but a fig leaf, the League offered a place where its treacherous ways could be called to account. Indeed, when he reconquered the capital city of Addis Ababa at the helm of his 'Gideon Force' in 1941 with the support of his British allies as part of the UN military alliance against Fascism, Haile Selassie I (as many in

61 Schabas, *The International Legal Order's Colour Line*. 52–89.

62 W. E. B. Du Bois, 'Inter-Racial Implications of the Ethiopian Crisis: A Negro View', *Foreign Affairs* 14, no. 1 (1935): 82–92. 87. See also Richard Pankhurst, 'The Italo-Ethiopian War and League of Nations Sanctions, 1935–1936', *Genève-Afrique* 13, no. 2 (1974): 5–29.

63 W. E. B. Du Bois, 'The Negro and the League of Nations, ca. November 1921', Special Collections and University Archives, University of Massachusetts Amherst Libraries, accessed 13 June 2024, https://credo.library.umass.edu/view/full/mums312-b210-i073. See also Jake Hodder, 'African Americans at the League of Nations', paper delivered at the conference 'Global Histories of International Thought and Geopolitical Concepts' – University of Groningen, 23–24 May 2024.

64 Discours Prononcé Par Sa Majesté Haylé Sélassié Ier, Empereur d'Éthiopie, à l'Assemblée de La Société des Nations, à La Session de Juin-Juillet 1936 (Geneva: Nations Unies Bibliothèque, 1936). Library of Congress (USA), available online at www.loc.gov/item/2021667904

65 Zara Steiner, *The Triumph of the Dark: European International History 1933–1939* (Oxford: Oxford University Press, 2013). 100–66.

66 Donaldson, 'The League of Nations, Ethiopia, and the Making of States'. 21.

his generation) drew from the experience of the League's 'failure' lessons for the new post-war order.[67]

The First 'Ally': Ethiopia and International Order in WWII

Like Alice in Wonderland, Ethiopia was rescued by the White Knight during WWII. And yet, it would soon discover that the 'protection' of the 'White' UN was not too dissimilar from the occupation of the 'Black(shirt) Knight'. The wake of the Ethiopian Liberation campaign of 1941 had left the country as a thinly veiled British protectorate,[68] in which the emperor's patriots were but 'grudgingly recognised as allies'.[69] At first, key imperial policymakers sought to treat Ethiopia as a conquered Italian possession – some even aspired to create a united British East African colony as a post-war trusteeship territory ruled from Nairobi.[70] Even after some autonomy was devolved to the emperor's quasi-sovereign government, the British held on to the Somali-inhabited area of the Ogaden and the former Italian colony of Eritrea was war conquests. Moreover, the rump state was forced to use the East African shilling as its national currency (until 1945) and almost all the Italian industrial infrastructure was duly looted by its British 'allies'.[71] The emperor remained 'aware that his country was as much occupied as liberated' and 'remained doubtful of British intentions'.[72] Indeed, with friends like these, who needs enemies?

The emperor, who had neither forgotten (nor perhaps forgiven) Geneva, turned to the promise of a new international order to fight for his polity's sovereignty. Like many peoples of the colonised and

[67] Jean d'Aspremont, 'The League of Nations and the Power of "Experiment Narratives" in International Institutional Law', *International Community Law Review* 22, no. 3–4 (2020): 275–90.

[68] Harold G. Marcus, *Ethiopia, Great Britain, and the United States, 1941–1974: The Politics of Empire* (Berkeley: University of California Press, 1983).

[69] Richard Pankhurst, 'Post-World War II Ethiopia: British Military Policy and Action for The Dismantling and Acquisition of Italian Factories and Other Assets, 1941–2', *Journal of Ethiopian Studies* 29, no. 1 (1996): 35–77. 35.

[70] Ibid. 40.

[71] Befekadu Degefe, 'The Making of the Ethiopian National Currency 1941–45', *Journal of Ethiopian Studies* 26, no. 2 (1993): 23–51; Pankhurst, 'Post-World War II Ethiopia: British Military Policy and Action for The Dismantling and Acquisition of Italian Factories and Other Assets, 1941–2'. 42–43.

[72] Jacqueline Swansinger, 'A Three-Legged Race: Ethiopian Reconstruction, 1940–1944', *Journal of World History* 2, no. 2 (1991): 175–200. 177.

occupied world – both seen as racialised by either the Allied imperial or Axis war machines – the promises issued by the Atlantic Charter in 1941 and the Declaration of the United Nations in 1942 offered a glimpse of hope.[73] If all people had, pursuant to the clause three of the Charter, 'a right to self-determination', this had to be true both for the polities militarily occupied by the Fascist powers (say Poland and Ethiopia), and perhaps even for the whole colonised world. This expectation gained even more momentum when, in 1945, the military alliance of the UN was formally institutionalised into a new 'universal' IO – and one, moreover, that enshrined equal rights and self-determination of peoples as one of its cardinal values.[74]

In this spirit, as soon as he retook the capital, Haile Selassie I wrote to the US President Franklin Delano Roosevelt (FDR) arguing that Ethiopia should be seen as the first liberated polity of the UN alliance.[75] FDR reciprocated by inviting the emperor to meet him personally aboard the *USS Quincy* near Cairo, where he would stop after the Yalta conference of 1945.[76] From then onwards, the US became a key supporter of Ethiopian independence. Ethiopia, in turn, committed fully to the UN (being, with Egypt and Liberia, the only three independent African countries that participated in the San Francisco Conference of 1945) and to the idea of the US-led international order.[77] Translating words into deeds, the Ethiopian army answered the military call of the UN by sending its forces to peacekeeping operations in Korea (1950) and the Congo (1960).[78] This gambit paid off,

[73] Daniel R. Quiroga-Villamarín, '"Holding Fast to the Heritage of Freedom": The Grotian Moment(s) of the Universal Declaration of Human Rights and the Early United Nations (1941–1949)', *Grotiana* 44, no. 1 (2023): 94–115.

[74] Marcelo G. Kohen, 'Self-Determination', in *The UN Friendly Relations Declaration at 50*, ed. Jorge E. Viñuales (Cambridge: Cambridge University Press, 2020), 133–65.

[75] Marcus, *Ethiopia, Great Britain, and the United States, 1941–1974*. 14.

[76] Ibid. 48–50. See also Herbert A. Fine et al., eds., 'The Minister in Ethiopia (Caldwell) to the Secretary of State', in *Foreign Relations of the United States: Diplomatic Papers, 1945, The Near East and Africa, Volume VIII* (Washington, DC: United States Government Printing Office, 1969), 5–7.

[77] Thomas Hovet, 'The Role of Africa in the United Nations', *The Annals of the American Academy of Political and Social Science* 354 (1964): 122–34. 123. I am not including South Africa here.

[78] Cynthia Tse Kimberlin, 'The Korean War (1950–1953) and the Kagnew Battalion: Music, War, and the Concept of Collective Security', in *Movements in Ethiopia, Ethiopia in Movement. Vol I*, ed. Thomas Osmond, Éloi Ficquet, and Ahmed Hassen Omer (Addis Abeba: Centre français des études

as it was untenable for the British to colonise a (nominally) equal ally and fellow UN member. As a British colonial officer noted, 'the fact that we surround [Ethiopia] and could in the old days have squeezed [it] flat with very little difficulty, is of course irrelevant in the age of Lake Something'.[79] This is a reference to 'Lake Success' – where, as we saw in my earlier chapter in this volume, the UN had its interim headquarters during this period.[80] The ambiguities of the White Knight, here, appear in their full colours.

Of course, this change in the nature of the liberal international order had more to do with the vanquished than with the victors. Given that the Axis powers had made racial superiority a central banner of their war effort, the allies included an 'equality of race' provision in their post-war settlement.[81] The inclusion of this, however, was not without frictions. Indeed, as I noted elsewhere, the Soviet Union 'rarely lost an opportunity to embarrass its erstwhile allies by highlighting the persistence of racial discrimination in the US to critique the use of the trope of "civilization" by European empires'.[82] Indeed, colonial powers frequently invoked the cover of sovereignty to shield themselves from UN criticism over entrenched racial hierarchies – with, of course, South Africa being the most obvious example.[83] Immigration policy was – and continues to be – a thorny issue in our allegedly post-racial world.

And yet, at the same time that the UN's notion of sovereignty provided cover for racialised hierarchies, it also created opportunities for those who wanted to challenge the global colour line. The General Assembly, in particular, became a key site of struggle – especially as the increasing tempo of decolonisation added more and more formerly

éthiopiennes, 2016), 273–86; Alan Karabus, 'United Nations Activities in the Congo', *Proceedings of the American Society of International Law at Its Annual Meeting (1921–1969)* 55 (1961): 30–40. 34.

79 As cited by Marcus, *Ethiopia, Great Britain, and the United States, 1941–1974*. 76.

80 Daniel R. Quiroga-Villamarín, 'Placeholders'. See further Daniel R. Quiroga-Villamarín, *'Architects of a Better World'*.

81 Paul Gordon Lauren, 'First Principles of Racial Equality: History and the Politics and Diplomacy of Human Rights Provisions in the United Nations Charter', *Human Rights Quarterly* 5, no. 1 (1983): 1–26.

82 Quiroga-Villamarín, '"Holding Fast to the Heritage of Freedom"'.

83 Corrie Gerald Haines, 'The United Nations Challenge to Racial Discrimination in South Africa 1946–1950', *African Studies* 60, no. 2 (2001): 185–204.

colonised peoples to its ranks.[84] In time, this IO – and its family of institutions, UNESCO in particular – has developed a series of mechanisms and procedures to highlight the persistence of racial discrimination and the unfulfilled promises of the post-war settlement.[85] Ethiopia, in particular, became a fervent supporter of the institution's work in general – and, in particular, became the host of its Economic Commission for Africa (UNECA).

In fact, it was in UNECA's building ('Africa Hall', as we saw earlier), that the UN's Security Council met in 1972 for the first time on African soil.[86] After an extensive diplomatic campaign coordinated with other African member states (and with the Organisation of African Unity (OAU) – created in the wake of a summit held in that same building in 1963), Haile Selassie I managed to convince the UN to discuss African problems within the continent itself. A US diplomat, anonymously quoted in the *New York Times*, candidly confessed that this was 'a silly idea, but if you object to it you're a racist, so naturally we didn't'.[87] The agenda was dominated by the thorny issues of Zimbabwe/Rhodesia, South Africa, and the Portuguese colonies that remained on the African continent. Unsurprisingly, the session ended in disappointment after the UK vetoed any resolution that threatened white supremacy in their former colonial holdings. Be that as it may, Haile Selassie I and his African allies saw the Council meeting as a triumph. Somalia and Sudan rotated the Council's Presidency, and in that capacity, they invited Haile Selassie I to address the international community – ultimately, for the last time. For the ageing emperor, the Council session's highlight was the ceremony held in his palace where the UN Secretary-General Kurt Waldheim awarded him the 'Peace Medal for his contributions to international peace and justice'.[88] A fitting end for a monarch who had invested many of his early years in convincing

[84] P. D. Kausik and Mansha Ram Singh, 'The UN General Assembly and Racial Discrimination', *Social Scientist* 1, no. 6 (1973): 42–48.

[85] Rosana Garciandia and Philippa Webb, 'The UN's Work on Racial Discrimination: Achievements and Challenges', *Max Planck Yearbook of United Nations Law Online* 25, no. 1 (2022): 216–45. See further Schabas, *The International Legal Order's Colour Line*. 90–243.

[86] William Borders, 'U.N. Security Council Meets in Addis Ababa Today to Discuss the Problems of Africa', *The New York Times*, 28 January 1972.

[87] Ibid. 10.

[88] Derrick M. Nault, *Africa and the Shaping of International Human Rights* (Oxford: Oxford University Press, 2020). 64–95.

his polity, perhaps somewhat naively, to believe in the promises of a so-called post-racial liberal rules-based international order.

Concluding Remarks: The Star of Ethiopia

The Star of Ethiopia: A Pageant, of 1911, was Du Bois' debut as a playwriter.[89] While it had been presented to audiences before, its presentation in Philadelphia in 1916 (to commemorate the passage of the Fourteenth Amendment to the US Constitution) represented its theatrical climax.[90] The plot was simple: merely 'the history and development of the black race from prehistoric times to the present'.[91] The involved cast mirrored the play's ambitions, with at least 1,000 actors involved in different capacities. The result, in Du Bois' mind, was a pedagogical *tour de force* that would teach 'on the one hand the colored people themselves the meaning of their history and their rich emotional life through a new theatre, and on the other, to reveal the Negro to the white world as a human, feeling thing'.[92] Ethiopia, in this perspective, appeared as 'the mother of men': a polity that could claim to be the true cradle not only of humankind as a whole but of the coloured peoples of the world in particular. In this same vein, the anthem of the Universal Negro Improvement Association (led by the famous Afro-Jamaican thinker Marcus Garvey) adopted as its anthem the song 'Ethiopia, Thou Land of Our Fathers'.[93]

Indeed, for Du Bois and many other anti-racist and pan-African thinkers, Ethiopia remained a 'northern star' in their struggle.[94] The Italian war of aggression against this polity in the interwar years, in

[89] W. E. B. Du Bois, 'The Star of Ethiopia: A Pageant, 1914', Special Collections and University Archives, University of Massachusetts Amherst Libraries, n.d., https://credo.library.umass.edu/view/full/mums312-b233-i083.

[90] W. E. B. Du Bois, 'Star of Ethiopia Brochure, 1916', Special Collections and University Archives, University of Massachusetts Amherst Libraries, n.d., https://credo.library.umass.edu/view/full/mums312-x01-i008.

[91] Ibid.

[92] As cited in Errol Hill and James V. Hatch, *A History of African American Theatre* (Cambridge: Cambridge University Press, 2005). 201.

[93] Robert G. Weisbord, 'Black America and the Italian-Ethiopian Crisis: An Episode in Pan-Negroism', *The Historian* 34, no. 2 (1972): 230–41. 231.

[94] Ras Wayne A. Rose, *W. E. B. Du Bois, Ethiopianism, and Black Internationalism: A New Interpretation of the Global Color Line* (Lanham: Rowman & Littlefield, 2024).

particular, became a galvanising call to arms for future generations of anticolonial actors. Haile Selassie I, years later, would also come to adopt the pan-African agenda with the zeal of the convert, becoming one of the architects of the aforementioned OAU in 1963. And yet, any recovery of this polity's legacy of anti-racist struggle cannot be complete without a mention of the ways in which the Ethiopian Empire, itself, reproduced racial hierarchies within its own borders. As Asseraf well reminds us (in relation to Arabic feelings of ethnic animosity against 'black' Africans in French-colonised Algeria), notions of racial hierarchy were not solely a European invention.[95] Imperialism, no doubt, ossified (and even radicalised) certain 'racial' tensions in the colonised world – with lasting consequences to our days.[96] But we also ought to remember that 'some of the most vocal "anticolonial states" – such as Indonesia and India – simultaneously repressed independence campaigns *and* pursued imperial expansion'.[97] The same was true of the mid-century Ethiopian polity. Ultimately, for 'the wretched of the earth', the day will not be saved by any dazzling Knight: white, black, or otherwise.[98]

[95] Arthur Asseraf, *Le désinformateur: sur les traces de Messaoud Djebari, Algérien dans un monde colonial* (Paris: Fayard, 2022).

[96] UN Human Rights Council, 'Summary of the Panel Discussion on the Negative Impact of the Legacies of Colonialism on the Enjoyment of Human Rights', A/HRC/54/4, 1 June 2023, www.ohchr.org/sites/default/files/documents/hrbodies/hrcouncil/sessions-regular/session54/A_HRC_54_4_accessible.pdf.

[97] Tudor, *Blue Helmet Bureaucrats*. 164. The same, of course, was true for the Japanese Empire in the so-called interwar period. See Xu Guoqi, *Asia and the Great War: A Shared History* (Oxford: Oxford University Press, 2017). 185–210.

[98] Frantz Fanon, *The Wretched of the Earth* (New York: Grove Press, 2015).

PART III

Conclusion

16 *Examining Elephants in the Dark*

GUY FITI SINCLAIR

What is an international organisation? In an ancient parable recounted in several religious traditions, a group of blind men encounter an elephant for the first time – I personally prefer the telling of this parable by the Sufi poet Rumi in his *Masnavi*, in which the men are sighted but encounter the elephant in a dark room, but will mostly refer to the better-known version. Each man touches a different part of the elephant: one touches its leg, another its trunk, the third its tusk, the fourth its tail, and the last its ear. Each argues forcefully that an elephant is a different thing, depending on which part they have touched: the first says the elephant is like a tree; the next that it is like a snake; the third that it is a kind of spear; the fourth a rope; the last a fan. The men are unable to reach agreement; in some versions of the story, they come to blows. The story's moral is usually taken to be that truth is not absolute, that each person's understanding is relative to their standpoint, and that an attitude of intellectual humility is necessary in order to learn from the perspectives of others.

This stimulating volume invites us to see international organisations anew, from fresh angles and in new lights. In particular, the editors are keen to expand the horizons of mainstream scholars of international organisations law, who are accustomed to viewing their subject-matter through lenses that focus narrowly on the relationships between international organisations and their members. Many of the chapters gathered here explicitly or implicitly reject a 'functionalist' approach to international organisations (though precisely what that means seems to vary somewhat from author to author); even the *doyen* of international organisations law, Jan Klabbers, disavows functionalism in its barest form, proposing a 'supra-functionalist' alternative in its stead.[1] The themes of the volume – expertise, structures, performances, and

[1] J. Klabbers, 'Inter-disciplinarity and the Law of International Organizations' in this volume, pp. 38–56.

capital – deliberately push at the boundaries of mainstream thinking in international law; many of the contributions manifest a growing interest in questions of materiality among legal scholars;[2] and several of the authors reflect on international organisations from outside the discipline. The volume goes a long way to remedy the imbalance that the editors perceive in mainstream studies of international organisations law, offering an abundance of new (in)sights from anthropology, political science, and history.

The editors of this volume draw a sharp distinction between *doing* international organisations law and *thinking* about international organisations. Mainstream international lawyers approach international organisations with pragmatic ends in mind: they see legal problems to be solved, and they deploy their legal toolkit accordingly. This 'mono-disciplinary outlook' and ethos has, in the editors' view, led to an over-emphasis on 'doing' international organisations law at the expense of 'thinking' about international organisations.[3] The solution the editors propose is 'for the discipline to start seeing IO differently'.[4] Yet the sequence could just as easily be reversed: what one sees will inevitably be shaped by what one thinks, how one imagines the world, what one expects to see. This concluding chapter begins with 'ways of doing' scholarship on international organisations and proceeds to reflect on the diverse ways of seeing and thinking suggested by the preceding chapters in this volume, before making some tentative suggestions about possible ways forward.

Ways of Doing

How should we do the study of international organisations?[5] The blind men in the parable come at the elephant from different angles but share a single method of investigation – touch. In contrast, the

[2] H. Y. Kang and S. Kendall, 'Legal Materiality' in S. Stern, M. Del Mar, and B. Meyler (eds.), *The Oxford Handbook of Law and Humanities* (Oxford University Press, 2019), p. 21 (ch. 2); J. Hohmann and D. Joyce (eds.), *International Law's Objects* (Oxford University Press, 2019).

[3] N. Mansouri and D. R. Quiroga-Villamarin, 'Editorial Introduction: Seeing International Organizations Differently' in this volume, pp. 3–15.

[4] Mansouri and Quiroga-Villamarin, 'Editorial Introduction', pp. 3–15.

[5] With apologies to I. Hacking, 'How Should We Do the History of Statistics?' in G. Burchill, C. Gordon, and P. Miller (eds.), *The Foucault Effect: Studies in Governmentality* (University of Chicago Press, 1991), pp. 181–195.

assortment of methodologies on display in this volume is striking. Each author makes a compelling case, sometimes implicitly but often explicitly, for *their* way of studying international organisations. Broadly, however, the approaches adopted here may be seen as resolving into two distinct ways of doing the study of international organisations.

The first approach is essentially deconstructivist, aiming to expose the blindspots and biases of international organisations, and perhaps also of those who study them. In general terms this approach is well established in international law scholarship,[6] though more theorised versions remain rare, especially in international organisations law (before now). Chimni leads the way, recommending an expanded 'external critique' of the 'biased design and unjust distributional outcomes' of international organisations, together with an 'internal critique' that would show how they 'subserve the interests of powerful states over time'.[7] These forms of critique require digging past surface appearances, clearing away distracting epiphenomena, and unearthing the essential truth. Cutler engages in a similar exercise, showing how 'resilience talk' obscures 'underlying socio-political-economic causes of poverty, insecurity, and inequality' while 'depoliticis[ing] and naturalis[ing] deep structural inequalities in the governance activities of international organisations and law'.[8] Mansouri likewise takes up the critical project of uncovering 'hidden power relations', revealing how ostensibly 'technical' organisations embody certain hegemonic orders.[9] Klabbers' analysis of 'functionalism's limits', showing how it distorts and obscures important aspects of the operations of

6 See, e.g., S. Marks, *The Riddle of All Constitutions: International Law, Democracy, and the Critique of Ideology* (Oxford University Press, 2003).

7 B. S. Chimni, 'Critical Theory and International Organizations: The Need for an Integrated Approach' in this volume, pp. 16–37. See also B. S. Chimni, 'International Institutions Today: An Imperial Global State in the Making' (2004) 15 *European Journal of International Law* 1; B. S. Chimni, 'International Financial Institutions and International Law: A Third World Perspective' in D. D. Bradlow and D. B. Hunter (eds.), *International Financial Institutions and International Law* (Kluwer Law International, 2010) ch. 2.

8 A. C. Cutler, 'Deconstructing "Resilience Talk" in Global Governance: Toward a Critical Political Economy Approach' in this volume, pp. 271–90.

9 N. Mansouri, 'Laissez-Faire, State Capitalism, and the Making of International Organizations: The Dynamics of a Struggle' in this volume, pp. 248–70.

international organisations, serves as a kind of critique of ideology, in effect if not in name.[10]

The second broad way of doing the study of international organisations suggested in other chapters is (re)constructivist. Rather than taking them apart with the aim of exposing the falsity or fetishism of international organisations, these scholars trace how they are constituted through heterogenous practices and materials. Littoz-Monnet thus aims to show how expert knowledge is made in global governance;[11] Uribe traces the construction of 'hidden hunger' as a specific 'object of governance';[12] Soave seeks to account for the 'legal production of the international judiciary';[13] Santer carefully recounts the transnational legal conflicts arising over maritime rescues in the Central Mediterranean;[14] Quiroga-Villamarín reveals how the physical headquarters of organisations shape and constrain their expression of the international;[15] Halme-Tuomisaari urges focussing on 'the legal technicalities and practical materialities that define their operations';[16] and Clements describes reform in the International Criminal Court (ICC) as an 'infinite institutional becoming'.[17] As Van Den Meerssche argues in his account of shifting 'cultural techniques' of lawyering in

[10] Klabbers, 'Inter-disciplinarity and the Law of International Organizations', pp. 38–56. Elsewhere, Klabbers more directly describes functionalism as an ideology: 'Functionalism is best seen not as theory, but as ideology: a more or less coherent set of thoughts with little explanatory power but strong normative appeal, and working so as to legitimize the use of power.' J. Klabbers, 'Notes on the Ideology of International Organizations Law: The International Organization for Migration, State-Making, and the Market for Migration' (2019) 32 *Leiden Journal of International Law* 383–400, 385.

[11] A. Littoz-Monnet, 'Studying the Assembling of Expertise in Global Governance' in this volume, pp. 59–80.

[12] J. Uribe, 'Drawing the Contours of Hidden Hunger as an Object of Governance' in this volume, pp. 101–20.

[13] T. Soave, 'The Puzzle of Freedom: Structure and Agency in International Adjudication' in this volume, pp. 122–41.

[14] K. Santer, 'Reassembling Transnational Legal Conflicts across Global Institutions: Ethnographic Perspectives on Claims of Authority over the Mediterranean Sea' in this volume, pp. 142–65.

[15] D. Quiroga Villamarin, 'Placeholders: An Archival Journey into the Interim Histories of International Organizations' in this volume, pp. 166–84.

[16] M. Halme-Tuomisaari, 'Keeping Up Standards for a Better World: Anthropological Alternatives to the Study of International Organizations' in this volume, pp. 208–26.

[17] R. Clements, 'Experts, Practices, Power: The Work of International Criminal Court Reform' in this volume, pp. 81–100.

the World Bank, tracing the assemblages that make up international organisations offers an alternative form of critique, one that remains sensitive and response to 'the changing politics of law'.[18]

The distinction between deconstructive and reconstructive 'ways of doing' outlined here is no doubt overdrawn. To be sure, many of the chapters in this volume can be read as straddling both modes. Clements' attention to the 'notions of efficiency and cost-effectiveness' embedded in the ICC's 'organisation form' resonates with Cutler's deconstruction of 'resilience talk'.[19] Cutler in turn reminds us that ideology works to interpellate subjects as much as it inverts or distorts our image of reality.[20] Halme-Tuomisaari is concerned with uncovering the 'inner logic' of international organisations.[21] Chimni's 'internal critique' would include examining their 'everyday practices or organisational culture',[22] while his interest in proposals for reform suggests a fundamentally reconstructive impulse at play.[23] Other authors would almost certainly resist being pigeon-holed into one or other approach, and fairly so.

Ways of Seeing

What then does this volume reveal about international organisations? What is glimpsed here that was not seen before? The authors of these chapters are more modest than the blind men in the parable. None claims exclusive (in)sight into the nature of international organisations; several explicitly deny the possibility of turning on the lights, opening one's eyes, and seeing the elephant whole. One or two express mild misgivings about the overweening claims to special discernment by scholars in certain disciplines (not their own, of course). Instead,

18 D. Van Den Meerssche, '"The Critic Is Not the One Who Debunks, but the One Who Assembles": On Professional Performances and Material Practice' in this volume, pp. 227–46.

19 Clements, 'Experts, Practices, Power', pp. 81–100; Cutler, 'Deconstructing "Resilience Talk" in Global Governance', pp. 271–90.

20 Cutler, 'Deconstructing "Resilience Talk" in Global Governance', pp. 271–90.

21 Halme-Tuomisaari, 'Keeping Up Standards for a Better World, pp. 208–26.

22 Chimni, 'Critical Theory and International Organizations', pp. 16–37.

23 See generally G. F. Sinclair, "Between Salvation and Cynicism: TWAIL Perspectives on International Organizations", in A. Anghie, B. P. Chimni, M. Fakhri, K. Mickelson, and V. Nesiah (eds.), *Research Handbook on Third World Approaches to International Law* (Edward Elgar, in press).

most of the chapters self-consciously focus on specific episodes, mechanisms, or aspects of international organisations. In doing so, they present a kaleidoscope of images that transform how we view these entities.

Indeed, the international organisations seen through the chapters in this volume are startlingly heterogeneous in their composition and activities. As the editors note, mainstream international legal scholars tend to focus on international organisations as such – assumed to be discrete, self-contained, coherent entities – and their members, which are mostly states. In contrast, the chapters in this volume describe entities that are teeming with life – actors and actions, objects and projects, practices and performances. From the varied perspectives of the authors gathered here, international organisations are channels for the circulation of people, data, and documents through multiple 'crossing points', 'boundary sites', and 'material infrastructures';[24] producers of policies, programmes, committees, and documents;[25] 'socio-political machineries' that generate diverse 'governance objects' through the manipulation and deployment of knowledge;[26] targets of reform, carried out by 'a set of actors, arguments, and their tools';[27] physical sites, buildings, and other infrastructures,[28] constituted by the 'patterned practices', 'competent performances', and relationships of a community of legal professionals;[29] embodying professional cultures expressed in 'objects, rules-of-thumb, textual references and templates of analysis or documentation';[30] instruments for transnational capitalist class interests;[31] and more. As these chapters suggest, an international organisation will look very different depending on whether one is examining its (executive) head, its (operational) feet, or the (administrative) belly of the beast.

24 Littoz-Monnet, 'Studying the Assembling of Expertise in Global Governance', pp. 59–80.
25 Halme-Tuomisaari, 'Keeping Up Standards for a Better World', pp. 208–26.
26 Uribe, 'Drawing the Contours of Hidden Hunger as an Object of Governance', pp. 101–20.
27 Clements, 'Experts, Practices, Power', pp. 81–100.
28 Quiroga Villamarin, 'Placeholders', pp. 166–84.
29 Soave, 'The Puzzle of Freedom', pp. 122–41.
30 Van Den Meerssche, 'The Critic Is Not the One Who Debunks', pp. 227–46.
31 Chimni, 'Critical Theory and International Organizations', pp. 16–37; Mansouri, 'Laissez-Faire, State Capitalism, and the Making of International Organizations', pp. 248–70; Cutler, 'Deconstructing "Resilience Talk" in Global Governance', pp. 271–90.

With such diverse makeups, it is perhaps unsurprising that many of the chapters also depict international organisations and their constituent entities as engaged in more or less continuous processes of struggle. To some, the principal antagonists are those actors already recognised by mainstream international lawyers – international organisations and their member states – though the struggles should be understood as taking place both between and within them.[32] To others, more specific struggles warrant particular attention. International organisations like the World Bank or the International Monetary Fund thus incarnate contestations between classes, within classes, or between capitalist states. Bodies such as the International Maritime Organisation, the International Organisation for Migration, and the European Union engage in transnational legal conflicts among themselves, with state agencies, and with non-governmental agencies regarding the governance of international borders.[33] The struggles to reform the ICC are played out through reiterative interpretive work on 'legal materials'.[34] More concretely still, even the effort to obtain and maintain secure physical accommodations turns out to be an ongoing, uphill battle.[35] But what enables our authors to see such variety and turmoil in institutions that typically appear so flat and lifeless in legal texts?

Ways of Thinking

The blind men in the parable interpret their findings through mental models drawn from their prior experiences in the world. The one who touches the elephant's leg and declares that the elephant is like a tree is only able to do so because he has some experience (and thus expectation) of what a tree feels like. Indeed, he has probably touched several trees, so he has a sense that there are different kinds of trees; even if this tree is not quite the same as the others he has experienced, it shares enough of the common properties of a tree – for example, its vertical orientation, girth, and rough surface – for it to be classed as such. Likewise, the man who touches the elephant's ear must have some general sense of the possible range of forms and properties of a

[32] Klabbers, 'Inter-disciplinarity and the Law of International Organizations', pp. 38–56.
[33] Santer, 'Reassembling Transnational Legal Conflicts', pp. 142–65.
[34] Clements, 'Experts, Practices, Power', pp. 81–100.
[35] Quiroga Villamarin, 'Placeholders', pp. 166–84.

fan, to be able to assert confidently that an elephant is like a fan. Their different 'ways of seeing' the elephant are intimately tied to their 'ways of thinking' about the world: how they classify and categorise objects; how they analogise or distinguish between different instances or cases; what they are primed to 'see', and what their imaginations do not permit them to observe.

Our authors likewise employ a range of mental models – or, to extend the ocular metaphor, theoretical or interpretive lenses – that allow them to see different aspects of their objects of examination. With a wide-angle lens such as is provided by historical materialist or critical political economic terms of analysis, it is possible (in fact, one is almost compelled) to see how international organisations are implicated in broad, transhistorical patterns of domination, hegemony, and exploitation. The scholar who adopts a more microscopic lens, in contrast, will be likely to discover more of the unseen, everyday lives of international organisations.[36] An anthropologist's sensibility will be attuned to pluralism in law as in culture; an historian will observe contingency and change; a scholar steeped in practice theory will find, well, practices. The variety of lenses being deployed here is impressive, taking inspiration from Marx, Bourdieu, Foucault, and Latour, among others. Each of these lenses has its limitations: to see one part of the elephant clearly is to see the rest only fuzzily, or not at all.

The most dominant mental model of all, of course, is that of the international organisation itself. With all their great diversity, all the authors in this collection seem to agree, more or less, on their object of study; certainly, none fundamentally questions the usefulness of international organisations as a category of analysis. Once one has been taught to see an elephant, it seems, it is difficult to forget or push the image out of one's mind, even if one is told 'don't think of an elephant!' And yet, there may be good reason to question whether all of the entities under investigation in this volume belong to the same species. Is the many-limbed (and many-trunked, and many-tailed…) United Nations really the same kind of thing as the Organisation for the Prohibition of Chemical Weapons? Do the Universal Postal Union and the World Health Organisation belong in the same conceptual bucket as each other, the ICC, or the Appellate Body of the World Trade

[36] G. F. Sinclair, 'Unseen and Everyday: International Secretariats under the Spotlight' (2022) 116 *AJIL Unbound* 378.

Organisation? For all the attention to detail in practices, materiality, and processes found here, it may be surprising to find such consensus on an overarching concept that purports to unite them.

The division between macroscopic and microscopic views leads back to the distinction between deconstructivist and reconstructivist ways of doing the study of international organisations. The first element in each dyad imagines international organisations as real and complete entities, with capacity for sufficiently coherent will and action that they can be debunked or dismantled – or at least held responsible. The second imagines international organisations in the process of becoming or assemblage. This may at first blush seem less useful for accountability purposes, and therefore less appealing to a practising lawyer. But that judgement is probably premature; rather than undercut accountability, a more complex and fluid understanding of international organisations-in-the-making may eventually make possible a more precise schema of responsibility. These are early days as an exciting new wave of scholarship gathers: instead of closing down possibilities, why not catch the wave for a while and see where it takes us?

Ways Forward?

Ways of doing – ways of seeing – ways of thinking. Like the blind men in the parable, students of international organisations grasp at different parts of the objects of their study, observe distinct phenomena, and interpret their findings through diverse mental models. Indeed, all three are tightly interconnected and impossible to separate in practice. What, then, might the future hold for this flourishing field of scholarship and praxis? No one can say for sure, but here is a short wish list – as personal and idiosyncratic as any other – from a fellow dweller in the dark.

First, there is certainly room to push further in all of the directions pursued and advocated in these chapters, and to connect these with other streams of scholarship. Though a number of excellent ethnographic studies of international organisations have appeared,[37] much

[37] See, e.g., S. Block-Lieb and T. C. Halliday, *Global Lawmakers: International Organizations in the Crafting of World Markets* (Cambridge University Press, 2017); R. Niezen and M. Sapignoli (eds.), *Palaces of Hope: The Anthropology of Global Organizations* (Cambridge University Press, 2017); G. Sarfaty,

more is needed to understand their everyday, inner workings. Here, inspiration could be drawn from recent inquiries into, among other things, documents,[38] files,[39] and meetings[40] in other settings, as well as from the classic works of Max Weber, who is surprisingly little cited in this volume.[41] The relations among international organisations, mentioned in passing in only a few chapters, is a subject of increasing study by international lawyers and international relations scholars,[42] and could likewise offer opportunities for more focussed ethnographic and historical study. Rational choice and game-theoretic approaches, also under-represented here, might strengthen Marxian critiques of international organisations' role in entrenching the domination of powerful states.[43] Complementary ways of thinking about international organisations could be found in the academic discipline of public administration,[44] while

Values in Translation: Human Rights and the Culture of the World Bank (Stanford University Press, 2012).

[38] A. Riles, *Documents: Artifacts of Modern Knowledge* (University of Michigan Press, 2006); N. Mathur, *Paper Tiger: Law, Bureaucracy and the Developmental State in Himalayan India* (Cambridge University Press, 2006); R. H. R. Harper, *Inside the IMF: An Ethnography of Documents, Technology and Organisational Action* (Routledge, 1998).

[39] C. Vismann, *Files: Law and Media Technology* (Stanford University Press, 2008).

[40] J. Sandler and R. Thedvall (eds.), *Meeting Ethnography: Meetings as Key Technologies of Contemporary Governance, Development, and Resistance* (Routledge, 2017); H. Brown, A. Reed, and T. Yarrow, 'Introduction: Towards an Ethnography of Meeting' (2017) 23 *Journal of the Royal Anthropological Institute* 10–26; Special Issue: Meetings: Ethnographies of Organizational Process, Bureaucracy, and Assembly (2017) *Journal of the Royal Anthropological Institute* 23: S1.

[41] Max Weber, *Economy and Society*, 2 vols (G. Roth and C. Wittich eds., University of California Press, 1978).

[42] See, e.g., L. Boisson de Chazournes, *Interactions between Regional and Universal Organizations: A Legal Perspective* (Brill, 2016); H. Gött, *The Law of Interactions between International Organizations: A Framework for Multi-institutional Labour Governance* (Springer, 2020); R. Biermann and J. A. Koops (eds.), *The Palgrave Handbook of Inter-Organizational Relations in World Politics* (Palgrave, 2017).

[43] See, e.g., E. Benvenisti and G. W. Downs, 'The Empire's New Clothes: Political Economy and the Fragmentation of International Law' (2007) 60 *Stanford Law Review* 595.

[44] See, e.g., D. Stone and K. Moloney (eds.), *The Oxford Handbook of Global Policy and Transnational Administration* (Oxford University Press, 2019); M. W. Bauer, C. Knill, and S. Eckhard (eds.), *International Bureaucracy: Challenges and Lessons for Public Administration Research* (Palgrave

organisation studies might offer further critical and practice-oriented perspectives.[45]

Second, more efforts to bridge the gaps between apparent dichotomies in the field, building on those made in this volume, would be welcome. Productive linkages could be sought between the microscopic views provided by practice-theoretic approaches and the more macroscopic, diachronic perspectives offered by exciting new histories of international organisations during the interwar period, during the Cold War, and in the era of decolonisation.[46] There is ample scope for studies connecting the materiality of international organisations to the affective lives of the people who work in them.[47] Similarly, scholarship that bridges – and thus helps to explain – the gulf between the high ideals expressed by international organisations and their involvement in projects of imperialist domination or capitalist exploitation seems as necessary as ever.

Macmillan, 2017); S. Kim, S. Ashley, and H. W. Lambright (eds.), *Public Administration in the Context of Global Governance* (Edward Elgar, 2014).

45 See, e.g., B. Czarniawska, *A Theory of Organizing* (Edward Elgar, 2008); B. Czarniawska and G. Sevón (eds.), *Translating Organizational Change* (Walter de Gruyter, 1996).

46 See, e.g., M. Alacevich, *Political Economy of the World Bank: The Early Years* (World Bank, 2008); M. Schmelzer, *The Hegemony of Growth: The OECD and the Making of the Economic Growth Paradigm* (Cambridge University Press, 2016); P. Clavin, *Securing the World Economy: The Reinvention of the League of Nations, 1920–1946* (Oxford University Press, 2013); M. Christian, S. Kott, and O. Matějka (eds.), *Planning in Cold War Europe: Competition, Cooperation, Circulations (1950s–1970s)* (De Gruyter, 2018); K. Gram-Skjoldager, H. A. Ikonomou, and T. Kahlert (eds.), *Organizing the 20th Century World: International Organizations and the Emergence of International Public Administration, 1920–1960s* (Bloomsbury, 2020); O. Aloni, *The League of Nations and the Protection of the Environment* (Cambridge University Press, 2021); D. Stinsky, *International Cooperation in Cold War Europe: The United Nations Economic Commission for Europe, 1947–64* (Bloomsbury, 2021); E. Roehrlich, *Inspectors for Peace: A History of the International Atomic Energy Agency* (Johns Hopkins University Press, 2022); E.-M. Muschik, *Building States: The United Nations, Development, and Decolonization, 1945–1965* (Columbia University Press, 2022).

47 See, e.g., J. Billaud and J. K. Cowan, 'The Bureaucratisation of Utopia: Ethics, Affects and Subjectivities in International Governance Processes' (2020) 28 *Social Anthropology* 6–16; J. K. Cowan '"The Feeling of Pursuing an Ideal": A League of Nations Civil Servant Reflects on his Work' (2020) 28 *Social Anthropology* 17–34.

Third, a reflexive turn that accounts for the effects of scholarship on the practice of international organisations may be well overdue. There is something strange about the passivity of the elephant in the parable that opened this chapter. What are the chances that the elephant would not react in some way to all that prodding and poking of its ears, trunk, and tail? Similarly, scholarly probings of international organisations are more than likely to produce some kind of response, for better or for worse. This relationship between cause and effect can be seen most obviously in self-conscious efforts by international lawyers to promote new rules on decision-making in particular international organisations or to reform the law on responsibility, or to devise new mechanisms to hold them to account. But more subtle effects – though no less far-reaching – may arise from re-visioning international organisations, to take one example, as an actor in 'global administrative bodies' operating in a 'global administrative space'.[48] Exploring these effects promises to offer a new way of connecting the 'ways of seeing' explored in this volume with the 'ways of doing' in international organisations.

[48] B. Kingsbury, N. Krisch, and R. B. Stewart, 'The Emergence of Global Administrative Law' (2005) 68 *Law and Contemporary Problems* 15–61, at 17, 18; B. Kingsbury and L. Casini, 'Global Administrative Law Dimensions of International Organizations Law' (2009) 6 *International Organizations Law Review* 319–358.

Index

www.ingramcontent.com/pod-product-compliance
Lightning Source LLC
LaVergne TN
LVHW052034200926
848481LV00005B/1672
9781009552615